THE SHATTERING

ALSO BY KEVIN BOYLE

Arc of Justice:
A Saga of Race, Civil Rights, and Murder in the Jazz Age

The UAW and the Heyday of American Liberalism, 1945–1968

Muddy Boots and Ragged Aprons:
Images of Working-Class Detroit, 1900–1930 (coauthor)

Organized Labor and American Politics:
The Labor-Liberal Alliance, 1894–1994 (editor)

THE SHATTERING

AMERICA IN THE 1960S

KEVIN BOYLE

W. W. NORTON & COMPANY

Independent Publishers Since 1923

For information about permission to reproduce selections from this book,
write to Permissions, W. W. Norton & Company, Inc.,
500 Fifth Avenue, New York, NY 10110

For information about special discounts for bulk purchases, please contact
W. W. Norton Special Sales at specialsales@wwnorton.com or 800-233-4830

Maps by Mapping Specialists, Ltd.

Manufacturing by Lake Book Manufacturing
Book design by Chris Welch
Production manager: Lauren Abbate

Library of Congress Cataloging-in-Publication Data
Names: Boyle, Kevin, 1960– author.
Title: The shattering : America in the 1960s / Kevin Boyle.
Description: First edition. | New York : W. W. Norton & Company, [2021] |
Includes bibliographical references and index.
Identifiers: LCCN 2021022377 | ISBN 9780393355994 (hardcover) |
ISBN 9780393356076 (epub)
Subjects: LCSH: United States—History—1961–1969.
Classification: LCC E841 .B694 2021 | DDC 973.923—dc23
LC record available at https://lccn.loc.gov/2021022377

W. W. Norton & Company, Inc., 500 Fifth Avenue, New York, N.Y. 10110
www.wwnorton.com

W. W. Norton & Company Ltd., 15 Carlisle Street, London W1D 3BS

1 2 3 4 5 6 7 8 9 0

To Vicky, Abby, and Nan
with all my love and admiration

✦

and in memory of my parents, Kevin and Anne Boyle

CONTENTS

Illustrations follow pages 138 and 266

CHAPTER 1

EDDY STREET

It started with an accidental shaming. Ed Cahill was chatting with his neighbor from across the street, Clarence Miller, as they'd done thousands of times since they were kids. In the course of the conversation Ed happened to say something about how people didn't fly the flag as often as they used to. Clarence had to admit that he didn't have one to fly. But he promised to correct that by Independence Day. Then he did Ed one better, in the slightly competitive way of men who'd known each other forever. Why not drape the entire block in flags, he said. So they went door to door, offering to buy a flag for whoever didn't own one, and to hang it too. When they had almost everyone signed up, Ed wrote a letter to the *Chicago Tribune* inviting "all those who love Old Glory . . . to come take a peek at the 6100 block of West Eddy Street on the northwest side of Chicago on the Fourth of July. If the good Lord blesses us with a fine day, you'll find each and every home in the block proudly displaying the most beautiful flag in the world."[1]

As it happened, the Fourth was cool and damp. But the flags went up anyway, thirty-eight of them, though there were only thirty-six houses on the block. Having run Ed's letter, the *Trib* decided it might as well send a photographer out too. He lined up as many people as he could on the lawn next door to the Cahills' bungalow and asked them to look up at the flags strung above them. The next day, July 5, 1961, the folks on Eddy Street appeared on the *Trib*'s back page. Ed and Clarence got the photo's center, kneeling alongside each other. On Ed's other side crouched his daughter Kathy, her arms wrapped across her chest and her hair pulled into pigtails. His son Terry was standing on the top porch step. And way in the back row, barely visible over his shoulder, stood his wife Stella, smiling for the camera.

Stella

THEY'D MOVED TO Eddy Street in 1948, two years after Ed had returned from the war. Stella knew how much that bungalow in the middle of the block meant to him. Yet when he'd brought up the possibility, she'd hesitated. She had her mother to think about, and his father, and all the other moves her family had made, some in hopes that they'd get themselves on solid ground, some in desolation.

Stella's father had come to the States in 1908, the year he turned eighteen, from a town in what had once been southern Poland but had long since fallen under Austrian rule. More than likely he left because of the economic transformations that were then reaching into the Polish countryside—the age of machines pounding down from Warsaw and Lodz—and ended up in Chicago because it seemed better to be in the center of the industrial world than on its ragged edges. It was a common calculation. Forty years earlier there were 300,000 people living in Chicago. In 1909 there were 2.2 million, three-quarters of them foreign-born or the children of foreign-born parents, a solid portion of the rest migrants from America's own increasingly marginalized countryside.

They arrived in a city driven by the most modern forms of production. In its immense stockyards, meatpackers processed fifteen million head of cattle a year by moving their carcasses along a fully integrated assembly line. On its far south side a labyrinth of blast furnaces and rolling mills made almost half of the nation's steel. Across its western border, in suburban Cicero, Western Electric's innovative new Hawthorne Works put 20,000 people to work assembling the telephones and switching systems that were transforming human communication. In between, along Chicago's tangle of rail lines, lay hundreds of

PREFACE

THERE WERE 180 MILLION people living in the United States in 1961. *The Shattering* starts with a handful of them posing for a picture on the Fourth of July.

A number so small can't represent a nation so large, but they weren't a bad match. They were urban people in a nation dominated by cities and their surging suburbs, working people in an economy dominated by factories, native-born Americans in a country where immigrants' share of the population had tumbled to its lowest point in more than a century. They were husbands and wives in a country where 72 percent of adults were married, the younger couples raising their kids together at a time when 88 percent of parents with school-age children lived with their spouses. Every one of them was white, as were 85 percent of Americans. And they were to a striking degree safe and secure.

Then the sixties cracked their nation open. What follows is a history of that crack-up.

The idea is hardly new. For almost fifty years historians have seen the 1960s and early 1970s—what they've come to call the "long sixties"[1]— as the pivotal point in the fracturing of modern American public life. Over time their analyses have grown increasingly sophisticated, but the broad outlines have remained much the same. The United States emerged from World War II the most powerful nation on earth, the argument runs, its diplomatic reach genuinely global, its economy three times the size of its closest competitor, and its military capabilities almost beyond imagining. For a few postwar years politicians and

policy makers struggled to make sense of the nation's new position. In
the late 1940s they began to reach an understanding of what needed
to be done. Having failed to stand against Nazi Germany in the 1930s,
they decided that the United States would now stand against its rogue-
state successor, the Soviet Union, as it tried to spread Communism
across the wounded world. The expansion of the nation's international
commitments dovetailed with a drive toward domestic tranquility. The
Cold War crushed American radicalism, while the nation's unparalleled prosperity convinced the Republican Party finally to support the
liberal reforms of the 1930s and the Democrats to stop pushing for
more. "The ideological age has ended," wrote the brilliant social critic
Daniel Bell in 1959, the old passions of the Right and the Left having
been replaced by a relentlessly moderate consensus. A "middle way," he
said, "for the middle-aged."[2]

But not for the young. In the standard history the shattering started
with the idealism of a new generation unwilling to accept the com-
promises the consensus required. Bell had caught hints of it in 1959,
though he thought it nothing more than young intellectuals' yearning
for a cause to believe in. By the time his essay appeared, in April 1960,
it was already coursing through the South in a wave of sit-ins inspired
by four college freshmen, the oldest of them barely nineteen. Over the
next few years it surged across the country, pulling young pacifists into
the Freedom Rides, young organizers into Mississippi, young protesters into Birmingham's mean streets, young liberals into government
service, young hipsters into the avant-garde, and young radicals into
the open. In the rush of events that followed, they swept away the measured politics their elders had embraced.

Precisely when the postwar accord collapsed remains an open question. Some versions date its fall to the latter half of 1963, when the
civil rights movement broke the white South's grip on the Democratic
Party; others to the tensions that cut through the election of 1964; yet
others to the summer of 1965, when Lyndon Johnson escalated the war
in Vietnam and a portion of South Central Los Angeles—a neighborhood called Watts—went up in flames. From there the story lines shift:

first to the agonies of the Left, then to the resurgence of the Right, and ultimately to the intertwining of the two in the fiercely polarized politics of the Nixon years, a world removed from the 1950s. "A nation that had believed itself to be at consensus instead becoming one of . . . two loosely defined congeries of Americans, each convinced that should the other triumph, everything decent and true and worth preserving would end," says Rick Perlstein in his marvelous history of Richard Nixon's rise. "That was the 1960s."[3]

It's a powerful story, often beautifully told. But for a while now the best scholarship on postwar America has been moving in ways that challenge its central premises. How does a story that begins with consensus explain the rounds of repression and violence historians have uncovered in the 1950s, from the federal government's institutionalization of homophobia to whites' repeated assaults on African Americans who dared to move into their neighborhoods? How does a narrative that pivots on generational change incorporate historians' recent emphasis on the long histories of civil rights activism and modern conservatism? What happens to the polarization that closes the story, now that historians have developed a more subtle reading of the red/blue divide? How are we to understand the sixties, now that so much history has changed?

The first step, *The Shattering* argues, is to set aside the consensus politics and put in its place the particular interests of the postwar era's rapidly expanded middling classes: ordinary Americans with jobs to keep, kids to raise, pensions to build, mortgages to pay, and memories of harder times to put behind them. There the dominant politicians of the 1950s made their stand, in defense of that swath of the nation Dwight Eisenhower called "the common man."[4] That commitment helped to give his foreign policy the mix of caution and aggression he believed the middling classes wanted to see. And it defined the intense focus on security at home, anchored by the warfare state Ike came to fear, the middling culture he loved, and the quiet extension of the nation's racial regime.

Even at its mid-fifties peak, that political order was a fragile arrangement, its boundaries repeatedly tested and occasionally broken. In the first half of the 1960s they were fully breached. The young played a pivotal part in their wreckage, as the standard story says. So did older activists steeped in traditions the previous decade's politics had marginalized: people like Ella Baker, the radical democrat who gave the civil rights movement its vanguard organization; Estelle Griswold, the birth control advocate whose singular act of defiance won Americans a right they'd never had; Bayard Rustin, the radical pacifist who brought a quarter million Americans to the Lincoln Memorial on a brilliant summer day in 1963 to demand jobs and freedom; and Lloyd and Dolores Herbstreith, the veteran McCarthyites who on a snowy night in 1964 decided that Alabama's racist governor, George Wallace, ought to be president of the United States. As important as they were, though, activists alone didn't bring the order down. It also cracked from within, as some of its key constraints were stripped away by a transformative series of Supreme Court rulings, Lyndon Johnson's willingness to confront the nation's original sin, and his calculation that the country ought to fight a war he knew it couldn't win.

As the barriers fell, the forces they were meant to contain surged forward, some of them moving precisely as the 1950s' leading men had feared they would, others in directions they'd never imagined. It's true that the tumult plunged the Left into crisis and reinvigorated the Right, a process made plain in the chaotic summer of 1968, when millions of Americans responded to the violence engulfing the Democratic Party by taking up the Herbstreiths' dream of a Wallace presidency. But that November three times as many people voted for the candidate who'd painstakingly positioned himself as the champion of the embattled center, a politics he'd learned from the president he'd served. With that vote the 1960s took their final turn, not to the polarization of left and right—though during the Nixon years there were moments so divisive reasonable people feared that the nation was coming undone—but to a bitter, often brutal struggle between an administration determined to reconstruct the order the decade's upheavals had shattered and those forces the shattering had released: a struggle for the nation's future shaped by the enormous weight of its past, as the rest of the sixties had been.

That story can be told in any number of ways. I've given it a narrative form shaped from the intertwined histories of three of the 1960s' defining challenges: one shaped by the African American struggle to bring down the United States' long-standing racial system, another by the nation's foreign policy and the devastating war it produced, the third by the government's right to regulate its citizens' sexuality. My focus on those challenges inevitably crowds out others. I barely touch on the Latino, Asian-American, and Native American movements that developed during the decade. I give only passing attention to the campaign the resurgent women's movement waged to break gender discrimination in the workplace. And I spend no time at all on the United States' deepening role in the Middle East and environmentalism's remarkably broad-based challenge to corporate America, though the first Earth Day in April 1970 outdrew the era's largest anti-war protest by a margin of ten to one. Those were agonizing choices to make. But I'm convinced that the sixties are best revealed by diving deeply into those three defining struggles.

Much of the narrative revolves around the massive political, economic, and social structures that by the 1960s had come to dominate American life. I'll argue, for instance, that it's impossible to understand the course of the Vietnam War without seeing how it became entangled with the financial order that connected the United States to the rest of the Western world. History isn't shaped by structures alone, though, no matter how powerful they may be. Individual actions matter too, as do the complex mix of experiences, beliefs, and emotions that lie behind them. That is why *The Shattering* burrows again and again into the lives of activists, politicians, and policy makers, and why it opens with a small group of people the postwar order was meant to serve, posing for a picture on Eddy Street.

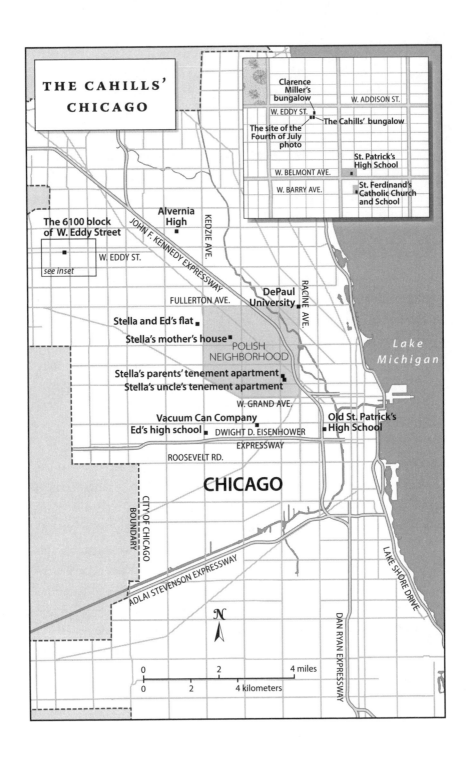

THE CAHILLS' CHICAGO

Clarence Miller's bungalow

W. ADDISON ST.

W. EDDY ST.

The site of the Fourth of July photo

The Cahills' bungalow

St. Patrick's High School

W. BELMONT AVE.

W. BARRY AVE.

St. Ferdinand's Catholic Church and School

Alvernia High

JOHN F. KENNEDY EXPRESSWAY

KEDZIE AVE.

The 6100 block of W. Eddy Street

W. EDDY ST.

see inset

FULLERTON AVE.

DePaul University

RACINE AVE.

Stella and Ed's flat

Stella's mother's house

POLISH NEIGHBORHOOD

Lake Michigan

Stella's parents' tenement apartment

Stella's uncle's tenement apartment

W. GRAND AVE.

Vacuum Can Company

Ed's high school

DWIGHT D. EISENHOWER

Old St. Patrick's High School

EXPRESSWAY

ROOSEVELT RD.

CHICAGO

CITY OF CHICAGO BOUNDARY

ADLAI STEVENSON EXPRESSWAY

N

DAN RYAN EXPRESSWAY

LAKE SHORE DRIVE

0   2   4 miles

0   2   4 kilometers

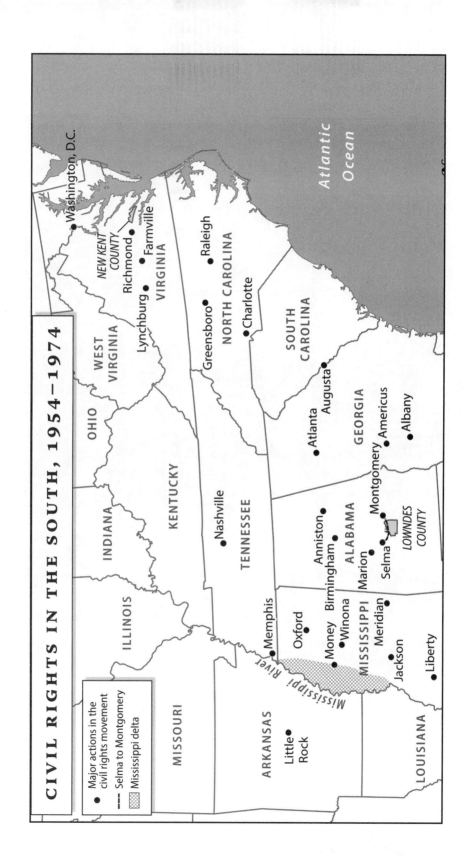

CIVIL RIGHTS IN THE SOUTH, 1954–1974

Major actions in the civil rights movement
Selma to Montgomery
Mississippi delta

Washington, D.C.

NEW KENT COUNTY
Richmond
Farmville
VIRGINIA
Lynchburg

WEST VIRGINIA

OHIO

Raleigh
Greensboro
NORTH CAROLINA
Charlotte

SOUTH CAROLINA

Augusta
Atlanta
GEORGIA
Americus
Albany
Montgomery

KENTUCKY

INDIANA

Nashville
TENNESSEE

Anniston
Birmingham
ALABAMA
Marion
Selma
LOWNDES COUNTY

Memphis
Oxford
Money
Winona
MISSISSIPPI
Meridian
Jackson
Liberty

ILLINOIS

MISSOURI

ARKANSAS
Little Rock

LOUISIANA

Mississippi River

Atlantic Ocean

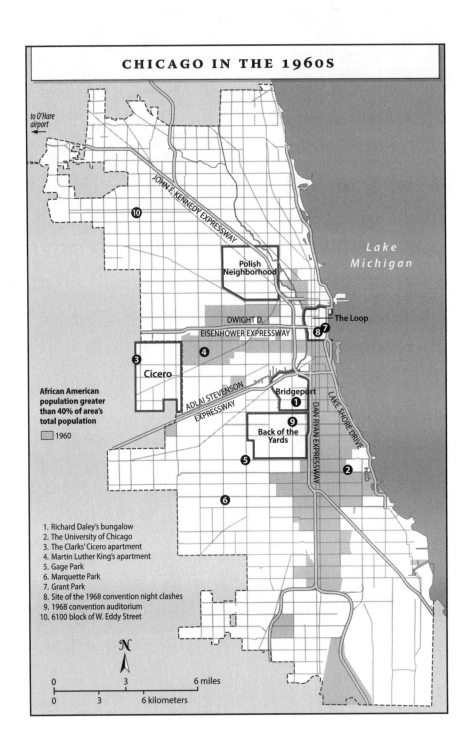

CHICAGO IN THE 1960S

to O'Hare airport

JOHN F. KENNEDY EXPRESSWAY

Lake Michigan

Polish Neighborhood

DWIGHT D. EISENHOWER EXPRESSWAY

The Loop

Cicero

ADLAI STEVENSON EXPRESSWAY

Bridgeport

DAN RYAN EXPRESSWAY

LAKE SHORE DRIVE

Back of the Yards

African American population greater than 40% of area's total population

1960

1. Richard Daley's bungalow
2. The University of Chicago
3. The Clarks' Cicero apartment
4. Martin Luther King's apartment
5. Gage Park
6. Marquette Park
7. Grant Park
8. Site of the 1968 convention night clashes
9. 1968 convention auditorium
10. 6100 block of W. Eddy Street

N

0   3   6 miles
0   3   6 kilometers

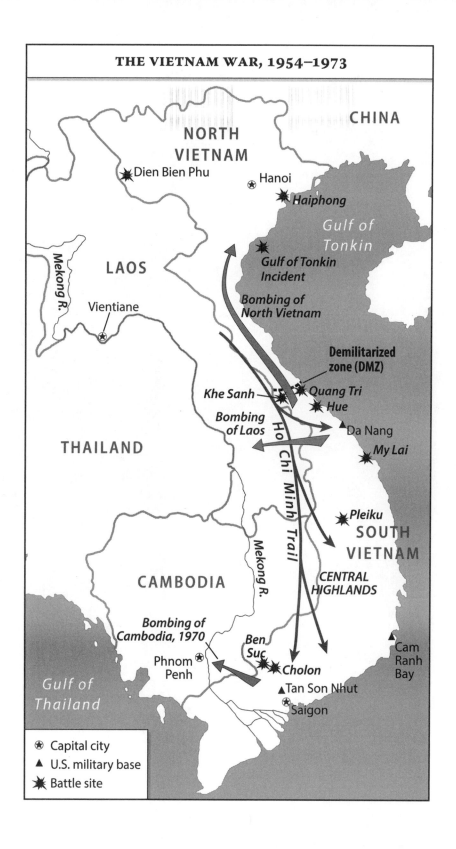

THE VIETNAM WAR, 1954–1973

CHINA

NORTH VIETNAM

⋇ Dien Bien Phu

⊛ Hanoi

⋇ *Haiphong*

Gulf of Tonkin

LAOS

⊛ Vientiane

Mekong R.

⋇ *Gulf of Tonkin Incident*

Bombing of North Vietnam

Demilitarized zone (DMZ)

Khe Sanh ⋇ ⋇ *Quang Tri*
Hue

Bombing of Laos

▲ Da Nang

Ho Chi Minh Trail

⋇ *My Lai*

THAILAND

⋇ *Pleiku*

SOUTH VIETNAM

Mekong R.

CENTRAL HIGHLANDS

CAMBODIA

Bombing of Cambodia, 1970

Ben Suc ⋇

⊛ Phnom Penh

⋇ *Cholon*

▲ Cam Ranh Bay

▲ Tan Son Nhut

⊛ Saigon

Gulf of Thailand

⊛ Capital city
▲ U.S. military base
⋇ Battle site

THE SHATTERING

smaller factories making whatever the market would bear, from chewing gum to women's wear.

Around them circled the city's patchwork of neighborhoods. The fabulously wealthy held the Gold Coast, north of downtown; the cultural avant-garde the less genteel area immediately to its west, where they celebrated anarchism, feminism, free love, and whatever else would shock the mainstream; the businessmen the Loop, with its towering office blocks and Tiffany-encrusted department stores. The middle class claimed a ring of neighborhoods a respectable distance from the inner city, while the working class sliced Chicago's center into a series of ethnic and racial enclaves: Poles northwest of downtown, Italians due west, Russian Jews to the south of them, Czechs to the southwest, Slovaks back of the stockyards, the Irish in nearby Bridgeport, and a growing number of African Americans, most of them refugees from the horrors of the white supremacist South, in a narrow band on the south side and two much smaller blocs on the west.

Through those neighborhoods threaded the conflicts that gave Chicago's public life a furious feel. There was the city's long tradition of class conflict, stretching back to the earliest days of its breakneck industrialization. There was the intensifying violence along its racial borders as the Black migration accelerated. And more and more there were clashes over its raucous sexuality. Since the mid-nineteenth century a nationwide corps of solidly middle class, overwhelmingly Protestant social reformers had been trying to prohibit practices that they saw as violations of the proper moral order. They'd had their successes: by 1890 the federal government had banned pornography from the mail; twenty-four states had outlawed the distribution of birth control; and abortion, once accepted as legitimate until the fetus started to move, had become illegal everywhere. But there was still plenty of work to do, the most pressing of it in cities like Chicago, where the reformers' order ran up against the breadth of American sexuality.

Much of their energy went into shutting down the city's sprawling sex trade. Some 5,000 prostitutes serviced five million customers a year, many of them down in the Levee, the thicket of brothels, dance halls, gambling parlors, and drug dens squeezed between downtown and the African American South Side; others in flats, saloons, and cheap hotels scattered around the center city's neighborhoods. Alongside that crusade the reformers built a campaign against Chicago's wide-ranging sites of sexual display: the strip shows, the drag balls, the dive bars, the bathhouses, and—on technology's cutting edge—a wave of titillating movies they tried to block by getting city hall to set up the nation's first film censorship board.

The reformers' high profile eclipsed the quieter struggles that ran through the working-class wards. At their center lay the network of institutions that tied Chicago's migrants to the worlds they'd left behind, from the South Side's Masonic lodges and storefront churches through the West Side's transplanted synagogues and ethnic halls to the enormous national parishes the Catholic archdiocese built across the inner city. Occasionally one or another would add its name to a reformer's campaign. For the most part, though, they traded politics for the intimate work of preserving their communities' traditional, often intensely conservative sense of propriety, order, and obligation against the corrosive power of distance, displacement, temptation, and the poverty that clung to the working classes even in the center of the industrial world.

It clung to Stella's father too. He'd probably left home with at least some training as a tailor, maybe even with a formal apprenticeship behind him. But he had to settle for running a sewing machine in a downtown sweatshop, a job that paid for repetition rather than skill: two cents a jacket lining properly sewed, four cents a pant seam, the weekly total reduced by the cost of whatever cloth he spoiled with an errant stitch. At some point the orders would stop coming in and his boss would shut the sweatshop down to let his inventory clear; his first full year in Chicago her father went ten weeks without any work whatsoever. The only way to manage was to cut costs to the bone, which was undoubtedly why he took the cheapest housing he could find, renting out a bed from a presser and his wife in one of the five apartments someone had squeezed into a narrow old two-story deep in the Polish ghetto.

He was still there five years later, when he met Stella's mother. She was a country girl, raised in a backwater village eighty miles south of Krakow, in a family that seemed to hemorrhage its sons and daughters. Her brother had left in 1908, her sister in 1909, she and another brother in October 1912, following the trail the other two had set from their slowly shrinking home, through Hamburg and Ellis Island, to the same corner of Chicago Stella's father had settled into. Their courtship should have been policed by her siblings and the Polish priests who ran the three mammoth Catholic churches that dominated the streets around the flat she shared with her sister. But in the ghetto traditional authority didn't always hold. Stella's mother and father were married in the baroque splendor of the Church of the Holy Innocents on June 24, 1914, a twenty-four-year-old tailor clinging to his tattered trade and his eighteen-year-old bride, who on her wedding day was at least six weeks pregnant.

The following February their son Chester was born. The next year—two days after Christmas 1916—they had Stella. A few months later the United States went to war. The mobilization stretched across the country, through draft calls, bond drives, and feverish demonstrations of Americanism. But it only reached her family in the cataclysmic autumn of 1918, when the Spanish flu came roaring down from the army camps north of the city.

They buried Stella's father in a spitting October rain. Afterward her uncle took them in, because somebody had to save them from tumbling into destitution. But he couldn't keep them forever, not with four children of his own to raise. So, in January 1920 Stella's mother married again. Her new husband was also a Polish immigrant, who'd come to the States ten years before without a trace of skill to sell. Sometimes a man in his position pulled himself up into factory work. He had stayed mired in the vast pool of common laborers who filled the lowest level of the working class, where a man took the sort of job that required nothing more than a strong back—hauling bricks, shoveling snow, laying streetcar lines—and hoped to hold it until the weather turned or someone stronger came along to replace him. The burden of his working day he softened with nights of drinking he couldn't control, which must have cost him a share of jobs he couldn't afford to lose. Maybe Stella's mother married him out of love, though it looked like desperation.

If the strains that ran through Stella's new family had an obvious marker, it was their shuffling from place to place. The year she turned seven they spent in a four-flat five blocks back of the stockyards, close enough that she must have gone to school each morning reeking of the pens. The next year they were in a carved-up workman's cottage in the Polish ghetto, close to where her father had died; the year after that down near the yards again; and the following year in another carved-up cottage in the West Side Jewish enclave. The other strains she was too young to understand. But there was some reason why her mother never had another baby, though she was only twenty-five when she remarried, and why she never gave Stella and her brother their stepfather's name.

Then the economy collapsed. When the slide started in the summer of 1929 they were living in an overflowing three-flat in the Czech neighborhood, her stepfather hauling furniture and her mother packing boxes in a candy factory to cover the rent. By the spring of 1930 he'd been let go, and the family was getting by on her paycheck alone. It wasn't enough. Stella's brother left school first, for a job out in a Cicero metal plant he probably landed because of the half-finished shop course he was leaving behind. Stella stayed long enough to complete the school's two-year commercial course. As soon as she was finished, in June 1932, she went to work too, in one of the city's secretarial pools. She was fifteen.

They were lucky to find anything at all. In April 1930 Chicago's unemployment rate reached 10.8 percent; eighteen months later it was at 40 percent. Other cities were hit just as hard. Gary, Indiana, lost 90,000 jobs in 1930 and 1931 as the demand for steel crumbled; Detroit a quarter million as the auto industry slashed into payrolls; and New York so many that the school board reported having 200,000 malnourished children in its classrooms. From there the contagion spread to the countryside, where already depressed farm prices plunged so low they didn't come close to covering the cost of the crops' planting, and into the financial system, which buckled beneath a crush of bank failures. Constricting credit sent the crisis surging through the networks that tied the American economy to the rest of the industrial world. By the summer of 1931 a quarter of British workers were unemployed. Germany's jobless rate had reached a crippling 34 percent. Central Europe's finances were in free fall. And Japan was being whipsawed by the foreign capital it couldn't raise and the exports it couldn't sell.

The political order couldn't stand the strain. In the final months of the year a hastily arranged coalition cabinet abandoned Britain's century-long commitment to free trade in a startling set of moves meant to wall off the empire from foreign competition. In May 1932 ultranationalists within Japan's fiercely imperialistic military all but destroyed the country's tenuous democracy by assassinating the prime minister who had tried to rein them in. Two months later Adolf Hitler's National Socialists took the largest share of seats in Germany's parliamentary elections, a victory that put one of Europe's most militaristic, racist, and incessantly violent political parties one step away from forming a government. Four months after that—in November 1932—a Democratic landslide made Franklin Roosevelt president of the United States.

It was the shape of the returns that seemed so stunning. For more than seventy years the Republicans had been the nation's dominant party, its majorities built on a fusing of the free-market principles the business class loved and the Protestant pieties that pulled in much of the middle class. The combination created its share of tensions—Wall Street financiers and small-town grocers didn't see the world in quite the same way—but it also gave the party an enormous reach: in the previous three presidential elections the Republicans had carried almost every state outside the Democrats' southern stronghold, often by massive margins.

In the 1920s the Republicans had used their power to sharply constrict the immigration that had filled the cities with people far different than their party's rank and file. The decisive law didn't limit the relatively small migration from Latin America—most of it from Mexico—which was inching Latinos' portion of the nation's population toward a still minuscule 1.5 percent. But it closed off Asian immigration entirely, a prohibition that for decades afterward kept Asian Americans' share of the population at about half a percent. And it eviscerated European immigration by imposing a set of national quotas calculated to dramatically reduce the number of people coming from the continent's southern and eastern rim. Stella's parents had both arrived in the States in the midst of a movement that was bringing in at least 100,000 Poles a year. The new rules sliced the allowable number to 6,000, so low that within a generation the Polish-born population would all but disappear, wiped out by a law designed to tell the immigrant masses that the nation wasn't theirs to shape.

That message didn't carry into 1932. Roosevelt swept the South, as a Democrat was expected to do. He also broke the Republicans' grip on the Plains and took the entire West Coast. But the most important turn came in neighborhoods like Stella's. The Democratic candidate hadn't won Chicago in 1928. Four years later Roosevelt piled up so many votes in its ethnic wards that he overwhelmed the Republican returns in the rest of Illinois. The same dynamic played out across the other major industrial states: Massachusetts, New York, Pennsylvania, Ohio, and Michigan all went Democratic because of the mobilization of the immigrant masses and their American-born sons and daughters on behalf of a patrician politician who promised to give their devastated communities a new deal.

FDR took office on March 4, 1933. That afternoon he launched an extraordinary stretch of experimentation and innovation in government power. Some of it aimed to reform malfunctioning markets. Banks were placed under tight new regulations, and the electrical grid extended into parts of the country that privately owned companies had refused to reach. The housing industry was transformed by Washington's willingness to insure mortgages in exchange for lenders lowering the down payments they required and stretching out the terms of their loans. But the bulk of Roosevelt's policies had a simpler purpose. The country wasn't going to be pulled out of its depression, administration officials decided, until ordinary Americans could afford to buy the huge quantities of goods its factories produced. So the federal government was going to get them the money they needed.

The most obvious way to do that was to give them jobs. State and local governments had long met economic downturns with public works programs. That's what FDR did too, through a welter of newly created agencies that pumped billions of dollars into projects the unemployed could be hired to do. What Roosevelt really wanted, though, was to get money into people's hands without the government having to put them to work. From that principle flowed the administration's most dramatic policies. It would pay farmers not to plant a portion of their fields, and by so doing drive up their incomes through the higher prices they could charge and the government checks they'd receive. It would guarantee industrial workers the right to unionize, in hopes that once they did they'd pull into their own paychecks a share of the profits their employers would otherwise keep for themselves. And in a single sprawling bill signed into law in August 1935, the administration provided monthly payments to workers facing a short stretch of joblessness, poor single mothers with dependent children, and most Americans over sixty-five: a stitched-together welfare state whose most far-reaching provision everyone took to calling Social Security.

It took a few months to put the first of Roosevelt's policies into place. Then the economy began to turn. Financial markets stabilized. Farm prices steadied. The industrial sector started to expand again. And the unemployment rate started to fall, from 25 percent in 1933 to 22 percent in 1934, 20 percent in 1935, and 17 percent in 1936. As the hiring gates opened, so did hopes that the industrial order could be transformed. By the summer of 1936 a group of insurgent unions had several hundred organizers out in strategically selected factory towns, telling workers there that they ought to claim the rights the New Deal had guaranteed them. And FDR was on the stump, lacerating the Republicans' most powerful businessmen, who were insisting that his reelection would turn the nation toward socialism. "These economic royalists complain that we seek to overthrow the institutions of America," he told the convention that had just nominated him for a second term. "What they really complain of is that we seek to take away their power" and to put in its place "a democracy of opportunity"—as militant a message as a president had ever delivered.[2]

But democracy had its limits. In the early nineteenth century the Democrats' defense of slavery had given them control of southern politics. The Civil War and its extraordinary aftermath had broken their grip; for a while it seemed that the South might build a multiparty, multiracial democracy. But in the century's last years the Democrats had reclaimed their hold on the region by creating a comprehensive system of racial domination. One part of that system required the strict segregation of social space: wherever whites and Blacks might interact—in schools and stores and streetcar lines—African Americans were to be shunted to the side, separate and unequal. The second part stripped African Americans of their vote through the flagrant manipulation of their states' electoral processes. The third buttressed the other two with the constant threat of white violence, its most severe form stunning in its barbarism.

African Americans had tried to block the system's brutal abrogation of their rights. When they were defeated—most devastatingly by the seven Supreme Court justices who decided in 1896 that "separate but equal" met the Constitution's standard—they pieced together a multisided movement to break down the system. But the political dynamics ran against them. The southern Democrats' exploitation of racism's poisonous appeal bound whites so tightly to them that most of the region became a one-party state. In much of the South the Republicans stopped even nominating candidates for office, since they had no chance of winning.

Decades of lopsided or uncontested elections gave the southern Democrats outsized influence on Capitol Hill: in Roosevelt's first term, the Speaker of the House came from Texas, the Senate majority leader from Arkansas, and most of the major committee chairmen from one southern state or another. In general they liked FDR's reforms, but they weren't going to let them become law unless they conformed to the South's racist regime. So Roosevelt looked away as they blocked their states' African American communities from the federal aid they desperately needed or used his programs to deepen their marginalization, because among the South's most powerful men nothing mattered more than preserving the color line.

Outside the South the New Deal's racial politics moved in more complicated ways. Thirty years of African American migration, the last fifteen of them at a furious pace, hadn't had any impact on much of the North and West: there were still ten times as many African Americans living in Georgia as in New England, on the Great Plains, or along the Pacific Coast. The migration had changed the nation's major cities, though. Since 1900 Detroit's Black population had shot up from 4,000 to 120,000, Chicago's from 30,000 to almost a quarter million, New York's from 60,000 to a third of a million. In none of those cities did African Americans face the legal humiliations that ran through the South. Nor were they stripped of their right to vote. Instead they were cordoned off by the private actions of whites who saw in their rising numbers a threat to their own social standing.

In the cities' public places the restrictions grew so haphazardly they seemed almost arbitrary, since everything pivoted on what a store owner or bartender might do when an African American walked in the door. At work the rules took a firmer form, though they still weren't perfectly clear. A Black doctor was never going to be hired into a white hospital, a Black attorney into a white law firm, or a Black working-woman into practically anything other than a service trade. But an African American workingman might get into a lower-end factory job, where the supply of white workers began to trickle out. Or he might be turned away, depending on where the hiring boss had decided to draw his color line.

That left one last division to define. As the Black migration intensified so had whites' insistence on the segregation of their neighborhoods. The pressure swelled up from the streets, nowhere more dangerously than in Chicago in the summer of 1919, when a Black teenager acci-

dently crossing one of the South Side's long-standing racial divides triggered a week-long pogrom that killed twenty-three African Americans.
But the crucial step came in the 1920s, as the businessmen who dominated the real estate markets of every major city systematized the segregation whites were demanding: realtors by refusing to show African
Americans properties in white neighborhoods, landlords by refusing
to rent to them there, bankers by refusing to give them mortgages, and
developers by barring them from ever buying homes in the tracts they
were building. In the process they locked Blacks into those areas whites
had already conceded—New York's Harlem, Detroit's Black Bottom,
Chicago's embattled South Side strip and West Side enclaves—and told
whites on the other side that the value of their homes now depended on
the color of their neighbors' skin.

African Americans pushed against that system of segregation as
forcefully as they did the southern version. But the New Dealers had no
intention of supporting demands to dismantle a racial system their white
voters embraced. Instead they made most of their reforms conform to
the restrictions already in place, sometimes by omission—nowhere in
their new labor laws did they mention employers' discriminatory hiring
practices—and sometimes by blatant commission: when they remade
the housing market they adopted as their own the racist lending policies bankers had used to harden the cities' segregation, and by so doing
made that segregation stronger still. They also didn't want to give up
on the bloc of African American votes the migration had created. And
some administration officials, at least, were genuinely concerned about
the Depression's intense effect on Black neighborhoods. So as they
reinforced the color line they made sure that their relief and recovery
programs crossed it. By late 1933 almost half of the African American
families in New York and Chicago were getting some share of their
income from New Deal agencies, the first time in half a century that
federal power had reached into their communities with anything other
than the back of its hand.

They reciprocated as the New Dealers had hoped they would. Roosevelt swept the white South again in the 1936 election. He also took

the cities' ethnic wards by even larger margins than he had four years before. This time the African American neighborhoods swung to him too. Together they pushed his share of the urban returns to stratospheric levels. He won 65 percent of the vote in Chicago, 70 percent in Cleveland, and 72 percent in New York, which made the country's most cosmopolitan city almost as solidly Democratic as Mississippi, where African Americans couldn't vote at all. That crush of support overwhelmed the Republicans' solidly conservative candidate, who took just 36.5 percent of the vote nationwide, the party's worst showing in eighty years. Eight weeks later a confrontation in a corner of General Motors' automaking empire triggered the decade's great strike wave. For almost a year it rolled through the nation's industrial core. When it finally receded more than three million workers had been unionized, more than enough to make the New Deal's realignment of public life seem complete.

By then Stella had been working for five years, her brother for six. The first few years must have been the hardest. They were teenagers, after all, holding on to jobs they had to have in what turned out to be the Depression's most devastating stretch. When the economy started to recover the fear probably faded a bit, though a lifetime of insecurity wasn't going to disappear with a drop in the unemployment rate. It certainly didn't for their mother. Every paycheck they received they undoubtedly handed to her, in the working-class tradition. Some portion she set aside, up to the spring of 1935, when she had enough for a down payment on a house.

She found a fifty-year-old cottage on the northwest edge of the Polish ghetto. It had long ago been cut into three apartments, one in the basement, one on the first floor, and the third in the attic. Her family could take the middle and let out the other two, so the rent would flow in rather than out. And after a quarter century of living in other people's houses she'd finally been able to give her family a home of their own. But a down payment alone couldn't buy her the house. And there wasn't a bank in the city that would loan her the rest, since the New Deal's housing agencies had decided that the neighborhood was too poor to insure any mortgages issued there. That left her to the informal money markets that snaked through the center city. She chose one run by a Polish-American lawyer—a man of considerable standing—who owned a real estate office in the heart of her old neighborhood. He was willing to give her the money she needed, as long as she'd agree to pay him back on a strict schedule and let him put his name alongside hers on the deed. Chances are the lawyer didn't tell her the meaning of those terms, nor would she have been willing to risk his offer by asking. She took possession of her new home on April 15, 1935, a triumph under-written by an arrangement that gave her co-owner the legal right to sell the property out from under her the moment she missed a payment.

Ed

STELLA MET ED CAHILL three years later, on a blind date a girl from the neighborhood had arranged because she thought he was too short to date him herself. He took her to one of the city's most popular ven-ues, the elegant Aragon ballroom, its lobby lit by crystal chandeliers, its ceiling painted to look like you were dancing under the stars, and its little corps of chaperones circulating around the dance floor to keep it free of any impropriety. An evening meant to dazzle her, in a safe sort of way.

That was Ed. Compared to Stella he was an old-line American, on his father's side at least, his great-grandparents having come to the States from famine-ravaged Ireland in the 1840s. They'd made their way to tiny Ashkum, Illinois, eighty miles south of Chicago. There they built a prairie version of Irish peasant life, bounded by the land they farmed and the Catholicism they'd carried from home. When they got too old to manage the farm anymore they passed it to Ed's grandfather, who eventually would have passed it to Ed's father had his dad not decided, in the first few years of the new century, to go looking for work up in Chicago instead. The Catholicism he took with him.

He'd had only eight years of schooling, none of them spent learning a trade, which should have put him a rung below Stella's father. But he was a native English speaker with an Irish name, which was enough to get him hired as a foreman with a road construction company that made its money contracting with the city. It was a solid, dependable job at the upper end of the working class, far above the pick-and-shovel men he supervised, and once he had it he held on to it, through his marriage to an Irish girl in 1906, the birth of their sons—William in 1908, Ed in 1917—and the pandemic that took their mother from them in December 1918, two months after it had taken Stella's father from her.

Ed's father remarried in May 1920. There was a transactional sense to it. He was a forty-year-old widower who'd spent the previous year and a half crammed into his sister and brother-in-law's apartment because he couldn't imagine how he'd raise two boys on his own. She was a thirty-four-year-old living with her mother in the apartment next door, staring into a life alone. Whatever they each took from the wedding, though, their marriage worked: they had their first child in 1921, their second in 1924, and their third in 1927. About a year before her last delivery they left the row house they had been renting in an Irish-American neighborhood on the West Side and bought a home of their own at 6131 West Eddy Street.

It was a little brick bungalow set on a narrow lot in one of the many tracts builders were putting up in a massive band of development along Chicago's western edge. For $9,000, half of it covered by the sort of conventional mortgage Stella's mother couldn't secure, they got a single floor of living space, an attic they could turn into a bedroom for the kids, a small backyard, a patch of grass out front, and a neighborhood meant for that strata of the working class—craftsmen, foremen, machinists, and a scattering of low-end office workers—who could afford the order and respectability the center city couldn't provide. On the side streets the bungalows would be perfectly aligned, one a few feet from the next, without any apartment blocks or sweatshops squeezed in between. The business strips would have strings of small shops, some storefront offices, and on the busiest of them a fancy new movie theater that wouldn't have a hint of scandal about it. That was the plan, at least. In practice the area had a half-finished feel. A number of the lots along the Cahills' block had yet to be developed. The theater had yet to open. And the neighborhood's Catholic parish was so new it had a priest and a patron saint—Ferdinand of Castile—but had yet to build a church or a school.

Ed's father was willing to wait on the church, since a priest could say Mass anywhere. The school was a necessity. Catholic parents might have to send their kids to the public schools, the nation's bishops had said. If they could manage it, though, they ought to put them into the parochial school system the Church maintained in every city with a sizable immigrant population. Ed's parents weren't given to defying the faithful's obligations. And with almost 250 schools in operation, Chicago's system was far too vast for them to pretend they couldn't find a way to fit Ed in. So they enrolled him in the grade school of the next parish over. When he finished they sent him to a boys' high school back in their old neighborhood, since there wasn't one anywhere near Eddy Street. He graduated in 1935, steeped in the tradition, discipline, decorum, and respect for authority the hierarchy expected a son of the Church to have.

The timing was just about perfect. For three years Chicago's mayor, Edward Kelly, had been funneling New Deal money into a vast patronage system that would turn the city into a Democratic machine. The system ran along Chicago's numerous ethnic lines. But as a proud product of Bridgeport, Kelly tilted it toward the Irish, which is undoubtedly why a kid with nothing more to offer than a set of commercial courses with the priests at St. Philip's High managed to get hired as a file clerk in the Chicago office of the New Deal's principal relief agency. It was routine work, but it paid a government wage and promised a government pension, remarkable things in the midst of the Depression. And Ed couldn't have gotten it without the connections that coiled through his parochial world.

There was something else about the timing as well. In the 1920s the moral reformers' urban crusades had stalled out. Now they were back, revived by a new generation of ethnic politicians brought to power by the same immigrant wards that had given FDR the presidency. On economic issues they were almost uniformly liberal. But they also carried with them the traditional sense of morality that ran through their communities. So it wasn't New York's middle class that finally suppressed the city's long-vibrant gay street life; it was its progressive new mayor, Fiorello La Guardia, the aspiring son of immigrants from Apulia and Trieste. Cities and states had been trying to censor Hollywood's films for a quarter century. But it wasn't until a well-placed group of Catholics threatened action in 1934 that the studios adopted the draconian production code that stripped their movies of anything other than the mildest hints of desire. And in Chicago Mayor Kelly resurrected the reformers' old campaign against public shows of sexuality through a series of police raids meant to show that the city belonged to boys like Ed, who wanted nothing more than to take their girls to a night of chaperoned dancing under a starlit ceiling.

Ed and Stella were married on May 28, 1940. It was a peculiar spring, caught between the Depression that the New Deal had yet fully to defeat and the suddenly expanding war most Americans didn't want to fight. In Asia the bloodshed had been spreading since 1931, when the Japanese military launched the first stage of its imperialist assault on China. In Europe the route had been more circuitous. The conflict had started when Hitler assumed Germany's chancellorship in January 1933, passed through a series of provocations none of the other major powers were willing to confront, and turned into a continent-wide war in September 1939, when the Germans and Russians overran Poland: the village where Stella's mother had grown up fell to the Reich, her father's hometown to the Soviets. A month before her wedding day the German army struck to the west, through Norway, Denmark, the Netherlands, and Belgium to the French coast. Two weeks into her marriage the Germans took Paris, and FDR started the nation's torturous march toward intervention.

When Roosevelt's proposal to put in place a military draft reached Congress toward the end of June, Ed and Stella were settling into half of a two-flat a mile west of her parents' house. The vigorous, occasionally bitter debate over the propriety of conscripting men when the country wasn't at war ran through the summer, as her mother grappled with what seems to have been her stepfather's sudden illness, though twenty years of living with his drinking must have given her plenty of experience in dealing with unwelcome turns. Congress passed a heavily amended version of Roosevelt's bill on September 14, 1940. Six days later Stella's stepfather died, leaving behind her forty-four-year-old mother, who'd now be making do on the little pension the government paid and the rents from the house she didn't quite own. Three weeks after her stepfather's passing Ed went over to the local draft board four blocks from their flat to fill in his registration form. It was a formality, since Congress had decided that drafting married men was a step too far for a nation at peace. But the army needed to know where to find him should his time ever come.

For the next three years the war metastasized, through Germany's invasion of the Soviet Union in June 1941, the Japanese attack on Pearl Harbor in December 1941, and the two years of fighting that followed, the worst of it—the siege of Leningrad, the Bataan death march, the war-induced famine in Bengal—staggering in its brutality. Roosevelt responded with a total mobilization of American power. A month after Pearl Harbor he told Congress that he wanted "a crushing superiority of equipment in any theater of the world war."[3] To get it, Washington essentially shut down the manufacturing of civilian goods and put in its place $110 billion in defense contracts in 1942 alone, mostly to major corporations that had the ability to produce the mammoth amounts of materiel the military needed. A solid share of the federal spending poured into Chicago's enormous industrial complex for freight cars, landing craft, airplane engines, metal sheeting, mosquito netting, processed cheese, and an obscure little South Side metallurgical lab of forty employees whose work would create a world of limitless destruction.

FDR portrayed the spending as a tactical turn, distinct from the New Deal's social engineering. In fact the two were intimately linked. The administration's wartime industrial mobilization was essentially a public works program so colossal it wiped out the joblessness the New

Deal version had spent eight years trying to break. The government paid about half its costs by borrowing the money it needed, the other half by revising federal taxes in an intensely progressive direction: the highest rate, on incomes over $200,000, hit 94 percent, four times the rate for the lowest earners. At the same time, the administration put provisions into its defense contracts that made it easier for the labor movement to add new members. Those rules interlaced with a plummeting unemployment rate to bring six million more workers into unions, among them Stella's brother, whose factory out in Cicero unionized in 1943. Once they were organized they could push up their wages for jobs that had been created in large part by taxing the well-to-do, an arrangement designed to shift income down the class structure, a New Deal policy through and through.

The spending had a geographic dimension too. Wherever the money went, people followed. Mostly they abandoned the countryside, the rural South especially, since there wasn't much point in staying in the Mississippi Delta or Alabama's Black Belt when there were high-paying jobs waiting for workers in Chicago or Detroit. So the biggest cities grew bigger still: Chicago's population shot up by about 175,000 during the war, its African American population by 60,000. Washington also used its funding to reconfigure the nation's industrial base, drawing it out from the cities to their suburbs, where there was plenty of land to build giant facilities, and into those parts of the country in desperate need of development. In 1940 Marietta, Georgia, was a fading mill town of 8,600. Then the federal government gave Bell Aircraft $75 million to build a bomber plant there, and Marietta wasn't fading anymore.

For all the opportunity war work opened, it also created enormous strains. The tension ran along factory floors packed with people who in harder times never would have been working side by side. It cut through the parks, the theaters, the diners, the corner bars, and the streetcars overwhelmed by the wartime migration. And it reached into those places where ordinary people lived. There'd been almost no new housing built during the Depression, certainly not in little towns that never dreamed of a sudden surge in their population or in those sections of the center cities most likely to draw in the working class. Washington tried to ease the pressure by slapping up a smattering of public housing for war workers—Chicago got four smallish projects, one of them on the eastern end of the Polish ghetto—but the demand overwhelmed the supply. So new arrivals pressed in wherever they could, doubling and tripling up in flats and tenements that hadn't been so crowded since the peak of immigration thirty years before.

The most severe conflicts followed the color line. During the war the long-struggling civil rights movement won some signal victories in the courts and the administrative structures of the mobilization. On the ground, though, whites resisted racial change as fiercely as they ever had. They lashed out at African Americans who moved into industrial jobs they hadn't been allowed to hold before the war, who dared to go into parks or stores whites claimed as their own, or who refused to sit in the back of a Jim Crow bus. And they insisted that the crush of African American migrants squeeze into the neighborhood boundaries that segregation had imposed. That particular restriction created intolerable pressures: by 1943 Chicago's Black South Side housed three times as many people per square mile as the white areas on its border, while the African American West Side strained at its seams. To find some relief on the other side of the boundary, though— even a block or two into the closest white neighborhood—meant putting your family at risk of having a brick thrown through the window of your new home, a fire set on your porch, or a mob form in the street in front of your door, a pattern repeated in cities across the nation.

The violence didn't reach the Cahills, who lived miles from the nearest color line. But the war itself closed in. Sometime in the spring of 1942—a few months after Pearl Harbor—Stella realized that she was pregnant. The military was even more reluctant to draft fathers than it was young married men. So Ed spent America's first long year of fighting safe at home, much of it waiting for his baby to be born. Then the army's casualties started to mount, the generals intensified their mobilization, and the draft's exemptions began to fall away. His call-up notice finally arrived in November 1943, with an induction date of

December 23, three days before Stella's twenty-seventh birthday and a month past their daughter Judy's first.

He was gone for two and a half years. In that time the Allies launched the blood-soaked campaigns that would topple Germany and Japan. Thirty-four thousand Americans were killed in the march up from Normandy's beaches in the summer of 1944; 200,000 Poles in that August's Warsaw uprising; another 20,000 Americans in the Wehrmacht's December counteroffensive in the Ardennes; 80,000 Germans in the Allied bombing campaign that ended the year; 250,000 Filipinos in the February 1945 battle for Manila; 100,000 Japanese in the American bombing that burned much of Tokyo to the ground in March 1945; 150,000 Okinawans in the carnage that consumed their island throughout the spring; 100,000 Russians in the April 1945 battle for Berlin, which reduced the Reich's last bastion to rubble.

From there the news grew even darker. During that final month of the European war the Americans reached Germany's western-most concentration camps. In the stacks of bodies they discovered there they confirmed the long-standing rumor that the Nazis were systematically annihilating European Jewry. Genocide, the experts called it, as if the only way to capture the enormity of a crime that murdered six million people was to give it a name no one had heard before. Four months later the United States ended the Pacific war by unleashing the power harnessed by that little South Side lab three years earlier. Some 70,000 people were killed in the first atomic blast, in Hiroshima on August 6, 1945; 40,000 in the second, in Nagasaki on August 9: another 110,000 victims added to the 60 million lives already lost.

Through it all Stella knew that Ed would be coming home. He said so in the sweet, often playful letters he sent from the training camp where the army decided he'd make a fine clerk for the Signal Corps, from the troop ship that took him to Europe, and from the desk job they gave him in newly liberated France once the Allied offensive had pushed the Germans back toward the Rhine. She said so whenever she showed Judy her photo of Ed in his uniform, something she did almost every day to make sure his daughter would know who he was when he returned. And she told herself that going back to the work she'd given up when Judy was born—she took a job as a secretary on the afternoon shift at a mechanical pencil factory—was a temporary arrangement to cover the income they'd lose while he was away.

But she couldn't have read through the newspaper without noticing the long lists of those killed in action, their next of kin listed alongside them; or gone to Sunday Mass without hearing the prayers for parish boys lost; or pushed a stroller around the neighborhood without seeing a gold star in somebody's front window. With all those marks of death around her, it would have taken an almost incomprehensible act of will for her not to imagine a Western Union messenger at her door handing her the government's regrets, and the spiral that would follow as she became her mother in the autumn of 1918, a far-too-young widow with a toddler clinging to her skirt, her fragile life lying in ruins around her.

Homecoming

THE EUROPEAN WAR ended in the wreckage of Berlin on May 8, 1945, the Pacific war on August 15, six days after Nagasaki's incineration. The military wanted to stretch its demobilization over a couple of years to make sure that the United States had enough troops to police its share of the vast territory the fighting had destroyed. But the idea of keeping the boys in uniform now that the war was over caused such outrage that the generals had to back down: within a year of Japan's surrender they'd discharged about 80 percent of the soldiers and sailors under their command. Ed's turn came on April 3, 1946. When he got home his three-year-old knew exactly who he was.

He had a bundle of veterans' benefits waiting for him, among them Washington's offer to pay for any more schooling he might want. For a little while he thought of using it to pick up a trade. Then they learned that Stella was expecting again and it seemed more important that he get a job. It was a tough time to be looking for work. But he managed to get hired as a clerk at the Vacuum Can Company, a manufacturer of heavy-grade thermoses and industrial-strength coffee urns with offices in a bleak little industrial strip squeezed between the lower West Side's African American neighborhood to its north and the Italian neighborhood to its south. A white-collar job in a blue-collar business set along the color line.

The Cahills settled into a less than complete peace. Ten years of depression had fundamentally undermined the international order. The war brought it crashing down. The world's other industrial powers had been bled white: Britain by the cost of the fighting, which had savaged its finances; France by the German and Allied eviscerations of its ports, factories, roads, rail lines, and honor; Germany and Japan by destruction so severe that in the months after their defeat large parts of their populations edged toward starvation. The Soviets had been bled worst of all. Still, they saw in the Western powers' fall their opportunity to consolidate their control over the Eastern European nations the Red Army had occupied on its drive to Berlin, a process shaped by Stalinist repression, appropriation, and the horrors of ethnic cleansing. In Japan's collapse China's Communist movement saw its path to power, though it would take three years of civil war and six million casualties for its forces to bring the revolution to its triumphant conclusion. And through the enormous stretches of the world the great powers had claimed as their empires—in the East Indies, the Philippines, Malaya, Indochina, Burma, India, Iraq, Iran, Algeria, Tunisia, Morocco, Ghana, Nigeria, Kenya, and Uganda—the colonized saw their chance to throw off their colonizers and claim the right to rule themselves.

The convulsions rattled through the United States too. Franklin Roosevelt had picked Harry Truman as his running mate in the 1944 election to please the party's southern wing, which had grown tired of his previous vice president's progressivism. But the implications of the choice reached much further, since it was plain to see that FDR was dying. The end came late on the afternoon of April 12, 1945, two hours after he'd suffered a massive cerebral hemorrhage. So it was Truman who had to guide the world's most powerful nation through the final months of the world war and the global crises that followed; who had to shape a foreign policy in the shadow of so many deaths; and who by the spring of 1947 had decided that the United States would define its place in the world in opposition to Soviet aggression, even if that meant fighting a long cold war of attrition.

And it was Truman who had to navigate the fierce politics peace unleashed. Almost as soon as the war was over he slashed military spending and lifted most of the government's restrictions on private production to induce a rapid return to the civilian economy the mobilization had shut down. He also wanted to temper that economy with the dramatically expanded New Deal Roosevelt had sketched out in his last year. Washington ought to be required to maintain the full employment the war had created, FDR had said then, so that every American could have a job at a living wage as a matter of right rather than luck. It ought to replace its patchwork of housing policies with a guarantee that every American would have a decent home. And it ought to assure every American a solid education and proper health care, two commitments that even in its most capacious moments the New Deal had never taken on. Gradually Truman added a third. The federal government had to secure the civil rights of those citizens who were now denied them, he told Congress in his 1948 State of the Union address, in direct defiance of the southerners sitting in front of him.

Nothing went to plan. Instead of reinvigorating the civilian economy, his defense cutbacks triggered a contraction so severe it took almost three years to reverse, while the end of wartime controls released a dramatic surge in prices. Through 1946 and 1947 the Republicans revived their 1930s assault on reform as a threat to free enterprise, an attack made all the more powerful by the anti-Communist fervor Truman himself was stoking. And as he closed in on the 1948 election his own party splintered beneath him. The revolt started in some of the country's most progressive districts, where his anti-Communism was anathema. But it reached dramatic proportions at the Municipal Auditorium in Birmingham, Alabama, where in the summer of 1948 the Democrats' most ardent segregationists formed a third party—fronted by South Carolina's Strom Thurmond—purely to deny Truman the southern states he had to carry, on the calculation that it was better to put a Republican in the presidency than to let the Democrats drift toward racial justice.

Truman hit back with a fall campaign designed to counter the party's divisions with a relentless appeal to the coalition Roosevelt had assembled. Across its strongholds he raced, from a massive Labor Day rally in downtown Detroit through a defiant Texas swing to a precedent-shattering appearance before 65,000 people in Harlem on a sparkling late October day. At almost every stop he pitted himself against the forces of reaction that wanted to rob the common man of the New Deal's protections and drive him back into the darkness of the Great Depression. It was an exhilarating, exhausting, occasionally demagogic performance that no one thought would work until the returns came in. Up on Capitol Hill, the southern bloc gave Truman the rest of the year to think that his victory had won him something beyond another term. Then he sent them the comprehensive reforms he wanted enacted, and they joined with their Republican colleagues to defeat them all: civil rights by filibuster, national health care by a burst of red-baiting that turned it into socialized medicine, and housing reform by a legislative transformation that made his bill into a boon for developers, a sign of things to come.

The Cahills probably weren't paying much attention. Stella delivered their son Terry in March 1947. Eight months later Ed's stepmother died. That an arrangement had to be made was obvious enough, since no one could remember a time when his father had managed on his own. Still, when Ed said that they ought to move in with him, Stella had every reason to refuse. She'd spent her entire married life a twenty-minute walk from her mother's house, a trip one or the other of them had made almost every day during the war, when Stella had a job to hold and a toddler to raise on her own. Out on Eddy Street she'd be six miles away, trying to fit a newborn and a five-year-old into an old man's house; adding his laundry, his meals, and his care to theirs; and filling the days they'd spend together while Ed was at work halfway across Chicago. But there was something driving the idea she couldn't resist: Ed's sense of obligation, a veteran's longing for home, the Cahills' intense attachment to whatever land they owned. So sometime in 1948 they cleared out their flat and moved into his dad's bungalow.

The neighborhood had had some additions over the years. The Cahills' parish, St. Ferdinand's, had opened a grade school in 1934, though it took the pastor another two years to move the kids from Quonset huts into a proper building. In 1938 Sears had put a new store on one of the shopping strips. And there'd been a little flurry of home building in 1940 and 1941, as contractors filled in some of the lots the original developer hadn't reached before the Depression shut him down. The war put a stop to that, and the postwar contraction slowed a revival; not until 1948 did home construction nationwide come close to matching the 1920s' peak years. The vast majority of those houses were being built in the suburbs the government's wartime investments had opened up, where there was still enough land for developers to lay out entire subdivisions. But there was a scattering of new homes going in around Eddy Street too, simple little ranches their builders could market to that portion of working people the bungalow belt had been designed to serve, a couple of dozen houses at most, barely enough to make the neighborhood feel as if it might finally be filling in.

The center city was moving in a decidedly different direction. Right after the war most major cities had adopted master plans to remake their poorest neighborhoods. There were touches of reform about them, particularly in their talk of easing the war's desperate overcrowding with a dramatic expansion of public housing, a step toward FDR's promise of a decent home for everyone. But they were far more focused on ripping out the blight that poverty created and putting in its place amenities that the experts believed a modern city had to have. Chicago's plan followed the pattern perfectly. It proposed two major projects, one to level entire stretches of cold-water flats and kitchenettes on the African American South Side to make room for developments that could draw in the middle class; the other to carve five huge gashes through the city, from downtown to the suburbs, and to lay in them a web of highways for the postwar auto age. Some of those displaced by the destruction could move into the public housing the plan called for. As for the rest, they'd be on their own.

Ed could see the consequences when he headed into work. The neighborhoods on either side of Vacuum Can were already caught in the war-hardened tangle of race, space, and violence when he hired in. Once the state approved Chicago's plan, the strains grew stronger still. In 1948 the city started to clear a two-block-wide strip through the Italian neighborhood—just a third of a mile south of Ed's office—for the first of its freeways, the bulldozers driving out eighty, ninety, sometimes a hundred families with every block they demolished. Around the same time the South Side projects issued their initial eviction notices, and suddenly the African American neighborhood to the north of Vacuum Can was hit with yet another wave of people searching for housing they had to find, in an area that had no place to put them. In the pressure of the moment some of them edged across the color line, just as a few Black families had during the war. There was another quick burst of violence. This time it was followed by something that hadn't happened with those first breaches a few years before. By 1950 almost 40 percent of the Italian families had moved away, leaving to the growing number of African Americans who took their place a neighborhood the city had devastated by slicing it in two.

That summer the international order lurched again. The *Tribune* delivered the first dispatch to the Cahills' door on Sunday morning, June 25, 1950, half a day after Communist North Korea had sent its military surging across the South Korean border. On Monday the story worsened. South Korean defenses were collapsing. The Communists had reached the capital. Seoul was about to fall. On Tuesday Truman committed the United States to beating back the North's aggression. On Wednesday American bombers made their first runs while Congress raced to pass a rapid expansion of the draft. The following day Truman told the press that the US intervention was purely "a police action" against a "bandit" regime. But as the *Trib* said in a searing editorial, it looked a lot like war.[4]

It felt like one too. In the first four months of its intervention the

United States lost 6,000 men, the two Koreas far more. Then the violence accelerated, through the Chinese offensive the Americans didn't see coming, the furious combat it took to escape it, and the strikes and counterstrikes that turned December's retreat into the following spring's stalemate. Through the balance of 1951 both sides tried to break the impasse with a series of assaults that, at their worst, bore a terrifying resemblance to World War I's marches toward the enemy's trenches and on the American side to the bombing campaigns that had incinerated much of Japan in the last months of World War II.

As the deadlock tightened, the Republican Right launched a feverish escalation of its anti-Communism, twisted around a scalding attack on Truman's handling of the war. The offensive raced through the 1950 congressional elections, led by the Republicans' new red-baiting star, Wisconsin's junior senator Joe McCarthy. The next spring it linked itself to the American forces' commanding officer, the old war hero Douglas MacArthur, whom Truman had abruptly ordered home when he dared to defy the president's orders. MacArthur should have returned in disgrace. Instead he strutted across the country, soaking up the public's adulation—in Chicago three million people came out just to see his motorcade pass by—while slashing away at Truman as too weak-willed to give Americans the victory they deserved.

He was still on tour in June 1951 when McCarthy took to the Senate floor to expose a Communist conspiracy so immense it beggared belief. Yet his colleagues on the Republican Right lined up behind him, assuming that the more outrageous his accusations became the more damage they'd do. So it seemed. By January 1952, 72 percent of Americans believed McCarthy's poisonous charge that the State Department was infested with subversives. And the first round of the year's presidential polling put Truman 16 points behind the Republicans' leading candidate, Ohio senator Robert Taft, who'd spent his entire career trying to roll back the New Deal and block the international commitments the Democrats had made.

In that catastrophic stretch Truman also lost control of the war's political economy. Shortly before he ordered the troops into Korea he'd proposed that the next year's defense budget be set at $13.5 billion, 85 percent below what it had been in World War II's final year. Once the troops went into Korea, the spending started to spiral, to $48 billion in 1951 and $60 billion in 1952, about half of what the United States had been spending on its military at the peak of World War II. The soldiers out in the field drew a portion of the money. But the greater pull came from the generals and their supporters inside the administration, who saw in Korea their chance to restore the massive material advantage the military had enjoyed before Truman had cut its budget down to size. Out poured a flood of corporate contracts for the tanks and jets and helicopters, computer banks and missile systems the Pentagon's planners believed would shape the wars to come. Within nine months of the US intervention General Motors had over a billion dollars in defense contracts secured, General Electric and Douglas Aircraft half a billion each, with plenty more to come. Even Vacuum Can got a little share, for the Aervoid model 901, its cutting-edge, vacuum-sealed, three-gallon coffee urn.

Truman established some controls to prevent the spending from triggering a repeat of the ruinous inflation of 1946 and 1947. But he didn't stop private production as Roosevelt had in World War II. So the portion of defense dollars that filtered into people's paychecks at GM, GE, or Vacuum Can could go out again, to buy houses or cars or even one of the fabulous new television sets everyone was talking about. Mounting sales pushed up production, which pushed up hiring, often at union wages. That gave yet more workers money to spend, which pushed production higher still. In 1949 the economy had contracted for the third time in four years. In 1950 it grew by 8.7 percent, and in 1951 by another 8 percent, enough to cut the unemployment rate to its lowest level since 1945. There was the self-sustaining cycle of production and consumption the New Dealers had envisioned in 1933. But the defeat of the universal protections Truman had hoped to put in place back in 1945 meant that the benefits of prosperity did not flow to everyone. Now some Americans were going to be shut out.

Geography helped to decide who they'd be. Some of the money coursing through the economy reached into the old industrial centers, whose factories were still producing a solid share of the goods people wanted to buy. Far more flowed along the suburban channels World War II had created. Bell Aircraft had shut down its Marietta bomber plant when the federal government canceled its contracts in 1945. In 1951 Lockheed used a portion of the $162 million it received from the Defense Department to open it up again. Douglas Aircraft used a portion of its contracts to expand the sprawling facility it had built ten years before in Long Beach, on suburban Los Angeles' southern coast. And GM poured $100 million into a gleaming new 38-building tech center five miles beyond Detroit's city limits, down the road from the tank plant Chrysler had been running since 1941. Wherever the defense dollars went, the housing market followed. Between the summer of 1950 and December 1952, developers built about 3.5 million new homes. About 80 percent of them went up in the suburbs. Almost all of them were sold to whites.

That wasn't accidental. In 1947 the Supreme Court had invalidated the legal restrictions developers had long used to block African Americans from buying their properties. But suburban realtors, bankers, and local officials embraced the other tactics their colleagues had deployed back in the 1920s to segregate city neighborhoods, while federal authorities laid across new subdivisions the same discriminatory rules they'd set over the cities in the 1930s. Together those barriers made it all but impossible for African Americans to move into most of the nation's suburbs. If they should somehow squeeze past them, their new neighbors had one last line of defense, as Harvey and Johnetta Clark learned in the summer of 1951.

The Clarks and their two children had come to Chicago from Mississippi in 1949, another tiny addition to the southern migration that four years after the war was showing no signs of abating. They'd gone to the South Side, where they rented half of a four-room apartment, a space far too small for a family of four. By the time they could afford something more, African Americans had pushed a bit farther south, into streets that whites were rapidly deserting. But the city had also used $9 million in federal funds it had taken from Congress's 1949 Housing Act to accelerate its clearance program; during the Clarks' first two years in Chicago, it razed a hundred acres of low-income housing on the South Side's northern end. At the same time officials stopped putting up new public housing while they looked for ways to appease whites outraged by the possibility of projects being built in their neighborhoods. So even with the South Side's expansion the Clarks couldn't find anything better than what they already had. Then a real estate broker told them about a spacious apartment out in Cicero.

They knew that renting there was a risky thing to do. Cicero wasn't one of the new developments. It was a bungalow-belt suburb, built around Western Electric's gargantuan plant in the 1910s and 1920s and filled with ethnic workers—tradesmen and factory hands—just a step above the whites who lived along Chicago's color lines. Still, the Clarks hadn't expected that on their move-in day, June 8, 1951, they'd be met by a squad of Cicero cops, who turned them away with threats and force and racial slurs. So they went to court to demand that Cicero's authorities respect their right to live wherever they pleased. The ruling came down toward the end of June, along with an order that the city give the Clarks the protection they needed. Two weeks later, on July 10, they moved their belongings into their new home. Then they drove away for the evening, having claimed what was theirs.

That night 500 people jammed the streets around the Clarks' building, more than enough to break the cordon the Cicero police and the county sheriff had put up to meet the court's order. But rather than test the cordon the angriest portions of the crowd settled for lobbing stones at the building's windows. The next night the mob swelled to 3,500, and the angriest took to stoning the police. In the melee some twenty young men breached the barrier; they were let through, the sheriff's men said afterward, by Cicero cops unwilling to beat back their neighbors. Into the building they raced, up the stairs, and into the Clarks' third-floor apartment. They ripped apart the furniture, wrenched the toilet from the floor and the stove from the gas line, slashed through the boxes packed with personal items—the children's clothes, the family photos, Harvey Clark's army discharge papers—and threw whatever they could out the windows the mob had shattered the night before, so that the throng in the street could see what they had done.

On the third night the mob swelled again, the Cicero police stepped down, and after an evening of almost constant attacks the sheriff's cordon finally cracked. This time the mob's vanguard surged through the line armed with cherry bombs and homemade Molotov cocktails that set the building to burning. When Cicero's firemen tried to put out the flames, the crowd stoned them too. Around 10:30 p.m. 500 National Guardsmen rolled in, under orders from Illinois' governor Adlai Stevenson—a Democrat of aristocratic mien and liberal leanings—to bring the rioting to an end. That they did, in a two-hour battle that hospitalized nine members of the mob, seven of them with bayonet wounds. Once they had the streets secured the guardsmen strung the block with barbed wire to protect the gutted apartment the Clarks would never make their home, seven miles due south of Eddy Street.

Security

WHATEVER HOPE TRUMAN had of being reelected collapsed on March 11, 1952, when he lost the New Hampshire primary to a first-term senator who'd had the audacity to challenge him for the Democratic nomination. Truman withdrew from the race two weeks later, his political life destroyed by forces he'd thought he could control. The fight to replace him stretched all the way to the summer's convention in Chicago's International Amphitheatre, hard alongside the stockyards. There the Democrats decided that the home state's governor could have the unenviable honor of leading their wounded party against another hero come home from the war, this one far more formidable than MacArthur had been.

Not that Dwight Eisenhower wanted to seem formidable. When FDR had named him the supreme commander of the US forces in Europe in

June 1942, almost no one outside the military knew who he was; in its first profile the *Washington Post* called him the army's "mystery man."[5] Through the campaigns that followed he became the European war's public face, the newsreel general in his trim field jacket guiding the troops with a cool efficiency that would bring most of them home when the fighting was done. By the war's end he'd become one of the nation's most admired men.

Talk of his running for president began within a few months of Germany's surrender. Whenever it swelled to serious proportions, as it did in 1948 and again in 1950 and 1951, Eisenhower deflated it with a powerful appeal to principle. He was an active-duty officer, he said, cycling through a series of crucial posts—army chief of staff, chairman of the Joint Chiefs, NATO's first supreme commander—and as such was obligated to avoid partisan politics, a responsibility he took so seriously he'd never even voted, much less joined a political party. But his sense of the nation's proper course he took from the most sophisticated members of the Republicans' corporate wing. The United States had to exercise the global power its position demanded of it, he believed, particularly in opposition to the Soviet threat. But it had to do so with much more subtlety than Truman had managed. And the federal government had to provide ordinary Americans the basic security they deserved, as the best of the New Deal had done. But to go any further would take the country toward socialist "statism," he wrote in his diary in January 1949, "and therefore slavery."[6]

At first the executives whose ideas he shared settled for earnest discussions with Ike over private dinners and the occasional round of golf at Augusta, his favorite course. As the Korean debacle deepened in 1951, they pushed for more. For much of the year, the letters and visits kept coming, from the presidents of General Electric, General Foods, and General Motors, Ford, Chrysler, Studebaker, Republic Steel, National Steel, CITGO, and IBM; the publishers of the *New York Times*, the *Washington Post*, *Time* magazine, and the Gannett newspaper chain; and the financiers of Chase Manhattan, Dillon Read, and the fabled House of Morgan. Each of them delivered a version of the same appeal. McCarthy's rampage through public life had given the Republican reactionaries control of the party, they said. They'll use it to nominate Taft, who'll run against the New Deal. When he does, he'll go tumbling down just as the Republicans had in 1948, because Americans won't vote for a candidate who promises to take away their Social Security checks. In defeat he'll give the Democrats four more years to destroy free enterprise. There was only one way to break that chain of events, they told him. The Republicans had to nominate someone who could calm the passions Korea had enflamed while maintaining American global commitments, who understood that what the Democrats had created couldn't be undone but shouldn't be extended, and who floated above politics to such an extent he didn't seem like a politician at all. Someone like Ike.

Eisenhower still couldn't bring himself to run, but in January 1952 he announced that he'd accept the nomination if the party were to offer it to him. He spent the next five months in NATO's Paris headquarters, completing his tour while his backers won him the primaries Taft had assumed were his to take. Only when the voting was done, in June, did he resign his commission and return to the States for a month of campaigning in advance of the Republican convention. Between the policy speeches and press conferences, his handlers scattered personal touches to make him into the ordinary American he'd never been: a day at his boyhood home in Abilene, Kansas; a round of golf in Denver; a stop at the Gettysburg farmhouse he'd bought a few years before but never managed to live in because he was too busy serving his country.

Privately Taft raged that Eisenhower was nothing more than a front man for the corporate elites who wanted to deny a real conservative the nomination. "The General himself, I think, has about the right attitude," he wrote the banker Prescott Bush, his old friend from their glory days at Yale, "but I have no confidence whatsoever in nine-tenths of his advisors; and I am afraid we are going to end up against a Republican New Deal."[7] Most of the regulars who filled the convention didn't seem to care; three-quarters of them swung to Eisenhower on its only ballot. After he'd made a nod to the right wing he'd just steamrolled with his choice of a vice president, the new nominee headed back to Colorado for yet more golf, a few days of fishing, and a good-bye lunch with his son, who was shipping off to Korea.

Adlai never stood a chance. Stevenson started the fall campaign six points behind Eisenhower in the polls and finished it eleven points behind in the returns, enough to cost him thirty-nine of forty-eight states, including four states in the Upper South that Democrats simply didn't lose. Behind those totals lay a racial and economic reconfiguration of the electoral order. Stevenson won 80 percent of the African American vote but took just 40 percent of the white vote, 13 points below Truman's share in 1948. While he held the lower end of the blue-collar vote—66 percent of the unskilled went Democratic—Eisenhower sheared off a portion of the upper end and added it to his overwhelming margin among white-collar families. That's what gave his election its sweep: Ike's ability to construct a coalition of middling Americans that stretched from the new housing tracts around Memphis and Houston to the booming suburbs south of Los Angeles and up to the Cahills' corner of the bungalow belt, which voted Republican for the first time since 1928.

Once he took office he moved with the same efficiency he'd brought to his previous commands. Within six months he ended the Korean conflict with an armistice no one liked and everyone desperately wanted. In 1954 he brought down McCarthy with a quietly ruthless set of maneuvers infused with gay-baiting. By the time that was done he'd toppled two heads of state—in oil-rich Iran and land-starved Guatemala—with covert interventions designed to hide his administration's most aggressive international actions from the public he served, so that the feverish politics he'd calmed with his other steps couldn't flare again. The appearance of peace gave him the chance to end the wartime regulations Truman had imposed. But he still spent $45 billion on defense in 1954, $36 billion in 1955, and a matching amount in 1956. Onto that spending he layered a major expansion of Social Security, another housing act to clear yet more poor neighborhoods, and $25 billion to subsidize the highway construction that cities and states had underway, the centerpiece of the very thing Taft had feared in 1952. Eisenhower was putting into place a New Deal for his emerging Republican majority.

The economic results followed the pattern set in Truman's last years. Up went corporate profits, anchored by the massive contracts coming out of the Pentagon's procurement office and the dizzying cycle of production and consumption Korea had created. Up went the median wage, by a stunning 23 percent in Eisenhower's first four years, as employers scrambled to keep their profits flowing in a full-employment economy with a record level of unionization. Up went $22 billion in new factories, office blocks, showrooms, and shopping strips to keep the cycle spiraling. Up went the sale of all the things good wages could buy. With their expanding paychecks Americans bought 25 million new cars, 15 million televisions, a hundred million TV dinners to eat in front of their sets, 33 million coonskin caps for little Davy Crocketts, and for the teenyboppers a million copies of the latest 45 from that kid out of Memphis with the funny name: a deluge of goods to fill the four million new homes developers added to the suburban tracts where so much of Washington's money flowed.

And down in the center cities the destruction intensified. New York City's master planner evicted 180,000 people from the tenements that stood in the way of his remade Manhattan. Detroit gutted its largest African American neighborhood to make room for a downtown freeway and a chic new development designed by Mies van der Rohe. In Chicago the Democratic machine kept pushing the center city's reconstruction. In 1947 Ed Kelly handed the mayoralty to Martin Kennelly, who got an eight-year run before being shoved out of the way by Richard Daley. Beyond their Irish roots they didn't have much in common. Kennelly was a well-to-do businessman who lived in a fancy apartment near the lake and liked to talk of reform. Daley, the thick-necked son of a sheet-metal worker, was a career pol who lived with his wife Sis and their seven children in a bungalow a block from his parents' house in blue-collar Bridgeport. Every morning Sis got their kids off to their parochial schools while Dick stopped at the parish church for Mass before heading down to city hall for an honest day's work that didn't have any room whatsoever for reform.

When it came to reshaping the city, though, their differences didn't matter. Together Kennelly and Daley finished the West Side highway and started to carve out a second freeway running north from the first, through that part of the old Polish neighborhood where Stella's mother had lived when she'd arrived in the States forty years before. They also leveled two more stretches of the South Side, one to give the University of Chicago a buffer zone from the poor and the other to put up the public housing projects city hall had decided could only be built in Black neighborhoods. All the while whites' flight from the city's racial boundaries mounted, on the South Side and the West Side both. Between 1953 and 1956 about 40,000 whites left Chicago for the suburbs, while an undetermined number more moved from the center city to the arc of neighborhoods that ran along Chicago's western edge, a fraction of them toward Eddy Street.

There was an obvious caution to Ed and Stella's first years in his father's bungalow. They enrolled Judy in St. Ferdinand's grade school as soon as they arrived and Terry four years later, when he reached kindergarten age. And they had another baby, a girl they named Kathleen, born in May 1952. Maybe it was the cost of the kids that made them careful with their money, though their own childhoods probably weighed on them too. In 1954 something shifted. That April they bought the bungalow from his dad for $11,000—a fair-market price— secured by a twenty-year mortgage, a transaction that assured them they could stay in the house once he passed away. In 1955 they bought their first car, so Ed wouldn't have to keep riding the streetcars down to work every morning. Not much later they got a television. By then two-thirds of the country's households had already put sets in their living rooms, so it was hardly an extravagance for the Cahills to do the same. But it must have seemed like one.

The sense of solidity didn't stop at their front door. Since the boom years began in the first year of the Korean fighting, contractors had filled almost all of the area's remaining lots with the same modest ranches they'd begun to build in the late 1940s, along with a scattering of modern two-flats—about 250 homes in all. The vast majority they sold to families moving out of the center city, mostly Polish Americans displaced by the new freeway and Italian Americans abandoning the near West Side. Pieces of their old neighborhoods followed them out. For ninety years the De La Salle Brothers had run St. Patrick's high school for working-class boys about a mile east of Vacuum Can's offices. In 1953 they moved it to a beautiful new building six blocks south of the Cahills' bungalow. In the spring of 1955 a group of investors announced that they were going to open a $7 million shopping center on the commercial strip between the Cahills' neighborhood and the first suburb to the west. It would have all the modern amenities, but it would be anchored by a department store whose reputation rested on seven decades of service down in the ethnic wards. And in April 1956, St. Ferdinand's pastor broke ground for the church that the parish had been waiting thirty years to build. It would take $850,000 to pay for the Mankato stone that would wrap its exterior, the marble that would run along its interior walls, the copper fittings for the stained-glass windows, and the bronze doors the pastor had planned for its main entryway. When it was done, the tiny outlying parish Ed's parents had joined back in 1926, its congregation now swollen to 3,800 families, would have a church as elegant as the ones that were emptying out in the old neighborhoods.

Two months later Judy finished eighth grade at St. Ferdinand's. In September she started at a Catholic high school for girls a few miles into the city, where she'd get the education her mom never managed to have and her dad took as a given. In October 1956 Ed's father died, eight years after they'd come out to care for him, and the bungalow they'd already bought finally became their own. In November Eisenhower won reelection in a landslide that reinforced the coalition he'd assembled four years before. This time his sweeping support among the middle classes gave him all but one of the states in the North and West and six states in the no-longer-solid South. In Chicago the rapidly expanding African American wards ran decisively against him. But

64 percent of the voters around Eddy Street went his way, ten percent more than in 1952.

There were still troubling moments in those years. Several times international tensions spiked for a week or two, until Eisenhower found a way to defuse them. Twice in his second term, in 1958 and 1960, the economy tumbled into short, sharp downturns triggered by a bewildering combination of dollars, gold, and global trade. Even in its boom years the economy's limits were plain to see, for anyone who cared to look: in 1959 18 percent of white Americans and 55 percent of African Americans still lived below the poverty line, many of them in decaying neighborhoods like the one around Vacuum Can. Through the latter half of the 1950s disturbing stories of racial violence kept filtering out of the South, far too many of them involving children. There was the horrific murder of that South Side boy, Emmett Till, down in Mississippi in the summer of 1955; the photo of the teenage girl walking stone-faced through a mob in front of her high school in Little Rock, Arkansas, in September 1957, the year Judy started her sophomore year at Alvernia High; and the white thugs attacking the college kids who were sitting down at lunch counters in the winter of 1960, just as Judy was trying to convince her parents that they ought to let her go to college too.

Then there were the moral panics, which seemed to come with an unnerving regularity. McCarthyism had battered the major cities' gay and lesbian communities, Washington's most of all, but it hadn't come close to shutting them down. And the surprisingly explicit sexual imagery that had passed through the ranks of straight men during the war followed them into the postwar world. It flowed through the highest and lowest levels of cultural production, from Norman Mailer's literary misogyny to the big-breasted women of the pulp magazines. And it aimed for the middle, nowhere more deliberately than in the airbrushed declaration of sexual liberation for frat boys and businessmen delivered by *Playboy*, first published in November 1953 by Hugh Hefner, a Catholic kid born and raised in the neighborhood next to the Cahills'. But it wasn't until the teenage girls started screaming that the panic set in.

It began in June 1956, when the Memphis kid with the record sales made his first major appearance on national television. He did a cover of "Hound Dog," a song that had been a hit for the rhythm-and-blues star Big Mama Thornton on the other side of the color line. If that weren't bad enough, he sang it while thrusting his hips in a way that looked like he'd spent too much time at the burlesque shows. Within a couple of days everyone seemed to be talking about the dangers of rock and roll. Popular music "has reached its lowest depths in the 'grunt and groin antics' of one Elvis Presley," wrote a reviewer. "Elvis, who rotates his pelvis . . . gave a performance that was suggestive and vulgar, tinged with the kind of animalism that should be confined to dives and bordellos."[8]

It turned out that they didn't have to worry about Elvis, who loved his mother with all his heart and wanted to be a movie star. The real threat came from the acts a little lower on the charts, like Chuck Berry, who came to Chicago to follow his idol, the great Muddy Waters, and ended up infusing a furious rush of the blues into facile songs about girls staying true; or devout Richard Penniman of Macon, Georgia, who didn't seem all that devout when he dropped his last name and his gospel repertoire and created the pulsing stage shows of androgynous Little Richard; or Jerry Lee Lewis, another Delta white boy like Elvis, who was so untamed he seemed downright dangerous even before he married his thirteen-year-old cousin. Maybe Chicago's cardinal knew what he was doing when he announced in 1957 that henceforth rock and roll would be banned from the city's Catholic schools.

The next year the beatnik panic hit. By then the Beats had spent almost a decade in the anonymity that tends to envelop artists committed to cultural rebellion. They'd come together at Columbia University in the late 1940s, young intellectuals largely from ethnic working-class families, searching for an alternative to mainstream America's crushing banality. They'd found their inspiration in the bebop revolution that was redefining jazz: the posture, the style—the goatees, the berets, the pot—and the rhythms too challenging for dancing. To that act of appropriation they added a heavy dose of polymorphous sexuality and a dash of mysticism. From that combination the Beats' most brilliant talent, Allen Ginsberg, produced his epic poem "Howl," which was published in 1956 by an obscure San Francisco press.

It probably would have remained obscure had the authorities not decided to charge the publisher with obscenity. The mainstream press picked up the trial, which the publisher's lawyers won by arguing for the poem's artistic merit. Along the way reporters discovered the vibrant little counterculture the Beats had created in New York's Greenwich Village—the ancestral home of the American avant-garde—and San Francisco's gay enclave of North Beach, where Ginsberg then lived. The sexuality they avoided in favor of breathless reports on the Beats' rejection of American values: one of San Francisco's favorite columnists gave them the "beatnik" name because he thought it sounded subversive, like Sputnik, though most commentators preferred to see in them a symbol of the younger generation's alienation rather than their Communism. That seemed reason enough to panic.

When the most significant shift occurred, though, it barely seemed to register. In 1950 Planned Parenthood of America, the nation's leading proponent of birth control, convinced one of Chicago's richest women, Katharine Dexter McCormick, to bankroll the development of an oral contraceptive. Planned Parenthood used the money to support a tiny group of superb scientists and doctors to do the bench work and conduct the clinical trials. One of the researchers had a connection to a Chicago pharmaceutical company, which added its support. When the trials were finished, in 1957, the company asked the Food and Drug Administration for approval to mass produce the pill, ostensibly as a treatment for menstrual irregularities, since that seemed a safer bet than saying it was going to be providing women a reliable way to avoid pregnancy. Once the approval came through, the company made sure to mention on the pill's packaging that it had a side effect of preventing ovulation, which probably explained why, by 1959, half a million women had prescriptions. A market that promising couldn't be ignored. So in May 1960 the company secured the FDA's approval to sell the pill explicitly as a means of birth control, a bureaucratic confirmation of a quiet revolution already three years underway. The *Times* put the news on page 75.

The Cahills didn't have anything to fear from it all. The biggest rebellions at Alvernia High involved the girls rolling their skirts above their knees on their way to school and sneaking the occasional cigarette as they headed home. And the nuns certainly weren't using class time to talk about birth control pills. As for Judy herself, the only time she pushed against her parents was in the spring of 1960, the tail end of her senior year, when she won a scholarship that would pay most of her way through college. Her dad pushed back. He just couldn't see why she needed a college education, he told her, an argument she took to mean that he didn't think much of girls, though more than likely he also couldn't stand the thought of losing her. In the end they agreed that she could stay at home and commute to DePaul, Chicago's largest Catholic university, where she planned to take a two-year commercial course, as safe within her parents' world as a seventeen-year-old could be.

That was a very safe place to be. The Cahills' block was still lined with the sort of people who'd always lived there, some of them—like Clarence Miller—in the houses their families had bought when the street was new. But its comforts had deepened. Since the early days of the boom in the summer of 1950 the neighborhood's average family income had gone up by 66 percent. Ed and Stella had probably done even better, since his bosses had rewarded his years of service to Vacuum Can by making him head of sales. They were almost a third of the way through paying off the mortgage they'd taken out to buy their bungalow, its monthly payments easier to carry with every bump in Ed's pay. They had the elegant church their pastor had promised them, opened since Holy Week of 1958, and St. Patrick's High, where Terry would go when he reached ninth grade in September 1961. They had a war-hero president who'd given them seven years of peace and prosperity. They had a mayor just like them. And in July 1960 the Democrats gave them John Kennedy as the party's presidential nominee, an Irish-American Catholic almost exactly Ed's age who loved his family and country—the latter so much that he'd come close to dying for it during the war—and whose election would confirm in the most public of ways that families like theirs had arrived.

The following June, Ed and Clarence had their somewhat awkward conversation about flying the flag. A few weeks later Ed wrote his letter to the editor inviting the city out to their block to see what they had done. When the *Trib*'s photographer lined up the neighbors for his back-page shot, Ed took his place up front, as he had every right to do. Ten-year-old Kathy plunked down on the lawn. Fourteen-year-old Terry staked out his spot on the neighbor's steps. Into the back row slipped forty-four-year-old Stella—forty-two years past the loss of the father she couldn't remember, forty years past the first of her childhood's perpetual moves, thirty years past the collapse of her family's finances, twenty-nine years past her last day of school, sixteen years past those wartime nights when she wondered if Ed would ever return, thirteen years past the decision to move out to what proved to be a solid, dependable life on Eddy Street. There she stood, almost hidden from view, smiling into the sixties.

CHAPTER 2

TWILIGHT WARS

Curtis LeMay hadn't been at the Joint Chiefs' first briefing, on October 16, 1962, when the Defense Intelligence Agency laid out the details of the Soviet buildup. The Russians had put three nuclear missile sites in the Cuban countryside, the agency's experts told the Joint Chiefs, and equipped them with missiles that had a range of 700 to 1,100 miles—far enough to reach central Virginia. Each of them was potentially operational within twenty-four hours. But by the time he joined the Joint Chiefs' discussion, on October 18, LeMay knew what had to be done. The air strike should come first, a surprise attack not only on the sites but on Cuba's entire military capability, followed by an invasion that would topple the Castro regime and put in its place an American occupation. Clearly there'd be casualties, possibly on a colossal scale. But wars weren't won with halfway measures. They were won with unrelenting violence.

It was the principle that had guided LeMay in 1942 and 1943, when he led a series of high-risk bombing runs over occupied Europe that traded cataclysmic losses among his own crews for the ability to batter Germany's industrial capacity. He'd pushed it even harder in 1945, when he ordered the firebombing of Japan. Night after night B-29s hit selected cities with incendiaries and napalm; 100,000 civilians were killed in the Tokyo raid alone, possibly half a million in the five months that the campaign ran. "I suppose if I had lost the war I would have been tried as a war criminal," LeMay said later. "But . . . if you let that bother you you're not a good soldier."[1]

The onset of the nuclear age didn't change the calculation. It had been his men who'd carried out the president's order to obliterate Hiroshima and Nagasaki in August 1945. The following year he was put in charge of the Strategic Air Command, whose bombers would deliver the next nuclear strike should that moment ever come. The Cold War defined his target. From the late 1940s onward LeMay argued that the United States ought to meet any indication of an impending Soviet attack with the full force of its nuclear arsenal. Assume he'd received the order this morning, he told the National War College in 1956. "Between sunset tonight and sunrise tomorrow the Soviet Union would cease to be a major military power or even a major nation. . . . Dawn would break over a nation infinitely poorer than China—less populated than the United States and condemned to an agrarian existence perhaps for generations to come."[2]

But the politicians didn't have the stomach for it. In 1954 his fellow general Dwight Eisenhower signed a directive declaring that the United States would not launch a preemptive war, a message meant to reassure the Soviets that they'd never have to mobilize toward a first strike of their own. LeMay tried to push back, mostly through apocalyptic speeches to military groups, a couple of times in dangerously provocative ways. No matter what he said or did, though, Washington wouldn't budge. When he was promoted to the Joint Chiefs in 1961, the directive was still in place. Worse, its implementation had passed from Ike to Jack Kennedy. Not quite two years later there were Soviet missiles ninety miles from Miami.

On LeMay's first day in the thick of the crisis, it seemed that the White House might give him what he wanted: definitely air strikes, the Joint Chiefs' chairman Maxwell Taylor said, and probably the invasion too. That evening, though, Kennedy's thinking started to shift from an assault toward a more cautious approach, centered on a naval blockade and a set of political maneuvers. General Taylor delivered the news at the next morning's briefing, forty-five minutes before the Joint Chiefs were to meet with the president himself. Taylor's colleagues spent the time planning their response. But LeMay wasn't interested in an exchange of views. At 9:45 he trooped into the Cabinet Room looking for a fight.

Kennedy opened the session with a careful, balanced review of the dangers the Cuban missiles created not only in the Western hemisphere but in Europe as well. Taylor, a confidant of the president's, said a few politic things about having to defend American credibility. "That's right, that's right," Kennedy said. "So that's why we've got to respond. Now the question is: what is our response?"

"I'd emphasize . . . that we don't have any choice but direct military action," LeMay replied. And he was off, racing through the practical reasons a blockade wouldn't work, sweeping past the international complications Kennedy had raised, heading straight for the confrontation he wanted. "So I see no other solution," he concluded. "This blockade and this political action I see leading into war. I don't see any other solution."

Then he delivered the crippling blow, as sharp and quick as he could make it. "This is almost as bad," he said of Kennedy's caution, "as the appeasement at Munich."[3]

The Cold War

IT WAS STRIKING how quickly Munich's meaning had changed. "Good man," Franklin Roosevelt had wired the British prime minister, Neville Chamberlain, on the day he agreed to meet with Adolf Hitler in late September 1938.[4] Within a year Europe was at war. Within two years the Germans had taken most of Western Europe and had set stretches of London to burning. Within three the Wehrmacht was 150 miles from Moscow, imperial Japan was barely two months from its attack on Pearl Harbor, and no one in Roosevelt's circle was praising Chamberlain's Munich meeting anymore.

In 1942 and 1943 it took on added significance, as Washington's most powerful policy makers scoured through the 1930s for the lessons they needed to remake a shattered world. They were sure that the descent into war had begun with the economic devastation of the Great

Depression, which destabilized every major industrial nation. Some, like the United States, had righted themselves through reform. But in their desperation Germany and Japan had fallen prey to extremists who promised regeneration through hyper-nationalism, militarism, imperialism, and racism so ferocious it pointed toward the genocidal. From that combination came acts of unconscionable aggression, much of it aimed at land the regimes thought ought to be theirs. Japan's belligerence stretched across the 1930s, while Germany's grew more intense from the mid-1930s on.

The other major powers had compounded the crisis, Washington's policy makers concluded, by trying to buy off the aggressors with concessions—to appease them, in the language of the time—never more callously than in the autumn of 1938. Through the summer Hitler had been threatening to seize the portion of Czechoslovakia that bordered Germany, by agreement if possible and by force if necessary. For weeks the other powers tried to negotiate, but Hitler kept hardening the terms as they closed in on the October 1 deadline he'd set. On September 29, Chamberlain and the French premier, Edouard Daladier, rushed to Munich for a last-minute summit. The talks started that afternoon. When they finished early the next morning Chamberlain and Daladier had given Hitler everything he demanded, in blatant violation of Czechoslovakian sovereignty and international law. Still Hitler wasn't appeased. For another year his aggression mounted, until the British and French finally decided in September 1939 that they had to meet force with force because, as the Munich meeting had made painfully clear, peace couldn't be won with weakness.

Out of those lessons the Roosevelt administration shaped its approach to the postwar world. In a series of complicated negotiations that stretched across the war years, it pieced together a new economic order meant to avoid another Great Depression by linking nations together in a globe-spanning system of free and open trade. The United States was to stand at its center, as the only major industrial power not devastated by the war. To make the system work, though, the other industrialized countries would have to be rebuilt, an extraordinarily expensive undertaking Washington committed itself to pursuing through a new international organization called the World Bank, with an initial capitalization of $714 million, 80 percent of it from the United States.

To anchor the global system of free trade, the United States pledged to set the dollar's value permanently at one thirty-fifth of an ounce of gold, the standard secured by Washington's guarantee that anyone holding a dollar could exchange it for its gold equivalent. In 1944 forty-three other nations agreed to set their currencies in relation to the dollar, in the process creating a network of firm exchange rates from Australia to Canada, South Africa to the Soviet Union. From that network—and the deals to follow—would eventually emerge a vibrant global economy, stabilized by its participants' interlocking interests. Or so Roosevelt's advisers decided in the course of the war.

Economic integration wasn't enough, though. The most powerful nations also had to sweep aside the timidity that had led them to Munich. But it wasn't clear precisely what ought to take its place. Publicly Roosevelt seemed to favor a system of global diplomatic cooperation much like the economic system his experts were building, to be implemented through another new international organization, the United Nations, which the United States helped to found in 1945. In private FDR took a tougher approach. Germany's aggression had pushed the United States into alliance with Great Britain and the Soviet Union. It wasn't an obvious combination, fusing as it did the world's foremost capitalist states and its only Communist one. Two of the powers operated by democratic principles, however imperfectly; the other was fiercely totalitarian, with a propensity for mass murder. But the alliance worked. In 1943 and 1944 the Soviets' enormous Red Army pressed in on Germany from the east, the Americans and the British from the south and the west. In the power of their combined forces Roosevelt seemed to see the future he wanted. When the war was won the United States and its allies could transform themselves into the world's policemen, standing up to aggressor states whenever they threatened the international order, the ghost of Munich laid to rest in the rubble of Hitler's criminal regime.

Then, in the war's last months, everything threatened to come undone. The trouble started in 1944, as the Red Army swept across Eastern Europe—through Poland, Hungary, Czechoslovakia, Yugoslavia, Romania, and Bulgaria—in pursuit of the retreating Wehrmacht. Instead of liberating those countries as they raced toward Berlin, the Soviets made it clear that they intended to occupy them, as if they had no right to rule themselves.

In Washington the Soviets' actions set off a furious debate. Were the Russians simply trying to shut down the corridors the Germans had used to invade in the summer of 1941, at the cost of 26 million Soviet lives? Or were they doing exactly what the Nazis and Japan's imperialists had done in the 1930s and early 1940s, extending their reach as far as force would carry them, their aggression driven by the Soviets' own toxic mix of militarism and Communism? If the latter were true, as some of the best minds in Washington thought it was, didn't the war's lessons require that the United States stand against them? Roosevelt's final round of wartime diplomacy, at the Russian resort of Yalta in the winter of 1945, seemed to suggest that he was leaning toward the softer reading of the Soviets' aims. Two months later FDR was dead. And the weight of the debate fell to his successor, Harry Truman.

Truman had no intention of overturning Roosevelt's approach to the postwar world. But he also had no experience in foreign affairs, no briefings from the president—in his three months as vice president he'd met with Roosevelt twice—and not a hint of the secrets FDR had kept. So he had to inch his way along, trying to balance the commitments Roosevelt had made with his own deepening sense that the Soviets couldn't be trusted, the course made all the more complex as the Allies rushed to the end of the war. Germany fell on May 8, 1945, two weeks after the Red Army breached the defenses the Reich had assembled around Berlin. Japan held out another three months, until the August destruction of Hiroshima and Nagasaki: the last of Curtis LeMay's bombing runs, driven partly by military calculation and partly by Truman's determination to impress the Russians with the awesome power he now had at his disposal.

But the Soviets weren't impressed enough to pull back from Eastern Europe. And Truman wasn't willing to use his new weapon to force them out, though a few of the military's more aggressive officers thought that he should, LeMay among them. Through 1946 the two powers circled around each other, the Soviets probing for openings, the Americans trying to shut them down, Truman struggling to shape a coherent policy from the rush of events. Not until the winter of 1947 did he manage to pull it together.

The fundamental principle came from one of the State Department's most experienced Soviet watchers, forty-four-year-old George Kennan. The Soviets were indeed aggressors, he argued in a long analysis that raced through official Washington in late 1946. But they couldn't afford to confront the United States directly, not when their industrial base was a fraction of America's, their military much less powerful, and their people exhausted by four years of horrific warfare. Given those conditions, Kennan argued, the Soviets' only option was to use the Communist parties they controlled around the world to take advantage of the West's economic and political weaknesses and the anticolonial movements sweeping through Asia and Africa: to spread their power not by invasion but by subversion. There wasn't any point in meeting that subversion with threats or military posturing, Kennan said. Rather, Washington ought to match every Russian move with a calm, cool countermove designed to close off whatever opening the Soviets hoped to exploit, and by so doing to seal them—to contain them, as Kennan put it—within the limited sphere they'd already established.

It was one thing to read a policy paper, though, another to push its principles through the political process. In March 1947 Truman went to Congress to ask for financial aid for Greece and Turkey, so as to block any Soviet expansion into the eastern Mediterranean. But he put his pitch in dramatically broader terms. The world was being divided into two "ways of life," he declared. One was "based upon the will of the majority and . . . distinguished by free institutions," the other "on the will of a minority forcibly imposed on the majority" through "terror and oppression . . . and the suppression of personal freedoms." A world so sharply split forced the United States to make the starkest choice. It could come to the defense of freedom wherever it was threatened, Truman said. Or it could shirk its responsibilities, as it had in the 1930s, and "endanger the peace of the world and . . . the welfare of our own nation," which was to say that it had no choice at all.[5]

It would be another month before someone thought of saying that the Truman Doctrine had taken the United States into a global cold war with the Soviets, a couple of months more until the term "cold war" entered common usage. But by universalizing the Soviet threat, that's what Truman had done. At first it seemed to go well enough. The Greeks and Turks got their aid. From that victory the administration pushed for a wave of economic programs meant to contain the Russians precisely as Kennan had suggested, most of them built on the structures Roosevelt's men had put in place. The most sweeping came from the former general and current secretary of state George Marshall, who in June 1947 called for a dramatic increase in reconstruction funds for almost all of Western Europe, a total of about $12 billion to build the roads and bridges, rail lines and factories that would keep the Soviets at bay. Reconstruction fed integration, nowhere more forcefully than in the western half of occupied Germany, where in 1948 the Americans used currency reform to create an entirely new non-Communist state that pressed up against the Soviet sphere: as sophisticated a countermove as Kennan could have hoped to see.

But wars—even cold ones—aren't easy to control. Kennan's emphasis on economic containment fit perfectly with Truman's commitment to shrinking the enormous armed forces the world war had created. By framing the Soviet threat so broadly, though, Truman gave his generals an opening to argue that economics alone wouldn't do; to face an enemy of such sweeping intent, they insisted, the United States had to maintain a devastating military capacity too. And by stressing Soviet subversion he gave the Republican Right another opportunity to turn on him. They'd embraced anti-Communism in 1946 to batter the Democrats' domestic agenda. As US-Soviet tensions mounted they gave the attack a conspiratorial twist. There were Communists and fellow travelers scattered throughout the New Deal's leading institutions, they suggested, and Truman and his liberal friends were too soft on radicalism to root them out.

Truman tried to ease the pressure with a series of concessions. To undercut the Right, he created an internal security system empowered to fire from government service anyone its investigators found to be subversive. And in 1948 he gave the generals back the military draft he'd taken from them two years before. But those moves weren't strong enough to withstand the twin shocks of 1949. On August 31 the Soviets tested their first atomic bomb, wiping out the security of the American nuclear monopoly in a single seismic blast. Four weeks later the Chinese revolutionary Mao Zedong announced from Beijing that after four brutal years of civil war the forces under his command had toppled the old regime and put in its place the People's Republic of China, the servant state of the liberated masses. Suddenly the American military was talking about the desperate need for a rapid buildup, while the Republican Right was demanding to know how the president had allowed the Soviets to steal America's atomic secrets and the Communists to seize control of the world's most populous nation.

As the furor grew, one of the Right's most obscure politicians saw his opening. Joe McCarthy had been elected to the U.S. Senate from Wisconsin in 1946. Five years into his first term he had yet to distinguish himself in any way, which is undoubtedly why the party asked him to headline a February 1950 fundraising dinner in Wheeling, West Virginia, about as far as a man could go from the Republicans' center of power and still be within the country's continental limits. But a stage was a stage, and McCarthy used his to charge that the secretary of state was allowing 205 Communists to work inside the State Department, despite—or perhaps because of—the threat they posed to the nation. He knew this to be true, McCarthy said, because he had a list of their names in his hand.

He didn't. But his claim was so spectacular that news outlets across the country picked it up. From the press it came rushing back to Washington, where it dominated the spring. The Democrats insisted that he make his list public or admit that it was a fraud. McCarthy fought back with obfuscation, more accusations, and an infusion of class resentment. "It's not the less fortunate who have been traitors to this nation," he insisted. "This is glaringly true in the State Department. There the bright young men who are born with silver spoons in their mouth are the ones who have been most traitorous." Some of his Republican colleagues pulled the charges in a different direction. The problem wasn't that State was full of rich young men, they said, but that it was full of gay young men, whom the Soviets could blackmail into espionage simply by threatening to expose the sexual orientation they were desperate to hide. "Certainly Harry Truman cannot like either Communists or homosexuals," one of the Right's best publicists wrote in April. "Why does he protect them?"[6]

Truman wasn't above a bit of counterpunching: Senator McCarthy was nothing more than a tool of those Republicans who wanted to retreat from the international commitments his administration had made, he told White House reporters at the end of March, and therefore was the Soviets' "greatest asset." But by then the president's approval rating had tumbled to 37 percent, 21 points below where it had been when the Soviets had set off their atomic bomb. With numbers so low, he couldn't take another blow like the ones the Russians, the Chinese, and McCarthy had delivered. So when the North Koreans invaded South Korea on June 25, he took just three days to order the sort of military action that Kennan had insisted the United States didn't have to pursue, a decision Truman wrapped in the most powerful justification he could imagine. "The free nations have learned the fateful lesson of the 1930s," he told the nation as the troops went in. "That lesson is that aggression must be met firmly. Appeasement leads only to further aggression and ultimately to war," as did the ferocious politics Truman had hoped to contain.[7]

Ike

"POOR [HARRY TRUMAN]," Dwight Eisenhower wrote in his diary in November 1950, a few weeks before the Korean campaign went hopelessly wrong. "A fine man who, in the middle of a stormy lake, knows nothing of swimming. Yet a lot of drowning people are forced to look to him as a lifeguard. If his wisdom could only equal his good intent."[8] Eisenhower wasn't normally so candid, even with himself. But these weren't normal times.

He'd decided that the Soviets were a threat to the United States in 1944 or 1945, he said later, though for years afterward he would be blamed for not pushing American troops on to Berlin before the Red Army arrived. By mid-1946 he'd settled on a strategic framework that looked almost exactly like the one Kennan had laid out a few months before. He agreed that the United States had to stop Soviet expansionism or risk repeating the disasters of the 1930s. And he decided, much as Kennan had, that the best way to block the Russians was with a concerted campaign to promote democracy and free enterprise in every country Washington could reach, and to bring those nations it could sway into the free-trade system the Americans had begun to build during the war, so that they'd be linked together in mutual prosperity.

Eisenhower certainly believed that Kennan-style containment had to be backed by military power; otherwise he wouldn't have accepted NATO's command when Truman offered it to him in 1950. He also believed that releasing that power was a very dangerous thing to do. "We are traveling a long and rocky road toward a satisfactory world order," he'd written his father-in-law in August 1946. "No war can be anything else but a grave setback to such progress. The one thing that disturbs me is the readiness of people to discuss war as a means of advancing peace. To me this is a contradiction in terms."[9] Four years later Truman had American troops clawing their way up the Korean peninsula toward the Chinese border. Ike dutifully gave the president his support, but he wasn't pleased.

When the Chinese army intervened a few weeks later, the situation grew darker still. The military setback was troubling enough. What really bothered Eisenhower was the assault's effect on America's already poisonous public life. He hated MacArthur's tumultuous return from Korea in the spring of 1951, with its overt politicization of the military. And he absolutely despised the Right's red-baiters, all the more so after McCarthy stood in the well of the Senate in June 1951 and accused Ike's longtime commanding officer and mentor George Marshall—now Truman's secretary of defense—of betraying his country on behalf of "the world-wide web of which has been spun from Moscow." It wasn't much later that Eisenhower began to seriously consider the presidential run his corporate supporters were pressing on him. He clearly was swayed by their insistence that his election could stop the Democratic drift toward socialism. But he also wanted to break the rising power of those Republicans he'd come to see as "disciples of hate."[10]

He had no intention of confronting them directly. In the winter and spring of 1952 he swept past the Republican Right on the strength of his name more than his policy positions. And in his first official act as the Republican nominee, he picked as his running mate one of their most promising young men. Richard Nixon had grown up in small-town Southern California, the son of a grocer and his sainted wife, whom her little boy adored. From that middle ground he took the same distrust of elites that McCarthy had taken from his parents' struggling Wisconsin farm. But Nixon combined it with a desperate desire to prove himself their equal. He started at little Whittier College down the road from home, moved on to Duke University's law school, and then, after wartime service in the navy, went into Congress in the Republican Right's 1946 resurgence, an interesting career choice for a man who everyone agreed wasn't particularly comfortable with people.

In the subsequent search for highly placed subversives, Nixon had the good luck to find Alger Hiss, whose suitably genteel family and impeccable credentials—Johns Hopkins undergrad, Harvard Law— had carried him into the State Department's upper ranks and whose hidden commitments had turned him into a Soviet spy. It didn't hurt that Nixon's pursuit of Hiss had a few spectacular turns, one of them involving a pumpkin full of microfilmed secrets. He used the enormous publicity the case generated, along with some vicious red-baiting, to get elected to the Senate in 1950 at the age of thirty-seven. Not quite two years later Eisenhower asked him to be the Republican vice-presidential nominee, the political equivalent of the general making sure that his right flank was secure.

The caution seemed to carry over to Eisenhower's first year in the Oval Office. In April 1953 he embraced the Right's combination of red- and gay-baiting by replacing Truman's loyalty program with a policy that gave the federal government the power to purge any employee who engaged in actions that made him or her a security risk. Within a year 2,200 people had been fired, at least a third of them not because they were Communists but because they were gay or lesbian. Eisenhower tried to ignore McCarthy—for a while the president refused to even speak his name—until late 1953, when the senator decided to take on the army, a line he really shouldn't have crossed. Eisenhower duly ordered his entire administration not to cooperate in any investigation, citing a little-known doctrine he called "executive privilege." And in the quiet, careful, essentially untraceable way that he preferred, he turned the Right's sexual politics inside out by leaking to the press a detailed report pointing to the homosexuality of McCarthy's leading aide, a young lawyer named Roy Cohn. McCarthy tried to push past it with yet more allegations and intimidation, much of it broadcast on what turned out to be a disastrous stretch of must-see TV. In July 1954 the Senate began censure proceedings, an unmistakable indication that McCarthy was through.

But Eisenhower's most important steps stretched far beyond breaking a single senator. There was never any doubt that he was going to maintain the international commitments the Democrats had made and the military modernization they'd gotten underway. Within that framework, though, he made two crucial changes. To implement his policies he turned to the business class that had elected him. His secretary of state and his CIA director both had been senior partners in one of Wall Street's most prominent law firms; his secretary of the treasury had headed a major steel company; and his secretary of defense had been the president of General Motors, the nation's largest defense contractor. And as soon as he took office, Eisenhower started to move the Cold War's confrontations into the shadows, so that the passions they'd released could finally be dampened down.

Korea came first. His guiding principle was straightforward. "People grow weary of war," Ike wrote in a private letter early in his term, "particularly when they see no decisive and victorious end to it." So he was going to stop it as quickly as he could. It took six months of negotiations intensified by another brutal American air assault—this one designed to push North Korea toward starvation—to finalize a settlement that put the two Koreas back to where they'd been before the fighting began, staring at each other across a border they'd killed 2.5 million people to move. On the night the armistice was signed, July 26, 1953, he issued a short statement his speechwriter wanted to close by quoting Abraham Lincoln's promise in the last days of the Civil War to pursue "a just and lasting peace among ourselves and with all nations." On the bottom of the draft Ike scrawled another line. "This is our resolve and our dedication," it read.[11]

A month later he ordered the CIA to overthrow the Iranian government. It was a classic application of containment, driven by the administration's fear that one of the world's most oil-rich nations was slipping into the Soviet sphere. But the operation was handled with such secrecy that no one in the United States knew that Americans had been involved. In 1954 the CIA staged its second coup, this time in Guatemala, whose democratically elected president had alarmed the White House by nationalizing swaths of land owned by the Boston-based United Fruit Company. Again no one back home cared to see the administration's hand, not even the august *New York Times*, which dutifully ignored its own columnist's hints of the agency's involvement.

The same year Eisenhower also committed the United States to building a brand-new nation in the southern half of Vietnam. The French had claimed Indochina as a colonial possession in the late nine-

teenth century. In the decades that followed, a wide variety of nationalist movements had challenged their rule. The most powerful came
from the Viet Minh, a coalition of revolutionary groups formed in 1941
under the direction of the Communist Ho Chi Minh. In the twisted
course of World War II, as Indochina's imperial power shifted from the
French to the Japanese, Ho built the Viet Minh a base in the countryside north of Hanoi, close to the Chinese border. When Japan collapsed
in 1945 and French forces returned to reclaim their possession, the Viet
Minh used their base to launch a war of independence.

For the next five years they fought on their own. That Ho had Soviet
connections was indisputable; he'd spent much of the 1920s and 1930s
as an agent of its international revolutionary apparatus. And in 1946
and 1947 he and his fellow Communists gradually, often brutally,
purged their non-Communist comrades from the Viet Minh's once-
expansive alliance. Still Ho couldn't convince the Soviet leadership to
support him, in large part because they feared that he wanted an independent Vietnam rather than a subservient one. So his Viet Minh had
to go it alone.

Ho handled the political side of the struggle. Its military strategy
he turned over to his hardened young general Vo Nguyen Giap, who
built the Viet Minh's war on a Maoist model of revolutionary struggle.
Instead of facing France's modern military head-on, a fight he was sure
to lose, Giap pulled his force back into its rural base. When the French
came in pursuit, the Viet Minh would hit them with bursts of guerrilla warfare that a highly mechanized military had no effective way
to counter. Giap then fed those small victories into a relentless propa-
ganda campaign in the villages beyond his base, to expand the support
he had to have for the war he wanted to fight. The model worked as Giap
hoped it would. By the end of 1948 the Viet Minh controlled much of
the countryside in northern and central Vietnam and had established
pockets of power in the south, while the 100,000 soldiers France had
dispatched were piling up casualties in an increasingly futile effort to
root them out.

It remained a colonial war on the far edge of world affairs until the

Communists' victory in China changed the major powers' calculations. In January 1950 the Soviets and the Chinese agreed to back the Viet Minh, the former with moral support, the latter with extensive military aid. Three months later—a month before his Korean intervention—Truman committed $23 million in American aid to the French, not because he wanted them to keep their colony but because he couldn't afford to have another Asian state fall to the Communists while he was being lacerated by the Right for letting China slip away. With that first installment he turned Vietnam into a proving ground for America's Cold War resolve.

There was a lot more to come. Through the last two years of the Truman administration the United States equipped the French with mounds of military equipment: more and more the French moved their troops on American trucks, struck Viet Minh strongholds with American bombers, waged firefights with American small arms, and burned stretches of the countryside with the incendiary jelly Americans called napalm. The Viet Minh struck back with the piles of materiel the Chinese provided, some 450 tons of it a month by the end of 1952. With the increase in supplies the bloodshed intensified, both forces—each grown to a quarter million men—inflicting enormous damage on the other, each side struggling to maintain morale as the body counts mounted.

There the war stood when Eisenhower took office in January 1953. "I'm convinced that no military victory is possible in that kind of theater," he'd written on the day in 1951 that the commanding officer of the French forces had come to call.[12] Yet he was also sure that the Communists had to be stopped, because once they'd seized power in Vietnam they'd move on to the rest of Southeast Asia and probably India too. So he spent his first year keeping the French aid flowing, since there wasn't anything else he could do. But in September 1953 the Soviets unexpectedly proposed that the world's major powers negotiate a peace deal. The Chinese, anxious to reduce the costs they were carrying, quickly agreed. Once his primary backer was committed, Ho had no choice but to join in. The British signed on. In February 1954 the

French did too, though they were then in the midst of a major military maneuver that they hoped would devastate the Viet Minh by luring them into an assault on their northern stronghold at Dien Bien Phu. And suddenly Eisenhower had an opening he didn't want—to solve a problem that had no solution.

The peace talks opened in Geneva in April 1954. They lasted through the French maneuver's catastrophic defeat, which convinced Paris that it was time to cut its losses; a few tense weeks in Washington as Eisenhower considered sending US forces into the fighting; and the summer's push to an agreement everyone was willing to sign, except for the Americans. The settlement split the western portion of French Indochina into two nations, Laos and Cambodia, both of which would be required to remain neutral in the Cold War's international alignments. As for Vietnam, it would be temporarily split in two. The Viet Minh would be given control of the northern half, the non-Communist independence groups the southern. There they could transform themselves into political parties, in preparation for the July 1956 elections that would decide which of them would govern a united Vietnam.

That sounded reasonable enough. But when the Vietnamese went to the polls, Ike estimated, 80 percent of them would vote for the Viet Minh, and another Asian nation would tumble into the Communist camp. So he decided that there wouldn't be any elections. Ho would simply hold the northern portion the agreement gave him, while the United States would use its unparalleled power to transform the southern portion into a nation of its own. North and South Vietnam would then become another North and South Korea, with the Communists contained in half the space they otherwise would have controlled—as much a victory as the Americans could manage under the circumstances.

But the maneuver would work only if the United States could make South Vietnam a viable country. The first step was to find it a head of state. Among the multiple factions that made up the non-Communist side of the anticolonial struggle, the administration settled on the longtime Catholic nationalist Ngo Dinh Diem. Those Americans who came into closest contact with him wondered whether he was up to the job.

One of the diplomats who staffed the US embassy described him as "a curious blend of heroism blended with a narrowness of view and egotism which will make him a difficult man to deal with."[13] But Diem was a virulent anti-Communist with strong connections to a number of influential Americans. And in Washington that's what mattered most.

Once they had a premier in place, Ike's men provided him with a torrent of support. The Joint Chiefs set up a program to create the army he'd need, which the Pentagon then flooded with the latest military equipment; within a couple of years he had 150,000 soldiers at his command. The State Department stabilized his economy with expansive financial aid and a special trade deal that filled Saigon, his new nation's capital city, with piles of American goods. And inside Diem's presidential palace the CIA counseled him on how to beat back whatever threats might arise. "Nation-building," administration insiders called their work, a process that most Americans had no idea was underway, which was exactly how Eisenhower wanted it to be.

Cracks

THE CRACKS STARTED to show as Ike reached the final stretch of his second term. In the years since Truman had turned the Cold War into a global struggle the costs had escalated dramatically. Though he liked to talk about keeping the federal budget under control, Eisenhower had never reined in defense spending: in 1958 the military's budget was $38 billion, $2 billion above the previous year's. Much of that money coursed through the American economy. But a solid share went abroad, to pay for the approximately 650,000 soldiers the United States had stationed in other countries and the military aid it provided to a growing number of allies such as Iran and South Vietnam. In the Cold War's early days the United States could bring back much of that money by selling the Europeans and the Japanese the steel and shoes and automobiles their shattered factories couldn't produce. By the late 1950s those economies had been largely restored, and the money wasn't flowing back anymore. The more imbalanced the accounts became, the more investors feared that the situation wasn't sustainable. So they did what the international financial system allowed them to do. They started to trade their dollars for gold.

At the same time the administration was hearing of serious troubles in the South Vietnamese countryside. No one in Eisenhower's inner circle had expected Diem to make South Vietnam a genuinely democratic nation. But even some of the most informed observers were surprised by how ruthlessly he suppressed dissent. His primary targets were the Viet Minh loyalists who remained in the South after the Geneva agreement was finalized; his government executed hundreds of suspected Communists in 1956 alone. He also turned against a number of the non-Communist groups who'd made up the South's fractious politics as he concentrated power in the small Catholic clique he'd assembled to help him rule. "South Vietnam today is a quasi-police state," said the prestigious journal *Foreign Affairs* in January 1957, "characterized by arbitrary arrests and imprisonment, strict censorship of the press, and the absence of an effective opposition."[14]

Late that year the CIA reported a rising number of guerrilla actions in the rural areas south of Saigon, where the Mekong River widened into its delta. They were coming from the tattered remains of the Viet Minh cadres that had once had a hold there, in alliance with some of the other groups Diem's repression had alienated. And they were aimed at government officials out in the field. The reports filtered up to North Vietnam as well. At first Ho was inclined to keep his distance. But others inside his government pushed him to see in the attacks an obligation and an opportunity. It took him more than a year to come around, but in January 1959 the North Vietnamese agreed to assist the southern struggle. Within a few months they started to ship arms and men secretly along the Laotian border into South Vietnam's militant villages, in support of what they took to calling the National Liberation Front (NLF). Diem preferred a term that implied the insurgents' traitorous intent. He called them the Viet Cong.

That same winter another insurgency came in from another countryside. Fidel Castro's revolutionary movement had spent the previous two years in Cuba's Sierra Maestra Mountains, waging a sporadic guerrilla war against the government of Fulgencio Batista, the island's military dictator. Batista had undermined his popular support by tying himself to the American mobsters who dominated Havana and the sugar company executives who dominated Cuba's rural areas. Still, even the rebels were surprised when Batista responded to a couple of admittedly serious military defeats in late 1958 by abruptly fleeing the country. Castro's men marched into Havana unopposed on January 2, 1959. Castro arrived six days later.

At first no one was sure what to make of him. By most accounts—including the Soviets'—Castro wasn't a Communist. But two of his closest advisers, his brother Raul and the Argentine Che Guevara, were. During the regime's first year in power they gradually moved Fidel toward Moscow, through the quiet diplomacy that brought their government mounting Soviet aid and the sweeping land reform Raul's Communist colleagues put in place to strip the sugar companies of 90 percent of their holdings. But it wasn't until a high-ranking Russian official made a very public visit to Havana in February 1960 that the White House knew the terrible truth. The Soviets had secured an ally ninety miles off the Florida coast.

Then there was the insurgency sweeping up from Arizona. In the Eisenhower years the Republican Right's old guard had collapsed. Taft had died of cancer in 1953, McCarthy from his drinking four years later. Even MacArthur was fading away. In their place a new generation had established itself. Most of them came from that segment of the business class where distrust of Eisenhower's corporate elites ran deep. Around them circled a superb group of publicists dedicated to polishing the Right's tarnished image, led by young William Buckley, whose *National Review* magazine had become the center of conservative intellectual life. And behind the scenes stood a handful of operatives who decided in 1959 to reclaim the party Eisenhower had taken from them.

Timing was everything. In 1951 the states had ratified a constitutional amendment limiting the president to two terms, so Ike couldn't run again in the 1960 election. Nixon was his obvious successor, a possibility that in 1952 would have thrilled the party's conservative wing. But eight years of loyalty to the president had turned Nixon into a charmless version of an Eisenhower Republican, committed to doggedly continuing what the general had done. And if there was one thing the Right hated more than having another moderate take the nomination in 1960, it was seeing it go to an apostate, particularly when they had a true believer in their sights.

Barry Goldwater was a square-jawed, blunt-talking businessman from Arizona—his family owned Phoenix's largest department store—who'd won a Senate seat in 1952 as part of Eisenhower's landslide. In the years since, he'd become the Republicans' leading advocate of the unfettered free market, the right of states to do as they pleased, and an anti-Communism so fervent he saw containment as dangerously close to capitulation. When the Right's insurgents took him aside to talk about his leading a right-wing charge at the Republican convention, he started to look an awful lot like a candidate. He let Bill Buckley's brother-in-law ghostwrite a little book that laid out his political positions, foremost among them the dismantling of the New Deal and the complete reconfiguration of Eisenhower's foreign policy. "If an enemy power is bent on conquering you he is at war with you," it read, "and you—unless you are contemplating surrender—are at war with him. Moreover, unless you contemplate treason—your objective, like his, will be victory." And he spent the first half of 1960 barnstorming the country, drawing adoring crowds wherever he went. So strong was the reaction Goldwater couldn't help but think that he had a path to the nomination, if not the White House. "I would rather see the Republican Party lose in 1960 fighting on principle," he wrote his Phoenix friend William Rehnquist shortly before the convention, "than I would care to see us win standing on grounds we know are wrong and on which we will ultimately destroy ourselves."[15]

But Eisenhower hadn't spent his presidency suppressing conflict only to let it flare again in his final days. He staunched the flow of gold with a set of economic maneuvers intended to convince investors that he would protect the dollar's value, even as those maneuvers pushed the economy into a recession. To counter the NLF he sent Diem yet more aid and told the Joint Chiefs that the several hundred US military advisers they had in that country were free to accompany the South Vietnamese army on their forays into the countryside to search out and destroy the Viet Cong. In March 1960 he approved a CIA plan to overthrow Castro just as they'd toppled the Iranian and Guatemalan governments during his first term. And though he had his doubts about Nixon—he doesn't have any friends, he told his longtime secretary—Ike quietly helped him to consolidate his control of the convention so completely that the Right had no room to maneuver. Having counted the delegates he wasn't going to win, Goldwater gave up the fight the night before his party nominated Nixon by acclamation.

By then the Democrats had already settled on their candidate, who had a few cracks of his own to seal. John Kennedy had grown up swathed in wealth and steeped in politics, thanks to his father Joseph P. Kennedy, one of the nation's richest men. Joe's grandparents had come to America from famine Ireland around the time Ed Cahill's great-grandparents had arrived. The families' trajectories had moved in very different directions. Joe's father had been a Boston ward boss, powerful enough to get his boy into Harvard—Class of 1912—though not powerful enough to get him accepted by the Brahmins who dominated the Yard. From there Joe raced up the social scale, marrying the daughter of Boston's former mayor and launching a hard-driving, wildly successful career as a stock market speculator, commodity trader, and Hollywood power broker. He invested a share of his money in Franklin Roosevelt's first two presidential campaigns, and in return received a series of high-level appointments, which he performed with such skill that there was talk of his running for the presidency himself—until Roosevelt asked him to serve as ambassador to Great Britain.

Joe Kennedy arrived in London in February 1938, eight months before the British prime minister went to meet Hitler in Munich. It was hardly surprising that Kennedy thoroughly approved of the appeasement that took place there; FDR approved of it too. His mistake was to cling to that view after the war began. Through its first catastrophic year he repeatedly urged Roosevelt to reach an accommodation with the Nazis in anticipation of Britain's impending defeat, even as the president was trying to pull American policy in precisely the opposite direction. His stack of confidential cables having failed to move Washington back to appeasement, Kennedy went public. "Democracy is finished in England," he told the *Boston Globe* in November 1940, in the midst of the German blitz. "If we get into war it will be [finished] in this country too."[16] He suffered through three weeks of relentless criticism before offering his resignation, long enough to destroy whatever was left of his political career.

So Kennedy transferred his ambitions to his sons. He began with his eldest, Joe Jr., the family's golden boy. When Joe was killed in the war his father had been desperate to avoid, Joe Sr. turned to his second son. John—Jack to his family and friends—had all the privileges fabulous wealth could buy: winters at his parents' Palm Beach mansion, summers at their compound on the Cape, school years at Choate and Harvard, where he turned his casual charm into a social whirl built around his relentless, often exploitative pursuit of women. What his father's fortune couldn't buy him was good health. As a teenager he was diagnosed with colitis, a debilitating disease of the digestive tract. His doctors tried to control it with an aggressive use of steroids that devastated his adrenal glands and caused a deterioration of his spinal column so severe there were times when he could barely walk.

His conditions should have kept him out of the war, but he was determined to serve. So in 1942 he used his father's connections to get a naval commission in a combat zone, as commander of a small patrol boat in the Pacific's Solomon Islands. He came home not quite two years later a national hero, celebrated in a slew of newspaper and magazine stories for the genuinely courageous actions he took to save most of his crew after a Japanese destroyer had split his boat in two. It was the first installment of a concerted campaign to turn Jack into the vigorous young man he'd never been.

Joe Jr. was killed in August 1944. By that December Joe Sr. was pushing Jack to run for office. "It was like being drafted," he told a reporter a decade later. "My father wanted his eldest son in politics. 'Wanted' isn't the right word. He demanded it. You know my father."[17] In 1946 his family name, his dad's money, and a lot of copies of John Hersey's *New Yorker* story on his wartime heroism won him Boston's Eleventh Congressional District, though he hadn't lived in the city for almost twenty years. The House was just a way station; as soon as he could, in 1952, he ran for a Massachusetts Senate seat. It was a Republican year. But Jack took 51.5 percent of the vote: a testament, the experts said, to the candidate's magnetism and his father's checkbook.

Over the next eight years Jack polished his image to a blinding sheen. On domestic policy he was a moderate Democrat, supportive of reform but suitably solicitous of his party's southern wing. Internationally he accepted containment as the core principle of foreign policy, though the only time that Eisenhower seriously considered military intervention—in Vietnam in 1954—Kennedy opposed it. The reservation seemed to come from a distrust of the military establishment, a view a lot of veterans brought home from the war, but it was hard not to see in it a hint of his father too.

Politics didn't power his image, though, as much as celebrity did. *Life* ran a photo spread of his 1953 marriage to Jacqueline Bouvier, an elegant twenty-two-year-old raised in almost as much comfort as he had been. When he wrote a book in 1956—some of it, anyway—it became a bestseller and, with a little prodding from some well-placed supporters, won the Pulitzer Prize. *Time* put him on its cover twice, the women's magazines ran so many stories it was impossible to keep track, the television networks loved him, and Harvard professors swooned. "Jack is the greatest attraction in the country today," Joe said in 1959. "He can draw more people to a fundraising dinner than Cary Grant or Jimmy Stewart. Why is that? He has more universal appeal."[18]

Yet there was an audacity in his decision to run for the presidency in 1960. He was only forty-two when the campaign started, four years younger than the youngest man ever elected president. He was a Catholic, which a quarter of Americans thought disqualified him from office, on the assumption that he'd be more loyal to the pope than to his nation. He was still suffering from the agonizing back pain that the steroids had caused, along with the full onset of Addison's disease. Washington was filled with rumors of the obsessive womanizing his marriage hadn't stopped. And behind him lurked his father the appeaser.

So Joe slipped as far into the background as he could, while his third son stepped to the front. Twenty-six-year-old Robert Kennedy had been a year out of law school when his father insisted that he manage Jack's first Senate campaign. The idea appalled him. But Joe wanted to be sure that the family had complete control over Jack's career. And harddriving, quick-tempered, fiercely loyal Bobby was the perfect person to make that happen. He ran Jack's 1958 reelection campaign too, with what turned out to be an impressive organizational ability. And there was never any doubt that he'd manage Jack's run for the presidency, because if there was one thing Bobby believed in above all else, it was his duty to promote and protect his brother.

Together Jack, Joe, Bobby, and the rest of their inner circle hid Jack's secrets behind a carefully crafted campaign of counter-imaging. Out went the flood of stories of his contented life with his beautiful wife, who was now expecting their second child. Out went the photos of an obviously healthy JFK—a marketer's perfectly fashioned echo of FDR— playing touch football on the lawn of his family's compound and sailing off the Cape. And out went reports that the back pain the photos couldn't completely hide was the result of the injuries he'd suffered in the Pacific: a war hero's wounds that he eased simply by sitting in a rocking chair.

The weaknesses they couldn't mask they turned to his advantage. Kennedy wasn't too young to be president, the campaign said. He was exactly what the country needed to move past the sclerotic administration Eisenhower was running as he closed in on seventy. His Catholicism wasn't a problem. It was an opportunity for Americans to prove that they weren't so bigoted as to vote against a man simply because of his faith. And he certainly wasn't going to show any weakness in defending the nation against foreign threats. In fact Eisenhower had weakened those defenses, Kennedy said, by not spending enough on the missile systems that the nation had to have to keep pace with the Soviets, a charge so baseless Ike found it absolutely enraging.

Kennedy wasn't running against an aging Eisenhower, though. He was running against a candidate just four years older than he was, whose eight years of service to a widely popular president had given him a depth of executive experience JFK didn't have. But Nixon was hobbled by the economic slowdown Ike had accepted to keep the gold supply in place. And experience couldn't substitute for charm. Nixon plodded through the fall of 1960 with a grim determination and obvious discomfort that seemed almost depressing when it was set alongside Kennedy's glittering image. In late September they met in the nation's first televised presidential debate. Kennedy was confident, cool, and marvelously telegenic; Nixon tired, nervous, and caked in makeup. "My God," said Chicago mayor Dick Daley, who was all-in for JFK, "they've embalmed him before he even died."[19]

Nixon had one last line of defense in the electoral coalition that Eisenhower had assembled. In the end he held a good portion of it, carrying three of the four southern states Ike had won in 1952 and barely losing the fourth, though Kennedy had made its senator his running mate. He swept the West. And he came close to taking the industrial Midwest as well, had old pols like Daley not stopped him with a Democratic firewall. Nixon carried the white vote, though not as strongly as Eisenhower had, and held on to the Republicans' share of the Black vote. Then there was the question of religion. Studies showed that JFK lost 6.5 percent of the Protestant vote that a Democrat normally won. But he took 78 percent of Catholic ballots, 37 points above Stevenson's total in 1956. Some of that surge came in just the right places, like the Cahills' Chicago ward, where JFK won 10,000 more votes than Stevenson had: nine percent of the nationwide margin of 112,000 votes that gave John Kennedy the presidency.

When Nixon finally conceded defeat on the afternoon after the election, JFK was at the Kennedys' Cape Cod compound. The entire family gathered in their parents' living room for a photo shoot, then headed to a row of limousines waiting to take them to the president-elect's first public appearance. "Everybody but Dad," Jack's sister Patricia recalled, "who was on the front porch, back a little in the shadows, looking very happy. . . . He had decided to stay at home out of the range of photographers and reporters. Jack suddenly realized what was happening. He got out of the car, went back up on the porch, and told Dad to come along. . . . Jack insisted on it," since it wouldn't have been right to leave behind the man who had made him president.[20]

To the Brink

EISENHOWER HAD KENNEDY into the White House twice after the election, once in December and again in January 1961. He spent a lot of their first meeting going over the White House's organizational chart, which Kennedy didn't find the most scintillating way to spend an afternoon. But Eisenhower also made a special mention of the drain on gold and the steps Washington might have to take to keep it under control. In their second session JFK asked about Vietnam and Laos, which was struggling with a Communist insurgency of its own. And Ike told him about the CIA's plan to overthrow Castro, though Kennedy already knew the details from the agency briefings he'd received. There were covert operations underway on the island. But the major initiative was in development in Guatemala, where the CIA was training 1,500 anti-Communist Cubans to conduct a spring invasion.

In between their meetings Ike offered Kennedy a public warning, wrapped inside his farewell address. It was a tradition stretching back to George Washington, who'd used his final speech as president to warn against entangling alliances. Eisenhower used his to warn about the rising danger of what he called "the military-industrial complex": the "conjunction of an immense military establishment and a large arms industry" whose influence was so vast, he said, it could "endanger our liberties or our democratic processes."[21] No doubt he was thinking about the pressure for yet more spending that JFK had created with his campaign talk of a missile gap and the gold rush that the spending could cause. But he was also telling the new president not to repeat the mistake he'd made by tying the nation's course to a corporatized warfare state.

Kennedy certainly wasn't as beholden to the corporate world as Ike had been. He handed the Treasury Department to a Wall Street banker—a Republican no less—and Defense to the president of Ford, the nation's second-largest automaker and a major defense contractor. But forty-four-year-old Robert McNamara wasn't a typical car guy. A product of Stanford and the Harvard Business School who'd helped Curtis LeMay optimize his bombing runs during World War II, he was an expert in the science of statistical control: rigorously, relentlessly, some thought excessively analytical; a thinking man's businessman whom Kennedy hoped could control a military establishment he didn't quite trust. The same analytical bent defined some of the president's other key appointments. His secretary of state was a career diplomat, his national security advisor a Harvard dean. And his most important appointment was familial. At his father's insistence Jack named Bobby attorney general, for all the same reasons Joe had wanted his third son managing Jack's election.

But changing personnel wasn't the same as changing policy. Though he couldn't bring himself to cut the defense budget—he spent $4 billion more in his first year than Ike had in his last—Kennedy made a concerted effort to correct the balance-of-payments deficit that had created the pressure on gold, just as Eisenhower had urged him to do. He followed Ike on Vietnam too. In the course of 1960 the NLF had used relentless attacks on Diem's local officials to take control of some rural areas south of Saigon and scattered parts of South Vietnam's narrow center. The losses were so extensive that the entire country was in "critical condition . . . needing emergency treatment," one of the army's more knowledgeable observers told JFK in January 1961.[22] But Kennedy wasn't interested in moving beyond the parameters Eisenhower had set. So he promised Diem the aid he needed to increase his military by another 30,000 men and upped the number of American advisers from 700 to 1,200, in hopes that small steps could stave off whatever disaster seemed to be heading his way.

Instead the disaster hit in Cuba. Kennedy began reviewing the CIA's proposed invasion within a few weeks of his inauguration. The agency planned to put its rebels ashore in a daylight beach landing about two hundred miles from Havana. There was a good chance they'd run into Cuban troops. But that wasn't necessarily a problem, the CIA said, since the resulting firefight might trigger the general uprising that would bring Castro down. If it didn't, American air support could give the rebels the cover they needed to escape to the nearby mountains, where they could build the anti-Communist version of Castro's revolutionary movement.

Kennedy wasn't convinced. A daytime landing was too risky. And he wanted a covert operation, without any indication of American involvement, not one that could depend on American fighter jets strafing Cuban troops. So the agency's planners quickly reworked the plan. They'd land the rebels at night on an isolated stretch of beach along the *Bahia de Cochinos*—the Bay of Pigs—where Cuban soldiers weren't likely to notice. From there they'd slip into the mountains without the firefight, the jets, or the spark of rebellion. Kennedy gave his approval over Easter weekend, two weeks before the invasion date of April 17.

The CIA started the landing at midnight. But the beaches weren't as isolated as the agency had thought they were. Within a few hours local militias had notified Havana that an invasion was underway. By dawn Castro's meager air force had the rebels pinned down, while his ground forces closed in. Agency operatives spent the day tracking the fighting. The next morning they told the White House that the invasion wasn't going to get beyond the beach unless the president ordered the air assault he'd been determined to avoid. Kennedy had every reason to hesitate. And he did, until early the following morning, April 19, when he ordered a limited attack that stripped away what little was left of his ability to deny that the United States was behind the entire operation. It was also too late: the Cubans crushed the CIA's collapsing force later that day. A hundred rebels had been killed. Almost all the rest were taken as prisoners of the Americans' undeclared war.

She'd never seen Jack so upset, Jackie Kennedy told his mother that day. For weeks afterward he was haunted by the men who'd died on the beach; when he brought a few of their families to the White House he made a point of telling them about his brother Joe, so they'd know that he understood the depth of their loss. He worried that both the Soviets and the Republicans would assume from his hesitation that he wasn't tough enough for the job. He was convinced that the CIA had misled him. And he hated the thought that three months into his presidency he'd let the Cold War's cruelties come out of the shadows and into view.

He spent the rest of the year trying to put them back again. Kennedy had no intention of letting the Castro government stand. But there'd be no more invasions. Now the entire battle would be fought in secret, in the Eisenhower way. And it wouldn't be run by the CIA but by the one person he knew he could trust. Bobby took over the fight with the devotion he always brought to Jack's causes. "My idea is to stir things up on the island with espionage, sabotage, general disorder, run & operated by Cuban themselves," he wrote in a note to himself that November.[23] He also seemed to embrace an ongoing CIA effort to assassinate Castro. The plots twisted and turned in various directions, one of them passing through the American mobsters whose casinos Castro had driven out of Havana. Bobby probably didn't know that part of the agency's plans. But he knew enough to accede to the idea of murdering a head of state, as long as it was done without anyone seeing the president's hand in it.

JFK also tried to keep his Vietnamese commitments as covert as he could. In October 1961 he sent his favorite general, iconoclastic Maxwell Taylor, to Saigon to assess Diem's standing. He came back with news of the NLF's expanding support and the South Vietnamese army's sagging morale. Both of those problems could be solved, Taylor thought, with an infusion of 6,000 to 8,000 American military advisers who could show Diem's troops how a war ought to be fought. The Joint Chiefs of Staff, which Taylor had yet to join—Kennedy would make him chairman in October 1962—argued that a force that small wouldn't do: they proposed that the president send 200,000 men to take the fight straight to the Viet Cong, a complete misreading of Kennedy's intentions. In November he told Diem that he was increasing the number of

American advisers in South Vietnam from 1,200 to 3,400, and sending still more military equipment, the slightest ratcheting up of the policies he'd put in place at the beginning of the year.

But the most dangerous dynamic he'd set into motion couldn't be contained. Castro had come out of his victory at the Bay of Pigs convinced that Kennedy would eventually launch a full-scale invasion. As his intelligence services picked up traces of Bobby's plotting, his fears intensified. So he asked the Russians for protection. In April 1962 the Soviet premier, Nikita Khrushchev, handed him a proposal well beyond anything Castro had expected. The Soviets would be willing, he said, to build and staff nuclear missile bases on the island.

It was purely a power play, Khrushchev told the leading members of the Soviet Central Committee, meant "to scare [the Americans], to restrain them . . . to give them back some of their own medicine."[24] At first Castro wasn't sure whether he wanted to let the Soviets use him that way. But his fear of attack was too strong to let the offer go. In August Russian military technicians began building the missile sites in the Cuban countryside. The first of them were to be ready by October, in plenty of time for Khrushchev to reveal them right after the American midterm elections.

The Pentagon's high-tech spy planes photographed the work almost immediately. But they caught the antiaircraft emplacements the Russians were building around the sites rather than the missiles themselves, a worrying sign to be sure, but not a terrifying one. Not until October 14 did a flight get firm evidence that the Russians had put in place missiles capable of hitting the United States. It took another day to develop and analyze the film. JFK was sitting in bed on the morning of October 16, reading the newspapers, when his national security advisor told him the news. Kennedy asked him to assemble his foreign policy advisers as soon as possible, without letting anyone know its cause. Then he called Bobby.

The Executive Committee of the National Security Council—ExComm for short—began its first meeting in the Cabinet Room at 11:50 a.m. Bobby was there, of course, as were the vice president, the secretaries of state, defense, and the treasury, the chairman of the Joint Chiefs, and the national security advisor, along with a handful of high-ranking aides. Kennedy had already decided that the group would meet whenever possible over the next few days to settle on a response. Their sessions would be absolutely secret; he wouldn't even change his official schedule, since doing that would alert the press that something was wrong. Only when they had a policy set would Kennedy tell the public what was happening. With that understanding in place, they started to talk. And the Cold War's inexorable power closed in.

The first meeting was barely underway when the secretary of state, Dean Rusk, said that in his view Khrushchev was making a political move, not a military one. "He . . . knows that we don't really live under fear of his nuclear weapons to the extent that he has to live under the fear of ours," he said. "We have nuclear missiles nearby [the Soviet Union], in Turkey and places like that," while the Soviets' other missiles weren't anywhere near the United States.[25] It took Bob McNamara a little longer to point out that Khrushchev's moving the missiles closer to the United States didn't tip the balance of power; a nuclear warhead fired out of East Germany was going to be just as devastating as one fired out of Cuba. Yet the ExComm spent the next four days—while JFK made the public appearances that kept him out of the room—discussing how the administration had to eliminate the missiles, because even a symbolic Soviet victory was too much to bear.

The key question then became how the missiles might be purged. On that point the ExComm split in two. One side, led by Rusk and backed by Bobby and the Joint Chiefs, urged the president to launch an overwhelming air strike of 500 to 2,000 sorties against the missile sites and ancillary targets, to be followed within a few days by a full-scale invasion with a force of at least 100,000 men, two-thirds the number the Allies had sent onto Normandy's beaches on the first day of the European invasion in 1944. The power would be enormous, McNamara argued for the other side, but it would also carry tremendous risk. The air strikes would probably destroy the sites. They'd also kill the Russian soldiers stationed around them, which could force the Soviets to respond with an attack of their own, an escalation that could rapidly turn into a nuclear exchange. And 100,000 American troops wading ashore would undoubtedly make things worse. Better to give Khrushchev the chance to back down before the shooting started. American intelligence had reported that the Soviets were still shipping to Cuba what analysts assumed to be the nuclear warheads. The navy could put a blockade around Cuba to prevent those ships from arriving. If the Soviets tried to run the blockade, the American ships would have to sink them, McNamara conceded, and the United States and the USSR would again be on the path to nuclear annihilation. But if they turned around, the Americans would know that the Russians didn't really want a confrontation. Maybe then they could move toward some form of negotiation.

Through October 18 the assault side dominated. As the sessions dragged on, though, McNamara slowly brought the most influential person in the room over to his side. Around 8:00 p.m. that evening Bobby stopped by the Oval Office for a private conversation with his brother. The next morning the chairman of the Joint Chiefs told his colleagues of JFK's new inclination. And Curtis LeMay told the president that anything short of immediate military action was appeasement.

When Kennedy went on national television three days later—Monday night, October 22—to tell the American people about the missile sites, he talked of appeasement too. "The 1930s taught us a clear lesson," he said. "Aggressive conduct, if allowed to go unchecked, ultimately leads to war. This nation is opposed to war. We are also true to our word. Our unswerving objective, therefore, must be to prevent the use of these missiles against this or any other country, and to secure their withdrawal or elimination. . . ."[26] But he'd start with a blockade instead of the devastating assault LeMay wanted to lead.

The news shuddered through the nation. Eighty-four percent of Americans supported the blockade, according to Gallup's overnight poll. But they feared where it might lead. Seventy-five percent expected some shooting between American and Soviet forces. Twenty percent thought that World War III was about to begin. And 65 percent gave some thought to the possibility of nuclear war. JFK knew the feeling. On October 23 he set the military at its highest level of alert, one step short of nuclear war, in case the Soviets should defy him. That evening he asked Jackie whether she wanted to spend the night with their children in the White House bomb shelter. She said she'd stay with him.

The blockade went into effect at 10:00 the next morning. The Soviet signal arrived forty-five minutes later, when the CIA director informed the ExComm that the Russian ships that had been heading toward Cuba were reversing course. But no one knew what to do next. For three more days the Americans and the Soviets edged around each other, trying to puzzle through what the other intended. The longer the impasse lasted, the more the military pressure mounted. On October 27 the Joint Chiefs prepared a formal recommendation that Kennedy immediately order the air strike the blockade had superseded. That afternoon, just as the ExComm was beginning its second meeting of the day, word arrived that a Cuban antiaircraft battery had shot down one of the Americans' spy planes, killing the pilot in the process. In the taut conversation that ensued, even McNamara started talking about the need to prepare for the occupation that would follow the American bombing and the increasingly inevitable invasion.

The session ended around 7:45 p.m. As everyone was filing out, JFK asked a handful of them to join him in the Oval Office. They spent about twenty minutes settling on instructions. Once they had their message clear, Bobby went to see the Soviet ambassador.

They met alone in the attorney general's office down the street from the White House. Bobby started with the death of the American pilot. "I told him that this was an extremely serious turn in events," he wrote a few days later. "There was very little time left. If the Cubans were shooting down our planes, then we were going to shoot back. This could not help but bring on further incidents and he had better understand the full implications of this matter."[27] From the threat he moved to the offer. If the Soviets were to remove their missiles, the United States would guarantee that there'd be no invasion of Cuba. Then he cycled back to a point the secretary of state had raised on the crisis's opening day. Should the Cuban missiles be withdrawn, he said, the Soviets could expect that in four or five months the president would remove the Americans' missiles from Turkey. There'd be no formal deal, just a mutual understanding. And if the Russians ever spoke a word of it, the United States would deny everything. The next morning, October 28, Khrushchev announced that the Cuban missile sites would be dismantled, the missiles crated and returned to the Soviet Union. To the president he sent a highly confidential note accepting Bobby's terms.

In the secrecy that Kennedy wrapped around the settlement lay the crisis's final danger. It had been seventeen years since the Red Army rolled into the ruins of Berlin. In that time the world war's lessons had hardened into principles so absolute many of the nation's most powerful men had come to see caution as weakness and compromise as akin to surrender. Those principles had created the crisis that Kennedy had then solved by refusing to give in to its adherents' demand for violence on a staggering scale. Yet in the end he believed that he had to hide his path to peace as thoroughly as Eisenhower had hidden his harshest actions, for fear of being called his father's son.

CHAPTER 3

THE BELOVED COMMUNITY

If Elizabeth Eckford's family had had a phone, she would've gotten the evening call that went to the other kids, telling them where to meet their escorts in the morning. But her parents had six children to raise on working people's wages, and there wasn't room for extravagances. So Elizabeth got up earlier than normal to give herself time to get dressed in the outfit she'd picked out for the first day of school: a prim blouse, a skirt she'd sewn over the summer—white cotton on the upper half, blue gingham on the lower—and the bobby socks all the other fifteen-year-olds in the country seemed to be wearing. Her mother pulled the family together to recite the Twenty-Seventh Psalm. Once they were done, Elizabeth picked up the binder her mother had bought her, slipped on the sunglasses she hoped would hide how scared she was, and headed out on her own to catch the city bus to Central High.

It dropped her off two blocks north of the school. Right away she could tell that something was wrong, though at first it was hard to know what it was. As she got closer she could see the solid line of National Guardsmen on the sidewalk around the school and the crowd in the street in front of them. Because the guardsmen were letting the white kids through she thought that everything was going to be OK. But when she tried to pass through too they blocked her way.

Later some of the details of that moment slipped away. She seemed to have asked them where she was supposed to go. They pointed her to Central's main entrance, another block down the street. She followed their directions, walking along the line of troopers, a couple of feet from the curb. Now the crowd was following behind her, teenagers and adults together, the closest of them within arms' reach, though she didn't dare look around to see. A couple of the girls were chanting like they were at a football game: "Two, four, six, eight, we don't want to integrate!" Some of the grown-ups were calling her racial slurs and other names her family would never use. Others were yelling at her to go back to Africa. And someone was screaming, "Lynch her! Lynch her!"[1] The newspapermen fell in with them, the reporters walking next to her with their notepads flipped open, the photographers in front of her clicking away as she stared past them, doing her best not to show any emotion at all.

She stopped about halfway down the block to ask another group of guardsmen to let her through. This time they closed their ranks and crossed their rifles in front of her. The shock of it set her legs to shaking so badly she wasn't sure she could make it down to the entrance. But somehow she managed to walk the rest of the block as she had the first part, her face set, her binder pressed to her chest, the mob still screaming behind her. When she finally got to the stretch of sidewalk directly in front of the sweeping stairs that led up to Central's main doors, the troopers stationed there told her that she wasn't going to school that day and ordered her to step back from the line.

She stood in front of them for a moment more, unsure of what to do. Then she turned away and started walking in the only direction open to her, past the rest of the guardsmen, beyond the far end of the school, to the nearest bus stop. She sat on the edge of the bench, spread out her skirt as a proper young lady was supposed to do, folded her hands over the binder she'd set in her lap, and waited for her bus to arrive. The reporters circled around her in what one of them said later was an informal cordon that Elizabeth didn't notice, the mob just beyond them, still calling for someone to hang her from a tree.

How long she stayed there she couldn't say, though others thought it was close to half an hour. At some point an African American man came over to say he'd drive her home. But her parents having told her never to take rides from strangers, she politely declined. Not long after that a middle-aged white woman came out of the crowd to offer her protection. Elizabeth had no idea who she was or why she insisted on standing by her. But the woman's willingness to scold the mob—to tell them how sorry they'd be one day—made her fear that she was only going to make things worse, when all Elizabeth really wanted was for everyone to leave her alone: a hero of the movement, sitting silently on a bus-stop bench, trying not to cry.

Segregation Now, Segregation Forever

THEY CALLED IT Jim Crow, after a blackface character white audiences had flocked to see in the decades before the revolution southern Democrats wanted to undo.

The enslaved had started the transformation in the war's first years, when the Republicans still thought that they were fighting for something else. But so many slaves had come pouring toward the Union lines they'd forced the generals and the politicians to think about the contours of freedom, as a matter of practicality if not of principle. The greater the war's devastation grew, the more radical the Republicans' vision became. It wasn't enough to end slavery in the territories Union troops occupied; its complete abolition had to be written into the Constitution. It wasn't enough to free the enslaved from bondage; the Constitution had to guarantee them equal rights before the law in every state of the nation. And among those rights it had to guarantee was the right to vote, for African American men at least, since women couldn't vote anywhere at all.

It took three amendments—the thirteenth, the fourteenth, and the fifteenth—to secure those guarantees, the last of them ratified just five years after the Confederacy's defeat. On the ground the constitutional guarantees didn't always hold. Across the South, where more than 90 percent of African Americans lived, white landowners used the freedmen's desperate need for work to shape new forms of domination, while white terrorism drove down the Black vote in state after state.

As the Democrats clawed back into power in the 1870s and 1880s, they began to harden the South's racial regime. But they couldn't destroy the revolutionary changes the war had wrought without staging a counterrevolution.

They built it on the ruthless exploitation of whites' deep-seated racism. Slavery had kept Blacks in check, southern Democrats said again and again, but two decades of freedom had turned them into the threats whites had long feared them to be. From the many racist tropes available to them, the demagogues turned to the most inflammatory, repeatedly raising the specter of Black men as sexual predators, given to raping white women. "The poor African has become a fiend, a wild beast, seeking whom he may devour," proclaimed one-eyed Ben Tillman, the most fearsome of the South's demagogues, "lurking around to see if some helpless white woman may be murdered or brutalized."[2] Mob violence inevitably followed: whites lynched a thousand African Americans in the 1890s, an average of one racial murder every three and a half days for an entire decade. Behind those lynchings lay all sorts of power dynamics. But it was often the rumor of rape that turned them into spectacles of barbarism, with throngs of whites come to prove their superiority by sharing in the brutality.

Southern Democrats offered a way out of the crisis they'd created with a raft of racist laws. One set aimed to deny African Americans even the smallest share of political power by stripping them of the vote. Since they couldn't make that disenfranchisement explicitly racial without violating the Fifteenth Amendment, they put in place a series of restrictions designed to prevent African Americans from voting without mentioning race. Almost every southern state imposed a poll tax a voter had to pay before he could cast his ballot, a cost that many African Americans couldn't afford. Most states required voters to prove that they'd lived at the same address for a couple of years, knowing that poor people tended to move more often than that. And some required anyone who wanted to vote to appear before a registrar, who'd test the applicant's understanding of state law according to a standard that everyone knew was absolutely arbitrary.

The results were exactly what the Democrats wanted them to be. Mississippi's laws purged 94 percent of eligible African Americans from the voting rolls, Alabama's 98 percent. They also purged a lot of poor whites, a side effect the Democrats offset by the other set of laws they passed. Southern schools had been segregated since the 1860s, railroad cars since the 1870s and 1880s. But the color lines were haphazardly drawn and unevenly applied. In the 1890s and 1900s Democratic legislators made them as comprehensive as they could be. African Americans couldn't eat in the same restaurants as whites; couldn't drink from the same drinking fountains; couldn't wait in the same railway station waiting room; couldn't sit in the same section of a theater or alongside a white person on the streetcar line; couldn't even try on clothes in the stores, since a white person would then run the risk of buying a dress or a coat that had touched Black skin. Everywhere Blacks were allowed to go, the space was racialized, either explicitly by the "Colored" signs that became ubiquitous across the South or implicitly by understandings of an enforced spatial hierarchy. At the movies Blacks had to sit in the balcony, on buses in the last rows, on trains in the car directly behind the engine where the smoke came pouring in.

Some of the distinctions imposed enormous material costs on Black communities. With many of the laws, though, the placement was the point. Through its segregation of social space, the Jim Crow system imprinted on the southern landscape the inviolable hierarchy of the races. So when an African American did any one of a dozen ordinary things in the course of a day—catching a streetcar to work, taking a sip of water, walking her little boy past a park they couldn't enter—she would be humiliated. And when a white man took his little boy onto those segregated grounds he'd be reminded that no matter how poor he might be, there was always someone beneath him.

African Americans fought back by appealing to the constitutional rights they'd secured during Reconstruction. The defining case came out of Louisiana, where a group of Black activists fronted by Homer Plessy filed suit against the state's segregation of its railroad cars. Their segregation imprinted on African Americans a mark of inferiority, they argued, and therefore violated the equal protections the Fourteenth Amendment guaranteed. Their case reached the U.S. Supreme Court in April 1896. A month later the justices ruled against them by a margin of seven to one. Louisiana wasn't stopping Plessy from riding the railroad, their decision said. It was just requiring him to sit in a Black-only car, separate from but equal to the whites-only cars from which he was barred. If that requirement made him feel inferior, the justices said, that was his problem and not the Constitution's. Louisiana's law could stand, and with it the rest of Jim Crow.

Once the system's constitutionality was confirmed, the Democrats could consolidate their counterrevolution. It took some time. Georgia didn't complete its disenfranchisement of African American voters until 1908. And in the early 1910s legislators were still trying to extend segregation's boundaries in various directions. But by then the Democrats' relentless racial politics had turned the South into the one-party state that gave their senators and congressmen such inordinate power in Washington. And the system itself had expanded in the most malignant ways. Some whites rejected the state-sanctioned sense of superiority that Jim Crow created. But far more made it their own, building out from it a social structure of racial domination so complete it even defined how African Americans were supposed to stand in front of them, with their hats in their hands and their eyes downcast. Whites simply wouldn't tolerate any defiance of their domination, for the good of what they proudly came to call "the southern way of life."

But defiance there would be. It came through the small, often spontaneous acts of resistance African Americans dared to commit despite the catastrophic consequences they could face. It ran through the massive migration out of the South, even as northern cities hardened their racial regimes. And it took institutional form in the construction of a civil rights movement dedicated to beating back the racist tide.

The movement's foundational organizations pulled in decidedly different directions. The National Association for the Advancement of Colored People's inaugural platform of 1909 was so straightforward it fit on a single page. African Americans were citizens of the United States, it said, and therefore must be afforded all the rights that adhere thereto. But behind that demand lay a blistering sense of betrayal. For the white activists who controlled the NAACP in its first decade, the betrayal was often familial, their parents and grandparents having been among the radical Republicans who'd secured the constitutional guarantees that Jim Crow was now destroying. For the African Americans who replaced those activists in the late 1910s it was personal. They were professional men and women of stunning accomplishment, members of that strata of Black America the brilliant W. E. B. Du Bois condescendingly called "the Talented Tenth." But their elevated positions couldn't protect them. They'd seen their neighborhoods assaulted, their homes burned, their friends lynched, and, in Du Bois's case, his eighteen-month-old son killed by a fever that might have been cured had a white hospital been willing to take on his care. A structure that vicious could not be allowed to stand. So they would topple it with protests, political campaigns, and legal challenges to what the platform called "the systematic persecution of law-abiding citizens," a "crime that will ultimately drag down . . . any nation that allows it to be practiced."[3]

No one would have mistaken Marcus Garvey for a member of the Talented Tenth, least of all Du Bois. A printer by trade, born and raised in small-town Jamaica, Garvey had come to New York in 1916 to fundraise for the Universal Negro Improvement Association (UNIA), a small group he'd recently founded to promote Black self-determination. From Harlem's famous Speakers' Corner he sent his message surging across the country; by 1919 the UNIA was enrolling so many members it was on its way to becoming the nation's largest civil rights organization.

The NAACP's shocked leadership attributed that success to Garvey's indisputable charisma, which they considered dangerously close to demagoguery. But the UNIA's appeal ran far deeper than that. While the NAACP advocated protest marches and court cases as the path to equality, Garvey preached the power African Americans could claim for themselves by building communities completely free of white control, with their own businesses, social groups, political parties, and intense points of pride. It was an idea he'd come to through the Caribbean's anticolonial politics, and that thousands of African Americans had embraced through the brutal experience of living under Jim Crow's boot. In the late 1910s and early 1920s, the UNIA fused those two perspectives in the century's first Black nationalist breakthrough.

It didn't last. As the UNIA expanded, Garvey drew the attention of federal authorities, who saw in his promotion of self-determination a threat to the nation's order. In 1919 the FBI sent its first undercover agent into the organization to begin gathering the evidence they needed to break Garvey. Four years later Garvey was convicted of mail fraud and sentenced to a five-year prison term. Without him the UNIA all but collapsed. But the movement's two poles had been set. On one end stood the NAACP's dogged defense of equal rights, on the other the promise of Black power.

Between these poles other activists staked their ground. In the 1910s and 1920s a faction of African Americans argued that racial and economic domination were so intertwined that the struggle for civil rights had to be coupled with a fundamental transformation of the economic order. From there the faction split. One group joined the Soviet-inspired Communist Party, whose admittedly minute membership maintained an often-breathtaking commitment to racial egalitarianism. Another group followed the American socialist tradition, with its faith in democratic processes and grassroots organizing. In that faction of a faction no one mattered more than A. Philip Randolph, the dynamic editor of one of Harlem's most-respected monthly magazines. In 1925 Randolph agreed to lead a unionization campaign among the race men who worked as porters on the railroad's Pullman sleeping cars. Most of the porters weren't socialists, and Randolph was no porter. But he saw in the union campaign the fusing of race and class that was central to the socialist vision. So he signed on.

The movement's socialist strand intertwined with what may have been the most demanding of radical beliefs. American pacifism had its roots in those handful of faiths that rejected war as immoral and expected the devout to work for justice through nonviolent means. But its most profound inspiration came from the great revolutionary

Mohandas Gandhi, who in a series of brilliantly orchestrated mass confrontations—in South Africa in the 1910s and in his native India in the 1920s and 1930s—proved that the oppressed could use passive resistance and peaceful defiance to break their oppressors' grip. In Gandhi's movement the protests of the powerless could take various forms, from the burning of government-issued identity cards to the widespread refusal to obey unjust laws. At every step they had to be willing to endure, even welcome, the violence the powerful would inflict on them, because it was through their suffering that they demonstrated the "soul force" that Gandhi believed was at the movement's core. *Satyagraha*, he called it, though on the Black side of Jim Crow's color line it would come to be called redemption.[4]

The Quickening

THE MOVEMENT LIMPED through the 1920s and early 1930s. As the UNIA faded, the NAACP extended its reach: by 1933 it had 100,000 members in 327 branches around the country, a significant number of them in the South. But it had yet to build a sustained challenge to segregation in the courts or the streets. The Communists had won widespread praise for their defense of the Scottsboro Boys, nine young men imprisoned in Alabama in 1931 on an obviously trumped-up charge of rape. For all the Communists' efforts, though, the boys were still in prison. Eight years into his campaign, Randolph had yet to force the Pullman Company to recognize its porters' union. And the few activists attracted to pacifism were still watching Gandhi rather than bringing his protests home.

Then the New Deal came to Washington. FDR wasn't trying to give the movement the openings it needed, but that's what he did. Once the administration committed itself to supporting workers' right to unionize, Randolph could finally push Pullman into negotiations. It took until August 1937 to secure the Brotherhood of Sleeping Car Porters its first contract. With that long-awaited victory Randolph became one of the movement's leading men, a position he used to build a far larger challenge to the racial order. In January 1941 he announced that come summer he'd be mounting a massive March on Washington to demand equal access to the defense jobs the government was creating. The thought of 100,000 African Americans trooping down Pennsylvania Avenue so appalled FDR that he gave in to Randolph's demands before anybody arrived, a triumph for union brinksmanship that also had a Gandhian ring.

That was what drew Bayard Rustin in. He'd come to pacifism through his family's Quakerism and to socialism through a political journey that many engaged young men and women took in the 1930s. In 1942 he brought those commitments together by joining the staff of Randolph's March on Washington Movement—the inheritor of the previous year's rescinded protest—and the nonviolent vanguard of the Congress of Racial Equality (CORE), a tiny pacifist group dedicated to bringing Gandhism into the civil rights struggle. To the former Rustin brought organizational skills so superb he quickly became one of Randolph's most trusted advisers. To the latter he brought the audacity to confront Jim Crow with intimate acts of Gandhian resistance. He and his fellow pacifists demanded to be served in segregated restaurants, picketed segregated stores, and sat in the front row of segregated buses as they crossed the South, an action that in 1947 earned him twenty-two days at hard labor on a North Carolina chain gang.

As the New Dealers made room for protests they didn't want to see, they also widened the movement's ability to work within the legal system. FDR had spent his first term constrained by a staunchly conservative Supreme Court. In his second term he remade it with five progressive nominees. His goal was to get the justices' approval of his economic policies, but the NAACP saw in the Court's reconfiguration an opening for racial justice too. The fight would be led by the association's newly established legal department, through cases brought by members willing to risk the danger of demanding the rights denied them, both sides of the campaign—top-down and bottom-up—feeding off each other.

Howard University Law School dean Charles Hamilton Houston

set up the legal side and won its first breakthrough cases. In 1940 he turned its operation over to his protégé, thirty-two-year-old Thurgood Marshall, the son of a Pullman porter father and schoolteacher mother who brought to the campaign a common touch and a brilliant legal mind. That same year the association hired thirty-seven-year-old Ella Baker to help invigorate the grassroots side. Raised on the North Carolina farm that was her family's pride, Baker had carried her intense sense of social justice through her college years at Raleigh's Shaw University and then to New York City, where she spent the 1930s immersed in the political currents that swirled through Harlem. In December 1940 the NAACP's leadership brought her on as a "field secretary," its term for the handful of organizers it had on staff. Back into the South she plunged—to "barber shops, filling stations, grocery stores," and plenty of churches, she wrote from the road—for continuous rounds of organization-building premised on her faith in ordinary people's ability to define the issues that mattered to them.[5] That deeply democratic vision fed the NAACP's remarkable rise in membership, which hit almost half a million by 1945. From those numbers came the cases that sustained the campaign's synergy.

It helped that the association's lawyers kept winning. From 1938 on they chipped away at the nation's racial system, from Texas' all-white primary, which the Supreme Court declared unconstitutional in 1944, to the racial restrictions developers and homeowners put on their deeds, which the justices declared unenforceable in 1948. From the start, though, the NAACP's attorneys took as their primary target the legal segregation of schools. They couldn't have made a more provocative choice. By any measure schools were the nation's most pervasive public institutions, and the most strongly rooted in traditions of local control. Through that control whites infused their schools with the most egregious forms of discrimination: in the distribution of funding, the maintenance of facilities, the setting of teacher's salaries, and their dedication to the physical separation of the races, because there was no greater risk than letting kids of different color sit side by side. That was the system that the NAACP lawyers intended to break, if they had their way.

The question was how to get there. For a decade and a half the association's lawyers used a series of cases to gradually move the justices toward overturning *Plessy*. In 1950 Marshall finally decided that they'd gotten as close as they needed to be. So in his next school case he would argue that the legal segregation of schools made Black children feel that they were inferior to white children, a psychological burden a state should not be allowed to impose. Marshall wasn't particularly concerned that the claim was true, though he had to say it was. What mattered was the framing. By insisting on the damage segregation caused, he would be putting before the Court the same argument Homer Plessy had made about his streetcar ride in 1896. If the justices accepted that argument now, they'd be toppling the *Plessy* precedent, and with it Jim Crow's legal foundation.

Marshall found five cases to argue. All of them came up from the NAACP's branches in the pattern Ella Baker had set, though she had left the association by then: two of them from individual families, two from a number of parents banding together, and the fifth from a rural Virginia school strike organized by a remarkable sixteen-year-old, Barbara Johns, whose uncle was a prominent pastor of a church down in Montgomery, Alabama. As the cases worked their way to the Supreme Court, they were subsumed under the first to appear in the docket alphabetically: *Brown v. Board of Education of Topeka, Kansas*. Twice Marshall argued the case before the Court, in December 1952 and again in December 1953, a delay driven partly by the Court's internal politics and partly by Dwight Eisenhower's appointment of a new chief justice in the intervening year.

Earl Warren was sixty-two when Ike named him to the Court, old enough to be closing in on the end of a fine career. A working-class kid from Bakersfield, California, Warren had put himself through UC Berkeley, stayed on for law school, and then moved on to a life in politics. He spent thirteen years as the Alameda County district attorney, four as California's attorney general, and ten as governor, all of them marked by his commitment to good government and the Republican version of progressivism: a noble record stained by his unconscionable support for the wartime internment of Japanese Americans. *Brown* was reargued two months after he joined the Court. "On the merits," he said afterward, "the only way the case could be decided was clear. The question was how the decision was to be reached."[6] For the rest of the term he used the political skills honed over three decades to bring his fractious colleagues behind the unanimous ruling he thought a case with such explosive implications should have. Only when he had the votes did he issue the decision. On May 17, 1954, the Court ruled by the 9 to 0 margin Warren had created that any state, county, or municipality segregating its public schools by law was in violation of the Constitution.

"Once and for all it's decided," Marshall told the press when he had the opinion in his hands. "Completely decided." But it wasn't. Within a year about five hundred school boards, including three of the five test cases, agreed to desegregate their schools without further court orders. And the NAACP was working with hundreds of Black communities to demand that their districts do the same. In huge swaths of the South, though, whites were threatening massive resistance. *Brown* had turned the Constitution into "a mere scrap of paper," insisted Georgia's governor, Herman Talmadge. Virginia senator Harry Byrd declared it "the most serious blow that has yet been struck against the rights of the states." Mississippi's hyper-segregationist senator James Eastland went further. The South "will not abide by or obey this . . . decision," he said, a declaration that put him on the edge of rebellion.[7]

The Court tried to ease the pressure in May 1955 by announcing that its decision ought to be implemented with "all deliberate speed," a standard so vague it effectively gave the South unlimited time to desegregate its schools.[8] By then it was too late to rein in the backlash. From the politicians, talk of resistance had filtered down to the South's businessmen—a quarter million of them, at least—who'd rushed to form a region-wide network of White Citizens' Councils they could use to intimidate African Americans into silence with threats of economic retaliation. Below that layer of racist respectability lay the violence that had always been Jim Crow's default defense. In June 1955 white terrorists murdered Reverend George Lee, a central figure in the Mississippi NAACP. On August 13 three white men gunned down Lamar Smith while he helped Black voters to register at the courthouse in Brookhaven, Mississippi. And on August 28 a pair of cousins butchered a fourteen-year-old Chicago boy who had come to the Delta to visit family for a couple of weeks before the start of school. His name was Emmett Till. And he may or may not have whistled at a white woman in a ramshackle general store in Money, Mississippi.

Defiance

TILL WAS DEAD three months when African Americans in Montgomery, Alabama, launched a boycott of the city's buses. The timing wasn't coincidental. When forty-two-year-old Rosa Parks boarded her bus for the ride home from work on Thursday evening, December 1, 1955, she sat in the first row of the Black section. Gradually the bus filled in, Blacks in the back, whites in the front, with a white man standing. By law Parks's row belonged to him, so the bus driver told the people sitting there to give up their seats. Three of the four complied. But Parks thought of her grandfather, a loyal member of the UNIA, she said later, and of Emmett Till. And she refused to move.[9]

From that single act of defiance spun a perfect example of the grassroots action Ella Baker loved. Bus drivers had long used the power the law gave them to abuse African Americans, particularly the working-class women who made up much of the system's ridership. They'd pushed back with formal complaints, some political organizing, and the occasional act of impromptu resistance. But none of it worked. So one of Montgomery's most active civil rights groups, the solidly middle-class Women's Political Council, decided to up the pressure. In May 1954 the WPC's president Jo Ann Robinson, an English professor at Alabama State, the local Black college, informed the mayor that her organization was planning a bus boycott to demand that conditions be improved. Then she lined up the support of the local branch of the NAACP, whose longtime president, E. D. Nixon—a Pullman porter deeply devoted to his union—knew something about using economic pressure in pursuit of racial change.

What they needed was a galvanizing incident to get the boycott underway. Three times in 1955 the police arrested women for refusing to give up their seats on city buses. The first two were teenagers who, for one reason or another, Robinson and Nixon decided weren't respectable enough to rally around. The third was Mrs. Parks. She was a quiet, serious, church-going woman, a seamstress by trade, married to a barber who worked on a nearby military base. She was also the secretary of the Montgomery NAACP, a title that didn't come close to capturing the depth of her commitments. For more than a decade she'd taken on some of the branch's most dangerous assignments, foremost among them its explosive exposé of the sexual violence white men inflicted on Black women, an inversion of the story whites told themselves to justify Jim Crow's greatest terrors. The boycott hadn't been on her mind when she defied the bus's racial rules. But within hours of her arrest, she agreed to be its symbolic center. By the next morning Robinson had the first flyers going up on bus stops across the Black side of the city.

The boycott started on Monday, December 5, with the buses running empty of African American riders. Everyone assumed that the city couldn't hold out for long, since Blacks made up most of the system's customers. In the meantime the campaign had to have a coordinating committee. On Monday afternoon Nixon called together the community's leading figures to choose its chair. They passed over Robinson and Parks without a thought. And in a slight he never forgave, they passed over Nixon too, mostly because he'd made too many enemies over the years. In the place he thought was his they put a young man most of them didn't know particularly well.

Martin Luther King Jr. had been called to Montgomery's Dexter Avenue Baptist Church in May 1954 to replace the Reverend Vernon Johns, whose niece had organized the Virginia school strike that had led to one of the cases in *Brown*. Johns was a towering figure. But he was also a hard-driving advocate in a church that wasn't used to a politicized pastor. So after five tumultuous years the congregation let him go. For his successor they found a quintessential member of the Talented Tenth. Both King's grandfather and father had held one of Atlanta's most prestigious pulpits, at Ebenezer Baptist. For college he'd gone to Atlanta's elite Morehouse College, and from there to Philadelphia's Crozier Seminary and Boston University, which awarded him a PhD in theology in June 1955. He had a charming, sophisticated wife, the former Coretta Scott, who two weeks before the boycott had given birth to their first baby, Yolanda. While he had the proper political commitments—he expected his congregants to join the NAACP—he didn't have the hard edge that set people off. Then again, he was still a young man in the making, a fledgling pastor a month shy of twenty-seven, so it was nothing more than a guess what sort of leader he'd be.

He proved to have his share of skills. In front of the mass meeting the coordinating committee used to maintain the boycott's momentum he was electric, a preacher's preacher gathering his flock. Though he wasn't a particularly adept organizer, he was willing to surround himself with people who were; within a week or so the committee had an entire alternative transportation system operating out of Dexter Avenue's basement. What he couldn't do was get the city to budge. The economics were clear; a couple of weeks without Black riders and Montgomery's bus system was plunging toward bankruptcy. But the *Brown* backlash had choked off local officials' willingness to compromise. For more than a month King and his committee slogged through a useless set of negotiations, until, in the middle of January 1956, the authorities shut them down entirely in favor of a new wave of economic retaliation and police repression that they thought would break the boycott. In response King's committee authorized their attorney to ask the NAACP for its help in filing a federal suit against the bus system as the only way to bring the deepening confrontation to an end.

That was the dynamic that Ella Baker had created in the 1940s: ordinary people mobilizing around the issues that mattered to them, shaping a movement from the traditions and talents at hand—imperfectly, to be sure—pressing the cause as far as they could, and then bringing what they'd built to the association's lawyers so that they could use it to bring down another piece of Jim Crow. There the boycott's contribution to the struggle might have ended, had it not been for a couple of turns.

King had struggled with the boycott's burdens from the start. Somehow he was supposed to fit into his schedule night after night of rallies, committee meetings, and strategy sessions. He had to lead the negotiations and manage the politics that came with them. And he had to deal with the mounting harassment; by January he was getting thirty to forty threatening phone calls a day. The city's turn to intimidation made it worse. On January 26, 1956, he was arrested for the first time in his life: pulled over for speeding, shoved into the back seat of a cruiser, and hustled off to the Montgomery jail for booking. He was in custody for only a few hours in what was clearly a cheap show of force. But force in a system built on violence was a terrifying thing. During the twisting drive to jail King had wondered whether the cops were really just planning to lynch him.

That evening he had to attend seven mass rallies so that the community could see that he was safe. The next day was lost to another round of meetings shaped by the fear that the authorities had created. By the time he got to bed Coretta was already asleep. For a while he lay next to her, until the phone rang—another threatening call—and any hope of sleep was gone. He went into the kitchen, put on a pot of coffee, sat at the table to pray. And the silence cracked open. "It seemed at that moment," he said later, "that I could hear an inner voice saying to me, 'Martin Luther, stand up for righteousness. Stand up for justice. Stand up for truth. And lo I will be with you, even until the end of the world.' . . . I heard the voice of Jesus saying still to fight on. He promised never to leave me, never to leave me alone. No never alone. All at once my fears began to go. My uncertainty disappeared."[10]

Of course King had framed the boycott in religious terms before; he was a minister, after all. But this wasn't a rhetorical turn pulled from the Gospel to inspire the faithful. At his core he believed that God's only begotten son had given him His blessing and His commission in the words He'd used to send His apostles into the world. In the months that followed King would fit that sacred obligation into the framework the New Testament gave him. White Americans had embraced the sin of racism, he'd come to say. African Americans would walk into the face of that sin. They'd take it on their shoulders. They'd suffer for it. They'd die for it. And with that blood sacrifice they would redeem the soul of America, a vision of the movement formed by revelation.

A month later Bayard Rustin came to town. He'd heard of the boycott through the news stories that were filtering north and the activist networks he knew better than just about anyone else. He saw in it a nascent Gandhism he thought he could nurture. So in late February 1956 he headed down to Montgomery with an introduction from Randolph that was sure to make E. D. Nixon welcome him home. He showed up in a moment of crisis. As part of its hardening response, the authorities had convinced a Montgomery grand jury to indict 115 of the movement's leading figures for violating a little-used anti-boycott law, a move that sent the fear of mass arrests surging through the Black community. It also attracted the press's attention; a few of the nation's major papers had already dispatched reporters to watch the indictments unfold. In that confluence Rustin saw his opportunity.

His first day he spent in a flurry of consultations that Nixon opened up for him. The next morning Nixon appeared at the sheriff's office and voluntarily presented himself for booking. His pastor came next. Over the next few days a parade of the indicted appeared—Parks, Robinson, King's friend and associate the Reverend Ralph Abernathy of Montgomery's First Baptist Church, and eventually King himself— all formally dressed, all politely asking to be charged, all turning the city's attempt to decapitate the boycott into a demonstration of their resolve. As they left—their arrest photos taken, their fingerprints on file, and their bonds posted—they stepped into a growing crowd of supporters come to celebrate their courage. There stood Rustin too, in the cluster of reporters the indictments had drawn in. By the end of the week his Gandhian moment was on the front page of the *New York Times.*

He knew that he couldn't stay. He was a socialist, a pacifist, and a gay man from Harlem—almost a cliché of an outside agitator—and it wouldn't be long before the authorities figured out how to taint the boycott with his presence. In any case Montgomery wasn't where he needed to be. Ten days after his arrival he headed back to New York to take the story he'd started to shape up another level. It was fine to talk about the boycott, but a compelling story had to have a central character. Within a few weeks Rustin had ghostwritten the first article to ever appear under King's name. He published a pamphlet calling King "the American Gandhi" for circulation in his activist circles, and did his best to get the same image into the popular press.[11] As the attention intensified, he connected King to the progressive unions that could give the boycott the financial support it needed. He brought in a flood of cash with a summer rally at Madison Square Garden, headlined by the liberal icon Eleanor Roosevelt. He even managed to get King an appearance before the Democratic National Convention, not as the spokesman for a single city's protest but as the embodiment of a movement ready to sweep the South with the unstoppable force of Gandhi's *satyagraha*.

But King wasn't the head of a southern-wide movement of pacifist intent. He was the leader of an embattled bus boycott that had no hope of victory outside the courts. Through the spring of 1956 white Montgomery's assaults continued, through the indictments, the police harassment, the racist organizing—a Citizens' Council rally at the Montgomery Coliseum drew 10,000 people—and a series of bombings that by some miracle never killed anyone. On June 4 the NAACP got its first win in a two-to-one district court decision that declared the segregation of the city's buses unconstitutional. Montgomery's officials immediately appealed to the Supreme Court. So the boycott dragged on through King's summer of celebrity. In the fall the city made one last push to destroy the boycott before the justices ruled. But by then the movement had come too far to break. On November 13 the Court issued a single-sentence statement upholding the district court's ruling. It took another month for the implementation order to arrive and another little piece of Jim Crow to fall, in Ella Baker's way, 386 days after Mrs. Parks had refused to give up her seat on her evening ride home.

Momentum

BAYARD RUSTIN RETURNED to Montgomery three days after the buses were integrated to talk to King about building the region-wide movement he'd imagined. From that conversation came King's invitation to join a handpicked list of ministers in creating a new organization to spread Montgomery's momentum across the South. Sixty of them came to Daddy King's Atlanta church for what would be the founding meeting of the Southern Christian Leadership Conference (SCLC) on January 10, 1957. That Martin Luther King Jr. would lead the new group was a given, though exactly where he'd take it wasn't clear. He had a grand idea—inspired by Billy Graham—of staging a series of political revival meetings across the South to encourage African Americans to register to vote. Out of the revival tents the inspired would stream into workshops on navigating the byzantine requirements the white South had used to bolster disenfranchisement. Then they'd march to the registrars' offices to bring another piece of Jim Crow down, this one far more important than Montgomery's buses.

It was a stirring thought. But King's celebrity had created enormous demands on his time. He had speeches to give, sermons to deliver, interviews to grant—in 1957 *Time* magazine put him on its cover—articles to write, trips to take, and appearances to make, alongside the demands of running a church and raising a young family. Some of his work was the routine stuff of ministerial life, some of it political. A share of it sounded more like Rustin than King; *Time* loved the American Gandhi image. But the best of it was fused with the vision of redemptive suffering he'd derived from his kitchen revelation, an idea he honed with such care his wife Coretta thought it was becoming an obsession. Still, in a schedule that crushing something had to give. Almost a year after its founding, SCLC still didn't have a plan for putting King's crusade into action, a staff to develop one, or the money to get it up and running. For a while Rustin thought that he might have to take over SCLC's management himself just to keep it from collapsing, but he also knew that his personal background wasn't going to fit well with an organization full of ministers.

So, in January 1958 Rustin suggested to King that he hire as SCLC's executive director the best organizer he could imagine. Ella Baker was willing to take on the job. But when King finally got around to making a hire, his fellow ministers insisted that she be made assistant director, under the supervision of an elderly pastor who didn't have a tenth of her skills. And King had no more time to spare in 1958 than he'd had the year before. In those conditions Baker couldn't turn his registration drive into anything more than a shadow of what it ought to have been. More fundamentally, she knew that she was never going to make SCLC the force that King and Rustin wanted it to be until she found a way to link it up to the community activism that made a movement possible.

The first key step came in Little Rock, Arkansas, with a pivotal variation of the dynamic Baker had created inside the NAACP. When the Court handed down *Brown* in 1954, Little Rock's school board had been among those districts that decided to comply. Its agreeability wasn't too surprising. Arkansas was a Jim Crow state, but it wasn't a particularly rabid one. It had already desegregated its university, and no one saw much reason to make a fight of it at the lower levels of its public schools. By the spring of 1955 the Little Rock schools' superintendent had put together a painfully gradual plan. It would begin by bringing ten African American students into all-white Central High in September 1957, a step so small it barely marked any progress at all. The local NAACP clearly wasn't impressed: in February 1956 it helped a set of Black parents bring a federal court suit against the district, demanding the school's immediate integration. The judge split the difference. The board could follow its plan, he said, but it would do so under the court's mandate, so that it was now legally required to see the plan through to its implementation.

In the meantime the backlash against the *Brown* decision had raged across the state. Up went the Citizens' Councils, the Klan klaverns, the angry editorials, the panicked public meetings, and the intensifying demands that Arkansas' public officials do their duty in defense of the white race and its beloved children. The state's senators and congress-men fell into line, as did Orval Faubus, its feckless governor. Faubus had first been elected in 1954 as a moderate Democrat, more interested in economic reform than race-baiting. But when he ran for reelection in 1956 he swung to the right, pledging to protect the color line that Little Rock's school board planned to inch across.

The run-up to September 1957 was shot through with tension. The Little Rock NAACP took responsibility for identifying the ten kids who were to go to Central High, a selection process they built around the students' academic standing and their ability to withstand the abuse they were sure to suffer. The Little Rock Citizens' Council hammered the school board with demands that the desegregation be delayed. A handful of parents' groups filed restraining orders. Others circulated petitions pleading for the school board to back down. One of them held a very public meeting to discuss the dangers of miscegenation. And on Monday evening, September 2—the last day before schools opened—Governor Faubus went on local television to say that he was ordering the National Guard out to Central High to block those ten African American kids from entering the school.

The kids didn't try to get into Central High until September 4, when nine of them arrived and were turned away under an escort arranged by the local NAACP. Elizabeth Eckford came on her own. The next day every major paper in the country ran the photo of her walking down the street, the mob howling behind her. "Saw the awful pictures," Central's dean of girls wrote that night. "The dignity of the rejected Negro girl, the obscenity of the faces of her tormentors."[12] In that image millions of Americans came face-to-face with the searing moral contrast that the movement wanted them to witness. Not the individual one alone, as powerful as it was, but the systemic one, between a community that could produce a girl of such grace and a racial structure that twisted ordinary people into thugs in defense of the indefensible. That was the force Elizabeth Eckford had released in her terrifying walk along the guardsmen's line, much as Rosa Parks had with her quiet defiance in Montgomery two years before.

This time the force raced up to the nation's highest level. Dwight Eisenhower should have responded with federal power that day, since a state had no right to defy a federal court order. But Ike didn't believe in integrating schools—he'd decided that appointing Earl Warren as chief justice had been one of the biggest mistakes he'd made—and he wanted to avoid a confrontation. For two weeks he tried to talk Faubus into compliance, an approach that danced on the edge of domestic appeasement. Finally, on Friday, September 20, the federal court ordered the governor to stop obstructing Central's desegregation. Eisenhower assumed that Faubus would now use the guardsmen to protect the kids as they went into the school. But three hours after the court hearing, the governor went back on television to say that he'd be withdrawing the guardsmen and replacing them with a contingent of street cops. "I wouldn't think the parents of the Negro children would want their children in school with the situation that prevails now," he told reporters that evening, just in case anyone missed the point.[13]

The mob didn't. On Monday morning there were a thousand whites on the street in front of Central High, held back by a rank of policemen they could have easily overrun. Somehow the kids' handlers slipped them into the school unnoticed. As the word filtered out the crowd grew hysterical. Fearing a frontal assault, school officials pulled the kids out of their classes, rushed them into police cars waiting around back, and sped them out of the neighborhood.

That Eisenhower couldn't abide. The next day he ordered a thousand troops from the 101st Airborne into Little Rock. On Wednesday morning, September 25, the nine kids who'd made it through the previous weeks' upheavals walked up the sweeping stairs of Central High—where Elizabeth Eckford had been turned away three weeks before—safe within a phalanx of soldiers in full combat gear. It was a triumph of federal power over state defiance. But it was also something deeper. Since the 1940s Baker's brand of activism had fed into the courts. This time the Court's decision had created activism back on the ground. That activism, led by nine teenagers clutching their books in the face of hatred, had then created a crisis so profound that the president of the United States had been forced to intervene. There was a power even Baker hadn't imagined, on display for the nation to see.

John Lewis saw it. He was a freshman at Nashville's American Baptist College in the autumn of 1957. "It was that sense of mission, of involvement, of awareness that others were putting themselves on the line for the cause," he wrote later, "that moved me to do my part. I remember praying for those brave children of Little Rock. . . ."[14] He wasn't alone. Over the next few years there were sporadic community protests around the South: a handful of bus boycotts, a scattering of conflicts over school desegregation, a few singular challenges to restaurant segregation. And among young people there was a great deal of quiet organizing. Some of it was inspirational. After their first traumatic year at Central High was over, the Little Rock kids went on the lecture circuit, speaking to NAACP youth groups all over the South. Some of it was formal: down in Nashville, Lewis joined a cadre of committed college students being trained in Gandhian nonviolence by a charismatic Methodist minister named James Lawson, who'd come south because King had told him that was where he ought to be. And some of it was nothing more than conversation, like the long dorm-room talks four freshmen at North Carolina A&T had with each other through the fall of 1959, pushing and probing around the question of a young man's responsibility to confront injustice. When they felt they'd said enough, they walked into the Woolworth's store not far from campus, sat down at the lunch counter, and politely asked to be served four cups of coffee, just as Rustin and his colleagues had done in one of CORE's first acts twenty years before.

That first day, February 1, 1960, they just sat there, waiting for the service they knew was never coming. That evening almost everybody at A&T was talking about what they'd done. The next day, twenty-five men and four women from the college joined them at the lunch counter, and on the day after that sixty-three. The local newspapers and then the national press picked up the story. By the weekend hundreds of Black students were sitting in at lunch counters across downtown Greensboro. White kids were out too, shoving and shouting at the protesters while they sat in silence, as Elizabeth Eckford had showed them how to do. That night Woolworth's tried to erase the tension by shutting down its counter. But that just made the company look complicit. Across the country its sales started to tumble so precipitously that the store had to announce that it would desegregate its counters if other local businesses would do the same. One by one they agreed. Another victory for the cause, this one monumental.

Action fed action. Within a week of the A&T protest, African American students were occupying lunch counters in Durham, Charlotte, and Raleigh, North Carolina. By the end of the month, there were sit-ins in Hampton and Richmond, Virginia; Nashville and Chattanooga, Tennessee; Montgomery, Alabama; Lexington, Kentucky; and Baltimore, Maryland. By the end of April, 50,000 young people had joined a protest that no one had planned and no one was coordinating, the ultimate example of grassroots mobilization by young people willing to risk everything for principle. Back in SCLC's Atlanta headquarters, Ella Baker knew that she'd found exactly what she needed.

A little more than a month after the first sit-in began, she invited the leaders of the local campaigns to attend an Easter weekend retreat at Shaw University, her beloved alma mater. One hundred twenty-six people showed up, most of them students at the historically black colleges (HBCUs) that had been the sit-ins' incubators. As the featured speaker, King called on them to turn their protests into a mass movement premised on the power of redemptive suffering. But it was Nashville's Lawson who gave them their charge in an electrifying moment of Christian witness drawn on the vision that King had given him. "Love is the force by which God binds man to Himself and man to man," he told them. "Such love goes to the extreme. . . . It matches the capacity of evil to inflict suffering with an even more enduring capacity to absorb evil, all the while persisting in love." With that uncompromising love, he told them, the movement wouldn't just redeem the nation's soul. It would create on American soil the Beloved Community.[15]

Years later John Lewis tried to explain what the phrase meant. "According to this concept all human existence . . . has strived toward community, toward community together," he said. "Wherever it is interrupted or delayed by forces that would resist it—by evil or hatred, by greed, by the lust for power, by the need for revenge—believers in the Beloved Community insist that it is the moral responsibility of men and women with soul force, people of goodwill, to respond and to struggle nonviolently against the forces that stand between a society and the harmony it naturally seeks."[16] But definitional precision couldn't capture the emotion of the moment. By the conference's end Baker had guided her invitees through the intricacies of forming their own organization. They called it the Student Nonviolent Coordinating Committee (SNCC), an oddly functional choice for a vanguard of activists dedicated to creating the new world they believed to be within their reach.

The Lost-Found Nation

THE PASSION THAT ran through SNCC's founding session had its parallel in the one strand of African American political thought that the movement couldn't weave together. After Marcus Garvey's conviction and subsequent deportation back to Jamaica, Black nationalism slipped back to the local level, where it had always had its strongest appeal: to places like Detroit's African American ghetto, a neighborhood everyone called Black Bottom, where W. D. Fard came to live in 1930.

About Fard there was a great deal of controversy. It seemed that for much of his life his name had been Wallace Ford, that he was a light-skinned Black man—so light he could have passed for white had he been so inclined—that he'd once made his living running a restaurant in Los Angeles, and that he'd spent time in San Quentin Prison before moving to Chicago, where he became a central figure in a tiny African American religious community called the Moorish Science Temple, whose leaders preached that African Americans were descendants of the Moors and therefore Muslims. The connection was more stylistic than substantive. Members dressed in what they took to be North African clothes. They called their holy book the Qur'an, though the group's central figure had written it himself. And its key message was rooted in the Black separatist tradition more than in Islam. That's where Ford started his career, as a minister in the faith. But there was some sort of schism in the group in 1929, a split so violent that the temple's founding figure was convicted of murder. In the midst of the conflict Ford—or Fard—left Chicago for Detroit.

That's one version of events. The other version says that W. D. Fard appeared miraculously in Black Bottom in 1930. Upon his arrival he began preaching a messianic creed, a vision of history and salvation that combined evolution, genetics, early twentieth-century scientific racism—which he turned on its head—and the Christian story of the Fall. Allah made the first peoples Black, Fard said, and set them to living in the holy city of Mecca. But sixty-six hundred years ago one of their great minds, twisted by hatred, decided to create a devil race that would destroy the peaceful world Blacks had built. Through centuries of genetic manipulation he fashioned new peoples, each one lighter-skinned and therefore morally weaker than the previous: black to brown to red to yellow and finally to white. For two thousand years the white race lived in savagery, until Moses gave them the tools they needed to impose their evil on the world's other races. Prophecy said that they would do so for six thousand years, "down to our time," said Fard's most famous disciple, when "the black original race would give birth to one whose wisdom, knowledge and power would be infinite."[17] So Fard appeared in Black Bottom, come to free the Black race through his new community of faith, the Lost-Found Nation of Islam.

It wasn't enough to believe, though. To achieve the liberation he promised, Fard preached that Black men and women had to embrace the rigid discipline of traditional Islam. Believers weren't to drink, smoke, gamble, or fornicate. They were to dress conservatively, men in suits and ties, women in white robes. They were to work incredibly hard in Black-owned businesses, ideally owned by the Nation itself, saving what they could for the support of their families, giving as much as possible to their community. They were to attend the mosque—Fard set up the first in Detroit in 1931 or 1932—several times a week for prayer and instruction. And they were to keep their distance from the white devils, not dealing with them at all if possible and never, ever allowing themselves to be intimidated or abused, a Black separatist faith in word and deed.

That's what drew in Elijah Muhammad. He was Elijah Poole then, the son of a Baptist minister who made his living as a sharecropper. He'd grown up in Sandersville, Georgia, and came to Detroit in 1923 as part of the first great migration. The move didn't work out as he'd hoped: he apparently struggled to find work and maintain a stable personal life. But he did find something of value in Detroit. He'd become a devout Garveyite, a commitment he maintained even after the UNIA's collapse. He came to Fard's mosque for the first time in 1931 and was immediately entranced. At the end of the service, he said, he went up to Fard to ask him whether he was the redeemer. Fard told him he was, Poole reported, but his time had not yet come: a moment of revelation far more rooted in the New Testament than in Islam. Then again, that was the language of God Poole understood.

That quickly changed. Poole—renamed Elijah Muhammad, in keeping with the Nation's practice of rejecting slave names and adopting others more empowering—became one of Fard's most devoted disciples. Within a year he'd been named the Nation's supreme minister. Two years after that, in 1934, Fard disappeared as mysteriously as he'd come, taken up to Heaven, according to his followers, though there were other theories as well. Again there was something of a power struggle, out of which Muhammad emerged triumphant. But by then the Nation had come to the attention of the Detroit police, who wanted it out of the city. So in 1935 Muhammad moved his operation to South Side Chicago, which became the Nation of Islam's holy center.

For the rest of the 1930s the Nation of Islam remained a tiny organization, with only four mosques—in Chicago, Detroit, Milwaukee, and Washington, DC—and a total membership of maybe a thousand people. That's what the Nation might have remained had it not been for the war. When the Roosevelt administration started the draft, not only did Muhammad refuse to register but he told his followers not to register as well. It was an entirely logical thing to do: why would Black men risk their lives in a white devils' war? But that refusal made him a criminal, charged not simply with draft evasion but also with sedition. He was convicted in September 1942 and sent off to the federal prison in Milan, Michigan, fifty miles west of Detroit.

The Nation foundered without him: by one count its membership fell to about 500 people while he was serving out his sentence. Inside the penitentiary, though, the Nation flourished. Of course Muhammad spread the Nation's message to his fellow African American prisoners. As he did so, he found that the Nation's blend of self-pride, self-discipline, and a well-channeled rage had enormous appeal to the men he found there: almost by definition the most marginal men in America, lower even than the working people Garvey had organized or the poor Fard had recruited. And he found that, in Milan at least, some of them were willing to listen. When he was finally released in 1946, he set out to build his church upon that rock.

So he did. By 1960, as the sit-in movement was sweeping across the South, the Nation had an estimated 60,000 members, almost all of them young, many of them drawn from the urban poor, a share from the Nation's prison ministry. There were now dozens of mosques. And Muhammad had established himself as a man of wealth, power, and imposing religious authority. But it wasn't the number of followers that made Muhammad a public figure. It was the brilliance of his most important disciple, Malcolm X.

Malcolm X was born Malcolm Little in 1925 in Omaha, Nebraska. His mother was from Granada, his father a southern-born American, a Baptist minister and devoted member of Garvey's UNIA. Malcolm grew up in Lansing, Michigan, immersed in talk of racial pride channeled through the UNIA's local branch, where his parents were guiding figures. It was that activism that led to his father's murder in 1931, the family believed, killed by white supremacists for his separatist ideas, though the details of his death remained murky.

His loss threw the family into a vicious downward spiral. His mother ended up in a mental institution, his sisters and brothers scattered to various aunts and uncles. Malcolm himself drifted into drugs and crime, first in Boston, where he had family, then in Harlem as well. He was convicted of robbery in 1946, at the age of twenty-one, and sentenced to seven years in Boston's scabrous Charlestown State Prison, though he served most of his time in a prison colony outside of the city. That is to say he was the perfect candidate for the Nation's missionary work.

Malcolm learned of the faith through letters from his sister, who had become connected to the mosque in Detroit, where she lived. At her urging, Malcolm read some of Muhammad's teachings. He was so taken he began writing to Muhammad directly. Soon they were regular correspondents. And Malcolm, swept up in the Nation's ideas, began reading everything he could get his hands on. To everyone's surprise, he also took to the self-discipline that the Nation preached. The drugs, the women, the attraction of easy money that had defined his life as a young man: all of it Malcolm rejected once he'd discovered the truth.

As soon as he was released in the summer of 1952, Malcolm raced off to Chicago to meet Muhammad. Impressed by the young man's dedication and obvious ability, Muhammad appointed him assistant minister of the Nation's Detroit mosque. From there Malcolm began his meteoric rise through the hierarchy. Over the next few years he directed mosques in Boston and Philadelphia, both with great success driven in large part by his electric personality. Better than anyone else in the Nation, Malcolm—now officially Malcolm X—could command the stage, drawing in listeners with his marvelous mix of passion, humor, and bravado, winning converts wherever he went. In Detroit he'd tripled the mosque's membership, and in Boston and Philadelphia he'd turned deeply divided congregations into functioning, disciplined organizations. He was so successful that in 1954, just two years out of prison, Muhammad gave him one of the most important posts of them all, as minister for Mosque No. 7, in the one place in America where the media was sure to notice him. Muhammad sent him to Harlem.

It was a perfect match. First Malcolm established himself in Harlem's long-standing tradition of street-corner preachers, proclaiming the Nation's gospel for whoever cared to listen. Then, on April 26, 1957, he put on a display that made him a Harlem legend. The precipitating event was the sort of thing that happened in America's center cities all the time. A member of Malcolm's mosque, Johnson X, was walking down the street when he saw a couple of white policemen shoving around a Black suspect. He tried to intervene and for his trouble had his head split open by a nightstick. He should have been rushed to a hospital. But instead the cops handcuffed him and took him off to Harlem's precinct house. In short order several hundred angry people were gathered in front of the station to demand Johnson's release. Fearing that violence was about to break out, an African American newspaperman called Malcolm to help settle the situation. Half an hour later he arrived at the head of his mosque's paramilitary unit, the Fruit of Islam.

They lined up in precise military formation, fifty men strong standing stock-still across the precinct door, their arms crossed in front of them, while Malcolm went inside to insist that Johnson X be taken to the hospital. There was a good deal of discussion, but in the end the police agreed to Malcolm's demands. With their commitment secured, Malcolm walked out and whispered a few words to one of the young men standing guard. Immediately the entire unit pivoted and marched away. Suddenly, Malcolm said later, everyone was talking about the Muslims.

Then Malcolm crossed the color line. In July 1959, two years after Little Rock, CBS's New York affiliate ran a documentary—an exposé, really—on the Nation of Islam. It featured an interview with Elijah Muhammad. But its star was the young, handsome, insistently articulate Malcolm X, a striking figure on the screen, made all the more striking because, from CBS's perspective, he was saying such outrageous things. Is the white man evil? the interviewer asked him. "By nature he is evil," Malcolm replied. Do you teach your children that the white man is evil? the interviewer asked. "You can go to any little Muslim child and ask him where is hell and who is the devil," said Malcolm, "and he wouldn't tell you that hell was down in the ground and that the devil is something invisible and you can't see. He'll tell you that hell is right where he has been catching it and he'll tell you the one who is responsible for having received this hell is the devil." And the devil is the white man? asked the interviewer. "Yes," said Malcolm, without the slightest hesitation.[18]

The show's host framed the point he wanted his viewers to see. "While city officials, state agencies, white liberals, and sober-minded Negroes stand idly by," Mike Wallace said, "a group of Negro dissenters is taking to street-corner stepladders, church pulpits, sports arenas, and ballroom platforms across the United States to preach a gospel of hate that would set off federal investigation if it were preached by southern whites." There was the exposé CBS was looking for, the flip side of the sacrificial suffering that infused the southern struggle, the Black side of racial supremacy, "the hate," as the documentary put it, "that hate produced."[19]

Within the Nation Malcolm's star turn triggered talk of excess ambition, a dangerous thing in the byzantine politics that ran through its mosques. But Muhammad seemed well pleased. So Malcolm made the most of his moment. In came a steady stream of requests from the press to comment on the movement surging across the South, along with a slew of invitations to speak to audiences he never would have reached had it not been for his sudden celebrity. He gave the reporters the stinging analyses they wanted, delivered in finely fashioned sound bites. Anyone can sit down, he said of Greensboro. An old woman can sit down. A coward can sit down. It takes a real man to stand up. And he gave the whites in his audiences the chance to see a strand of Black politics many of them didn't know existed—though it scared them to learn of it—and African Americans to hear the power of that tradition renewed.

Later the writer James Baldwin remembered the first time he met Malcolm. He'd been asked to moderate a radio debate between Malcolm and a young man from the sit-in movement. "I was afraid that Malcolm would eat the boy alive," he wrote. But "Malcolm understood that child and talked to him as though he were talking to a younger brother, and with that same watchful attention. What struck me was that he wasn't at all trying to proselytize that child: he was trying to make him think. He was trying to do for that child what he supposed, for too long a time, that the Honorable Elijah had done for him. . . . 'If you are an American citizen,' Malcolm asked the boy, 'why have you got to fight for your rights as a citizen? To be a citizen means you have the rights of a citizen. If you haven't got the rights of a citizen then you're not a citizen.' 'It's not as simple as that,' the boy said. 'Why not?' asked Malcolm."[20]

New Frontiers

THE SAME QUESTION bled into the 1960 election, albeit in different form. For the Democrats the dilemma was the same as it had been since 1948: whoever the party nominated was going to have to please a liberal wing increasingly supportive of the civil rights movement and a southern wing violently opposed to it. The Republican situation wasn't much easier. The party didn't have a substantial southern faction to appease, but it did have an opportunity to exploit. Eisenhower had twice carried the Upper South—Virginia, Kentucky, and Tennessee—as well as Florida and Texas. If the Republicans could extend their reach in 1960, they could shatter the Democrats' increasingly fragile coalition.

Richard Nixon was going to have a hard time doing that. He'd been the point man for the Eisenhower administration's civil rights agenda, as thin as it was. And he carried with him the burden of Ike's intervention in Little Rock, a show of federal force that still enraged the white South two years after the troops had been withdrawn. His biggest challenge, though, came not from his own record but from Jack Kennedy, who had no intention of letting the Republicans drive any deeper into the South than they already had.

During the campaign JFK played on the themes of tolerance and decency, intended to undercut the idea that a Catholic couldn't be a loyal American. He was even willing on occasion to act on behalf of civil rights, most dramatically by having his brother Bobby secure Martin Luther King's release from a Georgia jail in October 1960. But his campaign's most meaningful move made clear where his strategy lay. In his first decision as the Democratic Party nominee, Kennedy selected as his running mate Texas' Lyndon Johnson, the Senate's immensely powerful majority leader. Campaign insiders would later claim that the choice was a mistake. It wasn't. JFK wanted white southerners to know that they had nothing to fear from his administration. And he wanted to take Texas back from the Republicans, as LBJ was sure to do.

It didn't quite work. Kennedy won Texas, but he still lost four of the five southern states Eisenhower had carried in the previous two elections. And a hunk of the Deep South fell away when half of Alabama's electoral votes went to a segregationist who had no party behind him and Mississippi managed the unusual feat of not voting for anyone at all. So JFK came into the Oval Office in January 1961 with the white South slowly slipping out of the Democrats' control. And the last thing he wanted to do was lose any more of it by letting his administration get tangled up in a movement that had proved its ability to draw a president in.

He got a three-month reprieve. Then, on May 4, thirteen Black and white activists working through CORE—Bayard Rustin's old organization—boarded two Greyhound buses in Washington, DC, to begin a meandering trip through the South to New Orleans. Their goal was to re-create the 1947 CORE protest that had gotten Rustin his month of hard labor. That trip had been designed to test a Supreme Court decision that outlawed the segregation of buses and trains that crossed state lines. In 1960 the Court had done the same for the stations and restrooms that served those buses and trains. CORE's volunteers were now going to test that ruling with a classic act of Gandhian disobedience. When the bus rolled into a southern station, the whites would walk into the Black waiting room, the Blacks into the white room. In 1947 CORE had called its challenge the Journey of Reconciliation. This time they called it a Freedom Ride.

Nothing much happened in the Upper South. When the group

reached Anniston, Alabama, on May 14, though, a white mob attacked one of their two buses, breaking its windows, setting it on fire, and then mercilessly beating the civil rights workers as they tried to escape the flames. The second bus pulled ahead to the next stop in Birmingham. There another mob descended, more vicious than the first. "Toughs grabbed the passengers into alleys and corridors," the CBS news reporter on the scene told his listeners, "pounding them with pipes, with key rings, and with fists. One passenger was knocked down at my feet by twelve of the hoodlums, and his face was beaten and kicked until it was a bloody pulp."[21] By the next morning photos of Jim Peck's shattered face had spread across the nation.

CORE promptly called off the rides. As soon as they heard of that decision, SNCC's most devoted chapter, James Lawson's Nashville group, decided to step in. "You realize it may be suicide," CORE's director told them when they called to tell him that they'd be completing the ride. "We fully realize that," Lawson's disciple Diane Nash replied, "but we can't let them stop us with violence. If we do, the movement is dead."[22] Early the next morning eleven new Freedom Riders headed to Birmingham to pick up the protest CORE had abandoned.

Suddenly JFK was trapped in precisely the same predicament that Eisenhower had faced in Little Rock. He couldn't allow mob violence to block the implementation of a Supreme Court ruling any more than Ike could. But he also didn't want another show of federal force. A round of presidential pressure and some less-than-subtle threats from the attorney general produced a promise from the governor that the state of Alabama would protect the new volunteers as they made the next leg of their journey, from Birmingham to Montgomery.

But when the buses pulled into the Montgomery station there wasn't a policeman in sight. Again the riders were assaulted in an attack of astonishing ferocity: one of them was beaten so badly—his attackers repeatedly hit him in the head with a baseball bat and tried to drive a metal spike into his ear—that he suffered permanent brain damage. This time the mob also assaulted a Justice Department official Bobby had sent along to make sure that peace was maintained. The attorney general was at an FBI baseball game when he got the news. Within a couple of hours he had 400 federal marshals heading to Montgomery to restore the order he'd thought the governor had guaranteed.

But the mobs, having tasted blood, simply shifted their target. Martin Luther King hadn't been a particularly strong supporter of the Freedom Riders. As the crisis escalated, he agreed to come to Montgomery to headline a mass meeting in their support. On Sunday evening, May 21, 1,500 African Americans filled First Baptist—Ralph Abernathy's church—to hear him and to honor the riders scattered among them. Outside, twice as many whites surrounded the church, their mood growing darker as the evening progressed. Shortly after 8:00 p.m. a group of them set a car on fire. Others started stoning the church. Molotov cocktails followed, the opening volley of a full-on assault that was broken only by the marshals' arrival and the repeated rounds of tear gas they fired into the mob. Not until four the following morning did the faithful manage to get out of the church, into a street strewn with the rubble of the mob.

A few hours later the Freedom Riders reboarded the buses, this time with the full protection of the federal government.

They got only as far as Jackson, Mississippi, where state authorities arrested them for trying to integrate the station's waiting rooms. But by then new waves of Freedom Riders were already pouring into the South. That was the last thing the Kennedys wanted to see. Bobby phoned King that afternoon to argue for a break in the campaign, a time for emotions to cool. King wouldn't hear of it. "It's a matter of conscience and morality," he said. "They must use their lives and their bodies to right a wrong. Our conscience tells us that the law is wrong and we must resist."

"But the problem won't be settled in Jackson, Mississippi," Kennedy countered, "but by strong federal action."[23] That wasn't the point. With the Freedom Rides, CORE and SNCC had created an international incident, forced the president to intervene on the movement's side, and shattered yet another segment of the South's racial regime. SNCC's Freedom Riders might have been stopped—they'd spend most of the summer locked away in Mississippi's infamous prison farms—but the movement had never had such momentum.

After the Freedom Rides SNCC shifted its focus, establishing several long-term projects in the most violent sections of the South, among them blood-soaked rural Mississippi. In the summer of 1961, SNCC's young field secretary Robert Moses, who'd come to the movement through Bayard Rustin, established a voter registration campaign in the heart of the Delta. But the campaign quickly morphed into something more than a voting drive: in his quiet, unassuming way, Moses set out to empower the South's most oppressed people. Whites saw the challenge for what it was. The local folks who rallied around Moses were assaulted, arrested, and imprisoned; their homes and churches attacked, their livelihoods threatened. And at least two of them were murdered, one gunned down by his state representative on the main street of Liberty, Mississippi, the other shot in the head for daring to say that the politician ought to be tried for the crime he'd committed. Instead of backing down, SNCC sent Moses a handful of reinforcements. By 1962 there were roughly twenty-five volunteers there, trying to build the Beloved Community bit by perilous bit.

In September 1962, the confrontation shifted to the all-white University of Mississippi. Eighteen months before, James Meredith, a twenty-seven-year-old air force veteran, decided to transfer from the Black college he had been attending to the state university. When Ole Miss rejected him, he went to court to force his admission, arguing that he had been turned down solely on the color of his skin. On September 10, 1962, Supreme Court justice Hugo Black—himself an Alabamian—ruled that Meredith had a right to be admitted. Three days later Mississippi's staunchly segregationist governor, Ross Barnett, went on television to announce that he would resist Black's order, which he claimed was the first step toward racial genocide. And the Kennedys were caught in another constitutional crisis, this one caused by one young veteran's desire to have his rights observed.

For two weeks Bobby tried to work out a deal with the university. Eventually they agreed that Meredith could register—not on the

Oxford campus but at a meeting of the board of trustees in Jackson on September 25. When Meredith arrived, though, accompanied by two Justice Department officials, Barnett personally blocked his way. "I won't agree to let that boy get to Ole Miss," the governor told Bobby in a heated phone call that evening. "I will never agree to that. I would rather spend the rest of my life in a penitentiary than agree to that."[24] That was a thought. On Friday, September 28, a federal court found Governor Barnett in contempt. Under the pressure of prison time, Barnett relented. He'd let Meredith register for classes the following Monday morning.

Meredith arrived on the Ole Miss campus Sunday evening, protected by five hundred federal marshals. They got him safely into a dorm, but they couldn't control the throng of whites that was gathering on the campus grounds. As darkness fell the violence began. First the mob attacked the newsmen who'd come to cover the next day's events. Then they turned on the marshals. At the White House the Kennedys received regular battle reports: the marshals were being hit by bricks and bottles; shots had been fired; a marshal had been hit in the neck; more were down. By midnight the news had become so dire that JFK had to order federal troops onto campus. It took another three hours for the 5,000 soldiers to arrive. By then 160 marshals had been wounded, twenty-eight of them by gunfire. Two people, a reporter and a jukebox repairman, had been killed. The next morning Meredith attended his first class—in American history.

For Kennedy, Ole Miss had been a disaster even greater than the Freedom Rides. As terrible as the violence had been in Birmingham and Montgomery, at least no one had been killed. And in its worst moments the administration had resorted only to the use of federal marshals; now JFK had been forced to use federal troops, with the symbolic weight they carried. But the president's problems extended beyond the immediate fallout. Two years into his term a movement of the marginal—of Baptist ministers, radical pacifists, legal tacticians, militant seamstresses, high school girls in homemade skirts, and young men and women willing to die for the cause—had pushed the question of racial justice into the center of American public life, where the Kennedys did not want it to be.

The pressure mounted through the rest of 1962 and early 1963. The major civil rights organizations called on Kennedy to mark the hundredth anniversary of the Emancipation Proclamation by condemning Jim Crow, a suggestion the president studiously ignored, while the movement's old socialist bloc revived its demand for the sweeping economic reforms that could break the fusion of racial injustice and Black poverty. On Capitol Hill, liberal Democrats and moderate Republicans demanded that JFK introduce vigorous civil rights legislation; when he didn't, the Republicans presented their own bill instead. Outside of Washington many liberals were growing even more frustrated with Kennedy's hesitation. "There is a need for a force to be ahead of the administration," complained Walter Reuther, the formidable president of the United Automobile Workers, one of the nation's most progressive unions, "to be pointing out that more has to be done toward creating pressure in the right direction to counteract pressure that is in the wrong direction." King agreed, quoting Saint Augustine for support. "Those that sit at rest while others take pains are tender turtles," he said, "and buy their quiet with disgrace."[25]

But words weren't enough. It was time to go to Birmingham.

CHAPTER 4

THE DEAD

Thursday, May 2, 1963. D-Day, the activists had taken to calling it, as if it were the beginning of a carefully planned campaign instead of a desperate gamble; as if they were storming the Normandy beaches instead of filling the streets of Birmingham, Alabama, with children.

They waited until around one o'clock to begin. Then they came out of the Sixteenth Street Baptist Church in waves, almost a thousand of them, girls and boys, teenagers and grade-school kids, the youngest eight, seven, six years old, marching in defiance of the authorities' orders. Down the church's grand stone steps they went, past Kelly Ingram Park across the street, toward downtown, into the police lines, where the arrests began. A dozen; two dozen; so many the police had to bring in school buses to carry them all. By evening they'd taken six hundred children into custody. One day down, and Birmingham's jails were already overflowing.

The protests started again on Friday afternoon, a column of sixty kids coming two by two out of the church; a thousand more still inside, waiting their turn. The first group marched a block, to the far edge of the park. There the police stopped them, not to arrest them—there was no point now that the jails were full—but to tell them they had to disperse. When they refused, the commanding officer nodded to the firemen lined up behind him and told them to turn on the hoses.

The first shock of water pushed most of the marchers back. But ten of the sixty held their ground, clasping hands and singing a single-word song—"Freedom"—while the spray soaked through them.[1] In response the firemen increased the water pressure, until the stream from the hoses was so intense it could rip bricks out of mortar. For an instant the kids withstood that too. Then the blast struck one of them—a wisp of a girl—straight on, and flung her off her feet. As she hit the ground the firemen concentrated their hoses on her, spinning her backward, rolling her body along the pavement.

Meanwhile, more children were pouring out of the church, swinging around the other side of the park, where the hoses couldn't reach them. To block their way the police rushed in the dogs: six German shepherds trained to attack on their handlers' command, straining on their leashes as they lunged, snarled, and snapped at the marchers. The sight of them sent the kids reeling, some of them racing into the park, others stumbling back toward the church, still others trapped in the crowd. Down went three teenagers who hadn't moved fast enough, their arms and legs torn open by the mauling dogs. And down went Jim Crow broken on the brutal streets of Birmingham.

Birmingham, 1963

MARTIN LUTHER KING knew the risks of mounting a major campaign in Birmingham. It was impossible not to know. Built as a steel town in the late 1800s, it had long been one of the most fiercely defended bastions of Jim Crow, the dark heart of one of the South's most segregated states. For years the Ku Klux Klan had dominated the city government, its power granted by Birmingham's elite, a collection of hard-nosed businessmen known as the Big Mules. Klan violence was endemic: the town was so violent its Black citizens grimly referred to it as Bombingham.

The terror was made possible by Birmingham's longtime police commissioner, Eugene "Bull" Connor. Put into office by the Big Mules in 1937, Connor took it as his personal mission to maintain segregation with the full force of the law; he once threatened to arrest the first lady of the United States, Eleanor Roosevelt, when she tried to sit on the Black side of a Birmingham conference hall. And he was more than willing to look the other way when white supremacists took the defense of Jim Crow into their own hands, as they had in their bloody assault on the Freedom Riders in 1961. There was a joke African Americans sometimes told. A Black man in Chicago woke up one morning and told his wife that Jesus came to him in a dream and told him to go to Birmingham. "Did Jesus say He'd go with you?" his wife asked. "Well," the husband replied, "He said He'd go as far as Memphis."[2]

The situation was made even worse by state politics. In November 1962 Alabama voters elected forty-three-year-old George Wallace as their new governor. Born and raised in Alabama's hardscrabble Black Belt, Wallace had started his political career as something of a populist, promising to address the obvious needs of the state's poor whites. When he'd first run for governor in 1958, though, his opponent had swept past him by claiming that Wallace was soft on race. It was a mistake Wallace wouldn't repeat. In his 1962 campaign he perfected a slashing assault on the civil rights movement, the liberals who supported it, and the federal government that, however reluctantly, had brought its weight to bear against the white South's obstruction of justice. On inauguration day, January 14, 1963, he made clear that he'd govern precisely as he'd campaigned. "In the name of the greatest people that have ever trod this earth," he proclaimed in his inaugural address, "I draw the line in the dust and toss down the gauntlet before the feet of tyranny . . . and I say segregation now . . . segregation tomorrow . . . segregation forever." Afterward a supporter complained about the speech's tenor. Wallace shrugged him off. "I started off talking about schools and highways and prisons and taxes—and I couldn't make them listen," he said. "Then I began talking about niggers—and they stomped the floor."[3]

Of course King knew the danger. But he went to Birmingham anyway. In part it was a matter of pride. As a public figure he towered over the movement. On the ground it had swept past him in waves of protest he'd inspired but rarely joined. The harder the movement pushed, the more glaring the gap became. Behind his back some of SNCC's most devoted activists had taken to calling him "De Lawd," for what they saw as his tendency to preach about suffering he wasn't willing to endure and his willingness to accept adulation he hadn't earned. He felt the gap too, though not just because it wounded his pride. "This is the only way to be delivered from evil," he told his congregation in early March 1963. "It can only be done when we allow the energy of God to be let loose in our souls."[4] In the end, King went to Birmingham because he'd been called to. The campaign's demands were humble enough: SCLC wanted Birmingham to desegregate the downtown stores, to hire at least some African Americans to work in those stores, and to establish a biracial committee to discuss ending segregation in other areas. Its explicitly Gandhian tactics were far more aggressive. First there would be small-scale sit-ins, to be coordinated with a series of mass meetings aimed at building community support for the campaign. Once that support was secure, the demonstrations would grow and be coupled with a boycott of the offending businesses. Only then would the mass marches—and the mass arrests—begin. If all else failed, SCLC would bring in busloads of supporters from across the South, fill the jails to overflowing, attract mass publicity, and cripple the city government. Out of that paralysis concessions were sure to come.

The campaign started on April 3, 1963. Immediately it floundered. Few of Birmingham's African Americans were willing to run the enormous risks that even the slightest protest would bring: arrest, possible beatings, perhaps death. For a week the campaign managed to mount a series of minor protests, none of them large enough to rouse the Black community, much less to threaten Birmingham's power structure. Another such week and the campaign would collapse. So King tried to create a catalytic event. On Good Friday, April 12, he led a small march, violating a hastily secured court order banning demonstrations. Bull Connor had him arrested.

Instead of winning the campaign support, though, King's jailing brought him a cascade of criticism. Many of the nation's major newspapers—the *Washington Post* and *New York Times* foremost among them—dismissed his actions as ill-conceived: designed, the *Post* suggested, to promote his standing rather than to serve the cause of racial justice. But it was an article in the local paper that stung King most.

A group of white ministers, moderate men, condemned his extremism, which they said incited hatred and violence. Sitting alone in his cell—Connor had put him into solitary confinement—King used the margins of the paper to scribble out his reply. The result was one of the movement's most powerful testaments, the struggle's justification by faith. "Though I was initially disappointed at being categorized an extremist . . . I gradually gained a measure of satisfaction from the label," he wrote. "Was not Jesus an extremist for love: 'Love your enemies, bless them that curse you, do good to them that hate you, and pray for them which despitefully use you, and persecute you.' Was not Amos an extremist for justice: 'Let justice roll down like waters and righteousness like an ever flowing stream.' Was not Paul an extremist for the Christian gospel: 'I bear in my body the marks of the Lord Jesus.' Was not Martin Luther an extremist: 'Here I stand; I cannot do otherwise, so help me God.'"[5]

King spent nine days in jail, long enough for the campaign to galvanize around him. But it didn't. For several days after his release the numbers of people attending the movement's mass meeting were dispiritingly small, too few to mount the next march, scheduled—in defiance of yet another court order—for May 2. And the national press, so critical to the movement's momentum, was losing interest in the protests. That's when one of King's most militant advisers, the electric James Bevel, proposed an extraordinarily dangerous step. Clearly Birmingham's adults were too scared to march, he said. But their children weren't. They had as much stake in the civil rights struggle as their parents did. They didn't have their parents' responsibilities, though—jobs to hold on to, rent to pay, families to support—that made the cost of defiance so high. Ask the children to march, said Bevel. They'd come. And if the police tried to stop them, as they were likely to do, the clash would be so powerful it would capture the nation's attention.

Some of King's advisers, particularly those from Birmingham, vigorously opposed the move. What right did the movement have to put children at risk? What if official violence escalated? What if a child were injured? What if she were killed? Others argued that children old enough to profess their faith were old enough to put it into action. King was torn. He knew that the campaign was failing, that something drastic had to be done. But the risk was so great, the possibility of tragedy so high. In the end he didn't formally endorse the tactic. But he let Bevel send out the word. On Thursday the children would march.

Hope

WITHIN HOURS OF the Friday afternoon assault grainy footage of the carnage was playing on the networks' evening news shows. The next morning photos of the dogs and the hoses were plastered across the front pages of the newspapers that a few weeks before were condemning the campaign: the *New York Times* ran not one but three photos, stacked one on top of another. The international press ran the images too, along with fierce condemnations of the southern racial regime. "To turn high pressure hoses on peaceful demonstrators is another act of calculated barbarity which besmirches Alabama," declared the editors of an Indian newspaper, "if that state had any reputation left to be besmirched at all."[6]

In Birmingham the protests intensified. There was another afternoon of marches on Saturday, May 4, the situation so tense King and Bevel feared the protesters might meet violence with violence. On Sunday the campaign took a day of rest, followed on Monday with the biggest march yet, adults now joining the children, at least a thousand people taking to the streets, eight hundred of them arrested and shipped off to jails that couldn't possibly hold them, their every move recorded by the army of reporters who had descended on the city over the weekend. Finally the Big Mules had had enough. In a series of tense negotiations brokered by Bobby Kennedy's Justice Department, they gave in to almost all of the campaign's original demands. But by then the movement had surged far past the desegregation of Birmingham's stores. For more than sixty years the nation had accommodated Jim Crow. And in a week of moral witness, of the boundless courage that redemptive suffering required, the children of Birmingham had released in America a force that sparkled with hope.

There were critics, of course. "I'll say this," Malcolm X told the press, "if anybody sets a dog on a black man, the black man should kill that dog—whether he is a four-legged dog or a two-legged dog."[7] But the doubters were overwhelmed by the movement's momentum. Its leaders saw it in the wave of protests that rolled across the towns of the South in Birmingham's wake, over a hundred of them by summer's end. They saw it in the money that was pouring into the movement, the donations arriving in such volume that SCLC's mailroom couldn't keep up with them all. They saw it in the outpouring of support from musicians and movie stars—from out of the Hollywood Hills came a $5,000 check from Marlon Brando—politicians and powerful public figures. They saw it in the sudden commitment of church groups inspired and more than a little shamed by the release of the letter King had written during his time in the Birmingham jail, which became an instant sensation. And they saw it in the massive crowds that came out to declare their solidarity with the struggle: 15,000 people at a rally in Los Angeles; 20,000 in San Francisco; an astonishing 125,000 at a June march through downtown Detroit, King at the front, striding as fast as he could to avoid being trampled by the throng behind him.

John Kennedy saw the momentum too. For two years he'd done what he could to avoid the issue, reacting only when activists forced his hand, and then going only as far as the situation required. But Birmingham had swept away the middle ground. He could offer no federal response to the movement's sudden power, which would in effect ally him to the white South. Or he could, at long last, commit his administration to racial justice.

He chose the latter. In late May, just two weeks after the Birmingham settlement, he told his advisers to begin drafting a civil rights bill stronger than anything a president had proposed in the course of the twentieth century. As they worked on the provisions, the movement again met the force of massive resistance. In Jackson, Mississippi, white thugs attacked five protesters who tried to desegregate a downtown lunch counter; in Greensboro, North Carolina—site of the original sit-in—the police arrested 278 student marchers; in Tallahassee, Florida, they tear-gassed demonstrators; in Danville, Virginia, they attacked with their nightsticks, injuring scores of marchers. And in Alabama, Governor Wallace triggered yet another constitutional crisis when he promised personally to block two African Americans from enrolling at the University of Alabama in accordance with a federal court order, a dangerous replaying of the previous fall's confrontation at Ole Miss.

At the last moment Wallace backed down. But his public belligerence forced JFK into the open. A few hours after the African American students were registered, on the evening of June 11, Kennedy went on national television to announce that his administration would send a civil rights bill to Congress, a decision he wrapped in language more reminiscent of King than of the Kennedys. "We are confronted primarily with a moral issue," he said. "It is as old as the scriptures and is as clear as the American Constitution. One hundred years of delay have passed since President Lincoln freed the slaves, yet their heirs, their grandsons, are not fully free. They are not yet free from the bonds of injustice. They are not yet free from social and economic oppression. And this nation, for all its hopes and its boasts, will not be free until all its citizens are free."[8]

The bill JFK sent up to Capitol Hill wasn't quite as courageous as his words suggested. It did include a number of far-reaching provisions. It banned discrimination in virtually all public accommodations, thus wiping out the segregation of drinking fountains, bus terminals, hotels, and restaurants. It threatened to cut off federal money to school districts that defied the Supreme Court's ruling in *Brown*. And it gave the attorney general the power to bring suit to protect the civil rights of African Americans if such help were requested. For all its positive provisions, though, it also neglected several measures that civil rights activists had long been advocating. Civil rights leaders wanted the federal government to create a Fair Employment Practices Commission to combat discrimination in hiring; Kennedy left it out. They wanted the attorney general to have the power to bring suit even if an African American didn't request it; Kennedy left it out. Most importantly, the bill made no mention whatsoever of protecting African Americans' right to vote.

Still, Kennedy's civil rights bill had dared to do something that no other Democrat—no other twentieth-century president—had been willing to do: to insist that Jim Crow be dismantled everywhere but at the voting booth. Politically the bill carried huge risks. Kennedy would be running for reelection in a year's time. No matter how carefully he moved, the bill would inevitably cost him countless white votes in the South, something no Democrat could afford. And there was every chance that southern congressmen would block its passage, as they had done almost every other time civil rights legislation had come up for consideration. Kennedy was gambling everything, in other words, for a bill he might never get to sign into law.

The civil rights forces wanted more. Once Kennedy's bill was delivered to the House of Representatives, the movement's leaders and its allies began an intense legislative campaign, not simply to push it through Congress but to strengthen it. Everyone understood that adding a voting provision would be a step too far: not only would southern Democrats oppose it, so too would Republicans, since it would bring millions of Black voters into the Democratic column. The other missing provisions, though, were within reach. Together lobbyists from the NAACP and the nation's most progressive labor unions, aided by suddenly mobilized church groups, convinced the liberals on the House Judiciary Committee—the bill's first stop—to add both the fair employment provision and the additional powers they thought the attorney general needed. But these changes simply made the bill's passage all the harder. By summer's end the administration's proposal, though stronger, was also still stuck in the Judiciary Committee, nowhere near a vote in the House or the Senate. So the movement upped its pressure.

The idea of a mass march on Washington had come from A. Philip Randolph and Bayard Rustin. When they'd started their discussions, in late 1962, they'd envisioned it as a two-day event: the first devoted to nonviolent protest, the second to a huge rally aimed at addressing the "economic subordination of the American Negro," as Rustin put it, a perfect phrasing of the socialist politics that Randolph had been championing for almost half a century. Gradually they brought into the planning some of the major civil rights organizations—SNCC and CORE both signed on in March 1963—but others kept their distance, among them the NAACP and SCLC, rejections that made Rustin wonder whether he ought to give up on the enterprise altogether. But then came Birmingham and the civil rights bill. Suddenly King and the NAACP saw the wisdom of some sort of mass action in the nation's capital, both as a demonstration of the movement's dedication and as a prod to Congress. By early July Rustin had brought both the SCLC and the NAACP into the march, along with another important civil rights organization, the National Urban League. The United Automobile Workers, which was deeply involved in the movement's lobbying, and several major religious figures—one each from the Protestant, Catholic, and Jewish traditions—also committed to the march. To keep his carefully constructed coalition together, Rustin scaled back the march from two days to one, set aside the promise of civil disobedience, and focused instead on a mass rally "for jobs and freedom," to be held at the end of August on the steps of the Lincoln Memorial.[9]

The Kennedys hated the idea. "We want success in Congress," JFK pointedly told Randolph, King, and their colleagues, "not just a big show at the Capitol. . . . The wrong kind of demonstration at the wrong time will give those fellows [in the House] a chance to say they have to prove their courage by voting against us."[10] But Rustin wasn't going to allow any mistakes. This was going to be the movement's golden moment.

So it was. August 28 turned out to be a perfect summer day in Washington, sunny and warm without a hint of rain. Before dawn the busloads of marchers began to arrive, thousands of people from across the country, the vast majority of them African American. By noon the crowd around the Lincoln Memorial had reached a quarter of a million, twice as many as Rustin had hoped would attend. Malcolm X was among them—the NAACP's Roger Wilkins saw him sitting under a tree, looking out over the throng—though Elijah Muhammad had explicitly forbidden anyone from the Nation to participate. Through the afternoon the program ran, Randolph serving as master of ceremonies, shuttling Rustin's lineup of speakers to the podium: the UAW's longtime president Walter Reuther, NAACP's president Roy Wilkins, SNCC's John Lewis, whose incendiary speech Rustin had insisted on editing, because it wouldn't do to have a young civil rights activist tell the nation that "the revolution is at hand."[11]

Even in their more tempered form, the day's speeches reflected the dynamics that Birmingham had created. The speakers demanded again and again that Kennedy's bill be strengthened and then signed into law. But legal rights were not enough: the nation needed to tackle the problem of economic inequality too. Poverty trapped millions of Americans as surely as Jim Crow did, and "we will not solve education or housing or public accommodations," Reuther proclaimed, "as long as millions of Americans, Negroes, are treated as second class economic citizens," a line of argument that led the movement exactly where Randolph and Rustin had always wanted it to go.[12]

Rustin left King to last, mostly because no other speaker wanted to follow him. He started slowly, reading the text he'd prepared, his delivery halting, almost labored. Then the pace began to change. He started with the sacrifice the movement demanded. "I am not unmindful," he said, "that some of you have come here out of great trials and tribulations. Some of you have come from narrow jail cells. Some of you have come from areas where your quest for freedom left you battered by the storms of persecution and staggered by the winds of police brutality. You have been the veterans of creative suffering." Now the nation ought to see what their suffering could do.

Much of what followed wasn't original. He'd used many of the same words, and the entire central imagery, at the Detroit march two months before. And he took his powerful closing almost word for word from a Chicago pastor's address to the 1952 Republican convention. But in the moment none of that mattered. He laid his foundation with a recitation of the self-evident truth that defined the American creed. From there he took the crowd through a new South, where the sons of slaves and the sons of slave owners sat together as equals, and little Black boys and

Black girls joined hands with little white boys and white girls as brothers and sisters. Then he moved them to Isaiah, the greatest of the Old Testament's prophets, and one creed fused with another, as it always had for King.

"I have a dream," he proclaimed, "that one day every valley shall be exalted, every hill and mountain shall be made low, the rough places made plain, and the crooked places will be made straight, and the glory of the Lord shall be revealed, and all flesh shall see it together. This is our hope. This is the faith with which I return to the South. With this faith we will be able to hew out of the mountain of despair a stone of hope.... With this faith we will be able to work together, to pray together, to struggle together, to stand up for freedom together, knowing that one day we will be free."[13]

In the decades to come King's speech would become a set piece, a string of overused phrases, some of them twisted and turned to purposes antithetical to their meaning. But in that moment, in that sacred spot, King was doing something extraordinary. He was drawing from the brutality of America's racial order a radical vision of a nation transformed, its sins redeemed by the suffering of its most courageous citizens, who dared to imagine that hatred could give way to love. The Beloved Community—glittering in the summer of 1963.

Dark Currents

THERE WERE OTHER currents swirling through the summer of 1963 too. Some white southerners were pleased with the movement's success, to be sure, while many more simply wanted the conflicts to go away. But it was the movement's violent opponents, defenders of a mortally wounded social order, who set the tone.

The brutality continued through the summer of 1963. Shortly after midnight on June 12, just hours after JFK announced his civil rights bill on television, a Klan sniper shot the Mississippi NAACP's Medgar Evers as he got out of his car in the driveway of his Jackson home. His wife and children watched him die. In Winona, Mississippi, deep in the Delta, SNCC workers and their local allies, among them a longtime sharecropper named Fannie Lou Hamer, were brutally beaten while in the custody of the local sheriff. In Americus, Georgia, authorities charged three other SNCC activists with inciting insurrection, a crime that carried the death penalty. In Birmingham itself, there were threats and intimidations, as the Klan tried to stem the tide that the children had unleashed.

Southern politicians fanned the resistance. In Alabama Wallace slashed away at the pending civil rights bill; if Congress dared to pass it, he said during a July appearance on Capitol Hill, "You should make preparations to withdraw all our troops from Berlin, Vietnam, and the rest of the world, because . . . they will be needed to police America." Other extremists added to the tension. For half a decade the John Birch Society had been building a mass audience for its brand of militant anti-Communism, thanks to the generous support of archconservative businessmen like Dallas' Bunker Hunt and Missouri's Fred Koch. By 1963 half a million Americans were receiving the group's literature, with its repeated attacks on the movement as nothing more than a Soviet front. "The trouble in our southern states has been fomented almost entirely by the Communists for this purpose," explained the society's Robert Welch, "to stir up such bitterness between whites and blacks in the South that small flames of civil disorder would inevitably result. They could then fan . . . these little flames into one great conflagration of civil war."[14]

The backlash even reached into the federal government. For years FBI director J. Edgar Hoover had been convinced that Martin Luther King was a tool of international Communism. He was so obsessed that he had maneuvered the Kennedys into authorizing wiretaps on King's phone and the placement of hidden listening devices in his bedroom. With the information he gathered Hoover began to compile a massive file that he planned to use to discredit King and destroy the movement he'd come to symbolize.

There was another dark current running through Washington that summer as well. For two years the Kennedy administration had grappled with the tangle left by Dwight Eisenhower in South Vietnam: an increasingly brutal guerrilla war pitting the unstable government of Ngo Dinh Diem, the president handpicked by the United States, against a Communist insurgency in the countryside, run by Ho Chi Minh's government in North Vietnam. Diem's dictatorship seemed too weak to combat the Communists, even with the mounting support of the American military. Bit by bit JFK had increased US involvement. By 1963 there were 16,000 American troops in South Vietnam, sixteen times the number that had been on the ground when Kennedy took office. Although the troops were technically advisers to the South Vietnamese military, in truth they were starting to fight alongside Diem's soldiers: in the course of 1963, 400 American troops were killed in combat. Still, the Diem regime struggled to hold on.

Then the situation began to spiral out of control. On May 8, 1963, six days after the start of the children's march in Birmingham, a group of Buddhist priests and their followers gathered in the old imperial city of Hue to protest Diem's decision to ban the display of flags on Buddha's birthday. Trying to break up the rally, South Vietnamese soldiers opened fire on the crowd. That triggered more protests, led by Buddhist monks opposing Diem, his high-handed ways, his connection to the Americans, and his lack of commitment to democracy. Rallies in Hue and Saigon— cities that were supposed to be Diem's strongholds—drew huge crowds.

On June 11—the day Kennedy announced his civil rights bill, the day George Wallace stood in the schoolhouse door, the night Medgar Evers was assassinated—the crisis reached a crescendo. That day an elderly Buddhist monk sat in a busy intersection in Saigon, drenched himself in gasoline, and set himself ablaze. That horrifying public sacrifice pushed the protests to an extraordinary level. College students, working people, even segments of the army rushed to join the Buddhists' campaign: Diem, it seemed, was on the brink of being toppled not by the Viet Cong but by his own people. If Diem were to fall, Kennedy and his advisers knew, the Communists would be ready to step into the void.

For JFK it was a dangerously precarious situation. Containment policy required that the United States prevent a Communist victory in

South Vietnam. Now Diem, by his arrogance and stupidity, was undermining all those efforts. But the Kennedys thought that the situation could be finessed. They began searching for other options.

The moment came at summer's end. On August 21, six days before the March on Washington, Diem struck back at his Buddhist opponents, staging a series of military raids against pagodas and arresting 1,400 monks. As the crisis in Vietnam spiraled downward, Kennedy took a weekend's vacation at the family compound on Cape Cod. As a result, it was his advisers who received secret word from some of the generals in Diem's army on August 23. They'd decided that Diem had no ability to lead the South Vietnamese anymore. Any government in South Vietnam had to have American backing and approval. So they were asking whether the Kennedy administration would approve a coup.

Without asking Kennedy's permission, the advisers crafted a meticulously worded reply. They wanted Diem to reform his ways and make peace with the Buddhists. But if a coup should occur, the United States would provide "direct support to any interim" government. They checked with the president quickly and sent off their answer. By the time Kennedy returned to the White House on Monday, August 26, he'd started to have second thoughts. His advisers had pushed him into a corner, he thought, just as the CIA had done with the Bay of Pigs two years before. "This shit has got to stop," he barked at them during a particularly tense meeting. But he didn't send word to the generals that he'd changed his mind. Over the next few days—as the civil rights forces gathered at the Lincoln Memorial, as King preached of right and justice—JFK simply waited for news of the coup to begin.[15]

Two currents running through the summer: one of boundless hope, the other of blood. The summer belonged to hope. In the fall the balance tipped.

Six Deaths

SEPTEMBER 15 WAS an ordinary Sunday in Birmingham. Sixteenth Street Baptist Church was holding its first Youth Day, an effort to expand its children's fellowship. The youngsters began arriving early, filing into the basement, where Sunday school was held. A few of the kids in the children's choir slipped into the women's lounge so they could spend a little while primping and priming for their featured performance at the eleven o'clock service. Four little girls, making themselves look pretty.

The bomb went off at 10:22 a.m. For a moment the great church shook, the force of the blast surging through the sanctuary, out to the street, into the morning sky. Then came the soot and the smoke, thick and white; chunks of plaster and shards of stained glass. The sanctuary stood. But a section of the basement, the epicenter of the explosion, had been blown away—the northeast portion, the corner with the women's lounge.

Desperately the church deacons dug through the rubble, scrambling through the piles of brick and stone until they found them: Addie Mae Collins, Cynthia Wesley, Carole Robertson, each of them just fourteen, and eleven-year-old Denise McNair. Four little girls, their clothes ripped off by the blast, their faces maimed by debris, their bodies so badly burned they could barely be recognized. "The slaughter of the innocents," the Vatican called it.[16] Four little girls on a Sunday morning, primping and priming for church. Pools of blood starting to spread.

After the flurry of messages in August, the South Vietnamese generals seemed to back down from their threat to overthrow Diem. For the next two months rumors of a coup circulated through Saigon, but nothing happened. Inside the Oval Office Kennedy's advisers vigorously debated the best route to follow. A few of them pressed the president to cut his losses, pull out the US troops, and find a way to settle South Vietnam's future peacefully. Others advised a deeper commitment: more troops, more money. JFK tried to maintain a middle path, applying pressure on Diem to improve his regime, keeping aid flowing as best he could, as he had since taking office.

Then, in late October, the dissident Vietnamese generals resurfaced, again asking for US support for a coup. They received the same reply as before: the president would not encourage the generals, but he would not oppose them, either. That was enough. On the afternoon of November 1, the officers made their move, seizing key buildings in Saigon and declaring themselves the new heads of state. All that afternoon Diem tried to regain control of his government, to save himself. At one point he called the American ambassador from his embattled presidential palace, desperate to know whether the United States still supported him. No, the ambassador told him. Nor would it ensure him safe passage out of the country.

He escaped the presidential palace through a series of underground tunnels and fled to a nearby Catholic church, where he went to confession and received communion. There the generals' forces found him. He was arrested, pushed into a personnel carrier with his hands tied behind his back, and shot in the head. His body was buried in an unmarked grave in a cemetery next door to the ambassador's residence.

Kennedy was informed of Diem's murder during a morning meeting on November 2, 1963. The president immediately "leapt to his feet and fled the meeting with a look of shock and dismay on his face," according to one of the participants.[17] If he hadn't intended the generals to murder Diem, he must have understood that his administration's willingness to go along with the coup carried that potential. There was one of the great tragedies of the Cold War: in the course of that struggle, the United States committed itself so singly, so purposefully to preventing Communist expansion that it repeatedly violated the basic principles of democracy. Nowhere was that contradiction clearer than in Vietnam. First the United States blocked the will of the Vietnamese people, who surely would have elected Ho Chi Minh as their president in the mid-1950s. Then the Americans created in South Vietnam a country that many of its people didn't support. Now that its policy was failing, the Kennedy administration acquiesced in the toppling of the government it had created and the murder of the man the United States had handpicked to run it.

Three weeks later John Kennedy went to Dallas. If it weren't for the political crises caused by the civil rights revolution, it is likely that Kennedy wouldn't have visited Texas that fall. But he had to carry Texas to win reelection in 1964, and his support for the movement's demands had put the state in jeopardy. So he planned the trip simply to rally support among Texas Democrats in preparation for the presidential campaign. Some of his advisers urged him not to go. Emotions were running too high in Dallas, they told him: just a few weeks before a rabid crowd of right-wing extremists had driven the US ambassador to the United Nations, Adlai Stevenson, off the stage when he'd tried to speak in the city. The atmosphere was so fevered, a Texas Democratic national committeeman wrote Robert Kennedy on November 4, "I would feel better if the President's itinerary did not include Dallas. Please give this your earnest consideration."[18]

But JFK refused to listen. It was a sign of just how important the trip was that Kennedy turned it into a state visit. His wife Jacqueline accompanied him, something she rarely did. So did Vice President Lyndon Johnson and his wife Lady Bird. They arrived in Texas on November 21, spent the night in Houston, then arrived in Dallas the next morning. They were met at the airport by the Texas governor and his wife. The whole entourage climbed into a string of convertibles for a noontime motorcade through the streets of downtown, a chance for the crowds to come out, for the cheers to begin, for the president to show that he could hold the South.

Along Main Street the motorcade went, the route lined with crowds four or five people deep. At Houston Street the cars made a short jog to the left, then left again onto Elm Street, almost through downtown, five minutes from the president's destination at the Dallas Trade Mart. Then there was a single sharp report—a firecracker, some people thought—and another and another. Kennedy had been sitting up straight in his seat, waving to the crowds on his left, his posture made rigid by the brace he was wearing to ease his chronic back pain. Immediately he turned to the right, in the direction of the sound, and his hands went up to his neck. Jackie, who was sitting next to him, reached out to see what was wrong. That's when the second shot hit, the fatal shot, to the back of the president's head.

News of Kennedy's assassination reached the public shortly after two o'clock Eastern time, half an hour after the gunfire in Dallas. For the next four days the entire nation shared in the trauma of the moment: the horrific news of his murder; the arrest of his alleged assassin; his assassin's murder just two days later, his shooting shown live on television; the elaborate rituals of a state funeral; the flag-draped coffin lying in the Capitol rotunda, the long line of mourners—a quarter of a million people came to pay their respects—the solemn procession from the White House to the Catholic cathedral, the Kennedy family trailing behind the caisson, the president's widow holding the hands of their young children.

In the years that followed, there were all sorts of theories about who killed Kennedy. Was there a single gunman or more than one? Was there a conspiracy? If so, who was involved? The answers are not conclusive, and perhaps never will be. But it seems clear that Kennedy wasn't killed by rabid racists or right-wing conspirators. He was murdered by a delusional twenty-year-old former marine, Lee Harvey Oswald, who was connected—weakly to be sure—to left-wing supporters of the Cuban government. In the late 1950s and early 1960s, Oswald had flirted with Communism, defecting to the USSR for a short time and marrying a young Russian woman. The Soviets kept tabs on him, eventually deciding that he was mentally unstable. In June 1962 the Oswalds returned to the United States. After that, he joined several tiny organizations opposing US policy in Cuba. But he was at best a small-time radical, the sort of man who stood on street corners handing out newspapers that nobody read. Then he heard Kennedy was coming to Dallas. He bought a high-powered rifle and took it with him to the job he held in a building along the president's motorcade route. From his perch at a sixth-floor window of the Texas School Book Depository, he shot and killed the president.

Addie Mae Collins, Cynthia Wesley, Carole Robertson, Denise McNair, Ngo Dinh Diem, John Fitzgerald Kennedy: six lives, six deaths. In the spring and summer of 1963, the southern civil rights movement proved that the powerless could lay the powerful low, that the country could be moved toward justice through the force of moral witness, that redemptive suffering might yet redeem the soul of America. Then came the autumn's horrors: an act of racial terrorism, a state-sanctioned murder, a political assassination. Together those events brought to the surface the dangerous currents that ran through the United States in the early 1960s: the sheer brutality of white supremacy, the amorality of American Cold War foreign policy, and the extreme political passions that policy unleashed. A season of hope and a season of blood.

CHAPTER 5

BENDING

Lyndon Johnson was riding in the second car behind the president's when the shots were fired. At first he couldn't make sense of the sound. Then the Secret Service agent who was sitting across from him shouted, "Get down! Get down!" He grabbed the vice president by the shoulder, flung him to the car floor, threw himself on top of him, and pressed his elbows into his back to pin him down. Johnson could feel the limousine accelerate, could hear its tires squealing beneath him as it swerved onto the freeway ramp, could catch snatches of the communications crackling over the Secret Service's radio, someone with the president screaming, "He's hit! Hurry, he's hit!" But Johnson couldn't move until the motorcade reached Parkland Memorial Hospital, the agent pulled him to his feet, and rushed him inside.

He was led down a series of corridors into a hastily arranged safe room cut off from the rest of the hospital by a wall of guards. For almost an hour he stood in the little space, barely more than a cubicle, the only updates coming from whatever the Secret Service managed to overhear. Finally, at 1:20 p.m., John Kennedy's aide and confidant Ken O'Donnell came over from the emergency room, where he'd been holding vigil. "He's gone," he said. That was all: no details, no assurances, no words of support, not even an acknowledgment that Lyndon Johnson had just become the president of the United States.[1]

"I found it hard to believe that this nightmare had actually happened," LBJ wrote later. "A few hours earlier I had been having breakfast with John Kennedy—alive, young, strong and vigorous. I could not

The Fourth of July 1961 on the 6100 block of West Eddy Street, Chicago, Illinois. Ed Cahill and Clarence Miller are kneeling at the center. Kathy Cahill kneels on the lawn, to the left of Ed. Terry Cahill stands on the top porch step, on the far left. Stella Cahill is in the back row, standing between Ed and Clarence. (MPI/GETTY IMAGES)

Dwight Eisenhower and John Kennedy at Kennedy's inauguration, January 20, 1961. Chief Justice Earl Warren sits directly behind them. (AP Photo)

John Kennedy meets in the Oval Office with Curtis LeMay, fourth from the left, and three Air Force pilots who participated in the aerial surveillance of Cuban missile sites, October 30, 1962. (AP Photo)

Elizabeth Eckford walks in front of Little Rock High School, Little Rock, Arkansas, on what was supposed to be her first day of school, September 4, 1957. (BETTMANN/GETTY IMAGES)

A young protester is battered by water from fire hoses, Birmingham, Alabama, May 3, 1963.
(Charles Moore/Getty Images)

The front line of the March on Washington for Jobs and Freedom, August 28, 1963. Jackie Robinson is at the center of the line. To the right of Robinson is his wife, Rachel, and Rosa Parks. (Steve Schapiro/Getty Images)

Freedom Summer volunteers singing "We Shall Overcome" in Oxford, Ohio, before boarding the buses that will take them to Mississippi, 1964. (Ted Polumbaum/Newseum Collection)

The Reverend Dr. Martin Luther King Jr., Chicago, Illinois, September 15, 1966. (AP Photo)

Malcolm X, New York City, September 7, 1963. (Adger Cowans/Getty Images)

Stokely Carmichael, 1966. (Flip Schulke/Corbis/ Getty Images)

Teenagers run from the police during racial disturbances in the Bedford-Stuyvesant neighborhood of New York City, July 21, 1964. The disturbances began in Harlem the night before.
(BETTMANN/GETTY IMAGES)

The culminating march of the Selma voting rights campaign, March 1965. Rev. Ralph Abernathy's children are in the lead. Rev. Abernathy and his wife, Juanita Jones Abernathy, are behind their children, as are Martin Luther King Jr. and his wife, Coretta Scott King.
(PHOTO IN THE PUBLIC DOMAIN, COURTESY OF ABERNATHY FAMILY PHOTOS)

Whites protesting civil rights marchers in the Gage Park neighborhood, Chicago, Illinois, August 15, 1966. (Underwood Archives/Getty Images)

believe he was dead. I was bewildered and distraught."[2] But he also understood that he had to take charge. And that's precisely what he did in the days that followed, grabbing hold of the national agenda and putting himself at the front of the social movements that were surging across the country. It was an extraordinary performance. But as hard as he tried, as deep as his commitment ran, Lyndon Johnson couldn't control the course of American public life.

Lyndon

HE KNEW THE Kennedys didn't think much of him. The president had been unfailingly polite, of course. But he'd also given Johnson almost nothing to do; for almost three years he'd been the administration's marginal man, a phantom haunting the glittering halls of Camelot. Bobby Kennedy didn't even try to be courteous. "Rufus Cornpone," Bobby called him behind his back, a slap at Johnson's small-town southern roots, his lack of sophistication, his oversized personality, and his desperation to please.[3] LBJ had his talents. On the critical point, though, Bobby was absolutely sure. Lyndon Johnson was no Jack Kennedy.

They were certainly different men. JFK had grown up in the rarified world of the rich and powerful, LBJ in an isolated region of central Texas, the son of a local politician. Kennedy had gone from Harvard to the ambassador's thirty-six-room mansion on London's elegant Kensington Road, overlooking Hyde Park. Johnson had attended Southwest Texas State Teachers College, then taken a job teaching poor Latino children at a segregated school in tiny Cotulla, Texas, down near the Rio Grande. There was another difference as well. JFK was wonderfully adept at charming a crowd. But LBJ knew how to wield power.

It was a skill he'd been honing for thirty years. He'd come to Washington in 1931, driven by an ambition so intense—and so open—people found it startling. For four years he worked as an aide to a Texas congressman, a position he used to make as many connections as possible, none more important than to Texas' powerful congressman Sam Rayburn. In 1935 Rayburn got him appointed as the state administrator for the National Youth Administration, a New Deal program designed to help poor young people like the kids he'd taught in Cotulla. Johnson loved the work. But running an agency wasn't going to take him in the direction he wanted to go. So in 1937 he ran for and won a seat in Congress, representing Austin and its outlying districts.

From the start he was a loyal New Dealer, dedicated to supporting the whole range of programs Franklin Roosevelt believed would promote prosperity. He also continued to cultivate powerful colleagues; he grew so close to Rayburn that the older man came to think of LBJ as the son he never had, no small matter given that, three years after Johnson's election, Rayburn became Speaker of the House. LBJ combined his sterling connections with a mastery of congressional procedures. He studied every rule, every maneuver, every member's strengths and weaknesses, until he became one of the House's most adept legislators.

It wasn't enough. As effective as he was, Johnson wanted a bigger stage than the House provided. He made his first—unsuccessful—bid for one of Texas' two Senate seats in 1941. He tried again seven years later. The pivotal election was the primary, since whoever won the Democratic Party's nomination was sure to win the general election. It was a bitterly fought campaign, mean-spirited and manipulative. But LBJ took it—by all of 87 votes, a margin that earned him the name of "Landslide Lyndon," the senator elected by the will of the people and a fair share of fraud.[4]

After such a tainted victory Johnson might have thought about lying low for a while. But that wasn't LBJ's way. Again he worked his way into the graces of an older man, this time Georgia's formidable senator Richard Russell. Again he mastered both his colleagues' tendencies and the institution's rules, which were even more arcane than the House's. So thoroughly did he prove himself that his fellow Democrats waited just four years to elect him their minority leader. When the party won control of the Senate in 1955 he became majority leader, one of the two most powerful positions in Congress.

By all accounts he was extraordinarily effective. He knew just how to flatter the senator who needed flattering and how to intimidate the senator who could be intimidated. "The Johnson treatment," people called it, equal parts debate, seduction, and intimidation. He'd carefully present arguments to colleagues who were deciding which way to vote on an issue, wooing them, gladhanding them, flattering them, making clear their importance to the nation. A hulk of a man—he stood six feet four—he liked to lean into his targets, looming over them, standing too close for comfort, talking and talking until he wore them down. Only then would Johnson walk away, taking their votes with him.

Once he'd established himself as majority leader, there was only one other office worth having. Though he liked to deny it, everyone in Washington knew that LBJ wanted to be president. But he had an enormous liability. Since the Civil War no southerner except Woodrow Wilson had been elected president, and he'd run not from his native Virginia but from his adopted state of New Jersey. The Senate's fissures made the problem worse. In the late 1940s Richard Russell had brokered a deal between the southern Democrats and the Republicans: southern support for Republican economic policies in exchange for Republican votes against any legislation that threatened segregation. Northern liberals were furious. But they didn't have the votes to break the conservative bloc Russell had created.

Unlike many southern senators, Johnson wasn't a fierce defender of Jim Crow. But he was beholden to Russell. And he did represent a segregated state. So in his first few years as majority leader, he used his enormous skills to keep civil rights legislation off the Senate's agenda. As the civil rights movement began to sweep across the South, though, the pressure for change became too great to ignore. So in 1957 he tried a different tactic. He pushed through the Senate a voting rights bill so weak it would have no effect whatsoever on the South's racial order, and then proudly proclaimed himself the first majority leader since Reconstruction to put civil rights legislation into law. The liberals weren't fooled. LBJ "was an enemy of the people," said one of the nation's most dedicated progressives.[5] And anyone the liberals considered an enemy was going to have a hard time winning the Democratic presidential nomination.

But it did make him a fine choice for the vice presidency. Kennedy knew he was too moderate, too Catholic, and too northern to run well in the South. Picking Johnson as his running mate would offset his weaknesses. The liberals would be livid—in fact, they threatened to block LBJ's nomination—but that problem could be handled. The harder step, he assumed, would be getting Johnson to agree. Why would he want to give up one of the federal government's most powerful positions for its most meaningless? But when Kennedy called in the midst of the 1960 Democratic National Convention to ask him to be his running mate, LBJ accepted.

He did his share to help Kennedy win key southern states and thus the presidency in November 1960. After that he faded into the miasma that is the vice presidency, lost in an endless round of ceremonial functions and pointless trips abroad. Even when he was included in top-level discussions—JFK made sure he served on the ExComm during the Cuban Missile Crisis—no one listened to him. By the winter of 1963 his stature had shrunk so dramatically that the editors of the *Reporter* wondered, "What Ever Happened to Lyndon Johnson?"[6]

Then came Dallas.

It wasn't simply the horror of the moment that made the situation so delicate. It was the timing. It had been only six months since the Children's Crusade; five months since JFK had sent to Congress a sweeping civil rights bill; three months since the March on Washington; and two months since the Birmingham bombing. Now the fate of Kennedy's bill lay in the hands of this son of the South, this master manipulator who'd undercut the movement again and again. "I knew if I didn't get out in front of this issue [the liberals] would get me," Johnson said later. "They'd throw up my background against me, they'd use it to prove that I was incapable of bringing unity to the land I loved so much . . . I couldn't let that happen."[7] Politics compounded the pressure. Kennedy would have been the Democrats' nominee in 1964. If Johnson wanted to run in his place—to make himself president not by tragedy but by popular vote—he had less than a year to do with the activists of the party's liberal wing what he'd done with Rayburn and Russell: not just to earn their trust but to make them love him.

All the Way with LBJ

HE STARTED WITH his first major address, in a dramatic appearance before Congress two days after Kennedy's funeral, the evening before Thanksgiving 1963. Compared to JFK, LBJ was a plodding speaker, his delivery uninspiring, his inflection off. But his message was clear. "No memorial oration or eulogy could more eloquently honor President Kennedy's memory than the earliest possible passage of the Civil Rights Bill for which he fought so long," Johnson said. "We have talked long enough in this country about equal rights. We have talked for a hundred years or more. It is time now to write the next chapter, and to write it into the books of law. . . . John Kennedy's death commands what his life conveyed—that America must move forward. The time has come for Americans of all races and creeds and political beliefs to understand and to respect one another. So let us put an end to the teaching and the preaching of hate and evil and violence. Let us turn away from the fanatics of the far left and the far right, from the apostles of bitterness and bigotry, from those defiant of law, and those who pour venom into our Nation's bloodstream. I profoundly hope that the tragedy and the torment of these terrible days will bind us together in new fellowship, making us one people in our hour of sorrow. So let us here highly resolve that John Fitzgerald Kennedy did not live—or die—in vain."[8]

Having embraced Kennedy's agenda, Johnson used his next appearance before Congress—his January 8, 1964, State of the Union address—to go well beyond it. Again he called for the swift passage of the pending civil rights bill. But some of the movement's most powerful voices had made it clear that civil rights alone weren't enough, that the struggle for racial justice had to be coupled with a struggle for economic justice. That had been the message that the movement's socialist wing had been promoting for years, the message Bayard Rustin had wanted the

March on Washington to deliver. Suddenly Lyndon Johnson was saying it, not as a demand but as a promise. "Unfortunately, many Americans live on the outskirts of hope," he told Congress, "some because of their poverty, and some because of their color, and all too many because of both. Our task is to help replace their despair with opportunity. This administration, here and now, declares unconditional war on poverty in America."

The plan's scope was stunning. In 1964 about 20 percent of Americans lived in poverty. Most were white, but a disproportionate number were people of color, not just African Americans but Latinos and Native Americans as well. They lived in areas closed to the prosperity that had come to define postwar America: in central cities, in rural backwaters, on reservations. Now Johnson was announcing that these people were to be brought from the margins into the mainstream, their way cleared by a host of programs he hoped to put into place. There'd be extensive federal aid to public schools in impoverished areas; government loans for poor kids who wanted to go to college and job training for those who didn't; expanded welfare programs for struggling families; a higher minimum wage so the worst-paid workers could make ends meet; initiatives to rebuild blighted areas not only in cities but in the countryside as well; and medical care for the poor and the aged. Out of those efforts would emerge "a nation free from want," said Johnson, committed "to peace and justice, and freedom and abundance, for our time and for all time to come."[9]

In making such a spectacular set of promises, Johnson was drawing on the memory of his New Deal days, when he saw the good that government could do in the hardscrabble heart of Texas. He was also playing politics, preparing for the November election by giving the party's liberals an agenda they were sure to rally around. But there was more to it than that. In Birmingham the civil rights movement had thrust into the center of public life the question of equality, perhaps the most volatile question the nation can face, since it cuts to the core of the American creed. In the process the movement unleashed a power so great John Kennedy had no choice but to respond. Now LBJ faced that power too. But he wasn't following JFK's example, moving only when forced to do so, picking his way forward with the caution of a man who didn't want to move at all. He was sweeping out in front of the activists, handing them a program as far-reaching as almost anything they were demanding, trying to set a path for them to follow. As unlikely as it seemed, Lyndon Johnson had decided to make the movement his.

He was good to his word. By the middle of March 1964, the administration had fashioned its first legislation for the war on poverty: the Economic Opportunity Act, which would create a new government agency to oversee all the programs that were to follow, with initial funding set at $962 million. The act also included the remarkable requirement that the poor themselves participate in the development and administration of future programs, their contributions to be channeled through locally based Community Action Agencies.

Meanwhile Johnson waged a relentless campaign to get the civil rights bill through Congress. It took a massive push to force the bill out of the House Rules Committee, where it had been trapped since the autumn. Once freed, it passed the full House by a two-to-one margin. The Senate was another matter. A parliamentary maneuver allowed the bill to bypass the Judiciary Committee, chaired by Mississippi senator James Eastland, who surely would have killed it. So it reached the Senate floor on March 20, 1964, barely a month after the House vote. Again the southerners tried to block it, this time by taking hold of the debate and refusing to let it go. Johnson countered with uncharacteristic patience: as far as he was concerned, he said, the South's senators could filibuster as long as they wanted. So they did. Through April and May the southerners controlled the floor, passing the right to speak among themselves, refusing to let the Senate conduct any other business until the majority agreed to withdraw the bill from consideration.

While they talked, the White House furiously lobbied Republican senators to join with liberal Democrats in voting to break the filibuster, a process called cloture. The civil rights movement and its labor allies did their part, bringing hundreds of church groups and community organizations that supported the civil rights bill to Capitol Hill, quickly teaching them the proper way to pressure a congressman, and then setting them on wavering senators. LBJ did his part too. Day after day he applied the Johnson treatment, pleading, cajoling, flattering, threatening, bribing, bullying, charming, or shaming any Republican who had the temerity to pick up the phone when the president called. Only when he was sure he had the required sixty-seven votes did he have the bill's manager, Minnesota's Hubert Humphrey, call for cloture. The vote came on the filibuster's fifty-seventh day, June 10, 1964. In the end 82 percent of Republicans supported the motion to end the debate, more than enough to give LBJ the margin he needed. Nine days later the Senate passed the complete bill. On the second of July—two days before Independence Day—Johnson signed it into law.

In that moment most of Jim Crow came tumbling down, its claim to legality finally shattered, its blatant discrimination and ritualized humiliations finally outlawed. Of course the civil rights movement had made it possible; without Birmingham's children there would have been no bill at all. But Johnson had turned the bill's promise into reality. He'd done it by managing one of the most difficult political maneuvers imaginable. For almost thirty years Republicans and southern Democrats had worked together to block reform, their alliance so enduring it had come to define Washington's sense of the possible. With two months of constant pressure LBJ had split it apart, isolated the southerners, and passed a law that largely destroyed a system they had devoted their careers to defending. It was a towering achievement, a triumph of politics to be sure, but also of courage and vision: Lyndon Johnson's vision—improbable as it was—of a nation bending toward justice.

Stand Up for America

IN JOHNSON'S TRIUMPH conservative activists saw their opportunity too. During their 1960 crusade on behalf of Barry Goldwater they'd seen a way to remake the electoral map by linking together the South and the West in a conservative coalition. But they couldn't get Goldwater the Republican nomination. So they decided to try again in 1964.

This time they'd start at the bottom, building blocs of supporters in the clubs and caucuses that made up the party's infrastructure. The moderates would do their best to stop them. But if all went according to plan, in 1964 the Republican Party would swing to the right, with Goldwater leading the way.

By early 1963 the insurgency was gaining momentum. Conservatives had taken control of the Young Republicans—the party's college arm— thanks to an influx of young free marketeers. Christian evangelicals were flocking into Goldwater Clubs, particularly in the western states, their newfound activism driven by a potent mix of anti-Communism and a deepening fear of moral decay. The John Birch Society's apocalyptic literature was drawing its share of converts too, nowhere more than in Southern California's sprawling suburbs. Business groups had started to donate the cash the campaign would need. Even Goldwater— who had repeatedly said he didn't want to be president—was sounding interested. Then the civil rights movement surged across the country: this "so-called . . . Negro rebellion," as one Republican operative put it, with "its strident militant actions seemingly undeterred by the antagonisms which these actions create."[10] And suddenly the insurgency's leaders saw a chance not simply to take the nomination but to win the general election.

The key lay in Goldwater's opposition to Kennedy's civil rights bill. It wasn't that Goldwater opposed racial equality. What he opposed was the federal government interfering in state affairs; if Alabama or Mississippi wanted to segregate its citizens, he believed, Washington had no right to stop them. By taking that stand Goldwater dramatically increased his chances of carrying not only the Upper South, as Republicans had done for three straight elections, but the Deep South as well—maybe even Lyndon Johnson's Texas. "As of this writing," warned a moderate Republican in late June 1963, shortly after JFK had introduced the civil rights bill, "Senator Goldwater . . . has apparently chosen a course of . . . reiterating the conviction that local problems must be solved locally. This course might get him elected."[11]

But carrying the South and a portion of the West wouldn't be enough; to win a majority of the electoral vote Goldwater had to take some northern states as well. There his opposition to the civil rights bill seemed a far less potent political weapon—until the spring of 1964, when George Wallace came marching across the Mason-Dixon Line.

It started with a phone call on a windswept February night in Madison, Wisconsin. That evening Wallace had given a speech at the University of Wisconsin, the latest stop in a round of appearances he was making on famously liberal campuses. Students made up most of the crowd. But tucked in among them were two longtime conservative activists, Lloyd and Dolores Herbstreith, who had driven all the way over from Oshkosh just to see Wallace in action. They were so enthralled they decided to call the governor with a proposal. The aide who answered the phone wasn't impressed. "This is some damn fool wanting George to run for president in Wisconsin," he told the colleague sitting nearby. "You talk to him."[12]

The Herbstreiths weren't damn fools, though. They'd been working for conservative causes for more than a decade, first as disciples of Joe McCarthy, then as fierce opponents of the federal income tax. They understood Wisconsin's electoral system inside and out, and they knew that with just a little bit of work they could put Wallace on the ballot for the upcoming Democratic Party primary. At first glance it seemed pointless. Primaries were nothing more than popularity contests, after all, designed to prove to party leaders that a candidate was electable; the nomination was going to be decided at the party's convention, which LBJ was sure to control. To make matters worse, Wisconsin was widely seen as a progressive state, without the tradition of the race-baiting politics that were Wallace's forte. But the Herbstreiths were convinced that Wallace could cut deeply enough into Johnson's vote to embarrass the president, if not to block his nomination. And when they sat down with the governor's aides the morning after their phone call, they convinced them too.

Wallace announced his candidacy on March 6, just three weeks after the civil rights bill had cleared the House of Representatives. No one paid much attention. Then he started barnstorming across Wisconsin, talking not about segregation but about the threat of protesters taking over the streets, the importance of maintaining law and order, and the right of states to decide how to handle their problems without the federal government interfering. Most of all he talked of the pending civil rights bill. He told the businessmen who packed the small-town luncheons the Herbstreiths had arranged that once the bill was passed the government would tell them who they had to hire. He told suburbanites that they wouldn't be able to sell their homes to whomever they pleased. And when he marched into Milwaukee's ethnic south side, throngs of workingmen turned out to hear how the bill would strip away the seniority rights their unions had won them and the property rights that kept their neighborhoods on the safe side of the color line. "A vote for this little governor will let the people in Washington know that we want them to leave our homes, schools, jobs, businesses, and farms alone," he told the seven hundred people pressed into the south side's Serb Hall.[13] They gave him a five-minute standing ovation.

Once they realized what was happening, Wisconsin's liberals tried to break his momentum by slashing away at his record in Alabama, calling him "a carpetbagger, a bigot, a racist" and "a threat to the moral quality of our nation."[14] But it was too late. On primary day, April 7, he won 264,000 votes, a third of the total cast. From there he swept on to the May 5 Indiana primary, where he took 30 percent of the vote. Then it was off to Maryland for the final primary he'd decided to contest. There he took a majority of the white vote and 43 percent of the total. "If it hadn't been for the nigger bloc," reporters overheard him say the following day, "we'd have won it all."[15]

But Wallace hadn't entered the race to win. He'd run to shake up the Democratic Party, to undercut the president's embrace of civil rights, and to make himself the national figure he wanted to be. His strut through the primaries had done all of that. It had done something else too. In Kenosha and Gary and blue-collar Baltimore Wallace had forged a political language that turned racist appeals into paeans to freedom and slashing attacks on federal power. And it sold just as well as segregation had sold in the white South, because—as Wallace had made painfully clear—Milwaukee wasn't as far from Montgomery as people liked to think.

For the Republican insurgents that was a very encouraging turn. Through the spring Goldwater held to his principles, voting against the cloture motion that shut down the southern filibuster and against the civil rights bill itself, one of only six Republican senators to do so. The insurgents' campaign, meanwhile, swept through the party, piling up delegates as it went, so that by the time the Republicans met in convention—two weeks after LBJ signed the Civil Rights Act— Goldwater had essentially locked in the nomination. The very thought of it terrified those closest to the civil rights movement. "The November outcome . . . may rest entirely with those millions of white Americans who are becoming increasingly apprehensive about the impact of civil rights legislation in their lives," wrote one of Martin Luther King's aides as the convention approached. "If they vote on that basis, all bets are off." That was exactly what the insurgents were counting on. "This isn't South Africa," one of them said. "The white man outnumbers the Negro 9 to 1 in this country."[16]

Freedom Summer

NOT IN THE Mississippi Delta, they didn't. Nor on Chicago's South Side or up in Harlem. In those places the demographics of race were decidedly different than they were in the nation at large. So were the politics that ran through them in the summer of 1964, as the movement that Lyndon Johnson hoped to lead surged in directions he'd never expected—and didn't want—to see.

It had been three years since SNCC's Bob Moses had come to the Delta to mount a voter registration campaign. Three years of painstaking work, three years of living under the crushing weight of violence, and in that time the campaign had managed to register only five percent of the Delta's eligible African American voters. Clearly Moses's quiet, courageous organizing wasn't going to transform the dark heart of Jim Crow. So at the end of 1963 he proposed a dramatic change in tactics.

His goal was to bring to Mississippi the sort of national attention the Children's Crusade had brought to Birmingham. Instead of putting kids in the streets Moses would bring white college students to the Delta: several hundred of them, recruited from the country's most prestigious schools and set to work for the summer of 1964 registering African Americans. A few years earlier the idea would have seemed preposterous. Without Black students there wouldn't have been a SNCC. But white colleges and universities were generally conservative places. Public schools were dependent on state funding that the mere whiff of controversy could threaten; private schools as often as not were swaddled in layers of propriety and tradition, and on campuses everywhere the vast majority of students spent more time worrying about their majors or their football teams than they did the struggle for racial justice.

One tiny group of white students didn't fit that profile, though. Later they'd come to be called "red diaper babies" in honor of their radical parents, many of whom had been Communists or socialists in the 1930s and 1940s, before McCarthyism had made those allegiances hard to sustain. And they arrived on campuses in the late 1950s and early 1960s determined to build a new Left to replace the one their parents had lost.

That was easier said than done. There were sporadic protests in the early days, the most dramatic pitting University of California, Berkeley students against the reactionary House Un-American Activities Committee in the spring of 1960. For the most part, though, college radicals spent the first years of the 1960s not in the streets but in long, fervent discussions of what was to be done. Nowhere was the conversation more thoughtful than at the University of Michigan, where a cadre of activist undergrads calling themselves Students for a Democratic Society (SDS) developed a sweeping critique of postwar America. Its central ideas they took from their parents' politics and the books they'd read on campus. But they gave those ideas a generational spin. When they were kids they believed in the American promise of freedom, equality, and democracy, they said. Now that they'd reached adulthood they realized that power rested not with the people but with the military-industrial complex that the Cold War had created. Across the nation its influence ran, from the Pentagon through the White House and up to Capitol Hill, where everyone agreed that the United States had to pay any price and bear any burden to keep Communism contained; out to the corporations that filled their coffers with defense dollars and the universities co-opted by federal research funds; into the slums and hollows that had been neglected because it was more important to pursue the Red Menace than to care for the poor. That was not the nation they'd been taught to believe in, SDS insisted. It was an authoritarian system ruled by a power elite. And it was their duty, the sons and daughters of the postwar era, to shatter its grip.

SDS balanced its dark analysis of the current system with a shining vision of the future. Once decision making had been wrenched out of the hands of politicians, CEOs, and military men, they said, it could be returned to the people. The result would be a genuine American democracy—a "participatory democracy," SDS's gifted polemicist, twenty-two-year-old Tom Hayden, called it, "rooted in love, reflectiveness, reason and creativity."[17] That was the sort of language a segment of the student population wanted to hear: by 1963 SDS had 2,000 members on thirty-two campuses, up from a handful of members on one campus three years before. But it was only language, a beautifully crafted rhetoric of radical change, far removed from the change itself. And for the most dedicated college activists that wasn't enough.

Hayden first encountered SNCC when he went south in early 1961 on a reporting trip for the University of Michigan's student newspaper. He was immediately enthralled. Here was a community of activists living the principles he was only proclaiming, a cadre of believers trying to topple an unjust social order through reflectiveness, creativity, reason, and love—most of all love. There were already a few whites working with SNCC, among them a young Texan, Casey Cason, who mesmerized Hayden with her electrifying call for white radicals to turn their slogans into reality and their decisions into actions. "It seems to me," she'd said on the day they met, "that is what life is all about."[18] By year's end they were married.

In 1962 and 1963 other aspiring white radicals headed South as well—Mary King from little Ohio Wesleyan; Paul Potter from Oberlin College, where the abolitionist spirit still burned—drawn as Hayden had been to SNCC's fusing of idealism and incomparable courage. It was a trickle of people really, the largest influx arriving in November 1963 when an activist professor brought sixty Yale men to Mississippi for a week of voter registration work. But it was enough to make Bob Moses believe SNCC could recruit hundreds of white students for the summer of 1964.

For the volunteers—in the end there were a thousand—Freedom Summer was an opportunity to share in the struggle. For the movement it was a provocation, since nothing was more likely to outrage the defenders of Mississippi's racial regime than the sight of young whites and Blacks laboring side by side in the summer sun. That was exactly what Moses wanted. "Only when metal has been brought to white heat, can it be shaped and molded," he told his SNCC colleagues. "This is what we intend to do to the South and the country, bring them to white heat and then remold them."[19]

Moses had another provocation in mind as well. In August 1964 the Democratic Party would be holding its national convention in Atlantic City, New Jersey. Mississippi's Democrats would send a segregationist delegation, of course. But Moses planned to send another delegation, made up of local people—the vast majority of them Black, though there'd also be a handful of progressive whites—who'd been chosen in elections SNCC would run in the summer of 1964. They'd call themselves the Mississippi Freedom Democratic Party (MFDP). And they'd demand that the convention seat them rather than the segregationists as the legitimate representatives of the state, selected in a fair and open election. Again Moses knew exactly what he was doing. The convention was one of the most high-profile events of the election year, with gavel-to-gavel television coverage. And the Mississippi campaign was going to crash it.

It didn't take long for things to go horribly wrong. From the start of Freedom Summer there were tensions. The newcomers—products of

Stanford and Yale, UC Berkeley and NYU—often assumed that they knew more than the African American activists who had been struggling in the Delta for years. Sometimes they blundered along, more hindrance than help. Far worse was the violence. Moses had hoped that the students' race and social standing would protect them. But the first volunteers had been in Mississippi less than a week when disaster struck. On the evening of June 21, news of a Black church burning in a tiny Delta town reached SNCC headquarters in Meridian, Mississippi. One of the recent arrivals, twenty-year-old Queens College student Andrew Goodman, drove off to investigate in the company of two more seasoned activists: James Chaney, an African American from the Delta, and Michael Schwerner, a white New Yorker who'd been in Mississippi since the start of the year. They didn't return.

The disappearance of the three young men had an electric effect. As soon as it reached the national news, LBJ ordered the FBI to launch a full investigation, something that had never happened during Moses's first three years working in Mississippi. The president dispatched military helicopters and armed forces to help in the search. He even sent the former head of the CIA to direct operations. Moses was too familiar with the Delta's brutality to hold out any hope. "The kids are dead," he told the next group of volunteers waiting to go to the Delta. But that was the cost of freedom, he insisted, because "no privileged group in history has ever given up anything without some kind of blood sacrifice."[20]

Three weeks later Harlem exploded.

Ever since Birmingham the pace of protest in the urban North had accelerated, as it had across the South. Some of the rhetorical energy came from Black radicals, Malcolm X most of all. In December 1963 Elijah Muhammad had stripped Malcolm of his right to speak for the Nation of Islam, the first move in what turned out to be an intensely bitter break fueled by jealousy, apostasy, and accusations of sexual impropriety. Malcolm was devastated by Muhammad's turn. But being purged from the faith that had saved him also gave him the opportunity to free his politics from the Nation's strictures. Where he was going wasn't completely clear. At times he talked about Black nationalism as a revolutionary force that "overturns and destroys everything in its way," a vision inspired by Algeria's long war against French colonial rule. Other times he talked about mobilizing African Americans into a separate political party as an alternative to revolutionary violence. "It'll be Molotov cocktails this month, hand grenades next month, something else next month," he told a CORE rally in April 1964. "It'll be ballots or it'll be bullets." If Malcolm wasn't quite sure where he wanted to move, though, there was no doubting his ability to take his audiences with him.[21]

On substance, the movement's integrationists took the lead. In Chicago activists tied to the teachers' union called on the city's kids to stage a one-day boycott to protest the segregation of the public schools: a quarter of a million youngsters participated. In Philadelphia protesters began to picket building sites to demand an end to the discrimination that kept African Americans out of the construction trades. In California civil rights advocates pushed through a state law prohibiting discrimination in the sale of housing, in hopes of shattering the barriers that locked African Americans into segregated neighborhoods. And in city after city there were calls to end the police brutality that had long plagued the nation's racial ghettos.

That's how the Harlem riot began, with an act of official violence. On July 16 a white police officer shot and killed a fifteen-year-old African American boy who'd done nothing more than get into a tussle with a white man. As news of the killing spread through New York's Black neighborhoods tensions mounted. But not until July 18—a stifling Saturday, with temperatures in the 90s—did they reach the boiling point. That evening hundreds of African Americans gathered in front of the Harlem police station to demand that the officer be arrested. When a contingent of policemen tried to create a cordon around the precinct, they were hit by a barrage of bottles and garbage-can lids. Out of the station poured more patrolmen, enough to push the crowd into the surrounding streets. There the protest turned into a rampage. Along Seventh and Lenox Avenues they surged, young people mostly, attacking cars, shattering shop windows, taking whatever goods they could grab, and fighting running battles with the cops who tried to stop them. Not until the early morning did the police manage to regain some semblance of control.

The next evening they lost it again. And for the four evenings that followed, as the rioting spread from Harlem to Brooklyn's Black neighborhood, Bedford-Stuyvesant. The police put on a massive show of force, with almost 1,000 officers on the streets of Harlem and Bed-Stuy and thousands more in reserve. But short of unleashing that force—and facing the bloody consequences—there was little they could do but wait for the rioters' rage to dissipate. Finally, on July 23, it rained. The heat wave broke. And the cops found themselves out on the streets alone. But by then at least a hundred people had been injured, 450 arrested. Across the country there was nervous talk of the violence spreading to other cities. "This weekend's rioting in Harlem is a hideous portent," wrote the *Washington Post*'s editorial board. "What one must understand . . . is the bitterness, the frustration, the sense of apartness that lies behind it."[22]

That same week, Bob Moses told his Mississippi volunteers to devote all their attention to building the Mississippi Freedom Democratic Party. Through the first half of the summer the campaign had limped along under the weight of white terror; as of mid-July only 20,000 people had registered for the SNCC-run elections, a tenth of the total Moses wanted to see. The last-minute push brought the numbers up for the precinct meetings the campaign held toward the end of the month—at Moses's request, Martin Luther King flew in to offer his endorsement— higher still for the county conventions that followed. These were the final steps before the August 6 state convention, at which the MFDP would pick the sixty-eight delegates it would send to Atlantic City.

On August 4 the FBI found Chaney, Schwerner, and Goodman. They had been murdered the night they disappeared, shot execution-style, Chaney three times, the final bullet fired into his brain. Then they'd been buried in a half-dug dam outside Philadelphia, Mississippi, in rural Neshoba County, plowed into the clay by a bulldozer. So deep were the makeshift graves that it took the agents most of the day to uncover their decomposing bodies.

Andrew Goodman's father responded to the news by quoting Lincoln—"it is for us the living to dedicate ourselves that these dead shall not have died in vain," he said—Mickey Schwerner's widow by saying she felt only pity for the men who killed her husband. Down in the Delta, though, the confirmation of James Chaney's murder triggered a rage the movement had long tried to sublimate. It cut through the MFDP's convention, where SCLC's Ella Baker delivered a slashing keynote address. "Until the killing of a Black mother's son becomes as important as the killing of a white mother's son," she told the 2,000 delegates crammed into the steaming hall, "we who believe in freedom can never rest." It ran through the slate the delegates elected to send to the convention, which was as militant as Moses could make it. And it pulsed through Chaney's memorial service, held the day after the convention closed. The preachers were polite enough. But CORE's Dave Dennis, who'd worked alongside Moses to shape Freedom Summer, was not. "I'm sick and tired of going to the funerals of Black men who have been murdered by white men," he told the mourners from the pulpit of Chaney's church in Meridian. "I've got vengeance in my heart tonight, and I ask you to feel angry with me. If you go back home and take what these white men in Mississippi are doing to us, if you take it and don't do something about it, then God damn your souls."[23]

Lyndon Johnson didn't understand. He knew all about the MFDP's convention challenge, had even asked the FBI to maintain surveillance of the campaign as it developed. And he wasn't pleased. In his drive for the civil rights bill he'd battered southern Democrats, defying them, isolating them, and eventually breaking their power. Now this clutch of activists was demanding that Mississippi's Democrats be expelled from the convention as well, to be replaced by the very people they had long dominated, just as the Republicans were trying to pull the Deep South away from the party. This wasn't a moral issue. It was simple, practical politics. The MFDP had to be turned away.

For the Freedom Democrats, though, their challenge was very much a moral issue. The delegation arrived in Atlantic City on August 21, three days before the convention opened, trailing behind them the burned-out hulk of the car James Chaney had been driving when his murderers had forced him off the road. Immediately they seized the media spotlight, most forcefully when the MFDP's vice-chair, Fannie Lou Hamer, told the credentials committee and a national television audience of the violence she'd endured since she joined the movement. How her landlord had driven her family off the land they'd cropped for eighteen years; how night riders had opened fire on her house; how, on her way back from a political workshop just a few months earlier, she'd been arrested, dragged off to jail, and brutally beaten. "All of this is on account we want to register, to become first-class citizens," she said, "and if the Freedom Democratic Party is not seated now, I question America, is this America, the land of the free and the home of the brave where . . . our lives be threatened daily because we want to live as decent human beings, in America?"[24]

LBJ responded with the skills he'd perfected up on Capitol Hill. First he sent word to the convention that he wanted to compromise: the regular Mississippi delegates would stay in place, while the MFDP would get two at-large seats, one going to a Black member of the party—but not Hamer—the other to a white member. To sweeten the deal, Johnson promised that at the next convention, in 1968, every state delegation would have to be integrated. Then he used every bit of pressure he could to push the offer through the convention. He threatened and cajoled the credentials committee to sign off on it. He sent UAW president Walter Reuther to strong-arm the MFDP's lawyer, who also happened to be on the union's payroll. And he brought the full force of the civil rights movement to bear on Moses. Martin Luther King pleaded with Moses to stand down, as did Bayard Rustin. Moses wasn't so inclined. "We're not here to bring politics to our morality," he told King, "but to bring morality to our politics." But he insisted that the decision wasn't his. When he turned the question over to the delegates, they had no hesitation whatsoever. "We have been treated like beasts in Mississippi," one of them declared. "They shot us down like animals. . . . Politics must corrupt if it don't care none about people down there." Hamer put the delegates' position even more bluntly. "We didn't come all this way," she said, "for no two seats." On the convention's last day, August 27, the MFDP walked away empty-handed.[25]

That evening the convention feted LBJ with a mammoth celebration on the boardwalk, in honor of his fifty-sixth birthday. There were kids in costume doing ethnic dances and thirty-one fife and drum corps marching in parade, a flotilla of boats beyond the breakers, a 350-pound birthday cake, and a grand finale of fireworks that ended with a 600-square-foot portrait of the president lighting up the night. He'd been to every convention since 1928, LBJ told the throng, "but this is the best of them all."[26] No doubt it was: a glorious end to a long, hot summer when the movement he thought he could lead slipped out of his control.

The Second Sex

BUT THE SUMMER didn't end. Not for Mary King, at least. A minister's daughter raised to believe in the equality of man, she'd joined the movement straight out of college in the spring of 1962, a white northerner come south to serve the cause. She started by working for Ella Baker and SCLC, before moving over to SNCC's staff as assistant press secretary in 1963. In her first year on the job she'd put in more than her share of sixteen-hour days trying to get SNCC's story the national attention it deserved. She had been forced to flee Danville, Virginia, under threat of indictment, and spent five days in an Atlanta jail. So she went to Mississippi in 1964 not as one of Moses's fresh-faced recruits but as an experienced hand, someone who understood the risks of organizing and the necessity of institutional support. Hunkered down in Jackson, she spent the summer documenting the violence the activists endured. On the night Andrew Goodman went missing, it fell to her to tell his parents. But when the MFDP came home from Atlantic City and the volunteers headed back to school, it wasn't the previous months' bloodshed that played on her mind. It was the dynamic she'd seen running through the movement, a question not of race but of gender.

Later she'd attribute her concerns to her reading of the great French feminist Simone de Beauvoir. But surely she was also influenced by the gender issues that were already rumbling through public life. Much of the discussion revolved around women's place in the workforce. Since the 1940s the percentage of women working outside the home had been steadily rising. But the change had done nothing to break down the blatant discrimination that blocked women from a wide range of jobs—from corporate offices down to the factory floor—and that often paid them less than men for the work they did do. Suddenly those practices had come under assault. Female union activists opened one line of attack in 1961, when they prodded John Kennedy to appoint a commission on the status of women. The commission's final report, issued in 1963, offered a raft of proposals meant to correct the inequities the activists had long been trying to battle on the shop floors and in their union halls, foremost among them equal pay for equal work.

That year a former union staffer turned magazine journalist, Betty Friedan, opened another front with her best-selling book, *The Feminine Mystique*. Written in the grand muckraking tradition, it offered a stinging exposé of what Friedan called "the problem with no name." Then she named it. Because they didn't work outside the home, she argued, middle-class women had become utterly dependent on their husbands—so dependent they had become infantilized, just as some social scientists were then saying the Holocaust had infantilized many of its victims. Friedan even dared to make the comparison explicit. The family wasn't the secure, stable institution Americans thought it to be, she insisted. It was "a comfortable concentration camp."[27]

The more important line of attack, though, came from the most unlikely of sources: an eighty-one-year-old segregationist from rural Virginia. On February 8, 1964, Congressman Howard W. Smith proposed adding a single word, "sex," to Title VII of the civil rights bill LBJ was then pushing through the House of Representatives. Title VII had been added to Kennedy's original bill by civil rights groups who wanted to prevent employers from discriminating against employees on the basis of "race, color, religion, and nation origin."[28] Now Smith was suggesting that it also ban discrimination against women.

Why he wanted the addition isn't clear. Some of his colleagues thought he was trying to undercut the bill by making it too extensive in its protections. Others knew that he had long supported women's rights, as long as they were set within the confines of Jim Crow. A number of his fellow congressmen thought it was a joke. But the small coterie of women who held House seats pushed the amendment through, to almost everyone's surprise. When Johnson signed the bill into law five months later it was still in place: a fundamental transformation in women's rights improbably, almost inexplicably, secured.

The push for equality in the workplace ran alongside a more intimate set of issues. By the early 1960s the cultural threat to traditional sexual standards had seemingly been contained. Hugh Hefner still sold a million copies of *Playboy* a month. And in 1962 a brilliant young ad writer, Helen Gurley Brown, put herself on the bestseller list with a female version of the *Playboy* philosophy, provocatively titled *Sex and the Single Girl*. But the hipsters had been reduced to a cliché, safe enough to be turned into stock characters on television sitcoms. And rock and roll had been tamed. Elvis Presley had been drafted into the military and then shuffled off to Hollywood, while the other raucous acts of the mid-1950s had given way to doo-wop bands, girl groups, and furiously scrubbed solo acts: at the start of 1964 the number-one single in the nation belonged to crooning Bobby Vinton, "the Polish Prince." He lost that spot to a British band called the Beatles, whose recent arrival in the States seemed to have touched off an orgiastic response from its female fans. But the boys' songs were gentle enough. In their first big hit, all they wanted to do was hold hands.

As the cultural front weakened, the legal challenge to traditional standards expanded. By 1964 millions of women were using the birth control pill Katharine Dexter McCormick's money had made possible, more than enough to plunge the birth rate into a notable decline. Within that sweeping change lay one legal impediment. When the pill first went into mass production in 1957, seventeen states still outlawed the sale and distribution of birth control, and a few of them its use as well. Over the next few years most states repealed those restrictions. But a few clung to them, nowhere more doggedly than in Connecticut, though even there no one bothered to enforce the ban. Still that left a legal claim of state authority that birth control activists were determined to overturn. So in 1961, the director of Planned Parenthood's Connecticut branch decided to test the constitutionality of her state's restrictions. Slowly her case wound its way through the legal system, losing every step of the way. In September 1964 her lawyers filed their final appeal.

Beyond that challenge lay a more difficult one, brought to national attention by a scared young mother of four. Sherri Finkbine lived in Phoenix, Arizona, where she hosted a popular children's show on a local television station. When her husband was chaperoning a high school trip to England in 1962, he bought a medication that was supposed to help with headaches and nausea. He brought the unused pills home. Feeling sick in the early weeks of her fifth pregnancy, Finkbine took a number of them. Then she read a news story about a drug used widely in Europe, thalidomide, that scientists had discovered caused severe birth defects. Finkbine began to worry that the medicine she'd taken had thalidomide in it. Her doctor's tests confirmed her fears. Rather than risk giving birth to a terribly deformed baby, he said, she should consider having an abortion.

To that point Finkbine's decision was an entirely private one. A couple of days before she was scheduled to have the procedure, though, she called the local newspaper to suggest that it warn other women about the dangers of thalidomide. The editor ran a front-page article describing what she was about to do. All of a sudden she was the center of a public scandal.

There'd been a time when abortion was legal in the United States. But in the mid-nineteenth century every state had outlawed the procedure, except in those cases when carrying a child to term threatened the life of the mother. Even then, states required that the abortion be performed only with the approval of a doctor; if he decided that the fetus shouldn't be aborted it couldn't be—legally, at least—no matter the mother's wishes. In the late 1950s a handful of doctors had started to argue that the laws ought to be reformed, not to make abortion readily available but to deal with other difficult cases, such as pregnancies that resulted from rape or incest. But they'd made no headway. Now Sherri Finkbine was raising the issue too, under terribly difficult circumstances. When her story went public, officials at her hospital announced they wouldn't let her have the abortion, since her life wasn't in danger. The Finkbines tried to take legal action to force the hospital to proceed, which only drew more attention. Newspapers across the country picked up her story, as did Vatican radio, which offered a stinging reminder that in the Catholic Church's view life began at conception and therefore couldn't be aborted without the doctor and the mother committing the most grievous of sins, while *Life* magazine ran a photo spread showing Finkbine playing with her toddlers.

When the courts turned them down, the Finkbines decided that they had no choice but to go abroad, where abortion laws weren't so strict. After a frantic search for alternatives they flew to Stockholm, with the press dogging their every step. There, in the thirteenth week of her pregnancy, Finkbine had the abortion that had been denied her in the United States. When the couple came home she was fired from her job, and her husband was suspended from his. But polls showed that 52 percent of Americans approved of what they'd done. And talk of reform, which a few months earlier had been restricted to the fringes of the medical profession, suddenly moved into the mainstream. As for Sherri Finkbine's fetus, he was indeed severely disabled, just as she had feared.

Mary King wasn't thinking about abortion or birth control in the autumn of 1964. What bothered her was the chasm between SNCC's commitment to equality and the treatment of the women in its ranks. Again and again she'd seen the movement's men assume that leadership was a male prerogative, that women ought to be responsible for the mundane work the organization required—the typing and filing— while the men set policy, and that the seasoned activists who ran the same risks the men did were really only "girls." Behind those specific concerns lay a deeper analysis. Gender inequality was so ingrained in American life that even the most fervently democratic men—men she deeply admired—accepted it as natural. Of course it wasn't. Women were relegated to second-class citizenship by "value and ideas," she wrote that November, that could and should be broken, "so that all of us come to understand that this is no more a man's world than it is a white world."[29] Then she sent her thoughts to her colleagues in SNCC anonymously, for fear that they would laugh at her.

The Gears of the Machine

WHILE MARY KING was turning her experiences into a quiet declaration of liberation, another veteran of Freedom Summer was bringing its spirit to a place so far from the Delta it could have been mistaken for another country. Mario Savio had gone down to Mississippi at the end of his junior year at the University of California, Berkeley. It was a frightening, inspiring, transformative experience. "Everyone joined hands to sing 'We Shall Overcome,'" he wrote to a friend after attending an MFDP local convention at the end of July. "And they shall! We shall. Someday white people will thank Negroes for saving America from the historical trashcan. Freedom and democracy are things to sing about, but what white northerner has not at some point felt uncomfortable when singing about freedom. . . . Down here I do not."[30]

When Savio returned to Berkeley in the fall of 1964, he discovered that university officials had shut down the campus's traditional free speech zone: a stretch of Telegraph Avenue, just outside the university's main gates, where students came to pass out political flyers, distribute petitions, and recruit volunteers for their causes. No one was sure why the administration had done such a thing. Some thought the university was trying to undercut the campus CORE chapter, which had taken to picketing local businesses that had discriminatory hiring practices; others thought it was a reaction to a group of students who had staged a protest against Barry Goldwater at that summer's Republican convention. Whatever the cause, though, campus activists decided that the ban had to be reversed.

For much of September they tried negotiating with the administration. But the discussions went nowhere. So they raised the stakes. On September 30 a group of students—Savio among them—set up recruitment tables on the campus's central plaza, right in front of Sproul Hall, the university's administration building. Several deans rushed out to tell the five students staffing the tables to stop. When they refused, the deans ordered them to appear at a disciplinary hearing that afternoon. The five showed up in the company of five hundred more students, who demanded that they be punished too. The administration obliged, suspending the five they'd called in along with Savio and two others they identified as organizing the supporting march.

The next day the protest turned into rebellion. That morning a dozen or so student groups set up tables on Sproul Plaza, with hundreds of students gathered around them, some come to support the activists, others simply out of curiosity. At 11:00 the campus police arrested the young man staffing the CORE table, Jack Weinberg, and marched him off to a waiting patrol car. As they put him into the back seat, the crowd surged around the car, blocking its path, chanting, "Let him go! Let him go!" At first Savio sat on the hood. Then he slipped off his shoes, climbed onto the roof, and started to speak. It had been a completely spontaneous decision. But it "had a kind of poetic rightness to it," he said later, an act of defiance that turned the soon-empty cruiser into a platform for the very thing the protesters were demanding, that created—without any sort of planning—a free speech zone that was perfectly, wonderfully democratic.[31]

As soon as Savio finished another student took his place. Then another and another, speech following speech for thirty-two hours, with thousands of people gathered to listen. Only when the university's chancellor, Clark Kerr, agreed to discuss the decision to close down the Telegraph Avenue zone did the demonstration end. Savio and his fellow activists quickly put together an umbrella organization, the Free Speech Movement (FSM), to lead the negotiations. But Kerr was more interested in stripping away the movement's momentum than he was in reaching an agreement. Through the rest of October and all of November the talks dragged on, the extraordinary energy of those thirty-two hours dissipating in a miasma of technicalities.

Finally, on December 2, FSM decided to wait no longer. That day six thousand students gathered on the plaza for another protest, pulled in by the administration's incomprehensible decision to renew disciplinary action against Savio and three of his fellow activists. On Sproul Hall's steps Savio declared his defiance, his metaphors more mechanical than Bob Moses or Martin Luther King would have used but his message perfectly in keeping with theirs. "There is a time," he shouted to the crowd, "when the operation of the machine becomes so odious, makes you so sick at heart, that you can't take part; you can't even passively take part, and you've got to put your bodies upon the gears and upon the wheels, upon the levers, upon all the apparatus, and you've got to make it stop. And you've got to indicate to the people who run it, to the people who own it, that unless you're free, the machine will be prevented from working at all!"[32] When he was done he marched into the building, a thousand students streaming in after him, singing the song he'd found so inspiring down in Mississippi.

For hours they filled the hallways, all four floors of them: a SNCC-style sit-in on a massive scale, committed to shutting down one of the nation's premier universities. Sometime around midnight the administration decided it had seen enough. Phone calls were made. And at 3:00 a.m., December 3, four hundred California highway patrolmen, Alameda County deputies, and campus policemen swept into Sproul Hall. It took them more than twelve hours to clear the building, but by midafternoon 773 students had been taken into custody, many of them dragged down the steps, past thousands of people still in the plaza—"a sea of outraged faces," said a participant—and jammed into the vans that would carry them off to jail.[33] It was the largest mass arrest in California history, meant to bring the FSM to its knees.

It had the opposite effect. Even as the students were being led away protests were sweeping across the campus. Undergraduates walked out of their classes; graduate students went on strike; even a portion of the faculty refused to teach, they were so outraged at the university's actions. Reeling, Chancellor Kerr called for a campus-wide meeting on December 7 "to inaugurate a new era of freedom under the law." Ten thousand students and faculty members filled the university's outdoor amphitheater. But Kerr wouldn't let anyone from the FSM speak to them. When Savio went up on stage to demand a turn at the microphone, two campus policemen grabbed hold of him, one with his arm around his neck, and dragged him off. It was the university's final, fatal blunder: "an accident," Kerr said later, "that looked like fascism."[34] The next day the administration surrendered. The activists would have their free speech zone restored, Kerr announced. The arrested protesters would face no charges. And for a while at least, Savio's fellow students would share in the spirit he'd carried back from the Delta.

A Choice, Not an Echo

BEYOND BERKELEY, THOUGH, the spirit waned: according to polls, 74 percent of Californians opposed the protests. "For our country's sake and as loyalty to the thousands who want no part of Savio's rebels, don't surrender," one of them wrote to California's Democratic governor, Pat Brown. "Expel all the rebels and make way for . . . decent boys and girls who are willing to obey the long established rules."[35] The same sentiment extended to the movement that had inspired Savio. A September survey showed that 73 percent of Americans thought Blacks should stop protesting for their rights. Even in reliably liberal New York City, 54 percent of whites believed that the movement should slow down. And 93 percent said that the Harlem riots had hurt the cause. Here was the backlash the conservatives had been counting on, stoked by the summer's upheavals, waiting for Barry Goldwater to exploit.

He tried. In his swing through the South he attacked the Civil Rights Act as "unfair discrimination in the private affairs of men," a pitch strong enough to win over one of the Democrats' staunchest segregationists, South Carolina senator Strom Thurmond, who in September abruptly announced that he was becoming a Republican. In the urban

North Goldwater adopted the language that had worked so well for George Wallace the previous spring, arguing that the law would lead to social engineering of the most frightful kind. "Why not move families from one neighborhood to another so that quotas set by some bureaucrat somewhere will be everywhere met? Or workers from one job to another?" he asked a crowd in Cleveland. "Is that what we have in mind when we speak of freedom and equal opportunity?" And everywhere he mentioned the breakdown of law and order, "the degradation we see going on in the large cities of the east," he said in Boise, "completely dominated by the Democratic Party." In case his audience missed the connection, he added, "with a sincerely heavy heart," that the harder the Johnson administration pushed for civil rights "the more it has actually incited hatred and violence."[36]

But LBJ knew precisely how to counterattack. Goldwater gave him the opening on the last night of the Republican convention—July 16, the same night Harlem started to smolder—when the senator came before a hall full of the insurgents who'd just won him the nomination. In his acceptance speech he gave them what they wanted to hear: a full-throated defense of the genius of the marketplace, a long paean to freedom, and an inspiring call for victory over the Soviet menace, brought together in a passage he knew would drive them wild. "I would remind you that extremism in the defense of liberty is no vice," he proclaimed in rebuke not of the true believers who filled the hall but of the millions of people watching on television. "And let me remind you also that moderation in the pursuit of justice is no virtue."[37]

Johnson loved those lines as much as the insurgents did; maybe more, because around them he could build his campaign. It started on Labor Day, September 7, when the Democrats ran a thirty-second television ad showing a pretty little girl picking petals from a flower while a male voice-over counted down from ten. At one the screen suddenly changed to footage of an atomic blast. Then came Johnson's Texas drawl. "These are the stakes," he said, "to make a world in which all of God's children can live, or to go into the dark. We must either love each other or we must die."[38] The ad ran only once. That was enough. Apparently extremism in the defense of liberty was indeed a vice.

Through the fall the president and his supporters hammered away at the theme. Goldwater lay so far to the right that he was dangerous, they said, a man so reckless, so unstable, that he couldn't be trusted with the awesome responsibility the presidency imposed. He'd destroy Social Security, take away the price supports that kept farmers afloat, deny workers their right to unionize, cut the minimum wage, and by doing all this ruin the economy that had made the nation more prosperous than anyone would have thought possible just thirty years before. And always there was the specter of the disembodied voice counting down while that pretty little girl pulled the petals off a daisy, just two years after the United States had come to the brink of nuclear war. "The one overriding issue is the handling of our fact of infinite power, our sense of responsibility of its use," Johnson said to reporters as he swept through San Diego. "Today the hand that pushes the button is the hand that could destroy the world."[39]

The harder the Democrats pushed, the more the election moved in their favor. By October civil rights was no longer the most important issue on most voters' minds, as it had been for more than a year; now they were more concerned with questions of war and peace. The Republicans' moderates were running from Goldwater: Michigan's popular governor George Romney refused to endorse him, even as they were standing on the same stage during a September campaign stop. The widely read *Saturday Evening Post*, which had always backed the Republican candidate, condemned him as "a wild man, a stray, an unprincipled and ruthless political jujitsu artist." Even Goldwater could see the end was near. "His speech at Madison Square Garden in New York last night had all the hope and enthusiasm of a suicide note," wrote the *Guardian*'s reporter in the campaign's final days. "All pretense of discussing issues is gone and he now simply calls for freedom from government."[40]

That was enough for the conservative base the insurgents had built. Goldwater easily carried the Southern California suburban belt, thanks to the intense mobilization of the evangelical churches and their Bircher brethren. He did just as well in those areas dominated by conservative businessmen, such as Illinois' DuPage County, just outside of Chicago. But his greatest triumph was the one the insurgents had dreamed of securing since the late 1950s. For the first time since Reconstruction almost a century before, a Republican swept the Deep South. South Carolina, Georgia, Alabama, Mississippi, and Louisiana: Goldwater won them all, most by startling margins. In South Carolina he took 59 percent of the ballots; in Alabama 69 percent; in Mississippi 87 percent. Down in Neshoba County, where four months before FBI agents had pulled the bodies of three young men out of Mississippi's blood-red soil, Barry Goldwater carried 94.9 percent of the vote.

Everywhere else, though, the insurgents' hopes were crushed beneath a Democratic landslide. The Upper South, which had been trending Republican since 1948, went to Johnson by a wide margin. So did the Northeast and the Midwest: in the Cahills' neighborhood Johnson beat John Kennedy's margin of victory by a full percentage point, a major accomplishment for a man who would have been as out of place on Eddy Street as almost anyone could be. Across the Plains the landslide ran, through the Rockies, out to the Pacific Coast, where Johnson carried California by more than a million votes. The only state he lost outside the Deep South was Goldwater's Arizona, and if 5,000 voters there had changed their minds he would have taken that too. The vote's demographics were every bit as lopsided. Sixty-two percent of women supported LBJ, 71 percent of the working class, 73 percent of union families, 76 percent of Catholics, 94 percent of nonwhites. Even 20 percent of Republicans voted for him. Perhaps the greatest surprise was the collapse of the racial backlash that had seemed so dangerous through much of the year. In the end LBJ won 59 percent of the white vote, ten percent more than JFK had won in 1960.

The landslide rumbled through Congress as well. In the Senate twenty-five Democrats were up for reelection. Twenty-four of them won, as did four newcomers, among them Robert Kennedy, who had resigned as attorney general to run for one of New York's seats. In the

House the Democrats added thirty-six new members, assuring them the largest majority they'd enjoyed since the height of the New Deal in the 1930s. That majority had given Franklin Roosevelt the leverage he needed to remake America. Now Johnson was in a position to do the same. Or so it seemed as the results rolled in. The nation had the opportunity "to move forward toward peace and a better life for all our people," he said that night, perhaps even "to heal our history," as if the year's upheavals—the tensions, the conflict, even the violence—could be set aside once the voters had spoken.[41]

CHAPTER 6

THE REVOLUTIONS OF 1965

As a young woman in the early 1920s Estelle Griswold had dreamed of being a professional singer; she had even spent some time in Paris trying to make a go of it. Then she'd come home to Connecticut, where she'd fallen in love with an aspiring ad man. They'd married in 1927. From then on she'd followed his career, moving from Hartford to New York to Washington, DC, and finally, in 1945, to war-ravaged Europe, where he'd been sent by the State Department. There she found work with various aid agencies that were dealing with the staggering number of refugees the war had caused. For the next five years she immersed herself in the world of public service organizations, helping to coordinate resettlement efforts around the globe, until her husband's assignment was done and they headed home.

She spent her first year back in Connecticut continuing the work she'd done abroad. But the agency was based in New York, she and her husband had settled in New Haven, and she quickly tired of commuting back and forth. She quit in 1951. New Haven wasn't brimming with demand for her particular set of skills. So it took her to the end of 1953 to get a suitable job offer. It came from the Connecticut branch of Planned Parenthood, the birth control advocacy group. Griswold didn't know much about the subject—when she was hired, she said later, she didn't even know what a diaphragm was—but the branch needed an executive director. She needed a job. And it would certainly be challenging work; that much was clear from the start.

For decades the branch had been trying to get state officials to repeal Connecticut's law prohibiting the sale, distribution, or use of any form of birth control, the most restrictive in the nation. But the law had been on the books since 1879 and no one was inclined to remove it. At first Griswold tried lobbying the legislature too. She didn't have any more luck than her predecessors. So, in 1958 she changed tactics. Rather than working to get the statute rescinded, she decided to challenge the law's constitutionality. She found four married couples—it never occurred to her to recruit single women—who were willing to claim in court that Connecticut had no right to deny them access to birth control. Slowly the case, *Poe v. Ullman*, worked its way through the legal system, until it reached the U.S. Supreme Court in March 1961. There it hit a wall. Four of the justices wanted to rule on the couples' case. But the other five pointed out that, while Connecticut had the law in place, no one actually enforced it. And without enforcement, the couples faced no real harm; they had come before the Court, read the majority opinion, to battle "harmless, empty shadows."[1]

That's when Griswold decided to get herself arrested. Through the summer of 1961 she made the necessary arrangements. On October 2 she announced through the local paper that her office was opening its own birth control clinic, where married couples could come to get whatever information or devices they needed—right in the heart of New Haven. She assumed that such public defiance of the law would force the police to respond. When they did she'd have another test case, this one based not on a couple's right to acquire birth control but on her right to distribute it.

On the clinic's first day of operations, though, the police didn't come by. Chances are they wouldn't have come the second day either, had it not been for James G. Morris. A forty-two-year-old father of five and a fiercely devout Catholic, Morris believed that using birth control was a grievous sin. As soon as he read Griswold's announcement of the clinic's opening, he decided that the authorities had to shut it down, just as they would a brothel. Immediately he ran into a wall of official indifference. First he tried to file a complaint with the Connecticut state police. They told him to contact the New Haven police. When he called the local station house, the officer who answered the phone said he had to talk to the police chief. Instead Morris called the mayor, whose secretary sent him back to the assistant chief of police, who promised to take up the matter with the circuit court prosecutor. Morris waited an hour and then called the prosecutor himself. He hadn't received a complaint, the prosecutor said. So Morris marched down to his office to make sure one was filed. Even then the prosecutor tried to put him off. But Morris was so insistent that the prosecutor finally agreed to investigate the situation. A few hours later two New Haven detectives walked into the clinic's waiting room and asked to talk to whoever was in charge.

Out bounded Griswold, who swept them into her office, sat them down, handed them a stack of birth control pamphlets, and launched into a detailed explanation of the clinic's services. For more than ninety minutes she talked, packing in "all the medical terminology I knew," she said later, while the detectives desperately tried to take notes. When she finished they stood up, shook hands, and left to file their report. A week later, on November 10, 1961, the detectives returned with a warrant charging that Griswold "did assist, counsel, cause and command certain married women to use a drug, medicinal article and instrument for the purpose of preventing conception."[2] Morris had his arrest. And Griswold had her test case.

Then everything slowed to a crawl. In January 1962 Griswold was convicted of violating Connecticut's birth control prohibition—a crime she readily admitted to committing—and was fined a hundred dollars. Her lawyers appealed to a three-judge state panel, as the rules required, arguing that her conviction should be overturned because the law itself was unconstitutional. There her case sat until January 1963, when the panel finally ruled against her. Again she appealed, this time to the Connecticut Supreme Court, which took another year and a half to affirm the lower court's decision. That left her one last appeal, to the U.S. Supreme Court. Her lawyers filed the necessary papers in September 1964. In early December the justices unanimously agreed to take her case, with oral arguments scheduled for the following March.

Bruce Scott came to his test case from a very different direction. Except for his time in the army in World War II, he'd worked for the U.S. Department of Labor for most of his adult life, first in its Chicago office and then—after the war—in Washington, DC. He undoubtedly would have stayed there, a middle-aged bureaucrat moving through an ordinary career, had his office not been ordered in 1956 to review its security procedures. In the process his boss discovered that on a Saturday night in October 1947 Scott had been arrested for loitering outside of the men's restroom in Lafayette Park, Washington's best-known gay cruising spot. It was the only time his sexual orientation had reached into the public record. Once was enough. The department told him that he should resign rather than face the firing that was sure to follow now that he'd been outed, another victim of the federal government's ongoing Lavender Scare.

Over the next five years he struggled through a string of short-lived jobs, each one ending with the revelation of his misdemeanor more than a decade before. But he didn't have any way to challenge what had happened to him, until the Mattachine Society of Washington offered him one. The society wasn't exactly a powerhouse: its founding meeting in August 1961 drew just sixteen people, one of them an undercover cop. It had a fine name, though, taken from a small national organization that since 1950 had been promoting the remarkable proposition that gay Americans ought to have equal rights. It had a few connections, the most important to the Washington office of the American Civil Liberties Union. And it had in Frank Kameny—a Harvard PhD who'd lost his government job over a single men's room arrest—a president determined to use those connections to confront the injustices that the Lavender Scare had created. Within a few weeks of their first meeting Scott had agreed to give Kameny the court case he wanted.

Three times in late 1961 and early 1962 Scott applied for positions the federal government had opened. He aced the required Civil Service exam. From there his applications went to the Civil Service Commission for review. On May 16, 1962 it sent the inevitable news that his "immoral conduct" disqualified him for government service. He spent the next five months pursuing the three appeals available to him, on the grounds that the commission hadn't spelled out what immoral acts he'd committed. They all failed. But along the way he got an official letter explaining that he'd been rejected because he'd engaged in homosexual conduct, in violation of social standards, a perfect piece of bureaucratic precision to take to court.

His ACLU lawyers filed suit against the Civil Service Commission in April 1963. At the center of their case they put the commission's clearly stated equation of homosexuality and immorality, which they said was arbitrary and discriminatory. Their position seem to baffle the government's blue-blooded attorney—the son of Dean Acheson, Harry Truman's secretary of state— who thought homosexuality was so obviously indecent he barely bothered to make a counterargument. The judge couldn't see the point either: on January 14, 1964, he summarily dismissed Scott's claim. Up the line his lawyers went, to the U.S. Court of Appeals, whose three-judge panel heard arguments in mid-December, 1964. Then the judges went silent while they decided how they wanted to rule.

So it was by chance of timing that Estelle Griswold and Bruce Scott came to trigger one of the revolutions of 1965.

The Dogs of War

FOR LYNDON JOHNSON 1965 began in triumph. His landslide victory over Barry Goldwater had given him the political stature he'd always dreamed of having. It had also handed him the most liberal Congress in thirty years. No more would he have to worry about breaking southern Democrats' grip on Capitol Hill, nor appeasing the Republicans, as he'd had to do in the long battle to pass the Civil Rights Act the previous year. Now he had all the votes he needed to turn his entire legislative agenda into law.

At its center stood the stunning array of programs LBJ saw as constituting his war on poverty. There'd be more funding for the Economic Opportunity Act, which had launched the war in 1964, and more innovative new programs as a result. There'd be national health care for the poor and the elderly—Medicaid and Medicare, the programs would be called—along with an increase in Social Security payments not only for retirees but for the poor and disabled as well. There'd be a billion dollars in federal aid for grade schools and high schools in impoverished areas, along with federal loans to help underprivileged kids go to college. There'd be a boost in the minimum wage and a broadening of its coverage to include nine million more workers. There'd be a raft of new public works programs in struggling sections of the country, which would come with a fair share of jobs. There might even be a chance to completely rebuild inner cities, to replace sagging tenements with new housing, crumbling streets with vibrant communities, isolation with integration.

In the flush of victory, though, Johnson's ambitions stretched beyond combating poverty. Liberals had talked about strengthening consumer protection laws; he'd support them. They'd said they wanted to deal with air and water pollution; so did he. And some of them, at least, had long wanted to reform the discriminatory immigration laws that had been put in place in the 1920s. Abandon the law's quotas, the reformers argued, and put in their place a process that favored immigrants with skills employers needed or with relatives already living in the United States. They were willing to accept one key new restriction: for the first time the United States would cap the number of people it accepted each year from the rest of the Western hemisphere, a revision that they assumed would slow a migration that had increased Latinos' share of the population to about four percent. The reform's other provisions would overturn the rules that had choked off immigration from much of Europe and almost of Asia—four decades after the quotas were put in place, Asian Americans still made up less than one percent of the population—while making the system more rational and more humane. That was good enough for LBJ. When the Senate Judiciary Committee took up their bill in February, they'd have the president's backing.

It wasn't simply a matter of passing laws, though, as much as Johnson loved the legislative process. Bill by bill, act by act, he could fulfill—and extend—the vision that had been guiding him since Dallas, to unleash the power of government in pursuit of justice. That was the mandate the voters had handed him. And he was going to seize it, as he made clear in his inaugural address, delivered on a sun-drenched day in late January. "Underneath the clamor of building and the rush of our day's pursuits, we are believers in justice and liberty and in our own union," he said. "We believe that every man must someday be free. And we believe in ourselves. . . . Is a new world coming? We welcome it, and we will bend it to the hopes of man. And to these trusted public servants and to my family, and those close friends of mine who have followed me down a long winding road, and to all the people of this Union and the world, I will repeat today what I said on that sorrowful day in November last year: I will lead and I will do the best I can." In such a glorious moment there was no need to raise the one danger he saw looming, not in a meaningful way at least. Better to brush past it with a reference to American lives being lost "in countries that we barely know."[3] Better not to say the word "Vietnam."

It was fifteen months since the Kennedy administration had acquiesced in the coup that toppled the government of Ngo Dinh Diem. Kennedy had hoped that the generals who would put themselves in his place could stabilize South Vietnam. But it was clearly a gamble; the generals had no experience running a government, no control over the bureaucracy Diem had built, and no plan for combating the Communist insurgency that by American estimates controlled almost half the South Vietnamese countryside. Nor did they get time to solve those problems. At the end of January 1964 they were themselves overthrown by yet another general, Nguyen Khanh.

The serial coups might have given LBJ the cover he needed to scale back the United States' commitment. Instead he embraced each new government as it came. "Go back and tell those generals in Saigon that Lyndon Johnson intends to stand by our word," he ordered his ambassador at the end of his first briefing on Vietnam, three days after Kennedy's assassination. When they were deposed he swung behind the new government just as quickly. "This Khanh is the toughest one they got and the ablest one they got," he told a sympathetic newspaper editor two days after the January coup. "Now it'll take him a little time to get his marbles in a row, just like it's taking me a little time. But . . . it's not the Americans' loss."[4]

Johnson's response reflected the particular circumstances of his early days in office: a president still learning how to handle international affairs, surrounded by the martyred Kennedy's brilliant advisers—the Rhodes scholars and Harvard professors, career diplomats and corporate whiz kids—who had handled the Cuban Missile Crisis with such skill just two years before. How could he possibly change the course they had set? But there was more to it than that. Johnson had seen how conservative Republicans had used Mao Zedong's 1949 triumph in China to batter away at Harry Truman, charging that he was too soft to stand up to the Communist threat, too weak to fight the Cold War as it ought to be fought, perhaps even complicit in China's fall. The assault had all but destroyed Truman's presidency. LBJ was sure the Republican Right would do the same to him, given half a chance. "I am not going to lose Vietnam," he said at the end of that first briefing. "I am not going to be the president who saw Southeast Asia go the way China went."[5]

At first Johnson thought he could manage the situation much as Kennedy had. "The only thing I know to do is more of the same," he told William Fulbright, the highly respected chair of the Senate Foreign Relations Committee, "and do it more efficiently and effectively."[6] So, in January 1964 he approved a plan to increase covert operations in North Vietnam. And over the next few months he sent more advisers and more financial aid to South Vietnam, in hopes that the help would stabilize the situation there. It didn't. Throughout the first half of 1964 Nguyen Khanh struggled to maintain even a minimal level of control over his government—rumors of yet another coup constantly crept through Saigon—while the Communist insurgency pushed farther and farther into the South Vietnamese countryside. By mid-May Johnson's key advisers were telling him that the war could be lost in six months, unless the administration forced the North Vietnamese government to end its aggression against the South. And the only way to do that, they said, was by unleashing American military power.

Together, Secretary of Defense Robert McNamara, Secretary of State Dean Rusk, and National Security Advisor McGeorge Bundy set the central strategy. Working through secret channels, the administration would tell the North Vietnamese that if they didn't stop supporting the southern insurgency they'd face serious consequences. When that warning failed, as it almost surely would, the United States would hit North Vietnam with an air war so punishing it would force the Communists to back down. The message was delivered to the North Vietnamese prime minister, Pham Van Dong, on June 18, 1964. As expected, he brushed it aside. But LBJ wasn't ready to begin a sustained assault on North Vietnam, not in the midst of a presidential campaign he planned to center on his opponent's frighteningly belligerent foreign policy. Instead he settled for a single strike, wrapped in layers of deception. The episode began on August 2, when three North Vietnamese patrol boats fired on the USS *Maddox*, an American destroyer operating in the Gulf of Tonkin, ten miles off the coast of North Vietnam. Immediately the White House warned the North Vietnamese that a second attack wouldn't be tolerated. Then it sent the *Maddox* back into the gulf, along with another warship, the USS *Turner Joy*. For the next two days the destroyers prowled along the edge of North Vietnam's territorial waters, while administration officials waited for word of another incident. On the morning of August 4—night in Vietnam—it arrived.

That evening the ships' crews had engaged in a furious firefight against what they believed to be North Vietnamese patrol boats. No one had actually seen the boats except on radar screens. It was the sort of night—moonless with heavy squalls—that could produce false readings. And neither ship had been hit, even by small arms fire. The reports were so weak even LBJ didn't believe them. But the truth didn't matter. Shortly before midnight Washington time, Johnson went on national television to announce that North Vietnam's "aggression by terror against peaceful villages of South Vietnam has now been joined by open aggression on the high seas against the United States of America. . . . Repeated acts of violence against the armed forces of the United States must be met not only with alert defense but with positive reply."[7] As he was speaking, eighteen American warplanes were bombing a North Vietnamese naval facility, a preview of the power the administration would bring to bear if the Communists didn't stand down.

The following day LBJ sent Congress a draft resolution authorizing the president "to take all necessary steps, including the use of armed force, to assist [South Vietnam] in defense of its freedom." It was a remarkably open-ended proposal; the equivalent, said one senator, to a "predated declaration of war."[8] But virtually no one wanted to go on record opposing freedom just as American sailors had come under fire. After a few hours of hearings and a lackluster debate, the Gulf of Tonkin Resolution sailed through the Senate by a vote of eighty-eight to two and through the House without any dissent at all. Afterward the president praised the process as a demonstration of national unity. Really it was a triumph of manipulation. With just a little bit of lying, LBJ had coerced Congress into handing him complete control over American policy in Vietnam.

There the administration's show of force had very different consequences. By all accounts North Vietnamese officials hoped to avoid a full-scale war with the United States. But they were also determined not to seem cowed by American threats. So, they decided, in their own show of bravado, to increase their support for the southern insurgency. Nguyen Khanh, meanwhile, used the Gulf of Tonkin raid to impose a state of emergency in South Vietnam, a move that gave him virtually dictatorial power. That decision triggered protests in the streets of Saigon as severe as the ones that had crippled the Diem government in 1963. Khanh responded by abruptly resigning. For a week or so at the end of August it seemed as if South Vietnam was about to collapse, until the American ambassador convinced Khanh to return. He did so having been stripped of what little popular support he'd once had;

had it not been for Washington's backing he wouldn't have been able to govern at all.

As it was, the White House spent the autumn hoping Khanh could hold on until Johnson was elected. Through September and October reports of impending disaster poured in. Many of South Vietnam's government offices were no longer functioning. The South Vietnamese military was refusing to fight the insurgency. The Viet Cong controlled 50 percent of South Vietnam's territory during the day and 75 percent at night. It wasn't even safe to travel some of the major roads leading out of Saigon. Still LBJ refused to start the bombing campaign McNamara, Rusk, and Bundy had proposed the previous spring. At times the president went further, explicitly running against the strategy his advisers had defined. "There are those who say you ought to go North and drop bombs to try to wipe out the supply lines, and they think that will escalate the war," he said at an Oklahoma campaign rally in late September. "We don't want our American boys to do the fighting for Asian boys. . . . We are not about to start another war. . . ."[9] On the day before the election, though—with Nguyen Khanh still in place and his own landslide assured—LBJ told his advisers to begin final planning for the bombing to come.

They set a tentative date of January 1, 1965. But Johnson wanted to launch the campaign only in response to a North Vietnamese provocation. He passed on his first opening—a Christmas Eve bombing of a Saigon hotel that killed two Americans—because it didn't seem right to wage war on a holiday. Six weeks later, on February 7, 1965, the Viet Cong handed him another. It was a typical insurgent action: a late-night guerrilla raid on a forward base in South Vietnam's highly contested Central Highlands, 250 miles north of Saigon. But this time the base was filled with American soldiers, eight of whom were killed in the attack. Within a few hours Johnson had ordered a retaliatory strike on a North Vietnamese military compound, to be carried out by 132 US warplanes, the first ferocious assault in what would quickly become Operation Rolling Thunder, the sustained bombing of North Vietnam.

A handful of advisers urged Johnson to back down, none more vigorously than his newly inaugurated vice president, Hubert Humphrey. "American wars have to be politically understandable by the American public," he wrote the president on February 11. "There has to be a cogent, convincing case if we are to enjoy sustained public support. . . . Politically, people can't understand why we would run grave risks to support a country which is totally unable to put its house in order."[10] But instead of slowing the administration's march toward war, the instability in South Vietnam pushed Johnson forward. On February 18 a junta of South Vietnamese army officers finally toppled Khanh from power. In the chaotic days that followed, American commanders began to fear that the South Vietnamese military couldn't be trusted to protect the sprawling US air base at Da Nang, from which the bombing runs would be launched. So, on February 22 they formally asked the president to send two marine landing teams—a total of 3,500 men—to South Vietnam to secure the base.

Again a few advisers objected. "As I analyze the pros and cons of placing any considerable number of Marines in Da Nang . . . I develop grave reservations as to the wisdom and necessity of so doing," cabled the US ambassador in Saigon, JFK's once-favorite general, Maxwell Taylor. "Such action would be [a] step in reversing long standing policy of avoiding commitment of ground combat forces in SVN. Once this policy is breached, it will be very difficult to hold [the] line."[11] But Johnson sided with the current military men. The marines would arrive in South Vietnam on March 8. After a year and a half of deliberation and deception, the American ground war in Vietnam was about to begin.

Democracy Itself

ON THE DAY of the officers' coup in South Vietnam, an Alabama state trooper shot twenty-six-year-old Jimmie Lee Jackson at point-blank range. The attack shouldn't have been a surprise, not after so much blood had already been shed. Still, it was appalling that a man could be murdered simply because he wanted to vote.

For months the civil rights movement had been roiled by politics.

For their part, SNCC's leading figures had spent the autumn of 1964 struggling to make sense of Freedom Summer. They'd seen the promise of democracy fulfilled in the 80,000 African Americans who'd defied Mississippi's terror to join the MFDP. Then they'd brought that idealism up to Lyndon Johnson's convention convinced, said a veteran organizer, "in the ultimate morality in national political institutions and practices—'They really didn't know, and once we bring the facts about Mississippi to national attention, justice must surely be swift and irrevocable.'" But LBJ had known, as had the liberals he'd dispatched to offer the activists their two symbolic seats. They just didn't care. "White liberals and the so-called affluent Negro leader . . . will sell us down the river for the hundredth time to protect themselves," insisted John Lewis. "We all saw this in Atlantic City."[12]

But it wasn't at all clear how SNCC could move forward now that its liberal allies had been exposed. Despite the convention's bitter turn, Lewis clung to his dream of building a Beloved Community. Bob Moses desperately wanted to keep the focus on grassroots organizing, though he feared that his celebrity had begun to overshadow the local people he'd devoted himself to empowering. Others talked of turning SNCC into a centralized, ideologically disciplined organization that could undertake radical political action, an American version of the revolutionary movements that were then sweeping across sub-Saharan Africa. "We want much more than token positions," one of SNCC's founding members said shortly after the Atlantic City debacle. "We want power."[13]

So did Bayard Rustin. But nationalism wasn't the way to secure it, he argued in a widely read article published in early 1965. In fact the March on Washington, the passage of the Civil Rights Act, even SNCC's convention challenge all proved what was possible when African Americans worked with liberal politicians, unionists, and church groups. LBJ's landslide opened still greater possibilities. With the Democrats' southern bloc broken, Rustin said, the civil rights movement could begin to demand of Congress "radical programs for full employment, abolition of slums, the reconstruction of our educational system, new definitions of work and leisure"—an agenda of revolutionary reach, to be secured through mainstream politics. But the movement could only do so in alliance with its progressive partners, he concluded, "for there is a limit to what Negroes can do alone."[14]

Martin Luther King believed in alliances too. From Atlantic City he'd been pulled into the presidential campaign, set on a schedule of appearances so grueling he ended up in an Atlanta hospital suffering from exhaustion. While there he learned that he'd won the Nobel Peace Prize, a triumph he celebrated by going back on the road, sweeping through the African American sections of Cleveland, Chicago, Detroit, New York, and Los Angeles on Johnson's behalf. On election night he wired the president his congratulations, politely passing up the chance to mention the huge margins LBJ had amassed in the areas King had visited. Then he announced that come January he would launch a new crusade, aimed at forcing the federal government to break that portion of the southern racial regime the Civil Rights Act had left untouched: the systematic denial of African Americans' right to vote, an injustice King planned to shatter with the power of redemptive suffering.

His most volcanic adviser, James Bevel—the architect of the 1963 Children's Crusade—picked the target. Since 1962 SNCC had been struggling to build a voter registration campaign in Selma, Alabama, a town of 28,000 deep in the Black Belt, fifty miles west of Montgomery. The campaign's organizers had managed to mobilize a portion of the African American population. But they'd been ground down by relentless intimidation—led by Selma's version of Bull Connor, Sheriff Jim Clark—and an intense level of legal repression, capped by a 1964 injunction that prohibited SNCC from holding a meeting of more than two people. Bringing King to Selma was sure to intensify white resistance, perhaps catastrophically, which was exactly why Bevel wanted him there.

And why Johnson wanted him to stay away. He agreed that the southern system wouldn't be broken until the federal government intervened. He'd even ordered his new attorney general, Nicholas Katzenbach, to secretly draft a voting rights bill. But he had a massive legislative agenda to pass before he was willing to start another fight over civil rights. After the Nobel ceremony LBJ invited King to the White House for a private discussion. The talk quickly turned to the movement's plans. "I'm going to do it eventually, but I can't get voting rights through in this session of Congress," Johnson insisted. "It's just not the wise and politically expedient thing to do," though he should have known by then that arguing for expediency wasn't the best way to stop the newest laureate from taking to the streets.[15]

King opened the campaign with a stirring appearance at Selma's Brown Chapel AME Church on January 2, 1965, in defiance of the previous year's injunction. "We must be ready to march," he told the 700 people jammed into the church to see him. "We must be ready to go to jail by the thousands."[16] The protests started in mid-January, after two weeks of whirlwind organizing. By early February more than 2,000 people had been arrested, most for marching on the registrar's office. As the numbers rose, so did Sheriff Clark's ferocity. One group of protesters he bashed down the courthouse steps. Another he pushed into a three-mile forced march; those who lagged behind his deputies were shocked with cattle prods. The worst he reserved for Bevel, who was arrested while leading a demonstration on February 8. That night Clark's men hosed Bevel down, then threw open his cell window to let in the winter air. By morning he was so feverish he had to be transferred to a local hospital. Clark insisted that Bevel be shackled to his bed.

The movement's spokesmen met the violence with defiance, promising to extend the campaign from Selma into the surrounding countryside, already on the edge of revolt. King himself drove down to tiny Camden, Alabama, forty miles south of Selma, to join the seventy protesters who'd decided to march on their registrar's office. His longtime aide Andrew Young slipped out to rural Lowndes County, east of Selma, to encourage the local folks who were thinking of taking on an electoral system that had prevented every African American in the county from voting in 1964, though Blacks made up 80 percent of its population. And another SCLC organizer headed twenty-seven miles northwest to Marion, Alabama, where community activists had been trying to mount a voter registration drive for the previous two years. Within days of his arrival he was leading protests almost as large as Selma's, though Marion was one-sixth the size.

It was 9:30 p.m. when they started the February 18 march, a dangerous time in an area where white vigilantes had always ruled the night. But they were only going two blocks, from the rally at Zion Methodist to the Perry County Jail. And all they wanted to do, once they got there, was to sing some freedom songs. When they started out of the church, though—400 protesters walking two by two—they were stopped by a phalanx of 200 Marion policemen, sheriff's deputies, and Alabama state troopers. The police chief told the marchers to turn around. Zion's minister asked if they might have a moment to pray. Then the streetlights went out and the policemen attacked, pummeling those in the front of the line, beating them down with their nightsticks, wading through the wounded to reach the marchers closer to the church doors.

That's where Jimmie Lee Jackson was standing, alongside his mother, sister, and eighty-two-year-old grandfather. In the chaos of the moment they stumbled back behind the church, following a dozen other panicked marchers into the safety of Mack's Café. They were there a minute or two when the troopers burst in. There'd be claims and counterclaims about what happened next. It seems that a trooper charged Jackson's grandfather. When Jackson's mother tried to pull him off, he threw her to the ground. Jimmie Lee rushed to protect her—some said he lunged for her—and three other troopers turned on him.

Jackson died early in the morning of February 26, eight days after the assault in Marion. All that week King had been haunted by violence. First came the news that Malcolm X had been murdered, shot while giving a speech at Harlem's Audubon Ballroom on Sunday afternoon, February 21. One of the assassins had been seized as he ran out of the building, the other two arrested shortly thereafter. All three were devout members of the Nation of Islam, acting—it was rumored—on Elijah Muhammad's wishes if not his command, the father claiming the life of his once-beloved son. On Monday the attorney general called King to warn him of death threats coming out of Marion. On Wednesday King flew to Los Angeles, the latest stop in an endless round of fundraising. At the airport he was told of yet another threat, this one from neo-Nazis, its details serious enough that the LA police gave him around-the-clock protection. When reporters picked up the story, they badgered him with questions of how nonviolence would survive should he be killed. Now the Selma campaign had claimed Jimmie Lee Jackson. And Martin Luther King was in a heavily guarded LA hotel room, two thousand miles away.

The idea was Bevel's. By all rights he should have cleared it with King. But he was swept up in the emotions of the day. And it wasn't his style to obey lines of authority. Instead he used that evening's mass meeting in Selma to express his grief. "I'll tell you," he said, "the death of that young man is pushing me kind of hard." He talked of the need to carry on. And he talked of George Wallace, who as governor commanded the troopers who'd killed Jackson. Then his address took a sudden turn. "I must go see the king!" he announced. "Be prepared to walk to Montgomery! Be prepared to sleep on the highway!"[17]

It was an utterly reckless proposal—a fifty-mile march from Selma to the state capital, across a countryside steeped in white violence, to honor the memory of a man who'd been killed for threatening to walk two blocks—and as soon as he heard of it King doubted its wisdom. But he'd also been unsure of Bevel's decision to bring children into the streets of Birmingham in 1963, and that had changed the nation. On the day of Jackson's funeral King announced that the march would leave Selma the following Sunday, March 7.

King was in Atlanta, preaching at Ebenezer Baptist, when the protesters started out of Brown Chapel on Sunday afternoon. His colleague Hosea Williams took his place at the head of the line, alongside John Lewis, who was marching despite SNCC's official decision not to participate, the result of a bitter Friday night debate that had pivoted on the pointlessness of pushing Washington for meaningful change. Behind them trailed 600 men, women, and children set in the same formation as the Marion marchers. They walked five blocks east on Water Street, then turned right onto the Edmund Pettus Bridge, which curved over the Alabama River on the edge of town. "I noticed how steep it was as we climbed toward the steel canopy at the top of the arched bridge," Lewis said later. "It was too steep to see the other side. . . . When we reached the crest of the bridge I stopped dead still. So did Hosea."[18]

Just beyond the bridge's end stood a solid wall of state troopers dressed in riot gear, gas masks in place; behind them were Sheriff Clark's men, some on horseback, their nightsticks already drawn. There was a network news van pulled off to the side, around it a cache of reporters and cameramen waiting for the confrontation to come.

Slowly, silently, Williams and Lewis led the line to within fifty feet of the troopers. Again they stopped, as one of the officers started to speak to them through a bullhorn. "It would be detrimental to your safety to continue this march," he said. "And I'm saying this is an unlawful assembly. You are to disperse. You are ordered to disperse. Go home or go to your church. This march will not continue. Is that clear to you?"

For a minute nobody moved. Lewis suggested to Williams that they pray. Then the officer put down the bullhorn and turned to the men behind him. "Troopers, advance," he shouted.[19]

Across the fifty feet they moved in tight formation. Lewis and Williams took the first hit, a vicious cross block that sent them tumbling into the row behind them. As the first bodies fell the troopers' discipline broke. Into the crumbling line they waded, assaulting whoever got in their way, Clark's deputies rushing to join them, spurring their horses into a gallop, pounding through the tear gas the troopers had released—plumes of choking smoke—the clatter of hooves tangling with the screams of the crowd. For half an hour the assault went on, until the marchers had been beaten back to Selma and the wounded cleared from the streets.

Lyndon Johnson was hosting a small dinner party when the three major television networks interrupted their regular evening broadcasts with footage of the troopers' attack. But he didn't want to think about Selma that night, not when he was waiting to hear that the first battalion of American marines had arrived safely in South Vietnam. The soldiers sloshed ashore at 9:30 p.m. Washington time. Not long after, the president said goodnight to his guests and went straight to bed. In the morning he awoke to national outrage.

By then there were pickets outside the Justice Department, demanding federal intervention in Selma, with a SNCC-led occupation of the attorney general's office soon to follow. All day telegrams condemning the violence poured into the White House—from the Los Angeles City Council, the New Jersey State Assembly, the Anti-Defamation League, the Harvard Law faculty, the Jewish War Veterans, the ACLU, the Young Businessmen's Club of Montgomery, the mayor of New York, the governor of Massachusetts, and thousands of ordinary Americans. On the Senate floor Texas' Ralph Yarborough urged George Wallace to atone for Alabama's sins, while on the House side Michigan's James O'Hara called the assault "a savage action, stormtrooper style, under direction of a reckless demagogue." But by far the most important news came from Atlanta, where Martin Luther King told the press that he was heading back to Selma to continue the protests. And he was asking "clergy of all faiths, representatives of every part of the country" to join him, so that together they could "testify to the fact that the struggle in Selma is for the survival of democracy everywhere in our land."[20]

It was as if he had issued a call to prayer. By Tuesday morning some 450 ministers, rabbis, priests, and nuns had poured into Selma: prominent men come to lend their prestige—Lyndon Johnson's pastor among them—as well as ordinary religious people come to bear witness. There was a tense afternoon march, a symbolic turn across the bridge and back. Then evening fell and the danger rose.

James Reeb was a thirty-eight-year-old white Unitarian minister who'd rushed down from Boston when he heard of King's call. He'd had supper with two fellow clergymen at a Black-owned diner. When they were done the three of them headed toward SCLC's makeshift office nearby. Along the way four white men descended on them. The other ministers they beat to the ground. Reeb took a club to the head, a blow so vicious his colleagues had to support him as they stumbled to safety, though they were bleeding profusely themselves. By morning

Reeb was on life support in a Montgomery hospital. By Thursday night he was dead.

All week the national outcry mounted. On Tuesday 10,000 people marched on the federal building in Detroit to demand a voting rights bill, the procession led by Michigan's Republican governor, George Romney, and the city's Democratic mayor, Jerome Cavanagh. On Wednesday protesters established around-the-clock pickets at the White House. On Thursday, as Reeb was dying, twelve activists slipped into the tour line and launched a sit-in that shut off part of the East Wing for most of the day. News of the campaign's latest martyr pushed the protests to a fever pitch. Through the nation's smaller cities the rallies ran: 1,500 people marching in New Haven, Connecticut; 2,500 in Poughkeepsie, New York; 3,000 in Columbus, Ohio; 3,500 in Louisville, Kentucky. In major urban centers the turnouts were massive. That weekend 15,000 people paraded through Harlem to demand a voting rights bill, with Bayard Rustin at the front of the line. Another 15,000 filled Washington's Lafayette Park, close enough to the Oval Office that LBJ could hear their chants. Twenty-five thousand packed Boston Common. And down in Selma the clerics kept coming, until the Black side of town was awash in yarmulkes, habits, and pectoral crosses. "There is a time," a New Jersey rabbi told a reporter, "when man must choose between man's law and God's law."[21]

For Johnson the time had come. Later his aides would point to Saturday afternoon as the pivotal point. He'd suffered through a series of painful meetings with civil rights advocates, followed by a three-hour session with George Wallace that he dominated as only LBJ could, his chair pulled uncomfortably close to the governor, his face pulled closer still, his message blunt and brutal. "George, you're fucking over your president," he said to Wallace at one point. "Why are you fucking over your president?"[22] When they were done Wallace slunk away, while Johnson went before the press corps to announce that on Monday, March 15, he'd be submitting a comprehensive voting rights bill to Congress, the very step he'd refused to take three months before. And he'd be doing so with a personal appearance on Capitol Hill, to be tele-vised live to the nation, wisdom and expediency be damned.

It was an electric evening, the president marching down to the House floor, past the seats left empty by the congressmen from Mississippi and Alabama, who refused to attend; past the justices of the Supreme Court and the president's cabinet; up to the podium where the Speaker of the House was waiting to gavel the night to order; beneath the gal-leries where Lady Bird sat with a coterie of priests and ministers. As the applause died down he opened the speech in front of him and started to speak.

The president talked of the assault on the Edmund Pettus Bridge and of the death of Reverend Reeb, of the nation's values and purposes, of the rank injustice of denying any American the right to vote. He laid out the barriers that Jim Crow had created and outlined the remedy he'd be proposing, which would give the federal government the power to register voters when the states refused. He called on Congress to pass his proposal as quickly as possible. Then he reached beyond the moment. "What happened in Selma," he said, "is part of a far larger movement which reaches into every section and state of America. It is the effort of American Negroes to secure for themselves the full bless-ings of American life. Their cause must be our cause, too. Because it is not just Negroes, but really it's all of us, who must overcome the crip-pling legacy of bigotry and injustice. And we shall overcome."[23]

They were just song lyrics: three words to anchor the chorus. But behind them lay the promise that had sustained the movement for so many years. That someday justice would roll like a river and righ-teousness like a mighty stream, that the crooked places could be made straight and the rough places plain. That someday we—not you, not they, but we—shall overcome. Martin Luther King was watching the speech in Selma. When he heard the president use those three sacred words, he wept.

A Penumbra

GRISWOLD V. CONNECTICUT reached the Supreme Court two weeks after Johnson's brilliant performance on Capitol Hill. The proceedings were swaddled in the Court's decorous traditions, a world removed from Selma's brutality. There'd be two hours of oral argument, evenly divided between the two sides, after which the justices would retreat to their chambers to begin shaping a decision, leaving no indication of what they were thinking except for the clues they'd dropped during the lawyers' presentations.

But the justices weren't ciphers. They were nine white men, all of them married—William O. Douglas, three times. One was Catholic, one Jewish, the remainder Protestant. Four had been appointed by a Republican president, Dwight Eisenhower, five by Democrats, the most recent by LBJ. And though they didn't share a judicial philosophy, in recent years they had demonstrated a decided commitment to civil liberties. There was the epic *Brown* decision, of course. But in the previous three years alone the Court had also handed down landmark rulings protecting the rights of accused criminals, prohibiting prayer in public schools, defending freedom of the press, loosening obscenity laws, and undercutting states' manipulation of the vote. If the lawyers wanted to win the justices over, it was best to play to their proclivities.

From the start almost everything went Estelle Griswold's way. Her attorney, Yale Law professor Thomas Emerson, opened his argument by reviewing the facts of the case, stressing that Griswold's clinic offered contraception only to married women. How did the clinic know its clients were married? asked Justice Arthur Goldberg. The staff asked them, Emerson replied. Justice Hugo Black cut in. Why draw a distinction between married and unmarried women? Wouldn't it be discriminatory to allow married women to use birth control and prohibit single women from doing so? Maybe, Emerson said. But he wasn't asking the Court to settle that question. This was a case about marital rights.

There the justices kept the discussion, despite the efforts of Connecticut's attorney, Joseph Clark, to move it in other directions. He tried to argue that the statute prohibiting the distribution and use of birth control was meant to prevent sexual intercourse outside of marriage. "Well, the trouble with the argument is that, on the record, this involves married women," Justice Potter Stewart countered. Clark shifted to the question of religious liberty, arguing that the statute reflected the views of Connecticut's many Catholics and Jews. Again Stewart stepped in. "Well, you would have had quite a different case if the State of Connecticut compelled all married couples to use them," he said. "That's when you'd run into the argument you're now making, that this violates the religious precepts and beliefs of certain groups. . . . We're dealing here, by definition and on this record, with advice and the furnishing of devices to married women who asked for such advice." Finally Clark tried to question the validity of the medical testimony Griswold's lawyers had collected. This time Stewart wouldn't let him even pursue the point. "What we have here," the justice insisted, "is the freedom of people, of married couples to do this just as they want and therefore I don't quite see the relevance of what you're telling us now, when you remember what this case is about."

Clark knew he'd been pushed into a corner. "Well, if your Honor please," he replied, "I can only say that married couples do not have the freedom to do what they want."[24]

Griswold's lawyer couldn't have asked for a more helpful response than that. "I would be much surprised if we didn't win," he wrote his client shortly after oral arguments, most likely by a margin of seven to two.[25]

He had the count exactly right. The justices met to share their views of the case three days after the lawyers' presentation. Around the table they went in the order tradition required, beginning with the chief justice, Earl Warren, and ending with the Court's newest member, Arthur Goldberg. The only votes to support Connecticut's claim came from Hugo Black and Potter Stewart. Neither supported the law—Stewart called it "uncommonly silly"—but they didn't see a legal basis for declaring it unconstitutional.[26] The others thought that it ought to be voided, though they didn't agree on the grounds for doing so: some wanted a sweeping ruling, others a narrow one. It was something of a surprise, therefore, that after the justices took their vote Warren assigned the opinion to the most ardent of the Court's civil libertarians, William O. Douglas.

Douglas was famous—some said infamous—among Court insiders for the speed with which he wrote opinions. This time he took ten days to finish a draft. It was only six pages, double-spaced, but it had an imposing reach. "The association of husband and wife is not mentioned in the Constitution nor in the Bill of Rights," Douglas wrote. But the Court had already identified a general right of association as a "penumbra" to the First Amendment, not explicitly listed in the text but logically extending from those rights that were. Now the Court should extend that right to married couples, to protect "the sacred precincts of marital bedrooms."[27]

When Douglas circulated his draft, his fellow liberal, William Brennan, found the argument strained. The Court had defined free association in political terms: states couldn't prevent someone from joining the NAACP, for instance. That hardly seemed applicable to the highly personal relationships that lay at the heart of the *Griswold* case. Within a few days Brennan's clerks had come up with a new formula. Just as the Court had identified free association as being derived from the First Amendment, the revision read, so should the Court identify the right to privacy as an extension of the Third, Fourth, and Fifth Amendments. Brennan sent the suggestions back to Douglas, who was more than pleased with what he read. Little wonder. His first version had tried to apply an existing right. Brennan's approach created an entirely new one, a civil libertarian's dream made real by the logic of the law.

The Court handed down its decision on June 7. The opinion followed Brennan's reasoning almost entirely. But the words were Douglas's. "We deal with a right of privacy older than the Bill of Rights," he wrote, "older than our political parties, older than our school system. Marriage is a coming together for better or for worse, hopefully enduring and intimate to the degree of being sacred."[28] And the sacred ought not to be profaned by the state's intrusion. By order of the Court Connecticut's eighty-six-year-old ban on birth control was to be set aside, the marital bed pro-tected by a constitutional right that until that moment hadn't existed.

Nine days later the U.S. Court of Appeals handed down its ruling in Bruce Scott's test case. Compared to *Griswold* it was a spare decision, laid out in six straightforward paragraphs. Scott certainly didn't have a right to be hired by the federal government, it read. But he did have a right to have his application treated fairly. The government could have done that by saying precisely what immoral acts he had committed and why those acts made him ineligible for the jobs he wanted. Instead it had rejected him purely on its assumption that homosexuality was by definition immoral. That was discriminatory, the appeals court con-cluded, because even a gay man had rights that had to be respected.

Three Revolutions

THE INITIAL RESPONSE to the two cases was decidedly underwhelming. "The impact of the decision . . . is likely to be very limited," wrote the *Washington Post*'s reporter on the day that *Griswold* came down, since it had nothing to say about unmarried women's use of contraception. The Catholic Church's spokesman said the American bishops weren't concerned. Although Catholics consider birth control to be sinful, he told the press, "The Church does not seek to use the power of the state to compel compliance with its moral views."[29] Even Estelle Griswold didn't seem particularly excited. She dutifully posed for photographs holding the *New Haven Register*'s front page, where the Court's ruling had been given second billing to news of the latest space flight. But her primary reaction was a matter-of-fact announcement that she'd be reopening her clinic as soon as possible. At least *Griswold* made the front pages. Only the *Post* reported on the *Scott* ruling, in a page three story that never mentioned his name, much less asked him to comment on his victory.

In any case *Griswold* and *Scott* weren't likely to have riveted pub-lic attention, not when there were far more compelling stories to follow. Through the spring the nation's major news outlets had detailed the inexo-rable bombing campaign the United States waged against North Vietnam:

3,600 sorties flown in April, 4,000 in May, 4,800 in June. The more dramatic news came on the ground. Just as Ambassador Taylor had argued in March, once the administration committed the first contingent of combat troops to South Vietnam it wouldn't be able to resist the military's request for more. In April Lyndon Johnson agreed to deploy 40,000 additional American soldiers, enough for the United States to launch limited excursions against the Viet Cong in the South Vietnamese countryside.

As American troop levels rose, the South Vietnamese military buckled. In May the National Liberation Front launched an offensive in the Central Highlands that devastated South Vietnam's forces. Surging casualties pushed up the desertion rate—in some sections of the South Vietnamese army it reached 50 percent—and undercut the government's already tenuous will to fight. Again the White House was consumed by talk of imminent collapse, unless the United States was willing to intensify its bombing of North Vietnam and dramatically expand its combat operations in the South. "You must take the fight to the enemy," insisted the chairman of the Joint Chiefs of Staff. "No one ever won a battle sitting on his ass."[30] And no one fought a land war without troops. On the day the Court issued its ruling in *Griswold*, the Joint Chiefs asked the president for another 150,000 men. LBJ hesitated—already the death toll was mounting, with 141 Americans killed in April and May alone—and then authorized the deployment of 100,000, with the implicit promise of more to come.

Up on Capitol Hill, meanwhile, Johnson's voting rights bill raced toward passage. The Selma campaign had created such overwhelming support that the administration's proposal went to the Senate with 66 sponsors, just one vote shy of the number needed to defeat a filibuster. The southerners tried anyway, but it was nothing more than posturing for the folks back home. On May 25, after five weeks of debate, 70 senators voted cloture. The following day the Senate passed the bill itself, 77 to 19, the only opposition coming from below the Mason-Dixon Line. The vote might have been just a little less humiliating had three southerners—Texas' Ralph Yarborough and Tennessee's Ross Bass and Al Gore—not sided with the majority.

For another month the bill languished in the House Rules Committee, under the thumb of Virginia's Howard Smith. But the pressure was too great to resist for long. On July 1 Smith's committee sent the proposal to the House floor. Eight days of maneuvering followed before the Speaker felt confident enough to call for a vote. "It's going to be close and it's going to be dangerous," LBJ told Martin Luther King as the roll call approached.[31] It was neither. On July 9 the House approved its version of the bill by a margin of 333 to 85.

Off it went to a conference committee, whose members spent three weeks smoothing out the differences with the Senate bill. The reconciled version cleared the House on August 3, the Senate on the 4th. At noon on the 6th Johnson went back up to the Capitol for the signing ceremony, this time to the Rotunda. His handlers had placed the presidential podium directly beneath John Trumbull's great painting of Cornwallis's surrender at Yorktown, a pointed reminder of the moment's revolutionary antecedents. Johnson drew the connection tighter still. "Today is a triumph for freedom as huge as any victory that has ever been won on any battlefield," he told the guests the White House had assembled. "Yet to seize the meaning of this day, we must recall darker times. Three and a half centuries ago the first Negroes arrived at Jamestown. They came in darkness and they came in chains. And today we strike away the last major shackle of those fierce and ancient bonds. Today the Negro story and the American story fuse and blend."[32]

On that last point the president was clearly wrong: the Negro story and the American story had been fused for centuries, the nation's fate shaped to a dramatic degree by the darkness and the chains. But he was right to see the Voting Rights Act as revolutionary. For more than sixty years the South's embrace of Jim Crow had made a mockery of the American promise. Now the southern system's central structures had been shattered, its legal authority destroyed by the blood sacrifice of ordinary people who dared to believe that they had, in fact, been endowed by their creator with certain inalienable rights. There were other bonds yet to break, as activists well knew. But in 1965 the civil rights movement had brought the American Revolution a dramatic step closer to fulfillment.

LBJ's decision to escalate the war in Vietnam marked a very different sort of revolution. For a decade American policy makers had tried to keep the Vietnamese tangle within the standard practices of containment. The United States would embrace a friendly government, even if it didn't enjoy public support. It would give that government considerable financial and military aid. It would dispatch American troops in a limited way to bolster a failing regime or block an insurgency it believed to be threatening. It had even followed the containment strategy to the edge of nuclear annihilation. Only once since the onset of the Cold War, though—in Korea in 1950—had a president committed the country to a full-scale war. And in that case he was reacting to a Communist state's unprovoked invasion of its neighbor. Johnson didn't think of himself as breaking with past policy. He believed, fairly enough, that he was keeping his predecessor's promises. But he was doing so in a new and horrifically dangerous way.

Then there was Estelle Griswold, committing a crime that no one wanted to prosecute on behalf of a practice that by the time her case was settled had become commonplace, and Bruce Scott, challenging a fragment of the federal government's sprawling bureaucracy. Yet they'd triggered a revolution too. Griswold hadn't changed American women's use of birth control; the pill had done that. She hadn't even changed Connecticut women's practices, though she undoubtedly made their decisions a bit easier. But she had fundamentally transformed the relationship between the government and a wide swath of its citizens. Gone was the state's right to police the morality of married couples' most intimate choices. In its place stood their right to be left alone. Scott hadn't come close to extending that right to gay Americans: he'd simply forced the government to be more precise in saying why it wouldn't hire him. Still, by breaking the government's linkage of homosexuality and immorality he'd opened the tiniest crack in its criminalization of gay life. And there could always be another Scott, and another Griswold, willing to push against the boundaries the justices had set, to see how far they could be moved, because once a revolution starts, there's no saying where it might end.

CHAPTER 7

TURNING AND TURNING

S omething was wrong. They were living in a graciously aging mansion at the foot of the Hollywood Hills, a seven-bedroom Spanish revival with fan-lit French doors, faded hardwood floors, and a tennis court nobody used. Her husband was at work on a book, his first, while Joan Didion paid the rent by writing articles for widely read magazines. Though the subjects were often prosaic—a profile of John Wayne, a trip to Hawaii, a weekend with the baby at her parents' house—she brought to them a distinctly literary sensibility, the details so carefully chosen, the sense of place so well developed, the prose so luminous they hardly seemed like magazine pieces at all. Editors had taken notice. There was talk of collecting her best articles into a book, to be published by one of the nation's most prestigious presses, the unmistakable sign of a career in ascent. Yet she was tumbling down.

It had happened before, in 1963. Didion had been in New York for seven years by then, most of that time on the staff of *Vogue*. That summer she'd cut herself off from her friends, left her phone unanswered, cried in the back seat of taxis and on the elevator up to her apartment, a twenty-eight-year-old overwhelmed by doubt and failure. Now the darkness was descending again, with one critical difference. This time the breakdown wasn't hers alone.

She was a fifth-generation Californian, raised on stories of her ancestors' long, lonely struggles to break the land they had crossed the continent to claim, to transform the arid Central Valley into the golden West. From their struggles came wealth, social standing—one of her earliest memories was of a crystal bottle of Elizabeth Arden perfume, a gift from her grandmother when she was six—and an abiding faith in individual achievement rooted in discipline, sacrifice, and strength of character. "Wagon-train morality," she'd called it in 1965, the year after she'd voted, passionately, for Barry Goldwater, and the year she began to fear that America was coming undone.[1]

For a while the feeling floated around the edges of her articles, seeping into her reporting in small, sad ways. She wrote of the pregnant bride too young to sip the cheap champagne the waiter poured to celebrate her Las Vegas wedding; the late-night caller on the LA radio show, talking of pornography; the drunken sailors in Honolulu, chatting up the girls. But it wasn't sufficient; more and more nothing she wrote seemed sufficient. Then, in the spring of 1967, her editor at the *Saturday Evening Post* suggested that she write a piece on the hippies who were pouring into San Francisco's Haight-Ashbury neighborhood. It struck her as an assignment she had to accept, a story she had to tell. So she packed her bags and drove up the coast.

She spent several weeks in the Haight, filling her notebooks with snatches of days that drifted away in the company of addicts and dealers, activists and manipulators, teenage deadheads and runaways so young they couldn't say with any conviction what they were running from. When she had enough she came home to her mansion at the foot of the Hollywood Hills, fought off her mounting desolation with gin and Dexedrine, and set to work, the article's crucial opening line waiting for her in a poem written half a century before, in another nation sliding into anarchy.

"The center was not holding," she wrote.[2]

Twist and Shout

BY THE TIME the Supreme Court handed down its *Griswold* ruling in June 1965, the contours of private life were already shifting. That year the birth rate fell to its lowest level since 1940, thanks in large part to the widening popularity of the pill. The taboo against premarital sex continued to erode: almost eight percent of the babies born that year had been conceived out of wedlock, the highest percentage ever recorded by the U.S. Census Bureau. The divorce rate rose as well, to a figure unmatched in more than a decade. And another health scare over birth defects, this one driven by a virulent strain of measles, intensified the interest in easing abortion restrictions that had started with Sherri Finkbine's ordeal with thalidomide three years earlier. Three days before the justices announced *Griswold*, the editors of *Life* put another young mother like Finkbine on their cover, one of two the magazine had followed in the same California hospital on the day they had abortions for fear of the measles they'd contracted. Technically they'd broken California law, which didn't allow for abortions in cases of fetal abnormalities. But according to subsequent polls, 56 percent of Americans thought that such laws ought to be changed.

In its popular culture, though, the United States clung to traditional standards. The nation's most watched television show was a Western about a widowed father and his three grown sons in 1860s Nevada; the most popular movie a musical about a widowed military man in 1930s Austria, the nanny he hired straight from the convent, and the seven charming children he placed in her care, who had a remarkable ability to harmonize while dressed in the drapes. Even rock and roll kept to the safe side. For a month in mid-1965 a new British band, the Rolling Stones, snarled its way to the top of the charts with a song steeped in the overt sexuality of the Delta blues. But the Stones were no match for the Beatles, who mounted a record-breaking tour that summer in support of their two latest albums, both packed with hits innocent enough to play at the most sheltered teenybopper's slumber party.

Then again, maybe there was more to the Beatles than catchy choruses and incessant merchandising. That's what Ken Kesey decided, at least, as he sat up near the rafters of San Francisco's cavernous concert hall, the Cow Palace, on the last day of August 1965, listening to the teenyboppers scream.

Not that Kesey was a fan. There was a time when he might have liked the Beatles, back in his all-American days in suburban Springfield,

Oregon, when he was wrestling for his high school team, starring in the plays, and dating the girl he'd marry a year after graduation. But that was in the early 1950s, when the Fab Four were still in knee socks and Kesey hadn't yet decided to be a novelist. Only after he'd finished his degree at the University of Oregon in 1957 had the idea taken hold of him. Somehow he'd managed to win a fellowship to the creative writing program at Stanford, a major coup by any standard. They'd arrived in the autumn of 1958, he and his high school sweetheart, into the rarified world of Stanford's young sophisticates, where everyone despised pop culture's soul-crushing banality. Had the Beatles been touring in 1958, Kesey's new friends would have hated them.

The problem was the sophisticates didn't have a clear sense of how to break free of the mainstream. Allen Ginsberg and his acolytes had established a little colony in San Francisco's North Beach neighborhood, an easy drive from campus. But full-fledged hipsters were a bit too avant-garde for the university set. Instead they settled for earnest talk of an artist's responsibility to challenge the status quo, their conviction fueled by artfully prepared dinners in the peasant tradition and bottles of red wine: a tasteful rebellion, suitable for someone who one day might want tenure—until it was interrupted by Kesey's discovery of LSD.

Lysergic acid diethylamide, the synthetic version of a chemical compound found in a fungus, causes overpowering hallucinations when ingested: "an uninterrupted stream of fantastic pictures, extraordinary shapes with intense kaleidoscopic plays of colors," as its creator, Albert Hofmann, put it after his first LSD trip in April 1943. In the 1950s the drug seeped into psychiatry, where it was used to treat the emotionally stunted; into psychology, where clinicians used it to study psychotic states; and into the CIA, whose operatives thought it might be used to enhance interrogation techniques. And it secured a toehold in the literary world, thanks to British writer Aldous Huxley, who took a variant under a psychiatrist's care in 1953. Huxley decided that he wasn't simply hallucinating—he was opening his mind to a level of consciousness the modern world had blocked, "a radical self-transcendence and a deeper understanding of the nature of things," as he put it in his book on the experience, *The Doors of Perception.*[3]

In 1960 Kesey walked through the door too, with a little help from his friends at the CIA. The agency was secretly funding a research project on hallucinogenics at the VA hospital near the Stanford campus. The researchers needed observable subjects—needed them so badly they were offering volunteers $75 a day. So Kesey signed up. At first it was all tightly controlled: the subjects lying in hospital beds, watching the colors cascading in front of them and the walls bending around them, while the doctors took notes. But Kesey was feeling an overwhelming sense of freedom. "We were beautiful," he said of his first LSD trips. "Naked and helpless and sensitive as a snake after skinning, but far more human than the shining knightmare that had stood creaking in previous parade rest. We were alive and life was us."[4] Naturally he wanted to share the wonder. The doctors weren't offering free samples. Not long after he started the tests, though, he got a part-time job as a night attendant on the psych ward, just for the extra income of course. There the control wasn't tight at all.

Some of his Stanford clique weren't interested in trying the capsules Kesey brought home. But there were takers enough that he soon had his own little turned-on colony, the finely crafted dinners tossed aside for vats of venison chili laced with LSD, the earnest talk replaced by technicolor visions of liberation. He was writing a new novel too, better than anything he'd written before, a riotous book set in a ward modeled on the one where he'd been spending his nights, its narrator and single triumphant character a schizophrenic Native American taken straight from a phantasm he'd seen during one of his now-regular trips. *One Flew Over the Cuckoo's Nest* was published in 1962 to rapturous reviews. It was a "brilliant first novel," gushed *Time*, "a roar of protest against middlebrow society's Rules and the invisible Rulers who enforce them."[5]

In *Cuckoo's Nest* San Francisco's rebels saw a kindred spirit. So they started drifting down from North Beach and its even hipper offshoot around Haight and Ashbury Streets, where the art-school kids had traded the beatniks' beloved jazz for a blast of rock and roll and their somber style for a burst of flamboyant Victoriana—young men in stiff-collared shirts and riding coats, young women in flowing velvet dresses and lace-up boots, and everybody with their hair way too long—a generational shift the older hipsters marked by calling the new kids hippies. One by one they found their way to Kesey's door: fabled figures like Neal Cassady, the model for the central character in Jack Kerouac's *On the Road*; up-and-comers like Jerry Garcia, a wild-haired young guitarist who was trying to get a band together; aspiring writers who wanted a piece of *Cuckoo's Nest* magic; and assorted hangers-on whose only goal was to be on the cutting edge of cool. Kesey was happy to have them all. So happy, in fact, that in 1963 he used the book's royalties to buy a comfortable cabin on a secluded lot in the hills fifteen miles east of Stanford and invited anyone who wanted to come along with him. Off they went, the entire ragged clan, up to the redwoods to write and create and bend their minds whichever way they felt like going.

By then others were picking up on LSD too, so much so that authorities began to fear that they were losing control of the drug. So they tried to rein it in, not by banning it but by insisting that it be administered by professionals. In the summer of 1962 the American Medical Association issued a public warning that recreational use could lead to prolonged psychotic states. Los Angeles County sheriffs raided a church in South Gate whose pastor was supposedly tripping out his congregants. There was even a scandal at Harvard, where a young lecturer in psychology, Timothy Leary, was accused of administering the drug to subjects without a doctor's supervision, and of using it himself.

In fact he'd done more than that. Since 1960, when he'd first taken an LSD variant, Leary had been proselytizing for the mystical power of hallucinogens, an idea he took straight from his reading of Huxley. Partly he spread the word through lectures and articles in scholarly journals; in one he suggested that public officials spike the nation's water supply with LSD. But nothing could match the real thing. In private Leary became something of a high-end distributor, using the connections Harvard gave him to quietly offer the hallucinogenic experience to those culture brokers he thought would benefit most from the transformation of consciousness: among his most devout converts was Allen Ginsberg, whose first Leary-induced trip was so enlightening he stripped off his clothes and said that he was going to teach the world how to love. It was one thing to turn on a hipster poet, though, another to turn on the undergrads. When Harvard officials learned in April 1963 that Leary's closest collaborator had given a student LSD, the university fired them both. But Leary refused to surrender. Within a few months he'd convinced an heir to the Mellon family fortune to underwrite an independent institute where his work could continue unimpeded. "LSD," Leary told the press, "is more important than Harvard."[6]

Kesey couldn't help but hear about Leary; his firing made all the papers, as did his fancy new institute. Kesey appreciated the effort, but he also had some reservations. The point wasn't to move LSD from one lab to another but to break it out of the lab altogether, to carry it to freedom, and to let it carry its users to freedom too. That's what people needed to see: not some pseudoscientific study but the whole freaking, mind-blowing freedom Kesey had slipped out of the psych ward. The AMA didn't get that. Harvard didn't get that. Even Leary didn't get that. But Kesey's crew did.

The first road show set off in the summer of 1964. Kesey's second novel was to appear in July, and somebody suggested that they drive to the publisher's New York office to celebrate. They bought an old school bus fitted out with beds and a stove, wired it for sound, carved a hole in the roof so they could climb outside whenever they wanted, and one afternoon painted the thing wild colors like the ones that flashed before them when they were tripping. In the end it was such a howl, twenty zoned-out hipsters careening across the country on a psychedelic freedom ride, pranking the multitudes as they went: Cassady racing the bus backward through downtown Phoenix; the whole stoned crew taking a dip on the Black side of a segregated beach in Louisiana; Kesey up on the roof playing the flute for the stiffs on the streets of Manhattan; Cassady again, wheeling the bus up to one of New York's most exclusive restaurants so its tight-assed diners could see what they were missing.

Then they were home, back among the redwoods, and it wasn't

enough to ride in a painted bus anymore. Now they painted the trees too, and sometimes their faces. They bought trunk-loads of costume-shop clothes: not the Haight's Oscar Wilde imitation but plumes and boas, sashes and epaulets, bright green tights and tricornered hats that no one in his right mind would wear. Kesey stopped writing so he could concentrate on making a movie about their epic bus ride. But nothing happened, because making a movie wasn't enough either. He wanted something more, something bigger, though he couldn't say precisely what it was until the Beatles came to town to close out the summer of 1965.

Going to the concert was meant to be another prank: the famous novelist and his ultra-cool friends rolling into San Francisco already stoned, strolling into the Cow Palace in their tights and boas, floating through a sea of teenyboppers. But when the Beatles bounded on stage everything flipped around. The boppers started screaming, a piercing squeal that rose from the floor to where Kesey's crew was sitting, high above them. Once they got going they couldn't stop, not even when the boys launched into their set. And then there were the lights. Not the stage lights, which were bright enough, but the flashbulbs of the girls' Instamatics, thousands of them, bursting at random around the arena. Now some of the boppers down front were passing out and had to be carried off, and a few others were scrambling up out of the audience, security guards scrambling after them, the girls weaving and shrieking across the stage. They were tripping. That's what he was seeing, Kesey decided: ten thousand orgiastic teenyboppers on a pop-induced trip. If the Beatles could create such a scene—the squeaky-clean Beatles—imagine what he could do.

The Next Step

DREAMS OF A decidedly different sort had floated among Martin Luther King's advisers in the summer of 1965. Bayard Rustin was still calling for the movement to replace protest with politics, and SNCC was still sniping about SCLC's tendency to favor dramatic confrontations over the hard work of organizing the grass roots. But King's inner circle was convinced that the Selma campaign had elevated him to an extraordinary level, turning him into "a leader now not merely of Negroes," his aide Stanley Levison wrote in April, "but of millions of whites in motion."[7] Surely the moment demanded that he extend nonviolent protest, not back away from it. It was time, they decided, for King to turn his enormous moral power against the racial injustices that ran through the urban North.

Experience dictated that protests be focused on a single site. King spent most of July touring possibilities, starting with three promising days in Chicago—fifteen thousand people turned out to hear him speak in downtown's Grant Park—followed by a swing through Cleveland, Philadelphia, and New York: the last an obvious choice, except that Harlem's powerful congressman, Adam Clayton Powell, made it clear he didn't want King invading his turf. He finished with a stop in Washington, DC, on August 6, so he could stand by Lyndon Johnson's side as the president signed the Voting Rights Act, the final triumph of the Selma campaign. Five days later a California highway patrolman pulled over a ten-year-old Buick he saw weaving down Avalon Boulevard, on the southeastern edge of Los Angeles' sprawling African American neighborhood, an area called Watts.

It was hard to say when things went wrong. Maybe when the patrolman asked the driver, twenty-one-year-old Marquette Frye, to walk a straight line and he offered to do it backward, playing to the crowd that had gathered round, and they laughed, which got the cop's back up. Maybe when Frye's mother appeared, screaming at both her son and the patrolman, and the cop arrested her too, manhandling her into the patrol car, and the laughing stopped. Maybe when Frye refused to get into the car with her and the cop hit him in the head and the jeering started. Maybe when the backups arrived, driving the motorcycles onto the sidewalk to split open the crowd, and someone picked up a rock and hurled it at the officers. Or maybe it had started decades earlier, when the authorities decided to treat the city's African Americans as if they were a colonized people, the police their occupying army.

After the Fryes were taken away the rage raced along Avalon, where there were buses to stone, cars to assault, and shop windows to shatter. That night the Los Angeles police cordoned off the surrounding eight blocks, in hopes that the unrest would play itself out, as it had in Harlem the year before. But the next day was worse, the night cataclysmic. At dusk the crowds took control of the streets across Watts: sweeping down its business strips, attacking the few whites who happened to be in the area, looting and torching white-owned stores, then driving off the firefighters so the blazes would burn through the night. Around 3:00 a.m. on August 13 the LAPD tried to reclaim the neighborhood with a massive show of force. But the crowds were larger, and more than willing to meet violence with violence. By morning more than a dozen policemen had been injured, and the streets weren't close to clear.

Shortly thereafter the mayor formally requested that the governor send in the National Guard. The first of 14,000 heavily armed soldiers began arriving in Watts that evening. Immediately the death toll started to rise: at least fourteen African Americans were killed on the troops' first two nights on the street, more than double the number of Americans killed in Vietnam that week. By August 17 the area had been pacified. But emotions hadn't. In white neighborhoods people raced to buy guns amid rumors that Black mobs were going to stream across the color line, while Watts burned with talk of the fires next time. King heard the threats himself during a hastily arranged appearance at a Watts social center on August 18. He'd come at the request of a group of LA ministers, who thought his presence might calm the community. It didn't. "All over America, the Negro must join hands . . . ," he began. "And burn," someone shouted from the crowd. King left seriously shaken, and more convinced than ever that his next step had to be out of the South. "If [we] don't go north," he told Levison as he headed home to Atlanta, "we're damned."[8]

For the balance of the month King's advisers worked through their options. Los Angeles was too tense to manage a movement, New York too politicized, Cleveland and Philadelphia not big enough media draws. That left Chicago: three and a half million people, a quarter of them African Americans, spread among a 234-square-mile patchwork of hyper-segregated neighborhoods; another three million whites in the segregated suburbs; one of the country's most powerful politicians, Richard J. Daley, in the mayor's office; and a vibrant civil rights campaign already in motion. On September 1—the day after Ken Kesey's revelation at the Cow Palace—King made the official announcement. "I have faith," he told reporters, "that Chicago could . . . well become the metropolis where a meaningful nonviolent movement could arouse the conscience of this nation to deal realistically with the northern ghetto."[9]

But faith alone wouldn't do. King and his advisers had built their campaigns in Birmingham and Selma on a single central demand each—desegregating downtown stores, registering to vote—that they knew would trigger official resistance. In Chicago local activists had spent the previous three years locked in a bitter battle with city hall over the discriminatory policies of the public schools. The logical step was to follow their lead. But the autumn's planning sessions swept right by that possibility. Obviously King would take on the schools, argued the project's director, James Bevel, along with the segregation of housing, the high rate of unemployment, the concentration of poverty, and the injustices that ran through the welfare system. Precisely how they'd tackle such a tangle of issues wasn't clear. Bevel was sure of the outcome, though. "We're going to create a new city," he told the SCLC staff in October. "Nobody will stop us."[10]

The campaign began with a perfectly choreographed move. Around the first of the year Bevel's staffers surreptitiously rented King a $90 a month apartment in the middle of Chicago's West Side ghetto. On a frigid day in late January 1966 King brought a scrum of reporters through the urine-stained hallway—a consequence of the lockless front door, which permitted street-corner drunks to come in when they needed to relieve themselves—up three flights of creaking stairs, to his bare-boned new home. His first evening he opened his door to whoever wanted to stop by; for a while he sat with six members of the local gang, the Vice Lords, talking about nonviolence. The following morning he walked the neighborhood in the bitter cold, while the trailing reporters ferreted out the stories he hoped would illustrate the burdens poverty imposed.

The momentum soon faded. Part of the problem was King's crushing schedule. He was constantly slipping out of Chicago for appearances around the country, and when he was in town he spent much of his time at events that didn't fuel the movement: a lecture on the Black family at the University of Chicago; dinner with Mahalia Jackson; a courtesy call at Elijah Muhammad's South Side mansion. Worse, SCLC couldn't always read the complex dynamics that shaped urban inequality. In his first major move King led a dramatic takeover of a dilapidated apartment building near his, claiming that the tenants' right to decent living conditions trumped the owner's right to profit from their rents. But it turned out he wasn't the slumlord King needed him to be; he was an eighty-one-year-old invalid saddled with a property that didn't cover his costs. He'd be happy to give King title to the building, he said, as long as SCLC paid the mortgage.

Nothing hurt the campaign more, though, than its breadth. With so many issues to tackle, it couldn't focus its energies. For his part, Dick Daley wanted to make sure it stayed that way. In private the mayor was livid that King had come to Chicago. But in public he was conciliatory, even supportive. "All of us, like Dr. King, are trying to end slums," he told the press when King moved in. "We are not perfect but we feel we have done more than any other metropolitan city in the country."[11] To prove his continuing commitment, he unveiled a major initiative he said would eliminate blight citywide by the end of 1967. It was a ridiculous pledge, given that 40 percent of African American housing didn't meet minimal standards. But the point wasn't to turn Chicago into a model city; it was to make clear that Daley was no Bull Connor. And without a Bull Connor there'd be no confrontation, no spectacular footage playing on the nightly news, no sympathy marches sweeping the country, no proof that nonviolence offered African Americans a better alternative than the rage that had swept through Watts, no way to begin building the new city Bevel had promised.

King's advisers weren't worried. Hadn't Birmingham been on the brink of collapse right before its transformative moment? Hadn't the Selma campaign stumbled toward its defining event? What was to say that Chicago wouldn't work that way too? "We haven't gotten things under control," Andrew Young admitted in a late winter staff meeting. "The strategy hasn't emerged yet, but now we know what we're dealing with and eventually we'll come up with the answers."[12]

Sweet Home Chicago

ONE OF KING's aides had suggested the idea in February 1966, less than a month after King's arrival. But the campaign was considering so many approaches then, it was hard for one particular tactic to gain much traction. Into the mix it went, along with the proposed tenant union and the mass rally at Soldier Field and the march on city hall, until everything started coming undone, and the staffers knew they had to do something dramatic.

The first crisis no one saw coming. Since the debacle at the 1964 Democratic convention, SNCC's factions had been arguing over the organization's direction. Still, most of the activists who came to its annual election of officers in mid-May 1966 assumed they'd be reelecting the current chairman, John Lewis. In the first round of voting they did just that. But someone demanded another vote, and in the chaos that followed differences turned into wrenching divisions. Well into the night the factions fought it out, Lewis clinging to the group's founding principles, his opponents insisting that the time had come to abandon dreams of the Beloved Community for the hard work of empowering Black America. In the end Lewis came toppling down, replaced by a relentlessly charismatic twenty-four-year-old named Stokely Carmichael.

Carmichael couldn't quite match Lewis's extraordinary commitment to the cause. But he came close. Born in Trinidad, raised largely in Harlem, he'd first come into contact with the civil rights movement through New York's radical circles. He'd joined SNCC as a Freedom Rider in 1961, then spent portions of three years organizing in the Mississippi Delta, the most dangerous work the movement had to offer, before becoming director of a new grassroots campaign in rural Lowndes County, Alabama, in 1965. There his signal achievement was the creation of an all-Black political party designed to give the county's African American majority control of public affairs, its fearlessness represented by the sinewy black panther Carmichael chose at its symbol. Eleven days before the SNCC elections the Lowndes County Freedom Organization put together its first slate of candidates, a milestone Carmichael marked with a blistering declaration of independence. "We're going to take power in Lowndes County and rule," he declared. "We don't even want to integrate. . . . Integration is a subterfuge for white supremacy."[13]

Then he was just another activist, drawing on the Black nationalist tradition to imagine a dramatic reworking of the deep South's political order. Two weeks later he was the public face of SNCC's militant turn. The press's take was almost universally hostile. Here was the new Malcolm X, the reports ran, the latest manifestation of the hate that hate produced. Carmichael countered with a spectacular display of defiance. He was in the middle of a highly publicized march across Mississippi in mid-June—for several days King had walked alongside him—when the local sheriff arrested him for lack of a permit. He spent the afternoon in jail, made bail, and was back with the march in time for its evening rally. About 600 people were waiting for him. "This is the twenty-seventh time I've been arrested, and I ain't going to jail no more!" he shouted from the makeshift stage. "What we gonna start saying now is 'Black Power.'"

"Black Power!" the crowd roared back.

"That's right," he replied. "That's what we want, Black Power. We don't have to be ashamed of it. . . . We have begged the president. We've begged the federal government—that's all we've been doing, begging and begging. It's time we stand up and take over. Every courthouse in Mississippi ought to be burned down tomorrow to get rid of the dirt and the mess. From now on, when they ask you what you want, you know what to tell 'em. What do you want?"

"Black Power!" they shouted again and again and again.[14]

The firestorm started the following morning. Sparked by the *New York Times*'s front-page story on the previous evening's rally, it leaped from paper to paper, magazine to magazine, onto the nightly news, and into national politics; the outrage intensifying with each repetition of Carmichael's incendiary phrase. This was more than militancy, opinion makers insisted. It was the poisonous politics of extremists "inching dangerously toward a philosophy of black separatism . . . almost indistinguishable from the wild-eyed doctrines of the Black Muslims and heavy with intimations of racial hatred," as *Time* magazine put it in its blistering story. "In this context the Gandhian concept of nonviolence espoused by Martin Luther King is in danger of crumbling."[15]

At first King's advisers weren't sure how to respond. They tried quiet diplomacy, hoping that Carmichael might be reined in by a well-placed word. They tried carefully constructed public statements meant to reassure whites that Black Power was an aberration, a reflection of frustration rather than a wholesale rejection of integration. They even tried moral condemnation, the most powerful rhetorical weapon King could wield. None of it worked. By the end of June, Black Power had swept from SNCC to CORE, whose chairman dismissed nonviolence as "a dying philosophy," a striking turn for an organization founded by radical pacifists. The NAACP's director, Roy Wilkins, replied with the flat of his hand. Black Power is "a reverse Mississippi," he said, "a reverse Hitler, a reverse Ku Klux Klan. . . . We of the NAACP will have none of this."[16]

That's when King's analysis sharpened, just as the movement seemed to be breaking apart. Sharp words weren't enough, he told the *Times* on July 9. Black Power's militancy had to be met with "militant nonviolence," acts of civil disobedience "extreme enough to stop the flow of a city." Precisely what those acts might be he couldn't yet say. But whatever the tactic, the campaign wouldn't stop until local, state, and federal authorities had taken vigorous action against the structures that sustained the ghettos. Anything less wouldn't do, not if the nation wanted to defuse the anger on which Black Power rested. "Now people have to understand the choice is no longer between nice little meetings or nonviolence," he insisted. "It is between militant nonviolence and riots."[17]

Two days later the violence came home. It started with a tussle over a fire hydrant in a poor Black neighborhood a mile or so west of downtown Chicago: cops on one side, kids on another, both sides' emotions frayed by the heat. By the time King stumbled onto the conflict while driving to the evening's mass meeting, there were six kids in jail and angry crowds in the street. He spent the rest of the night trying to defuse the situation with talk of meaningful reform peacefully secured, mostly from the sweltering sanctuary of the local Baptist church. But a portion of the people he'd drawn to his impromptu rally walked out on him, while others laughed at his naivete. And when the reporters left to file their stories around midnight, they had to be escorted out of the church under armed guard.

The crowds came out again the next night, ripping through the neighborhood shopping strip, smashing windows, looting stores, pelting the cops with bricks and stones when they tried to intervene. On the third night the police brought out the heavy weapons—shotguns, machine guns, and thousands of rounds of ammunition—so they could reclaim the streets. Instead the violence surged along the ghetto's sinews: north to the projects, where the cops engaged in an hour-long battle with snipers, and three miles west into the area where SCLC had rooted itself six months before. King spent the evening driving the neighborhood with Andrew Young, pleading for peace. But no one was listening. In the course of the night dozens of people were injured, two killed. One was a twenty-eight-year-old man gunned down while looting, the other a fourteen-year-old girl hit by a random shot while walking with friends three blocks from King's apartment.

King came home to an early morning strategy session, a first attempt to shape the response he had to make. Through the next day the discussions ran, as the governor flooded the West Side with a hundred truckloads of National Guardsmen whose presence reduced the night's troubles to a sprinkling of incidents. The planning continued through the tense weekend that followed, when everyone feared that the violence would flare again, and into the following week, when there was more and more talk of the Chicago campaign's failures. Gradually the focus tightened on to a single dramatic tactic. At the end of July, King said, SCLC would launch a series of marches into white neighborhoods on the city's far West Side. The demonstrations would target realtors who refused to serve African Americans looking for homes, the front line in a series of barriers sustaining the urban color line. But confronting realtors wasn't really the point. By marching into the bungalow belt the movement would seize up the city, just as King had said it would.

King was in Atlanta when 250 protesters headed into the Gage Park neighborhood, due west of Chicago's sprawling South Side ghetto, on Saturday morning, July 30. They marched almost three miles—along a business strip and through a large public park—without any trouble. From there it was only four blocks to the realty office they planned to picket. But the way was mobbed with some 400 whites. At first they settled for booing and jeering and the occasional chant of "white power" from behind the thin line the police had established in the middle of the street. Then the protesters reached the realtor's shuttered storefront, and the whites started throwing rocks and bottles. Both of the march's leaders were hit, one of them knocked to the ground. With the march broken by the violence, the protesters rushed out of Gage Park under police protection.

On Sunday afternoon they returned. This time they came prepared for trouble: instead of walking into the neighborhood they drove in a seventy-car caravan to the public park, so they'd only have four blocks to march. But there were even more whites waiting for them than there had been the day before: upwards of 3,000, the police said later, though the streets were so packed no one could know for sure. Into the thick of them the marchers moved, surrounded by cops in riot gear, as the chants grew louder—"Burn them like Jews!" some shouted—and the rocks and bottles came raining down again, now with beer cans and cherry bombs scattered in.[18] Down went a twenty-two-year-old patrolman, his hand cut open by shattering glass; a fifty-seven-year-old minister struck in the face with a brick; a middle-aged nun, blood soaking through her habit. Still the line kept moving. Twice the cops had to break blockades the mob set up in the protesters' path. But they couldn't—or wouldn't—stop the whites who swarmed into the park as soon as the marchers had cleared it, surged around the cars they'd left behind, and set two dozen of them on fire. In the end forty-five protesters were rushed to the local emergency room. Most of the rest had to slog back to the ghetto on foot. When they reached the color line a knot of supporters was waiting for them, singing "We Shall Overcome."

Suddenly SCLC had the confrontation the Chicago campaign had been missing: peaceful protesters on one side, rabid racists on the other, with the resulting bloodshed splashed across the nation's front pages. But a weekend wasn't enough. On Tuesday and Wednesday, August 2 and 3, organizers sent marchers into the north West Side, less than three miles south of the Cahills' house on Eddy Street. Again massive white mobs filled the streets, shouting the same vicious taunts and slogans, but they stopped short of the South Side's violence. So the movement swung the protests back to Gage Park. The next march would be on Friday, August 5, King announced. It would follow the same route as the previous Sunday, with one critical addition. He would lead it.

There were already thousands of whites in the park when King arrived late that afternoon. As soon as they saw him getting out of his car they started chanting, "Kill the niggers! Kill the niggers!" and "We Want Martin Luther Coon!" Then the debris arced over the police lines—more rocks and bottles and cherry bombs—and something hit him above the base of his neck, a blow hard enough he stumbled a step and fell to one knee. There he stayed for a moment or two, the nation's Nobel laureate with his head bowed down and his hand splayed out on the trampled grass, until he felt strong enough to get back on his feet and march into the mob he'd come to save from itself. "I have never in my life seen such hatred," he declared at the protest's end. "Not in Mississippi or Alabama. This is a terrible thing."[19]

There were more marches over the weekend, more mobs, more violence, North Side and South Side both, the ugliness now set against the news of King's stoning, which rocketed around the world. In the chaos at least one of his aides could see the spirit of Selma descending. So he took that campaign's pivotal decision and brought it up to Chicago. "I have counted up the costs," Jesse Jackson proclaimed at a Monday night rally. "My life. Bevel's life. Even Dr. King's life. Over and against the generation and the continuation of a kind of sin that's going to internally disrupt this country and possibly the world. I have counted the cost! I'm going to Cicero!"[20]

In form and function it was pure imitation, a mimicking of the recklessly brilliant move Bevel had made after the first burst of violence in Selma, when he announced that the movement would march to Montgomery, a fifty-mile trek across Klan country. Now Jackson had announced that protesters would march into Chicago's most notoriously racist suburb while the cops who'd surrounded them in Gage Park stood on the other side of the city line, prevented by law and reason from following along. There'd be massive mobs waiting, just as there had been in 1951, when the Clark family's arrival at their newly rented apartment had triggered rioting so severe the governor had had to call out the National Guard. In the years since, the hatred had shown no signs of abating: only three months earlier four white teenagers had bludgeoned a Black seventeen-year-old to death with a baseball bat simply because he'd been walking down the street alone. The Cook County sheriff matched Jackson's counting with his own calculation. If the movement marched into Cicero, he told reporters, someone was going to be killed.

That possibility city hall couldn't abide. Since the marches had started, Dick Daley had offered the movement nothing beyond police protection. Less than a day after Jackson's announcement he called in the press to say that while he fully supported the right to protest, it would be far better to negotiate a solution to the movement's demands. He'd already arranged for some of Chicago's most influential men to meet the following week. He sincerely hoped that King and his aides would come too, along with representatives of the city's realtors, so that they could all sit and reason together. In the meantime SCLC ought to hold off on its Cicero march, so as not to put lives at risk when discussions would do. Surely Dr. King could see the logic of that.

He could. In every campaign he'd waged, there had come a point when the pressure became too great for the authorities to bear. The Montgomery buses running empty. Kids in the streets of Birmingham. A line of marchers on the Edmund Pettus Bridge. That's when the breakthroughs came: when the powerful couldn't withstand the powerless anymore. For the balance of the week the movement staged some of its largest protests yet around Chicago, though none near Cicero, in a final push before the negotiations began, while King's closest advisers hammered out a list of demands meant to open up the city's housing market. On Wednesday morning, August 17—eighteen days after the first cataclysmic march into Gage Park—they walked into the suitably neutral ground of the Episcopal diocese's elegant cathedral house and took their seats among the bankers, industrialists, labor leaders, and clergymen the mayor had handpicked to attend.

There were some preliminaries, the predictable posturing of powerful men in each other's company. Then one of King's aides presented the movement's demands. Would the marches end if these demands were met? Daley asked.

Yes, King replied. Was the mayor ready to do so?

Daley picked up the sheet the aide handed to him, read it aloud so everyone in the room could hear the terms again, and said that he was.

It took only a moment for King's circle to realize what had happened. Daley had given them everything—and nothing at all: no guarantees, no timetables, not a single assurance beyond his word that he would fulfill the promises he'd just made. As they started to press him on implementation, though, the realtors' representatives cut in to say that they couldn't go along with the mayor's appeasement of the protesters. Immediately the conversation swung around to the realtors' intransigence. Through the rest of the morning session the pressure built, not only from Daley but also from the clergymen and businessmen he'd brought in to back him, the weight of consensus crushing down until the realtors finally buckled. The meeting's chair, the president of a major railroad line, gave them some time to caucus. When they returned they put on the table two concessions that dovetailed with Daley's: they'd publicly support the principle of neighborhood integration, they said, and they'd urge their members not to discriminate against African American customers. "This is nothing," King hissed to a colleague.[21] But the chair pointed out that both the mayor and the realtors had now accepted the demands King had presented, so there were no grounds for continued demonstrations. And the trap Daley had set snapped shut.

They staved off defeat for a week, first by insisting that a subcommittee draw up the details of a settlement, then by reviving the threat of Cicero. But the threat had been hollowed out: SCLC couldn't possibly mount the march, not when any one of fifty prominent Chicagoans could say to the press that SCLC was inviting horrific violence in pursuit of goals it had already won. On Thursday, August 25, the subcommittee finalized a ten-point accord that codified the pledges made at the previous week's meeting. On Friday King signed it.

At the subsequent news conference he gave the deal a furious spin. "The total eradication of housing discrimination has been made possible," he said. "Never before has such a far-reaching move been made."[22] But anyone who read the accord knew better. After six months of organizing and a month of marches, after the bricks and bottles and howling mobs, the movement had come away with a set of paper promises. That evening King led the campaign's final, tepid rally. In the morning he flew home to Atlanta, leaving behind a color line he hadn't been able to break, a system of segregation and domination he couldn't destroy, a city he couldn't transform, and festering wounds he had failed to salve.

The Acid Test

KESEY IMAGINED A happening. There'd be rock and roll to bring in the kids, and a light show so wild it would blow their minds, and surreal images flashing up on the walls—snatches of his half-made movie, maybe—and loops of prerecorded sound when the bands weren't play-ing, and lots of LSD, and everyone would be dancing and tripping in a psychedelic bacchanal. But organization wasn't Kesey's forte, so the first attempts were little more than house parties. Then he connected with a couple of conceptual artists from Haight-Ashbury who knew this young promoter looking for his big break. Together they actually did the things you had to do, like renting a performance space and put-ting out advertising. And in one insane weekend in January 1966, at a hulking old union hall down near San Francisco's Fisherman's Wharf, the whole damn thing came together.

The artists gave the weekend its name—the Trips Festival, they called it—the promoter its headliners: the Grateful Dead, fronted by that Gar-cia kid who used to hang around Kesey's house; and Big Brother and the Holding Company, who could have used a better vocalist, if only one were available. Kesey's crew delivered the hallucinogenic light show, the dizzying images on the vaulted ceiling, the synthesized soundtrack, and the fistfuls of acid they passed around in a shopping bag. The final touch was brought by the thousands of people who crushed into the hall every night, a mass of sweat-soaked flesh out on the dance floor, who made the scene everything Kesey had hoped it would be.

After that the trips took on a life of their own. Almost every weekend the promoters put on another festival as frenzied as the first: Jefferson Airplane at the Fillmore, Great Society at the Avalon Ballroom, Coun-try Joe and the Fish at the Winterland, the Dead everywhere. From the concert halls the crowds poured into Haight-Ashbury's little hippie col-ony, the dabblers to wander through the thrift stores and head shops, the true believers to join the countercultural revolution the festivals had put on display. By the summer of 1966 the neighborhood was teem-ing with self-proclaimed poets, would-be musicians, radical actors and militant mimes, printmakers, shopkeepers, dope dealers, and a lot of kids from the 'burbs, come to the Haight to smash out the windows of mainstream America and climb through the gaping frame to freedom.

But even shattered windows can be barred. There was no saying what triggered the great acid panic of 1966. It wasn't Kesey, who two nights before the trip festival got arrested on a North Beach roof with three and half grams of marijuana in his possession, and rather than risk five years in prison fled down the coast to Mexico, leaving behind a blitzed-out suicide note no one believed. It wasn't the Haight either, since almost nobody beyond the hip noticed what was happening there. Somehow the panic just hit, fueled by breathless news reports of an LSD epidemic among the sons and daughters of the comfortable classes, complete with a *Life* photo spread featuring a pretty LA teenager writhing on the floor in the middle of a bad trip, and the lurid story of a New York City medical student too high to remember killing his mother. Not one but three congressional committees held highly publicized hearings, with the nation's leading acidhead, Timothy Leary, telling the Senate Subcommittee on Juvenile Delinquency that one in three undergrads had dropped acid. It was a ridiculously inflated estimate—the actual figure was around one percent—but the *New York Times* duly put it on its front page. In the end Congress decided not to take any action, for fear of criminalizing all those college kids. California's legislators didn't have the same compunction. At the height of the panic, in April 1966, they pushed through a law making the manufacturing and distribution of LSD a felony, its possession a misdemeanor, the prohibitions to take effect on October 6.

The obvious response was to pry apart the bars. In late September two of the Haight's more prominent figures sent around the neighborhood a declaration of independence. "We hold these experiences to be self-evident," the flyer read, "that all is equal, that the creation endows us with certain inalienable rights, that among these are: the freedom of the body, the pursuit of joy, and the expansion of consciousness, and that to secure these rights, we the citizens of the earth declare our love and compassion for all conflicting hate-carrying men and women of the world."[23] To celebrate their liberation, they were going to hold "a love pageant" in the neighborhood park on the day LSD became illegal. They gave it a few political touches, the best the bouquets they brought to give to the cops who'd been assigned to crowd control. For the most part, though, they simply carried the trips festivals out of the clubs and into public view. The

Dead and Big Brother each played a set, while seven or eight hundred of the Haight's devotees danced in the grass to prove they weren't afraid.

That was such an encouraging result that the Haight's activists decided to stage a bolder version. So they lined up the hipsters' great guru Allen Ginsberg, who said he'd do some ritual chanting; Timothy Leary, who wanted to lecture on acid's transcendence; a radical activist from Berkeley named Jerry Rubin, who'd recently discovered acid's revolutionary potential; and an assortment of hipster poets. To balance the talking heads they signed twice as many bands as they had for the love pageant, and to make it a full-fledged trip they convinced the Haight's leading LSD maker to contribute thousands of tabs for free distribution. Then they announced that on January 14, 1967, not just the Haight but the entire counterculture would be gathering at the Polo Fields in Golden Gate Park for the world's first Human Be-In. "For ten years a new nation has grown inside the robot flesh of the old," read their press release. "Before your eyes a new vital soul is reconnecting the living centers of the American body. . . . Hang your fear at the door and join the future."[24] Twenty-five thousand people showed up.

There was a peculiar little lag before the news hit the national press. The *Boston Globe* picked it up first, maybe because Boston had so many college kids. From there it flashed to Los Angeles' media market, and from there to just about everywhere. The be-in was only the hook. The real story was the alternative world the rush of reporters found in the Haight, the startling discovery of a strange new tribe that turned American values inside out, in defiance of law and reason. "The Haight-Ashbury district of San Francisco is not so much a neighborhood as a state of mindlessness," read *Time*'s version, which went out to the magazine's three and a half million subscribers in the middle of March. "The Erewhon of America's 'pot left' has over the past year become the center of a new utopianism, compounded of drugs and dreams, free love and LSD. It is a far cry from the original Utopia . . . whose denizens demanded six hours of work each day; the 7,000 mind-blown residents of San Francisco's 'Psychedelphia' demand a zero-hour day and free freak-outs for all."[25]

The effect wasn't precisely what the mainstream media had in mind. In late February Los Angeles' furiously expanding counterculture held its first be-in at Griffith Park, headlined by the Doors, a local band that had taken its name from Aldous Huxley's 1954 paean to psychedelic self-enlightenment. New York's waited until the end of March, when 10,000 people filled a corner of Central Park for a psychedelic Easter parade. But no place could match the Haight. On weekends the streets were so packed with gawkers, tourists, and hippie wannabes that the city had to reroute traffic. The Avalon and the Fillmore could barely keep up with the crowds, even with shows five nights a week. The major labels couldn't help but notice: by spring most of the Haight's favorite groups had record deals, the Airplane a single already getting a lot of airplay, courtesy of RCA. And every day, it seemed, there were more kids wandering in from the Greyhound station, refugees from small-town Ohio or suburban LA, come to settle into the utopia they'd read about in a magazine. How many had come no one could say. But by the end of March the neighborhood's most prominent spokesmen were telling reporters that as soon as school was out the numbers would shoot up, peaking at somewhere around 100,000, enough to create in the Haight a Summer of Love.

The more radical activists tried to warn them. The neighborhood couldn't absorb that many people, they said, not when it was already dangerously overcrowded. Once the word was out, though, there was no pulling it back. Through April and May the press gave the story prominent play—Hunter S. Thompson upped the number to 200,000 in his long article on the Haight in the *Times*'s Sunday magazine—while the music execs fed it into their spring marketing campaigns. Columbia had a huge hit with a Summer of Love song so insipid it had taken its composer twenty minutes to write. The Airplane's single tracked Columbia's single up the pop charts. And on June 1 EMI released the year's most shocking album, the Beatles' *Sgt. Pepper's Lonely Hearts Club Band*, with its eye-popping packaging, vertiginous swirl of sound, and LSD-laced lyrics, as sure a sign as anyone could want that the psychedelic moment had arrived. Word was the boys might even appear at the pop festival to be held in Monterey, down the coast from the Haight, the weekend before the Summer of Love was to begin. Little wonder the kids kept coming, with so many forces pulling them in.

The Beatles didn't show. But the crowds did: more than 55,000 of them on the festival's final night, when the Dead came out to play. Three days later the Haight took its turn, officially opening the summer with a free-form be-in celebrating the solstice in Golden Gate Park. The attendance was much smaller than it had been in Monterey, smaller than it had been at the January be-in, but the day had all the right touches, from paper flowers on the shrubs to a conch shell concert by a group of Tibetan monks. When it was over, those who were left wandered down to the beach at the end of the park to watch the sun set over the sea.

Then things started to unravel. It was the number of kids, who quickly overwhelmed the Haight's meager preparations. It was the predators—the hustlers, the hoods, the con men, and the psychopaths—who followed the kids in. It was the dealers, not just the familiar faces with the two-dollar tabs of LSD but the newcomers selling STP, PCP, and a pharmacopeia of amphetamines. It was the money that coursed through the drug trade, the competition for market share, and the inevitable violence: the threats; the muggings; the acid dealer everyone in the Haight claimed to know, found dead in his apartment on August 3, stabbed twelve times, his right arm severed. It was the spiraling risk: by late summer half the Haight's hippies were shooting meth, officials estimated, and 20 percent had tried heroin. It was the sixteen-year-old huddled in a doorway, staring into space. It was the fifteen-year-old crashing on the floor of someone she didn't know. It was the repeated rumors of rape. It was the freedom Kesey had dreamed of bringing out of the psych ward. But it wasn't liberation.

He wasn't there to see it. He'd come back from Mexico in time for the October 1966 love pageant. Shortly thereafter the FBI caught him while he was driving down the freeway. After two trials on the possession charges, and two hung juries, he reached a plea deal in April 1967 and was sentenced to six months in the San Mateo County jail, his term to begin on June 24, three days after the summer solstice.

Most of those months he spent on a work crew, clearing brush near his Day-Glo cabin in the woods. When he was released he gathered up his wife and kids, shuttered the cabin, and moved back to Oregon, to a dairy farm outside of his hometown, where he thought he might start writing again.

The Unheard

IN THE AUTUMN of 1966 Stokely Carmichael seemed to be everywhere. He appeared in the rarified pages of the *New York Review of Books* to explain Black Power to the intelligentsia, on NBC's *Meet the Press* to reach the nation's power brokers, and in front of Harlem's P.S. 201 to support local demands for community control of the city's schools. He lectured to ten thousand students at Berkeley, though the Republican candidate for governor, Ronald Reagan, asked to him to stay away, and to an overflow crowd at Yale. He crisscrossed the country—from Washington, DC, to San Francisco, Oakland to Detroit—to meet with Black activists; packed church halls in Columbus and Dayton, a lyceum in Boston, and a public park in Watts for a rally the city refused to sanction. In almost every venue he delivered a message of uncompromising militancy. "We are tired of trying to explain to white people that we're not going to hurt them," he told the crowd at Berkeley. "We are concerned with getting the things we want, the things that we have to have to be able to function. . . . The question is, will white people overcome their racism and allow for that to happen in this country? If that does not happen, brothers and sisters, we have no choice but to say very clearly, 'Move over, or we're going to move over you.'"[26] Twice he was arrested for inciting riots.

Most African Americans weren't impressed. Only 18 percent of those polled in December 1966 thought Carmichael was helping to advance civil rights, a figure that placed him at the bottom of a long list of Black activists, barely above Elijah Muhammad. For a portion of the African American Left, though, Carmichael's politics were electrifying. By the end of the year cadres of young radicals in New York,

Newark, Philadelphia, and Los Angeles had created political parties inspired by his Lowndes County campaign, as had two San Francisco–area militants, twenty-four-year-old Huey Newton and thirty-year-old Bobby Seale, who in October launched the Black Panther Party for Self-Defense in Oakland, across the bay from the Haight.

Beyond a few friends and colleagues, the party had no members. So Newton and Seale set to organizing, drawing not on the SNCC style of grassroots mobilization that had inspired Carmichael but on the power of self-presentation. They pieced together a uniform that combined an urban look of black pants, a crisp blue shirt, and a black leather jacket with the black beret favored by Latin American revolutionaries. Then they assembled a cache of weapons, loaded them into their cars, and established neighborhood patrols meant to protect Oakland's African Americans from the city's overwhelmingly white police force, an act of bravado made possible by a loophole in California law that allowed citizens to carry loaded guns as long as they weren't concealed. The inevitable confrontations with rattled cops brought in a fistful of recruits and a good deal of admiration. But the Panthers didn't have their breakthrough until the state assemblyman from Oakland's white suburbs introduced a bill to close the loophole. On May 2, 1967, Seale led twenty-nine of his heavily armed comrades—three-quarters of the Panthers' membership—into the state capitol to express their opposition to the move. As a lobbying tactic it left something to be desired. As guerrilla theater it was superb. The next day, news of the Panthers' "invasion" ran in newspapers across the country, usually alongside a photo of young Black Che Guevaras standing in Sacramento's marble halls with rifles slung over their shoulders, Black Power's revolutionary vanguard revealed.[27]

A month later urban America's racial wounds split open. On June 2, a police assault on a peaceful demonstration at a Boston welfare office sparked three nights of looting and burning in Roxbury. Tampa's Black neighborhood erupted on June 11, when a policeman shot and killed a nineteen-year-old he said had robbed a camera store; Cincinnati's on the twelfth, following a street-corner arrest gone wrong; and Buffalo's at the end of the month with another three nights of rioting, this time triggered by the police wading into a fight at a public housing project. After Buffalo there was a two-week lull. Then, on the evening of July 12, 1967, two white patrolmen stopped an African American cabbie for a routine traffic violation in Newark's Central Ward. Words were exchanged, the cabbie arrested. On the way to the precinct house the cops beat him up. As the news spread, people said the cabbie was dead.

Newark's agony began exactly as Harlem's had in the summer of 1964—with an impromptu rally in front of the local police station that the police decided to break up by wading into the crowd with nightsticks raised—but it spun out with the fury of Watts. The first night the rioting was localized. On the second night the mobs grew so large the police couldn't contain them. From the Central Ward the looting spread to downtown. Almost a hundred stripped stores were set ablaze, the fire crews pelted with bricks and bottles. And the cops on the street were reporting sporadic sniper fire coming from tenement rooftops. Early in the morning the mayor asked the governor to send in the National Guard, civil order having broken down.

The governor responded with 3,000 troops and a swaggering promise that "the line between the jungle and the law might as well be drawn here as well as any place in America." But the guardsmen weren't law-enforcement officers. They were weekend soldiers thrust into what city officials thought was an "open rebellion."[28] The first firefight came around 6:00 p.m. on the third day, a fierce exchange that began when a policeman was hit by a shot fired from the top floors of a housing project. For the next forty-eight hours the troopers turned central Newark into a war zone, suppressing the looting with mass arrests and increasingly undisciplined violence and the rooftop attacks with their own raking fire. Resistance finally collapsed on July 17. By then 1,500 people had been arrested, 725 injured, and twenty-six killed, the youngest just ten years old.

Five days later, in the early morning of July 23, the Detroit police raided an after-hours bar in a poor Black section of the city's West Side. In their rush to finish the operation the cops got rough with some of their prisoners, pushing and shoving and wielding their batons. A few onlookers started tossing insults at the officers, followed by bottles and stones. On the edge of the crowd a teenager launched a trash can through the window of Hardy's Drug Store, while someone else set a shoe shop ablaze. And it all started again.

This time the unrest moved with startling speed. Within half a day the looting had spread to the West Side's two major arteries, dozens of storefronts were burning, and sniper fire had begun. On Sunday afternoon the governor sent in the National Guard. But Detroit was a sprawling city, six times the size of Newark, and by evening there were outbreaks in neighborhoods so far apart they couldn't conceivably be contained, even by troops with the training the guardsmen didn't have. The night was horrific, the next day no better. By late Monday nineteen people had been killed, 800 injured, and hundreds more made homeless by the fires that were raging out of control. With reports pouring in of disturbances flaring in half a dozen smaller cities across the region, everyone knew there was worse to come.

Lyndon Johnson hated the thought of federal intervention. He could see the terrible image of combat troops fighting on the streets of Detroit, the horrifying possibility of a Black child killed by a white soldier he'd deployed, his administration's commitment to racial change and the eradication of poverty destroyed by his unleashing of state-sanctioned violence. When the governor's request arrived midday Monday, LBJ agreed only to send the soldiers to bases outside Detroit. There they sat through the evening, one brigade from the 82nd Airborne, another from the 101st—5,000 men in total—as the mayor and governor pleaded with the White House to use them. Johnson waited until 11:00 p.m. to issue the order. Even then he seemed desperate to distance himself from what he had done. "I am sure that the American people will realize that I take this action with the greatest regret," he said in an anguished midnight television address. "Pillage, looting, murder and arson have nothing to do with civil rights. They are criminal conduct. And the federal government in the circumstances here presented has no alternative but to respond. . . ."[29] Shortly thereafter armored personnel carriers rumbled into the East Side, the first time in a quarter century federal troops had been dispatched to crush an uprising in an American city.

Crush it they did. But it took three bloody days. When the city was finally brought under control, on July 28, the death toll had reached forty-three, and the number of injured had climbed to 1,200. Three-quarters of those killed were African American, among them three men executed by a contingent of cops during a raid on a seedy hotel on the upheaval's fourth night. In the five days of the rebellion 7,200 people had been arrested, 2,500 stores looted, 412 buildings burned, $50 million in property lost. Not since an anti-Black pogrom ripped through Tulsa in 1921 had an American city suffered such devastation.

Stokely Carmichael promised more. He was in Havana when Detroit exploded, attending an international conference of revolutionary movements. "We are moving to guerrilla warfare within the United States, since there is no other way to obtain our homes, our land, our rights," he told a packed news conference. "They have taught us to kill. Now the struggle is in the streets of the United States."[30] The vast majority of African Americans who lived in Detroit's riot-torn neighborhoods didn't agree. Only three percent thought that people had taken to the streets in pursuit of self-determination, according to surveys conducted shortly after the uprising ended, whereas 60 percent thought they'd come out to protest the police brutality, poor housing, unemployment, and poverty that afflicted their communities. Violence wasn't the answer, said 81 percent of those surveyed.

Yet violence there had been, just as Martin Luther King had feared there would be if the urban poor couldn't secure meaningful reform any other way. He'd tried: the evenings he'd spent in his ghetto apartment talking with gang members; the day his advisers had claimed control of a tenement on behalf of the people who lived there; the nights he'd driven through West Side Chicago pleading for peace; the afternoon he'd marched through the mobs in Gage Park. Now it had come to this. Not guerrilla warfare, though there were flashes of that. Not Black Power, though it had its adherents. But the enraged voice of the dispossessed, demanding to be heard.

Slouching Towards Bethlehem

THE EDITORS OF the *Saturday Evening Post* put a hippie on the cover of their late September issue, a close-up of a grinning young man with a garishly painted face, wearing a top hat he'd labeled LSD. But they opened the issue with a plea from Detroit's chief of police. A grizzled crime reporter turned reformer, he knew the city's troubles better than almost anyone. He'd seen the toxic mix of fear and aggression that had gripped its white neighborhoods since the summer's unrest: the surge of families moving to the suburbs, the angry talk of self-defense, the frightening spike in gun sales. And he must have read the national polls, which made clear that the same emotions were racing across the country. Forty-five percent of whites thought the riots had been caused by radical agitators trying to foment revolution. Thirty-four percent believed their neighborhoods might be threatened by a Black revolt, a ludicrously high figure given the extent to which residential segregation separated Blacks and whites. An overwhelming majority said looters ought to be shot. Thirty percent said they'd pull the trigger themselves if rioters came anywhere near them. The thought appalled him. "Does the public expect a policeman to be a public executioner who can inflict capital punishment for misdemeanors?" asked the chief. "It is one thing to shoot back at snipers and it is another thing to shoot down a child who is looting a pair of shoes or even a television set. Property can be restored, but not a life."[31]

Three pages later the *Post's* aristocratic columnist, Stewart Alsop, scion of Groton and Yale, offered a stinging rebuttal. He opened his essay with the story of Juanita, "a cheerful, rather charming sixteen-year-old Negro girl" he met while reporting on the looting of Watts in 1965. For Juanita the riot had been a carnival, said Alsop, "rather like a white middle-class child's Christmas Day, a day of excitement, of shared joy, and of all sorts of wonderful things for free," which was why the cops should do exactly what the majority of whites wanted them to do. "In the years to come," he said, "many sins of omission and commission by the white majority must be expiated and much money spent.

But for the short run there is only one way to make sure that next summer and the summer after that will not be repetitions of the ghastly summer now ending. Force must be used immediately and selectively, as soon as trouble starts. . . . Juanita and her contemporaries must be persuaded right at the beginning, before the carnival atmosphere has time to spread, that this riot will *not* be fun."[32]

After Alsop's essay the editors ran a torturous little poem about snails, followed by the article Joan Didion had written when she came back from the Haight. It was a stunningly elegant piece of precisely observed vignettes—the teenage girls trailing the Dead, the teenage boy with needle tracks up his arm, the mime troupe's racial provocation in the park, the five-year-old whose mother had given her acid—bound together by Didion's re-creation of the desolation she'd felt before she'd accepted the assignment. "It was not a country in revolution," she wrote. "It was not a country under enemy siege. It was the United States of America in the cold late spring of 1967, and the market was steady and the GNP high . . . and it might have been a spring of brave hopes and national promise, but it was not, and more and more people had the uneasy apprehension that it was not. All that seemed clear was that at some point we had aborted ourselves and butchered the job, and because nothing seemed so relevant I decided to go to San Francisco . . . where the social hemorrhaging was showing up."[33]

The nation wasn't hemorrhaging in the Haight alone, of course. It was also bleeding in the suburbs that fed kids into the Summer of Love; in Watts and West Side Chicago; in rabid Gage Park and along the Cicero line; in Newark's Central Ward, Detroit's center city, and the white neighborhoods that ringed them; in the pages of the *Saturday Evening Post*, where in the bitter aftermath of the summer's riots sober men could debate whether the police would be right to kill a cheerful, charming sixteen-year-old because she'd stolen a pair of shoes; and in Didion's rented mansion at the foot of the Hollywood Hills, where she'd sat with her gin and Dexedrine in the last days of spring and tried to warn her readers of the darkness descending.

CHAPTER 8

WAIST DEEP IN THE BIG MUDDY

Larry Burrows picked James Farley for his looks. "You're sort of all-American," he said. "You know, big ears, short hair. Yeah, you're the one I want."[1] That and the fact he'd be flying into a combat zone aboard helicopter thirteen. Yankee Papa 13: an unlucky number for an all-American boy.

The day before, Burrows followed Farley and his gunner as they wandered through the market that had grown up around the Da Nang air base, clicking away while they shopped for something to send to the folks back home. In the morning he was out on the tarmac early, three cameras slung around his neck. A fourth he anchored to the helicopter's struts, in hopes of getting a shot from the outside in. He photographed the last-minute preparations: the men sitting in the sun for their final briefing, Farley the grinning twenty-one-year-old lugging two M60s over to his helicopter, the crew chief slipping on his helmet. Burrows squeezed into the back, along with the South Vietnamese troops the Americans were ferrying out to the countryside: 465 soldiers spread over seventeen copters, nine of them in Farley's; twenty miles to the drop site; a few minutes on the ground while the South Vietnamese scrambled out; twenty miles home. A milk run.

But the Viet Cong knew they were coming. They set up in the tree lines that surrounded the landing zone: two companies with small arms, automatic weapons, and the advantage of surprise. The copters swooped down onto the elephant grass, into raking fire. The camera on the strut caught the South Vietnamese soldiers pushing past Farley, who was manning an M60 at the copter door. But Burrows missed the strafing up front. Ten hits in the time it took to unload and lift off again, one within centimeters of tearing out the pilot's throat.

They would have been clear, except that the pilot saw Yankee Papa 3 wasn't moving. So he swung back around, landing as close as he could to the wounded copter. Out of it sprinted two of her crew—the gunner and the copilot—across the twenty yards or so to Yankee Papa 13. But everybody could see that the pilot was still on board, slumped over his controls. And everybody knew that he wasn't to be left behind.

Farley went first, running low through the grass, Burrows right behind him. When they reached Yankee Papa 3 Farley climbed up the fuselage to the cockpit window, while Burrows knelt below, taking photo after photo. From that angle he could see Farley trying to drag the pilot out, pulling against what seemed to be his dead weight. But he couldn't see the head wound Farley could see—the entry hole in his cheek, the exit at the base of his neck—nor the blood that caked the pilot's face and throat. After a few frantic moments Farley dropped to the ground empty-handed and raced back toward his copter so quickly that Burrows barely managed to get him in the frame.

Only when they were airborne did anyone pay attention to the two crewmen who'd escaped Yankee Papa 3. The gunner was slumped against the copter's rear wall, in shock from taking a bullet in the shoulder, the copilot lying motionless at Farley's feet. Burrows got a brilliant shot of Farley screaming at his own gunner to hand him the first aid kit, then another of Farley desperately trying to staunch the wound in the copilot's chest, while the chopper dipped and bucked beneath him. Somewhere in the midst of it all Burrows saw the copilot's eyes glaze over. "Nobody spoke for a few seconds," he said afterward, until Burrows suggested that Farley cover the dead man's face.[2] He did as he was told, so Burrows could start taking photos again.

It was back in Da Nang, though, that he got the money shot. After the rush to get the wounded gunner to treatment; after the crew had time to talk over the details of what had happened; after the anxious trading of images and impressions, when Lance Corporal James Farley slipped into a supply shed, sat down on a packing crate, buried his head in his arms, and cried like the little boy he'd been not so long ago. That was the final image that appeared in Larry Burrows's photo essay, published in the April 16, 1965, issue of *Life*, the nation's preeminent news magazine. In the beginning a kid with oversized ears grinning as he prepared for battle, in the end wrenching sorrow: a few hours in a still-young war, a searing metaphor for the years to come.

The Vietnam Tangle

AT THE END of June 1965 Secretary of Defense Robert McNamara met with the British foreign secretary, Patrick Gordon Walker, to discuss the administration's decision to assume control of the Vietnam War. Lyndon Johnson was days away from announcing the deployment of 100,000 additional American soldiers. Yet, McNamara said, "none of us at the center of things talk about winning a victory." Then why not withdraw from Vietnam rather than escalate, asked Gordon Walker? Was the administration considering that possibility? Not at all, McNamara replied.[3]

There was the paradox of LBJ's war. The president and his advisers were painfully aware of the difficulties they faced in Vietnam. The most obvious were strategic. Lyndon Johnson could have unleashed American forces on North Vietnam, sending them across the border from the south just as the United States had pushed into North Korea in the autumn of 1950. The North Vietnamese would probably have buckled under the assault, like the North Koreans before them. But Johnson desperately wanted to avoid replicating the disaster that followed, when Chinese troops had come pouring across the border from the north in support of their fellow Communists, blocking the American advance and turning the Korean War into a brutal, bloody stalemate. So LBJ ordered his commanders to root out the Viet Cong in South Vietnam by almost any means necessary. But the Americans were not to set foot in North Vietnam.

Once those parameters were set, the problems deepened. No other nation on earth could put more powerful forces into the field. But American troops were trained and equipped to fight a conventional ground war, in which opposing armies battled each other in large-scale engagements. Vietnam was a dramatically different sort of conflict, fought mostly in the countryside by guerrilla units that staged lightning strikes and then faded away, disappearing into carefully concealed base camps or the elaborate tunnel systems they'd built beneath much of South Vietnam. Worse, they'd blend back into the villages from which they'd come, hidden among—and sometimes supported by—the very people the Americans were supposed to protect from Communist infiltration.

The diplomatic situation made matters more difficult still. The White House had virtually no confidence in the South Vietnamese government's ability to prosecute the war or its soldiers' willingness to fight it. Yet the administration had to act as if it did, a dynamic that sent US troops into combat alongside soldiers they didn't respect, and often didn't trust. Johnson tried to offset the problem by drawing more reputable allies into the war. Almost every head of state he approached, though, wanted no part of it; even the British prime minister turned him down, despite hints that the United States would give his flagging economy up to a billion dollars if he'd commit a brigade's worth of ground troops. In the end only the Australians sent any sizable force, and it amounted to a mere 7,000 men.

Then there was the home front. By the summer of 1965 LBJ was well on his way to passing the most sweeping reform agenda since Franklin Roosevelt's New Deal. On a few issues—civil rights most notably—he'd already surpassed FDR. And there was more to come: among the most pressing initiatives, an extended war on poverty, a long-awaited health care program for the poor and the elderly, federal aid to public schools, and the remaking of the nation's inner cities. He was moving that sweeping set of programs through Congress, moreover, with 70 percent of Americans approving of his performance, a rate that put him slightly below John Kennedy at the peak of his popularity and ahead of JFK's more difficult days.

But Johnson had seen the damage a war could do to a presidency. Harry Truman had never been particularly popular. When he'd committed US troops to the defense of South Korea in June 1950, though, the American people had rallied to him—until the war bogged down, the casualty count mounted, support gave way to frustration, and the Republican Right eviscerated him. By 1952 Truman's standing had fallen so far he didn't dare run for reelection.

The possibility that the pattern would repeat haunted Johnson. He'd already experienced the public's mood swings. In July 1964 only 38 percent of Americans thought he was handling Vietnam effectively. Then he ordered a single bombing raid of North Vietnam, in response to the Gulf of Tonkin incident, and suddenly 71 percent of Americans approved of his policies. Through the autumn of 1964 the numbers fell. In February 1965 he launched Operation Rolling Thunder and they shot up again. But Johnson knew they wouldn't stay up. Once they slipped, he was sure, the conservatives could make their move.

On Capitol Hill it would come down to money. Fighting a war, even a limited war, was an enormously expensive undertaking: by McNamara's estimate the Defense Department would spend $700 million on Vietnam in 1965, and $12 billion in 1966 as troop levels rose. And those were only estimates; actual costs could be much higher, depending on how the fighting went, with no accounting at all for the nonmilitary spending that would come through other departments. When the bills came due, conservatives would use the war's expense as an excuse to gut the social programs Johnson just put in place. On the stump they'd turn him into another Truman—too weak-willed to fight the Communist menace as vigorously as it ought to be fought, just as Goldwater had tried to do at the tail end of the 1964 campaign— though they knew as well as he did the dangers of additional escalation. Should that happen, he said later, "all my programs, all my hopes . . . all my dreams" would be lost to "that bitch of a war."[4]

Yet Johnson forged ahead. There was nothing else he could do, given the lessons World War II had imprinted on American policy makers. Secretary of State Dean Rusk made the stakes plain in a July 1, 1965, letter to the president. "The integrity of the U.S. commitment is the principal pillar of peace throughout the world," he wrote. "If that commitment becomes unreliable, the Communist world would draw conclusions that would lead to our ruin and almost certainly to a catastrophic war. . . . We cannot abandon [the South Vietnamese] without disaster to peace and to our interests throughout the world."[5]

If the war couldn't be avoided, then it had to be managed. Johnson decided to downplay the domestic strain, much as he had the civil rights question during his years as Senate majority leader. There was no way to deny the escalation, but he didn't have to dramatize it either, he decided. So he wouldn't tell the nation that the war would require real sacrifice—or even be much of an imposition. Instead he'd move quietly, increasing troop levels by stages, without a general call-up of reserves or a marked increase in draft rates. He'd pass on the cost in fragments, aided by financial assumptions that dramatically underestimated how much the military was going to spend. And he'd cloak it all in a steady flow of encouraging news, repeating as often as he could that the balance was tipping in the Americans' favor, the light at the end of the tunnel growing closer.

Actually fighting the war was another matter. The challenges were enormous, of course. But Johnson's key advisers had led JFK through those incredibly dangerous days in October 1962, when one wrong move would have triggered a nuclear war. And they believed that they could lead LBJ through the Vietnam tangle with the same precision, the same sophistication, the same combination of flexibility and resolve. No one could make those promises with greater assurance than Robert McNamara. "Our objective is to . . . expand substantially the US military pressure against the Viet Cong in the South and the North Vietnamese in the North and at the same time launch a vigorous effort on the political side to get negotiations started," he told the president in the early stages of escalation, as if he were writing an executive summary for his old bosses at Ford. "Even though casualties will increase and the war will continue for some time, the United States public will support this course of action because it is a combined military-political program designed and likely to bring about a favorable solution to the Vietnam problem."[6]

At the center of their strategy lay the air campaign the administration had launched in February 1965. On and on it went, month after punishing month. In 1965 the Americans dropped 63,000 tons of bombs on North Vietnam. In 1966 they more than doubled the number, to 136,000 tons. The following year they pushed it to 226,000 tons: one tenth of the total US bombing in all of World War II, inflicted in a single year on a country the size of Florida. The administration balanced the assault's intensity with specificity. Rather than devastate entire towns and cities, as the Americans had at the end of World War II, LBJ restricted the strikes to military bases and supply depots, factories and power plants, roads, bridges, rail lines, and the infiltration routes that led to the South. That way the United States could destroy the infrastructure the North Vietnamese used to support the Viet Cong without giving the Chinese cause to intervene. But precision bombing wasn't all that precise. By 1967 the campaign had inflicted so much collateral damage in the North Vietnamese countryside that signs of famine were seeping into Hanoi.

While the Americans battered the North, they took the fight directly to the Viet Cong in South Vietnam, using a tactic their commanding officer, General William Westmoreland, called "search and destroy." Destroy they did. First Westmoreland's men used computer simulations, mobile radars, and other cutting-edge technologies to identify likely Viet Cong bases and movements. Then they unleashed even more massive air power than they had in the North. Down rained the bombs— more than a million tons of them by 1967, twice the tonnage dropped on North Vietnam. Down came the chemicals too: the shells equipped with napalm, and the clouds of Agent Orange, a defoliant powerful enough to strip clean the dense forests the Viet Cong used for cover. The goal, an officer explained, was "to blow the hell out of them and police up."[7]

The policing fell to the ground troops. From their own increasingly elaborate bases they were sent in search of the enemy, sometimes in highly coordinated, large-scale operations meant to recapture vast swaths of territory from the Viet Cong; sometimes on targeted missions meant to destroy a particular Communist stronghold; often on vague patrols that their commanders hoped would flush out the enemy. Copter crews like Farley's would carry them out to their precisely defined landing zones. From there they'd head through the villages and rice paddies, forests and wetlands that dominated South Vietnam, looking for an enemy they couldn't identify, waiting for attacks they couldn't anticipate: the grunt work of a superb conventional army trying to fight an unconventional war.

At times the destruction turned strikingly systematic. Throughout 1965 and 1966 the army struggled to break the Viet Cong's control of an area known as the Iron Triangle, just thirty miles north of Saigon. Finally General Westmoreland decided to bring the military's full power to bear. Early in the morning of January 8, 1967, American forces swept into the triangle's primary village, Ben Suc. They brought its 3,000 people into the schoolyard. There they were sorted, the men of military age taken to be interrogated by South Vietnamese troops, on the assumption that they were Viet Cong, the women, children, and elderly men loaded onto the trucks and landing crafts that would move them, and whatever belongings they could carry, to a refugee camp at Phu Cuong, 15 miles away. Once Ben Suc was empty the American soldiers burned its houses to the ground. American bulldozers scraped the houses' foundations bare. And American bombers pulverized the rubble the bulldozers left behind, until the village—and four square miles around it—had been laid to waste. From its ruins the troops moved into the rest of the triangle in pursuit of the Viet Cong their officers believed were on the run, search and destroy having been turned on its head.

At least the operation's gains could be marked on a map. For the most part the military had no way of telling whether the enemy was being beaten back. The United States had no presence whatsoever in North Vietnam—not even any spies—so it had no ability to measure the effectiveness of its bombing campaign, except through whatever information the CIA could derive from indirect sources. The agency gave the Pentagon file after file of careful analyses, but they were really nothing more than estimates. The problem was no less complex in South Vietnam. Territory secured today could be lost tomorrow—as it was around Ben Suc—so gauging American progress in geographic terms produced nothing more than transitory results. Instead McNamara turned to his beloved statistics. By his calculations, the United States could break the enemy's ability to fight by killing ten Viet Cong for every American lost in combat. From his charts the order went into the field. In South Vietnam success was to be determined by a body count, each side's losses tallied every week, the resulting report placed on McNamara's desk so he could say with suitable precision that the war was being won.

And the North Vietnamese could stop it all, Johnson insisted—the bombings, the burnings, the mounting hunger, the devastation, the constantly expanding list of the dead—simply by letting the United States know that they would no longer try to topple the government of South Vietnam. They didn't even have to make a public declaration. A private promise would be sufficient, sent to Washington through the secret diplomatic channels LBJ repeatedly tried to open. As soon as the word reached the White House Johnson would ground his bombers, pull his troops back to base, and dispatch negotiators to wherever Ho Chi Minh's representatives wanted to meet, so the two sides could begin working on the settlement that would allow North and South Vietnam to live side by side in peace.

But the promise never came. As the Americans' bombing intensified, the North Vietnamese built up their air defenses with Soviet-supplied fighter jets and missile batteries. They drew on mammoth Chinese aid to continually rebuild their country's shattered infrastructure. And they stepped up their infiltration of South Vietnam. In 1965 the North Vietnamese military sent about 35,000 men across the border to join the Communist insurgency. By 1967 the number had risen to 90,000, enough to give the Viet Cong a fighting force in South Vietnam of 261,000 soldiers. The United States responded in kind, ratcheting up its deployment a step at a time through 1965, 1966, and 1967, until LBJ had committed almost half a million American men to that bitch of a war he said could be ended with nothing more than a word.

Our Boys

ON THE FOURTH of July, 1966, the flags went up on Eddy Street for the fifth straight year. Stella Cahill thought that things had gotten out of hand. But Ed loved every bit of it. Since 1961 he'd built an entire collection of American flags and made himself into an expert on the proper way to display them; almost every year he sent a letter to the *Trib* explaining one rule or another, and occasionally on the way to work he'd see a school or a business flying its flag incorrectly and stop to set them straight. On the Fourth his devotion turned into an extravaganza. With his collection added in, the number of flags draping the block hit a hundred. He had patriotic music blasting from the record player he set in the bungalow's front window. He arranged a bike parade for the kids and cookouts with the neighbors to mark what he proudly called "an old fashioned holiday." In 1966 the celebration had an added meaning. Of the thirty-six families on the block, three now had sons in the military. One was still in training stateside. Another was stationed in Germany. The third was in Vietnam. "God bless them all," Ed wrote as the Fourth of July approached, "and watch over them for us."[8]

Terry Cahill wasn't among them. He'd started at St. Patrick's High in September 1961 in a class of 435 boys, mostly from his end of the bungalow belt. The priests gave all of them the order and discipline that was to be expected and then sorted them into their futures: shop for the kids who were going to follow their fathers into the working class; typing and bookkeeping for those likely to make it into the middle; and an academic track for those they thought might have a shot at rising into the professions. Terry they slotted into the last group, where he got the grades that opened up a range of possibilities. By his senior year he'd decided he wanted to go on to Notre Dame to become an engineer.

Choosing a profoundly Catholic school a two-hour drive from home was hardly a dramatic move. But Ed didn't like it, not when his boy could stay at home and commute to a local college as his sister had a few years before. This time Stella intervened. She and Ed undoubtedly talked about the cost of sending him to Notre Dame and probably about the opportunities he'd find there, conversations they could have because Ed was bringing home such a solid income as head of sales at Vacuum Can. Maybe in their most private moments they also talked about his fear of their kids slipping from them—pulled away by the chance to move up from a world he couldn't imagine anyone wanting to leave. Judy was already gone, having moved to New Jersey shortly after her marriage in 1964 so that her new husband could pursue his corporate career. Whatever Stella said to soften the thought of Terry leaving too, it worked. In September 1965 Terry headed to South Bend while three of the kids he'd left behind headed into the army.

Three must have seemed like a small enough number, not even close to the great sweep that the draft had made through the neighborhood during World War II. Then the military was putting 12 million men into uniform. In 1966 it had a force of 2.7 million, 390,000 of whom were stationed in South Vietnam. That meant that only five percent of American families had a father, a son, or a brother in the service, and less than one percent had a loved one at war. All things being equal, the thirty-six families on the Cahills' block shouldn't have sent three boys into the military. They should have sent two. And neither should have been in Vietnam.

All things weren't equal, though. During World War II the draft had gathered up the rich and poor, the middle class and working class, on a fairly equitable basis. Since then the system had changed. When he turned eighteen a young man had to report to his local draft board. That board could declare him eligible for service, or it could give him one of the deferments it had at its disposal. Most of those deferments— for physical problems, for instance—could apply to any draftee. But one carried a distinct class bias. In 1951 the officials who directed the draft decided that they wouldn't take college students who were making progress toward their degrees. They thought the new rule would help the nation create the educated workforce it needed. In the process they shoved the weight of military service onto those young men whose families couldn't afford to send them to college as the Cahills could.

Not that the military was made up of draftees. In the 1950s and early 1960s, 75 to 80 percent of the men on active duty had volunteered. Some did so out of patriotism, others because they wanted steady work, still others for the discipline. There was a good bit of calculation involved as well. To keep the percentage of draftees as low as possible, the armed forces gave those who enlisted better assignments. So a young man about to be drafted had every incentive to sign up instead, a dynamic that extended the draft's class bias into the volunteer corps. It also gave that bias another spin, since those who didn't sidestep the draft were to be given the least desirable, most dangerous jobs the military had to offer.

From the start critics complained that those policies would turn the next conflict into a poor man's war. That's not exactly what happened in Vietnam, but it was close. According to the best assessments, 25 percent of the men who served there came from poor families, 55 percent from the working class, and only 20 percent from the middle and upper classes. Among combat troops the percentages may well have been even more skewed, particularly in the lower ranks, which the military tended to fill with draftees. The bias clearly took on a racial dimension. In 1965 and 1966 African Americans accounted for 11 percent of US forces in Vietnam, approximately their share of the population as a whole. But 31 percent of the soldiers in infantry units were Black.

Off they went, those vulnerable young men, many of them straight out of high school, into the incredibly complex war Washington had fashioned. Most had been given about sixteen weeks of training, the first half in the basics of military life—how to salute, how to march, how to obey orders instinctively—the second half in the particular skills they'd need, which for infantrymen meant learning how to use their weapons. About Vietnam they were taught virtually nothing, except what they learned from the rumors that swirled through the ranks, invariably based on Americans' long-standing belief in Asian duplicity: chilling stories of the Viet Cong's ability to hide just about anywhere, of their using women and kids as suicide bombers, of sappers killing Americans while they slept in their beds. So they came ashore at the sprawling US base at Cam Ranh Bay or onto the tarmac at Da Nang both ignorant of and terrified by the people they'd been sent to defend.

In-country the fear metastasized. Even front-line troops spent most of their tours in American-built base camps, shut off from the Vietnamese by rows of razor wire and a battery of creature comforts meant to give the men a touch of home. On the largest installations there were burgers in the mess hall, movies at the rec center, rock and roll on the radio, and a miniskirted young woman delivering the weather report on Armed Forces television. In the more remote camps conditions were tougher. But a soldier could still count on a hot meal, a cold beer, an occasional movie, and a heavily policed perimeter. "[W]e were in a three square mile piece of the United States of America," said a veteran of his time on a base halfway between Da Nang and Saigon.[9]

Beyond that piece of America, though, lay imminent danger, a message one soldier remembered receiving on the day he arrived. "We were loaded on an olive-drab school bus for the short ride from the airstrip over to the compound," he told an interviewer later. "There was wire mesh over the windows. I said to somebody, 'What the hell is the wire for?' 'It's the gooks, man, the gooks. . . . The gooks will throw grenades through the windows. See those gooks out there?' I look out and I see shriveled, little old men squatting beside the road in the fashion of the Vietnamese, filling sandbags. . . . Here we are at one of the largest military installations in the world and we have to cover the windows to protect ourselves from little old men."[10]

If the threat was so great just beyond the razor wire, there was no measuring the risk ground troops faced when they headed into the field. In theory search and destroy was a targeted strategy, driven by the best intelligence the military could muster. In practice Viet Cong forces were incredibly hard to find. For days on end infantrymen would trudge through their assigned areas in long thin columns, each man a few yards apart, his uniform drenched in sweat from the tropical heat, an eighty-pound pack on his back. Through the rice paddies they'd wade, up to their waists in stagnant water, because it wasn't safe to walk on the dikes the locals used; into elephant grass so thick they couldn't see the men in front of them; down roads they feared the Viet Cong had booby-trapped; into hamlets thick with alien sights and smells, among people who may well be the enemy they were searching for.

In the villages power and fear could create a toxic mix. A reporter from *The New Yorker* joined the troops who swept into Ben Suc in January 1967. His squad spent part of the morning scouring the villagers' houses, looking for traces of the Viet Cong. They spotted a young man riding a bicycle down the road away from Ben Suc. One of the soldiers opened fire, followed by another. The blast blew the man off the bike into a ditch by the side of the road. After a minute or so the two soldiers went to see what they'd done. "The Vietnamese . . . lay on his side without moving," the reporter wrote shortly thereafter, "blood flowing from his face, which, with the eyes open, was half buried in the dirt at the bottom of the ditch." The Americans stood over him for a while, arms crossed. "That's a VC for you," one of them finally said. "He's a VC, all right. . . . He was leaving town. He had to have some reason."

The other didn't seem so sure. "I saw this guy coming down the road," he replied. "And I thought, you know, is this it? Do I shoot?"

"I'm not worried," the first soldier said. "You know, that's the first time I've ever seen a dead guy, and I don't feel bad. I just don't, that's all. Actually, I'm glad. I'm glad we killed the little VC."[11]

Outside the villages the troops' power faded away, and only the fear remained. For the most part the Viet Cong avoided engaging the patrols. Instead they laced the countryside with explosives, many of them made from unexploded American ordnance, a tactic meant to terrorize as much as to maim and kill. In the end it did all three. "It's more than the fear of death that chews on your mind," said a marine. "It's an absurd combination of certainty and uncertainty; the certainty that you're walking in mine fields, walking past the things day after day; the uncertainty of your every movement, of which way to shift your weight, of where to sit down." For one soldier, it was simply a matter of glancing in the wrong direction. "It was real early, just after daybreak on a Sunday morning," he recalled. "We had just moved about a hundred feet when I hit it. Seems like I remember looking down at my watch. . . . I was unconscious for a couple of minutes. I come around and I was laying in a hot hole with my arms up on my side. There was absolutely no pain, just numbness—total numbness." For days he refused to believe that one wrong step had cost him both his legs and his eyes.[12]

When there was combat it almost always came at the Viet Cong's initiation. "You go out on patrol maybe twenty times or more and nothin', just nothin'," an infantryman told a reporter from *Time* in 1965. "Then, the twenty-first time, zap, zap, zap, you get hit."[13] Most of the assaults were ambushes: hit-and-run operations that US troops were supposed to counter by engaging the enemy long enough for artillery or air power to hit their position. In the middle of a firefight, though, it was hard for the men on the ground to know where exactly the Viet Cong were, much less to call in the coordinates necessary to pinpoint strikes. And bombers screaming overhead carried their own dangers. The military didn't count how many men were killed or wounded by friendly fire. But a controversial Pentagon study of the war's early years put the number in the thousands.

For many soldiers, though, the worst part of patrolling may have been the realization that they'd been put through such horror for cynical ends. "The purpose was for you to walk up on Charlie and for him to hit you, and then for our hardware to wipe them out," one of them said later. "That was all we were—bait. They couldn't find Charlie any other way. . . . They weren't looking for just a handful of VC. Actually, they'd love for us to run into a regiment which would just wipe us out. Then they could plaster the regiment and they'd have a big body count. The general gets another damn medal. He gets promoted. 'Oh, I only lost two hundred men, but I killed two thousand.'"[14]

Lose them they did. In 1965 1,928 Americans were killed in Vietnam; 6,350 in 1966; 11,363 in 1967. Back to the States they came, those whose remains could be found, their flag-draped coffins packed into the huge cargo planes that had brought some of them to the war. At their gravesides the honor guard would fold the flags into a tight triangle, as tradition required, and present it to their families. A flag for Jim Magel of St. Louis, Missouri, who died at James Farley's feet on March 31, 1965. A flag for Bentford Bennett of Lilesville, North Carolina, lost in a firefight on June 23, 1966. A flag for Arnoldo Carnevas of Uvalde, Texas, killed when he stepped on a mine on June 30, 1966. A flag for Gerald Krystoszek of Chicago's bungalow belt, shot in the Que Son Valley on April 21, 1967, three months short of his twentieth birthday, and buried in the same cemetery as Stella Cahill's father: a boy like the ones from Eddy Street, whom God in His infinite mystery chose not to watch over.

Give Peace a Chance

LATE ON THE afternoon of November 2, 1965, thirty-two-year-old Norman Morrison pulled the old Cadillac he'd borrowed from friends into the vast parking lot of the Pentagon, the command center of the American military, across the river from Washington, DC. Out of the car he lifted his daughter Emily—just nine days shy of her first birthday—along with a glass container full of gasoline. He carried them both to a little raised garden in clear view of Robert McNamara's third-floor office. What happened next is a matter of dispute. Morrison may have set his daughter down on the ground near him. He may have handed her off to a passerby. Or a security guard may have wrenched her away from him, so that the little girl in the light blue overalls wouldn't die in her father's arms.

It took Morrison a moment more to douse himself in the gasoline, sit down in the garden, light a match, and touch the flame to his foot. On contact the fire shot twelve feet into the air, a column of heat and light flaring into the darkening sky, filling the air with the stench of burning flesh. It was a ritual death modeled on the self-immolation Buddhist monks had performed in Saigon in the summer of 1963, a devout Quaker's solitary protest against the Vietnam War, and, some said, a heroic attempt to make the secretary of defense face the cost of the violence he had unleashed, though a Pentagon spokesman insisted that McNamara hadn't seen a thing.

Nor had he imagined that escalating the war would trigger such intense emotions. No one in the administration had, least of all the president. It was true that Americans almost always challenged their nation's wars. In 1863 Abraham Lincoln had to dispatch troops from Gettysburg's killing fields to the streets of New York to suppress massive riots against the draft. In the dying days of the Confederacy one out of three southern soldiers deserted. Some of the nation's most prominent figures—among them two former presidents—condemned the imperialist ambitions that drove the Spanish-American War. Woodrow Wilson had so feared the public turning against the United States' involvement in World War I that his administration had all but outlawed dissent. In the run-up to World War II the divisions had run almost as deep, though after Pearl Harbor the country had rallied. And then there was the Korean debacle. That's what LBJ expected: to be gibbeted by the Right—by Goldwater or Nixon or the hawks on Capitol Hill—for a conflict they claimed he'd been too weak to win.

But Johnson had spent his entire presidency courting the Left, from the day after JFK's funeral, when he'd promised to pass the civil rights bill then tangled up in Congress, through his extraordinary pledge to end the scourge of poverty and the flood of legislation that followed, to that electric evening a few weeks after the bombing of North Vietnam began when he made himself one with the civil rights movement. He'd heard of concerns from some progressives as he moved toward escalating the war in early 1965, read the occasional cautionary editorial in the liberal press. After everything he'd done, though, he never expected the Left to build a massive movement against him.

In fact they didn't. The war engendered a great deal of opposition in 1965, 1966, and 1967. But it sprawled across the political spectrum, drawing in people with radically different perspectives, goals, and standards. From their embattled offices it was easy for LBJ and his advisers to miss the distinctions. But the Johnson administration didn't face a single anti-war movement. It faced multiple movements connected to each other in complex, often contradictory ways.

The most conspicuous of those movements was itself an amalgam of forces. It drew much of its inspiration from the Left's most courageous—some would say most rigid—faction. When Bayard Rustin rushed down to Montgomery, Alabama, in search of an American Gandhi in the winter of 1956, radical pacifism had been on the fringes of public life, its principles far too demanding for most Americans to imagine, much less embrace. But in the struggles that followed, the civil rights movement had proved how powerful its vision of nonviolent witness could be. In the process pacifists had become the Left's moral exemplars. No one doubted how hard it was to meet oppression with passive resistance, to allow those in power to beat you and drag you off to jail, to love your enemy as yourself. By the mid-1960s, though, that had become the standard by which many radicals measured themselves. "Aren't activists martyrs?" asked one young woman. "Don't you give up everything and nail yourself to the cross?"[15]

Still, the pacifists' first attempts to oppose the Vietnam War had a lonely feel. No major newspaper bothered to report on the twelve young men who burned their draft cards in New York City in May 1964. Three months later Bayard Rustin headlined an anti-war rally that barely managed to fill a corner of Washington Square. The pacifists tried again in December 1964, just as the president was making the final decision for escalation, with the same feeble turnout. There they might have remained, back on the margins, had they not allied themselves with the rapidly swelling student movement.

It had been three years since Students for a Democratic Society's young radicals called on Americans to reclaim the democratic spirit the military-industrial complex had destroyed. In Mississippi and Berkeley they'd seen their words made flesh. But it wasn't their flesh. While the FBI was pulling bodies out of the Mississippi mud, while California state policemen were towing protesters down the steps of UC Berkeley's Sproul Hall, SDS's leading figures were still debating what role they should take in building a more democratic nation. At their December 1964 National Council meeting the conversation drifted to Vietnam. Everyone thought that the administration's impending escalation of the war was a bad idea. But they couldn't agree why. So they hammered out a less than scintillating statement. "SDS advocates that the US get out of Vietnam," it read. "It so advocates for the following reasons: a) The war hurts the Vietnamese people. b) The war hurts the American people. c) SDS is concerned about the Vietnamese and the American people."[16] Then they voted by a narrow margin to hold an anti-war march in Washington, DC, the following April, to coincide with Easter break.

Even inside SDS, though, the idea didn't generate great enthusiasm until the military launched its sustained bombing of North Vietnam in February 1965. Within a few weeks SDS activists were hearing of spontaneous protests around the country: a march in San Francisco, a sit-in at the federal court in St. Louis, a student-led picket line at the White House. On March 24 SDS brought the war home with a "teach-in" at the University of Michigan. Its format was hardly compelling: through the night professors and students would lecture on Vietnamese history and politics, American Cold War policy, and the terrible power of the military-industrial complex. Three thousand students showed up, more than enough to make the event national news.

Activists on other campuses immediately picked up the idea: 1,000 students came to the University of Wisconsin's teach-in, 1,200 to Harvard's, 2,500 to Columbia's. Those successes gave SDS's April march a prominence no one expected. The radical pacifists endorsed it. Alaska's Ernest Gruening, one of the two senators who had voted against the Gulf of Tonkin Resolution the previous year, agreed to speak, as did SNCC's Bob Moses, the patron saint of participatory democracy. Two weeks before the date of the march, SDS's organizers hoped it might attract 10,000 people. It drew twice that number. "It was unbearably moving to watch the sea of banners and signs move out from the Sylvan Theater toward the Capitol as Joan Baez, Judy Collins, and others sang 'We Shall Overcome,'" wrote one organizer a couple of weeks later. "Still more poignant was the perception—and I checked my reaction with many others who felt as I did—that as the crowd moved down the Mall toward the seat of government . . . our forward movement was irresistibly strong."[17]

So it seemed. The Washington march and its attendant publicity brought SDS a rush of recruits: by the end of the year it had 10,000 members, five times the number it had just two years before. Other organizations joined the movement too. Before April the handful of liberal groups willing to oppose the war had kept their distance from SDS; afterward they set their reservations aside. A bewildering array of radical groups did much the same, hoping to find in the movement the revolutionary fervor they'd long dreamed of reviving. As the movement swelled so did its protests. In October 1965, 10,000 people marched from Berkeley to Oakland's military induction center. A few days later an anti-war rally at the United Nations' Manhattan headquarters drew 20,000. And in November 30,000 protesters picketed the White House. LBJ wasn't in, having decided that it was a fine weekend to visit the folks back in Texas.

Mass marches mixed with acts of pacifist-style protest. Activists staged sit-ins at their local draft boards. A new round of draft card burnings brought out a crush of reporters. And on November 2, 1965, Norman Morrison set himself ablaze in the Pentagon parking lot. That morning he'd read an interview with a Catholic priest who lived in a South Vietnamese village American bombs had obliterated. "I have seen my faithful burned up in napalm," the priest told the reporter. "I have seen the bodies of women and children blown to bits. . . . By God, it's not possible!" By the time he'd finished the article Morrison was absolutely certain of what he had to do. "Know that I love thee," he wrote his wife in a letter he mailed on his way to Washington, "but must act for the children of the priest's village."[18]

There was the pacifist strain in its most extreme form, the ultimate witness against war's horrors. Morrison had "a moral call," said a friend and fellow Quaker. "The trajectory leads right down there. . . . The moral trajectory, right to its logical conclusion." That wasn't the trajectory SDS's leaders were following. They'd come to the movement not because they believed war was inherently wrong—"We're really not just a peace group," its vice president told the press—but because they saw in it a chance to expose the corruption of American society and create a genuine democracy. The first chance they got, they drove their message home. "What kind of system is it that justifies the United States or any country seizing the destinies of the Vietnamese people and using them callously for its own purposes?" SDS's Paul Potter asked in the closing speech of the April march on Washington. "What place is there for ordinary men in that system, and how are they to control it, make it bend itself to their wills rather than bending themselves to it?"[19]

SDS's democratic dreams ran up against the agendas its new allies brought to the movement. Most liberals supported the administration's decision to go to war. Many of those with doubts didn't want to attack the president's foreign policy just as he was putting into place the most sweeping domestic agenda since the New Deal. And everyone knew that LBJ's titanic insecurities made him interpret the slightest criticism as a personal betrayal. "You can't organize against Lyndon Johnson without getting bombed before breakfast," his national security advisor warned, "because in his view that's the . . . ultimate conspiracy."[20]

So, with a few exceptions—a couple of senators, a prominent newspaper columnist or two—those liberals who came out against the war in 1965 tended to be removed from the centers of power. And they staked out as moderate a position as they could manage. Of course the United States had to contain Communism, they said, but Vietnam was the wrong place to do it. The South Vietnamese government was too weak to be defended, the National Liberation Front too strong to be defeated, and the cost of an unwinnable war way too high. Far better for the administration to reach an agreement with the North Vietnamese that would give the United States the cover it needed to withdraw from the conflict gracefully. "The time has come," wrote one of the sharper liberal critics, "to stop beating our heads against stone walls under the illusion that we have been appointed policeman to the human race."[21]

If the liberals' careful critique fell short of SDS's condemnation of the nation's decaying democracy, the left-wing groups raced well beyond it. The old-style Communist blocs hoped the anti-war movement could be turned into a struggle against capitalism. Cadres of young militants wanted it to embrace the Viet Cong as heroic models of revolutionary commitment, a position that drew them toward the glorification of violence as long as it was sheathed in anticolonialism. Others believed that the movement ought to align itself with the cutting edge of pop culture, an idea particularly popular in Berkeley, where the brilliant provocateur Jerry Rubin saw the potential in bringing together anti-war protesters and the hippies by the bay.

Then there were the thousands of people who filled out the protests. Some shared the organizers' political commitments. Others feared the draft, or thought the country shouldn't go to war for a cause that wasn't clear, or wanted the money it was consuming to be spent at home, or were appalled by the graphic images seeping into their homes: the television news report showing American soldiers setting fire to a South Vietnamese hamlet; the newspaper account of a napalmed village; the photo essay of a young marine crying for the dead. "I'm not a marcher," one woman said later. "I'm not a marcher at all. I couldn't bear the thought of marching; but I did it. I mean, at least it was something to do—this horrible war had to be stopped."[22] On that point everyone could agree. But by the end of 1965 almost everything else about the movement—its tactics, its goals, the very purpose of its protest—was up for grabs.

We Are All Participants

NO ONE COULD take hold of it, though. For their part, the movement's liberals—people took to calling them doves—spent 1966 searching for ways to pressure Johnson into negotiations. They tried reasoned arguments, courtesy of the sterling set of academics the movement gathered to it. They tried moral suasion, pleading for peace in a two-page ad that appeared in the *New York Times* in January 1966, signed by 300 ministers, priests, and rabbis, some of them men of international reputation. They even took their campaign up to Capitol Hill early in February for days of blistering hearings on the conduct of the war, led by the chair of the Senate Foreign Relations Committee, J. William Fulbright of Arkansas. When he followed the hearings with a proposal that the Senate rescind the Gulf of Tonkin Resolution, though, almost every liberal senator voted against the move, most because they supported the president, others because they didn't dare to defy him however much they doubted the wisdom of the war he'd begun.

Of those votes, none mattered more than Robert Kennedy's. Not that he could swing his colleagues away from the president's policies: he was a second-year senator, after all, in an institution that honored seniority. Outside the Senate, though, Bobby Kennedy wielded enormous influence, secured by his famous name and the widespread assumption that he was heir to his brother's increasingly mythic legacy, the man who more than anyone else in Washington could lay claim to what might have been, had JFK not gone to Dallas.

The thought haunted him too. He'd spent the months after Jack's murder in a crippling grief shaped by a devastating sense of responsibility: for the cataclysmic failure of the protection he was supposed to provide his brother, and—worse—for the cycle of violence he feared he'd started when he'd pushed the CIA's pursuit of Fidel Castro back in 1961. His friends had hoped that a Senate seat would give him some direction. And it had, in a surprising way. He'd plunged into the roiling politics of race and poverty in New York City's Black neighborhoods; in the poorest portions of the South; and in 1966, out in California's Central Valley. The UAW's Walter Reuther had convinced him to make the trip in support of a farmworkers' strike being led by a young organizer named Cesar Chavez. Kennedy hadn't wanted to go. But once he was in the fields he was enthralled by the determination of the some of the nation's most exploited workers—almost all of them Filipino and Mexican American—to demand the decent treatment the major growers had long denied them. And he was completely taken with Chavez, who in his quietly charismatic manner was fusing unionism, Gandhism, and Catholic social action. The grief remained. But in his embrace of causes like the farmworkers Kennedy seemed to find some relief from the terrible burdens he bore.

The doves had reason to believe they could win him over to the antiwar movement too. Throughout the Fulbright hearings he sat in the back of the room, seething at LBJ's escalation of the war as a mindlessly militaristic response to a challenge his brother would have handled with subtlety and sophistication. He even offered a few oblique words about the need for negotiation. But then he voted against the motion to repeal the Gulf of Tonkin Resolution, and the next day he supported the administration's request for a $4.8 billion supplementary appropriation to pay for the rising costs of the year's combat. For the rest of the year he left the war alone in hopes of appeasing a president he despised.

But Vietnam wouldn't leave him alone. It seeped into the briefing books the young liberals on his Senate staff packed with reports of the military's faltering strategy. It ran through conversations over drinks with the more liberal of his political confidants, who pressed him to take a stand. It dominated his intensely private discussions with his only friend among the administration's policy makers, Robert McNamara, who told Kennedy that the bombing campaign wasn't working and that the war he was helping to direct couldn't be won. Finally, in February 1967, it burst wide open in a catastrophic meeting in the Oval Office, during which years of frustration exploded in a vicious presidential tirade, LBJ raging that RFK and his liberal friends were giving aid to the enemy and thus had the blood of American boys on their hands.

Kennedy waited almost a month to reply, long enough for his text to be perfected and the press informed of his intentions. When he rose from his desk to speak on March 2, 1967, the Senate floor was all but deserted, the gallery half full, mostly with the reporters who knew what was coming. In substance he followed the liberal line, carefully laying out a series of steps he hoped would lead Washington and Hanoi into negotiations, the crucial one an immediate end to the administration's bombing of North Vietnam. But he also insisted that he wasn't the only American whose hands were stained with blood. "All we say and all we do must be informed that this horror is our responsibility," he said in the first few minutes of an address that lasted almost an hour, "not just our nation's responsibility but yours and mine. It is we who live in abundance and send our young men out to die. It is our chemicals that scorch the children and our bombs that level the villages. We are all participants."[23] And for a moment, Bobby Kennedy sounded very much like Norman Morrison.

Four weeks later, on April 4, 1967, Martin Luther King strode into Riverside Church, the magnificent Gothic cathedral built by the Rockefellers on Manhattan's Upper West Side, for what turned out to be one of the most devoutly liberal congregations in the country. Through the nave he went, behind a solemn procession of a hundred clergymen, past the packed pews, up to its soaring sanctuary. He'd spoken from the church's pulpit a number of times before. This time he took his place at a makeshift lectern set in the center of the sanctuary, since he'd come not to preach the Gospel but to speak, he said, "from the burnings of my own heart."

Almost as soon as the United States began bombing North Vietnam in early 1965, King had wanted to object to the nation's descent into war. But his closest advisers pulled him back. After decades of presidential indifference and occasional hostility, they insisted, the civil rights movement finally had an ally in the White House; why risk alienating him by criticizing his foreign policy? King could have replied with a passage from the letter he'd written in Birmingham's jail two years before. "We will have to repent in this generation not merely for the hateful words and actions of the bad people," he'd said then, "but for the appalling silence of the good people."[24] Instead he gave his advisers what they wanted, with only occasional lapses—a call for negotiations in the summer of 1965, a condemnation of the South Vietnamese government in the spring of 1966—until he couldn't bear the weight of his own appalling silence anymore.

King's breaking point coincided with RFK's, though the timing was coincidental. His decision was driven not by LBJ—not directly at least—but by SCLC's most erratic organizer, James Bevel, who one day arrived uninvited at King's door speaking of revelation, and by a devastating photo essay of Vietnamese children mangled by American armaments that he stumbled across while sitting in an airport lounge. Again his inner circle tried to talk him down, but this time King wouldn't listen. So they insisted that if he had to speak he do so in a controlled setting, ideally somewhere that would give his message the gravitas it deserved. Somewhere like Riverside.

He began in the soft, somber voice of the penitent, hinting at the inner turmoil he'd felt over the previous two years and defending his right to speak out now. When he turned to the war itself his tone sharpened dramatically. He talked of "the madness" of US policy, of American troops herding the South Vietnamese "off the land of their fathers and into concentration camps"—a reference to the military's recent destruction of Ben Suc—and of a million civilian casualties, most of them children. Like Kennedy, he called for an immediate end to the bombing as a path to negotiations. Then he brought the conflict home in the same terms SDS had used in 1965, with a final twist of faith. "The war in Vietnam is but a symptom of a far deeper malady within the American spirit," he said. "It is a sad fact that because of comfort, complacency, a morbid fear of communism, and our proneness to adjust to injustice, the Western nations that initiated so much of the revolutionary spirit of the modern world have now become the arch antirevolutionaries. . . . Our only hope today lies in our ability to recapture the revolutionary spirit and go out into a sometimes hostile world declaring eternal hostility to poverty, racism, and militarism. . . . This is the calling of the sons of God."[25]

LBJ did what he could to limit the damage. On his order a line of powerful proxies—senior senators, the vice president, the secretary of state, General Westmoreland, the head of the NAACP, the only other African American Nobel Peace Prize winner as an obvious counterpoint to King—marched before the press to dismiss the possibility of a bombing pause as naive at best, dangerous at worst. Johnson himself worked the back channels, feeding friendly reporters damning stories of Kennedy's plotting to assassinate Fidel Castro and King's consorting with Communists. But it was too late. After two years of working on the periphery of power, the war's liberal critics had been cloaked in Camelot's aura and blessed by America's Gandhi, a combination of such force that LBJ couldn't contain it.

It didn't impress the movement's radicals, though. Maybe it would have in the spring of 1965, when militancy meant campus teach-ins and Easter marches led by earnest young men in suits and ties. But the tone had shifted in the months that followed, as SDS tried to accommodate the flood of recruits its protests had brought in. Participatory democracy demanded that the newcomers decide for themselves what politics they wanted to pursue. Some of its leading figures warned that the principle could be taken too far. "If God had meant us to be anarchists," said one, "we would have been born with beards."[26] But in democratic fashion they were outvoted: in late 1965 the central office turned control of its agenda over to its rapidly expanding chapters, a decision that tossed SDS into the maelstrom of radical actions that in the next two years gripped the movement's left wing.

There were still mass protests in 1966 and 1967, of course, but no longer was it enough to march on Washington. Now radicals confronted the military-industrial complex head-on, blocking recruiting offices and induction stations and throwing up pickets around Dow Chemical, the maker of napalm. There were still draft card burnings, but now they were accompanied by calls for a widespread defiance of the draft. Then there were the new initiatives, meant to shock and awe the mainstream. From the hippie contingent came a psychedelia of provocations, among them an absurdist assault on Wall Street—play money floating down on the trading floor—and a flower-strewn sit-in in the midst of New York's annual Armed Forces Day Parade, led by a SNCC-inspired organizer named Abbie Hoffman. And more and more the entire radical wing was infused with a revolutionary romanticism that not long before had been restricted to the Far Left. Even SDS's foremost theorist of participatory democracy was swept up in it. At the end of 1965 the North Vietnamese government invited Tom Hayden to visit Hanoi. He came back enthralled by the "socialism of the heart" that Ho Chi Minh and his comrades had created: "The unembarrassed handclasps among men," Hayden wrote the following year, "the poetry and song at the center of man-woman relationships, the freedom to weep practiced by everyone—from guerillas to generals, peasants to factory workers—as the Vietnamese speak of their country."[27] How could a radical not do what he could to stop the war being waged against a place so pure—not through negotiations but by confronting the American war machine?

Talk of an October march on the Pentagon began in May 1967, just a month after the liberals' breakthrough with Kennedy and King. The radical pacifists took charge of the initial organizing in hopes that it could be centered on dramatic acts of civil disobedience. But other groups objected, some arguing that confrontation would scare away many of the ordinary people who could make the march a mass event; others that peaceful protest, however noble, wasn't enough anymore. To keep the entire project from unraveling, the pacifists widened the scope: there'd be speeches and a solemn march on the Pentagon for those who didn't want to be arrested, civil disobedience for those who still believed in the power of moral witness, direct action against the Pentagon for those who didn't. Then they hired Jerry Rubin, San Francisco's impresario of hipster politics, to run the entire event. He promptly framed it in revolutionary terms. "We are now in the business of wholesale and widespread resistance and dislocation of American society," he told the press six weeks before the protest was to take place, to give the authorities plenty of time to panic.[28]

The run-up only increased the tension. In the week before the march waves of demonstrators tried to shut down the military induction center in Oakland, California. The police responded with the full force of the law, arresting hundreds of people, driving back the rest with tear gas and truncheons. On Wednesday, October 18, the violence spread to the heartland. At the University of Wisconsin, SDS activists tried to block Dow Chemical recruiters from interviewing job candidates.

They'd done it before. But this time the university chancellor called in the Madison police, who restored the company's right to hire with an assault so fierce it sent sixty-five students to the hospital.

Washington expected worse. Government officials had agreed that the protesters could hold their rally at the Lincoln Memorial, in imitation of the civil rights movement's transcendent moment four years before, and that they could then march to one of the Pentagon's parking lots, which would be cordoned off for the day. But no one expected the more militant among them to be restrained by a formal agreement and a chain-link fence. So Robert McNamara had ordered in the troops: some 2,500 military policemen, 2,000 National Guardsmen, 1,500 district policemen, and 200 federal marshals to protect the Pentagon's entrances, with 6,000 soldiers from the 82nd Airborne stationed inside its cavernous halls in case the front line was breached. All through Friday, October 20, military transports ferried them in, until the Pentagon began to feel like Da Nang.

The next day began with 50,000 people gathered for the morning rally. When the last speaker was done, the final folk song sung, the crowd started moving off the Mall, around the Lincoln Memorial to the Arlington Bridge, over the Potomac to the Pentagon, picking up marchers as it went, so that by the time the protesters reached the lot their numbers had almost doubled. "An army of amateur soldiers," wrote the novelist Norman Mailer, who was in the front of the line, made up of "college students from all over the East, and high school students and hippies" alongside "a smattering and a sprinkling of doctors, dentists, faculty, veterans' groups, housewives, accountants, trade unionists, Communists, socialists, pacifists, Trotskyists, anarchists, artists, and entertainers," all come to confront the war makers.[29]

But no one could agree on what form the confrontation should take. Defense Department officials had decided to put the protesters into the north lot, across a four-lane highway, another parking lot—the one where Morrison had set himself ablaze—and a plaza from the Pentagon's administrative entrance. In trooped Mailer's army, behind the chain-link fence the military had put up to keep them contained. The doctors and dentists, artists and accountants, and most of the students settled in for yet another round of speeches, while the hippies gathered off in a corner for a bit of ritual chanting they said would levitate the Pentagon three hundred feet into the air, spin it around, and expel the demons within. Others wanted to meet the demons face-to-face. Some of the students began rocking the fence, wrenching it back and forth until a section of it toppled. Through the gap surged two or three thousand protesters, the path now clear to the Pentagon's doors.

They quickly overran the plaza. On the steps leading up to the north entrance, though, stood 2,500 military policemen, each one armed with a bayoneted M14. From the back of the crowd came calls to storm the steps. The few protesters who tried were quickly arrested and hauled away. But most of those in the front stopped a few feet short of the troops. A man with a bullhorn tried to organize them, to get them to sit down and link arms in the classic pose of passive resistance, but no one listened. They just held their ragged line for a couple of minutes, as the soldiers held theirs. Then one of the marchers started to talk to the MPs across the divide, and others joined in, some lecturing them on the immorality of the war; others pleading with them to join the protest; still others insulting them, taunting them, burrowing under their skin, one poking at them with a pole, at the end of which he'd hung a North Vietnamese flag. And a handful of young people—some high schoolers, others barely old enough for college—came out of the crowd clutching bouquets of flowers. Down the line of troops they went, stopping in front of each soldier to place a single carnation in the barrel of his gun. This time Robert McNamara stood at his office window, half-hidden behind the barely parted curtains, and watched it all.

The Other Movement

THE TELEVISION NETWORKS didn't broadcast the march, for fear of the politics they'd put on display. But the major morning newspapers gave it full play. None of them went with young people slipping flowers into gun barrels. Instead the *Chicago Tribune* ran three front-page photos of marshals and soldiers beating back the mob, the *New York Times* a close-up of a young man snarling at the troops. And every paper ran at least one story of protesters chanting obscenities and urinating on the Pentagon's walls. "Demonstrations like these," wrote the *Times's* Russell Baker, "give peace a bad name."[30]

It was a sentiment widely shared. In the summer of 1965 pollsters first asked Americans what they thought of the anti-war movement. The majority of those surveyed didn't approve of it. But almost half believed that the protesters were acting out of "honest differences" with the administration.[31] That relatively benign interpretation quickly faded: by year's end only a quarter of Americans said the protesters had good intentions, while 63 percent thought they were Communists, dupes, or draft dodgers. Once set, the perception couldn't be dislodged. Sixty-seven percent of those polled in late October 1967 said that the march on the Pentagon wasn't a legitimate expression of alternative views. It was an act of disloyalty.

The more militant met protests with protests. In April 1967 a New York City firefighter organized a massive demonstration to counter, he said, "the impression given to the world of a people who opposed their country." Hour after hour they marched down Fifth Avenue, 70,000 of them—veterans in the uniforms they'd brought back from their wars; parents with babies in strollers and toddlers in sailor suits; longshoremen and pipe fitters, plumbers, teamsters, and cops; a contingent of nuns reciting the rosary; and two Medal of Honor recipients—in a defiant display of patriotism. Around the edges there was trouble: a few hippies assaulted, some anti-war protesters knocked to the ground, a young man tarred and feathered. But that wasn't enough to stop the organizers from promising to take to the streets again. They waited until the weekend of the Pentagon protests, when they staged rallies in half a dozen cities, the centerpieces a parade in Newark that drew 60,000 participants and a flag-draped vigil at New York's Battery Park meant to last as long as the Defense Department was besieged. A reporter from the *Village Voice* asked one of the protesters what he thought of his counterparts down in

DC. "I hope they all get shot on the steps of the Pentagon," he replied. "They're all commies anyway."[32]

Opposing the anti-war movement didn't correlate with supporting the war, though. In the first days of the 1965 escalation, 79 percent of Americans agreed that the United States had to hold the line in Vietnam or risk losing all of Asia to Communism, and only five percent disagreed. Relatively quickly, opinions began to shift. By the end of the year 21 percent thought that going to war in Vietnam had been a mistake, still a minority to be sure, but a dramatically expanded one. By March 1966 that number was up to 23 percent, by September 1966 33 percent, by May 1967 37 percent. That October it reached 46 percent, two points higher than the percentage who believed that the United States had done the right thing by sending in its boys.

The doubts grew even deeper when pollsters asked Americans what they thought of the way the administration was fighting the war. Eighty-three percent backed LBJ's decision to bomb North Vietnam in February 1965. Everyone understood that the support would drop once the rush to war faded. So it did: by spring about a quarter of those surveyed thought Johnson was mismanaging the conflict. There the proportion remained for the rest of the year. Then it began to rise. In April 1966 31 percent said they disapproved of LBJ's handling of the war, in June 37 percent, in September 40 percent. The following spring the opposition climbed to 49 percent. In the summer of 1967 it passed 50 percent. And in early October 1967, just a few weeks before the Pentagon protest, it peaked at 57 percent, double the number of those who approved of the administration's strategy.

Some of those who opposed LBJ's policies shared the anti-war movement's goals, of course. But the trend pulled in the opposite direction. In May 1965 about a quarter of Americans thought Johnson ought to intensify the war. Two years later 59 percent favored escalation. They wanted the United States to blockade the enemy's ports, they said; to step up the bombing campaign; even to launch a conventional invasion of North Vietnam. Twenty-seven percent thought the White House should take the ultimate step of unleashing the nation's nuclear arsenal,

almost the same share of the population as wanted Johnson to negotiate a settlement, and far beyond the portion who favored the immediate withdrawal of American troops. In the summer of 1967, in short,
most Americans weren't doves. They were hawks.

There was the politics LBJ had feared back in the winter of 1965,
before Rolling Thunder and all the steps that followed. He knew then
that Americans liked their wars to be short, their victories decisive, and
that if he didn't end Vietnam quickly and cleanly the patriotic surge
that invariably came with the start of combat would give way to a dangerous frustration. Now that his war had dragged into a third incon-
clusive year, the national mood was hardening, the public's toleration of
dissent shrinking, its determination to win the war at almost any cost
growing, both swings in opinion buttressed by a sense that the violence he had visited on Vietnam—as fearsome as it had been—wasn't
enough, that he'd been too soft on the Communists, just as Truman
had been too soft in Korea.

It was still nothing more than a sensibility, an expression, the experts
said, of a deepening weariness of Lyndon Johnson's war. But LBJ knew
how quickly that could change. Anyone who had a sense of the past
knew. Already it was moving from the polls into the streets. It appeared
in the "Bomb Hanoi" buttons that many of the marchers wore on their
lapels and in the homemade signs they hoisted over their heads—the
ones that read "Escalate, Don't Capitulate," "Down with the Reds," and
"My Country Right or Wrong"—as they paraded through Manhattan
in the spring sun; in the posters the Teamsters had printed that read,
"If your heart isn't in America you better get your ass out of here"; in
the talk of imposing "law and order" that dominated the October vigil,
and in the cheers of the crowd at the Newark parade when a group of
young men up on a rooftop set a Viet Cong flag on fire.[33] There was no
doubting the pressure the anti-war movement had brought to bear on
LBJ, the enormous force of King and Kennedy and those long-haired
kids that the newspapers vilified. But to his right there was another
movement in the making, another rough beast waiting to be born.

CHAPTER 9

THE CRUELEST MONTHS

George Wallace arrived in Chicago late in the morning of September 30, 1968. From the airport his motorcade raced downtown, where his staffers had a sleek open-topped limousine waiting for him, perfect for a brilliant autumn day. He climbed into the back, planted himself between the driver and passenger seats, and braced for the car to start moving. It had been barely a month since the mayhem at the Democratic National Convention: masses of protesters in the park along the lake; a confrontation in front of the nominee's hotel, the Chicago police wading into the throng, nightsticks drawn; brutality on Michigan Avenue. Now Wallace was ready to ride down State Street, two blocks to the west, waving to the 50,000 people who'd come out to catch a glimpse of him as he rolled by.

By all rights his political career should have been over after the Birmingham church bombing in September 1963, when *Time* put his scowling profile on its cover, superimposed over one of the church's shattered stained-glass windows. Or in March 1965, when state troopers under his command charged up the Edmund Pettus Bridge. Or in August of that year, when the attorney general used the power vested in him by the newly passed Voting Rights Act to send federal officials to Alabama to register what would turn out to be 100,000 African American voters. Or in the gubernatorial election of 1966, when state law prohibited him from seeking a second term, and rather than stepping aside he arranged for his wife Lurleen to run in his place, though she was dying of cancer.

Lyndon Johnson at Cam Ranh Bay Air Force Base, South Vietnam, October 26, 1966.
(Yoichi Okamoto/PhotoQuest/Getty Images)

Two of the villagers murdered by American soldiers in My Lai, South Vietnam, March 16, 1968. (Ronald Haeberle/The LIFE Images Collection/Getty Images)

Larry Burrows's final photo of James Farley after the return flight of Yankee Papa 13, Da Nang, South Vietnam, March 31, 1965. (Larry Burrows/The LIFE Picture Collection/Getty Images)

The remains of American soldiers killed in Vietnam arriving in the United States, February 11, 1965. (Bettmann/Getty Images)

The summer solstice celebration in Golden Gate Park, San Francisco, California, June 21, 1967. (The San Francisco Chronicle/Getty Images)

Sheri Finkbine packs for a trip to Sweden to secure the abortion she could not legally obtain in the United States, July 1962. (J.R. Eyerman/The LIFE Images Collection/Getty Images)

Estelle Griswold in front of the Planned Parenthood Center, New Haven, Connecticut, April 1, 1963. (Lee Lockwood/The LIFE Images Collection/Getty Images)

Robert Kennedy on the campaign trail, 1968.
(DECLAN HAUN/CHICAGO HISTORICAL SOCIETY)

George Wallace campaigning in Glen Burnie, Maryland, July 13, 1968.
(AP PHOTO)

A policeman assaults anti-war protests in Chicago's Grant Park during the Democratic National Convention, August 28, 1968. (PAUL SLADE/*PARIS MATCH* ARCHIVES/GETTY IMAGES)

Chicago Mayor Richard Daley shouts at Senator Abraham Ribicoff as he denounces the Chicago police assault on anti-war protesters at the Democratic National Convention, August 28, 1968.
(BETTMANN/GETTY IMAGES)

Allison Krause in her high school yearbook photo in the spring of 1969, and at an anti-war rally in October of that year.
(BETTMANN ARCHIVES/ GETTY IMAGES)

Richard Nixon's television announcement of the Cambodian invasion, April 30, 1970. (Bettmann/Getty Images)

Construction workers at New York City's hard-hat rebellion against anti-war activists, May 8, 1970. (Scott McPartland/Getty Images)

But Birmingham didn't ruin him. After Selma his support in the white South spiked. He shrugged off the federal registrars by adding 110,000 white voters to the rolls. And in November 1966 Lurleen Wallace won the governorship in a landslide. It was only the beginning, warned one of Alabama's rare white progressives. "I know you think I'm crazy when I say he expects to be president," she wrote a colleague. "But he actually does. He . . . is going to arouse hatred all over the whole country, and then pose as their Savior."[1] She had it just right. On the day Lurleen took the oath of office, January 16, 1967, her husband's most devoted supporters met at a Montgomery, Alabama, country club to begin planning his campaign for the White House. This time he wouldn't dabble in the Democratic primaries, as he had in 1964. He'd form his own party, run as he wanted to run, on a slogan they carried over from his first venture north. In 1968 George Wallace would stand up for America.

When the State Street parade was done he held a news conference for the crush of reporters who'd trailed him into Chicago. Then his motorcade was on the road again, heading west, past the neighborhood where Martin Luther King had lived during his 1966 crusade, through the bungalow belt that had tried to beat his protests back, to the only rally of the day, an outdoor event less than a block beyond the city limits, on the far side of the line King hadn't dared to cross. Of course Wallace would cross it. In the great sprawl of a city it was the most obvious place for him to be.

There were 8,000 people waiting to hear him, working-class folks mostly, a fair share of them from the giant General Electric plant down the street. He gave them his stump speech, a slashing attack on civil rights agitators and welfare cheats, radical longhairs and "silver-spooned" draft dodgers, closet Communists, government bureaucrats, "and some of these newspaper editors that look down their nose at every workingman . . . in the United States and calls them a group of rednecks or a group of punks because we want to defend America." That's exactly what he was going to do when he was president, he told them. Defend decent Americans' right to send their kids to the schools of their choice rather than have judges telling them where they had to go; their right to keep their tax dollars at home rather than have them shipped off to Ghana or Guinea or some other godforsaken place in the name of foreign aid; their right to be free of marches and riots and the crime liberals weren't willing to control; their right to live in neighborhoods filled with people like themselves because in America "a man's home is still his castle," no matter what Washington said.

"As he spoke the . . . crowd rocked with him," wrote the veteran reporter Theodore White, a portion of it with the rage Wallace unleashed—around the press pen swirled racial slurs and threats of violence—the balance with raw political passion. "He was saying what was on their minds," White decided, "saying it like it is, saying it in the way they said it to each other in the bars."[2] And they loved him for it, as Wallace knew they would, not just in Montgomery or Selma or the Alabama countryside but in the streets of Cicero, in the final weeks of an election year already drenched in bitterness and blood.

Gaping Wounds

BY THE AUTUMN of 1967 Lyndon Johnson had been through ten election campaigns, all but one a victory, with the most recent of mammoth proportions. That left him one last race to run. If he were reelected in 1968, as incumbent presidents generally were, he'd have four more years to extend the gains his sweeping reforms had secured—in the past two years alone the nation's poverty rate had fallen by two points, the African American rate by seven—to find a way out of the war in Vietnam, and to bind the nation's wounds. Then, in January 1973, after forty years in Washington, he'd hand the Oval Office to his successor and head back to his ranch, his place in history secured.

That was the plan, at least. The polls complicated the calculations. In June 1967, 52 percent of Americans approved of Johnson's performance as president. After Newark, Detroit, and another summer's violence in Vietnam, his approval rating tumbled to 38 percent, the lowest level recorded since 1952, when the public turned against Harry Truman's handling of the Korean War. LBJ was too practical a politician not to face the truth the numbers made plain. He could still win in 1968, but he was heading into his final campaign a far more wounded candidate than he had ever been before.

The Republicans certainly smelled blood. In 1964 the party's conservative wing had led it to crushing defeat. This time, its moderates were determined to grab hold of the nomination as quickly as they could. For a while in the autumn of 1967 the power brokers flirted with Michigan governor George Romney, until he showed an unsettling tendency to conduct his campaign with an openness and honesty they thought naive. So they began moving—slowly but inexorably—toward a man who wouldn't make the same mistake.

Richard Nixon had followed his razor-thin loss to John Kennedy in 1960 with a disastrous run for the governorship of California in 1962. In the postelection humiliation he let the public see the demons he'd tried to hide with a surly, self-pitying press conference that ended with his declaring that he was done with politics. The press took him at his word. The next week ABC News ran a half-hour report subtly titled, "The Political Obituary of Richard M. Nixon."[3] A couple of his longtime supporters duly appeared. But the show's star turn went to his most famous target, Alger Hiss, who calmly lacerated Nixon for the ruthless red-baiting he'd used to launch himself up the Republican ranks in the late 1940s: another reminder that now that his career was over there was no need to mourn it.

But Nixon wasn't done. Over the next five years he worked his way back to prominence by methodically remaking his brand. Away went the sullen loser of 1960 and 1962. In his place rose Nixon the party loyalist, crisscrossing the country in the elections of 1964 and 1966 to support other Republicans, raising them money, speaking on their behalf, piling up debts they'd have to repay. Away went Hiss's self-promoting McCarthyite, replaced by Nixon the statesman, writing about building ties to China in the prestigious pages of *Foreign Affairs*. Most importantly, away went the brooding loner who saw himself surrounded by enemies, replaced by a "New Nixon," steady, sober, and mature; his demons exorcised by the former advertising men to whom he'd entrusted his image.

His remade reputation slotted perfectly into the race he planned to run. Teddy White saw the essence of it in a February 1968 meet-and-greet in Manchester, New Hampshire, when he noticed how many people in the crowd were wearing "Ike and Dick" buttons from 1952. They were "mementos of a safer past, of the promise and then the delivery of tranquility," he wrote. "There is a nostalgia here, a reservoir of affection for [Nixon], for the Party, for his inheritance from Eisenhower."[4] That's what the New Nixon wanted to be: Ike's heir, the candidate of all those middling Americans who wanted to re-create the sense of security that the '60s had stripped away.

From that premise he and his handlers prepared their pitch. On Vietnam he drew the connection to Ike as tightly as he could. He'd end Johnson's mismanaged war, his stock speech promised, as he and Eisenhower had ended Truman's Korean debacle, with a quick and honorable peace. For his domestic agenda he combined Ike's commitment to preserving the Democrats' popular programs—no one had to fear Nixon dismantling Medicare—with a pledge to restore law and order through the decisive leadership that LBJ clearly couldn't provide. Precisely what form that leadership might take he didn't say, because as every ad man knew, a product's packaging was far more important than the list of ingredients on the side of the box.

George Wallace already had his image honed. What he needed was access. After its country club meeting in January 1967 his team set out to get their newly created American Independent Party onto the 1968 presidential ballot in fifty states, a prerequisite for a campaign premised on the national appeal of Wallace's racial populism. It was painstaking work, made more difficult by the party's lack of structure, a network of members it could call on, and even a slate of candidates for Congress: it was purely a vehicle for Wallace's race, run from a suite of offices outside of Montgomery. But one by one the states fell into line, won over by

Wallace's relentless campaigning among "the little people"—the white waitresses, machinists, cops, and cabbies—whose votes he planned to claim.[5] When California's officials announced that he'd qualified there, on January 2, 1968, the most difficult part of the job was done.

While Wallace mobilized, the Democrats divided. As LBJ struggled through the summer of 1967, a tiny cadre of youngish liberals launched a campaign to "dump Johnson" from the ticket in 1968 and put in his place an anti-war candidate. At first it seemed a ludicrous idea: not since 1896 had a sitting president been denied his party's nomination, in large part because the nominating system discouraged insurgencies. There were primaries, obviously, but they were showcases through which candidates could demonstrate their electability to the power brokers who would choose the nominee at the party's convention. And power brokers weren't generally given to turning their backs on incumbent presidents. But the more they talked to their fellow liberals, the greater the cadre's confidence grew. "We can do it," the group's leading figure, thirty-eight-year-old Allard Lowenstein, told his colleagues. "No one wants [Johnson] out there and all that we have to do is have someone say it. Like, 'The emperor has no clothes.' There's a movement inside the party that's dying for leadership."[6]

To move beyond talk, though, the insurgents had to find a candidate willing to challenge LBJ. They started with the obvious choice. Since his March speech on the Senate floor, Robert Kennedy had come to be seen as one of the nation's leading doves. He was undoubtedly its most electable: asked by pollsters whom they preferred to be the Democratic nominee in 1968, voters favored RFK over LBJ by twenty points. When Lowenstein raised the possibility of his running against Johnson as an anti-war candidate in the primaries, Kennedy gave him a hearing. But in the end he wasn't convinced that LBJ could be toppled. So Lowenstein had to turn elsewhere. He tried the Senate's other leading doves, South Dakota's George McGovern, Idaho's Frank Church, Oregon's Wayne Morse, piling up rejections as he went. Finally he reached the senior senator from Minnesota, Eugene McCarthy. Arrogant, acerbic, and unremittingly judgmental—before entering politics he'd been a college professor—he wasn't an easy man to love. Nor could he give the insurgency the cachet it needed, not when 58 percent of Americans had no clue who he was, much less what he stood for. But he was willing to run, and Lowenstein didn't have any other options. McCarthy declared his candidacy on November 30, 1967, three and a half months before the election's first primary, in New Hampshire, and almost nine months before the convention, set for Chicago at the end of August 1968.

Through the rest of the year and into the next the candidates did what they could to build their campaigns' momentum, Nixon moving methodically through the thoroughly controlled events his handlers had scheduled; Wallace firing up his base across the South, an emaciated Lurleen at his side for his most important appearances; McCarthy plodding around New Hampshire giving lackluster speeches; Johnson hunkered down in the White House, watching his opponents run. That's where he was on the afternoon of January 29, 1968—early the next morning in Vietnam—when the first bulletins came in from Saigon.

For months military intelligence had been picking up signs that the North Vietnamese were preparing for a major offensive in South Vietnam. But no one in the American command had expected it to start in the middle of a weeklong cease-fire meant to give Vietnam's beleaguered people the chance to celebrate Tet—the New Year holiday—in peace. Nor had anyone anticipated an assault on such a massive scale. It started at midnight on January 30 with attacks on eight towns along the coast. The following night some 80,000 troops from the National Liberation Front and the North Vietnamese army struck almost every major city and other strategic sites in the South. By dawn on the 31st they'd pushed deep into the ancient capital of Hue, onto the US air base at Tan Son Nhut, across the Mekong Delta, even onto the grounds of the US embassy in central Saigon, in a symbolic assault on American soil.

Analysts would later say that the furious counterattack by the United States turned North Vietnam's Tet Offensive into a rout. But that wasn't clear at the time. Some of the NLF's most audacious advances quickly crumbled: the marines reclaimed the embassy compound six hours after its walls had been breached. In much of the South, though, American forces met fierce resistance. It took twelve days of street fighting to drive the NLF out of Saigon's Cholon district. The battle for Hue stretched over a month. And in Khe Sanh, up near the Laotian border, 6,000 American and South Vietnamese troops endured week after week of a siege that at times bore an alarming resemblance to the French catastrophe at Dien Bien Phu in 1954. In the worst of the fighting the NLF and the North Vietnamese suffered devastating losses. They also inflicted them. In the first four weeks after the offensive began, 2,124 Americans were killed in action, 200 more than in all of 1965.

From the killing fields the conflict swept across the United States. It burst into public view through the evening news's Technicolor footage of the combat's carnage, a month's worth of mangled bodies and burning villages to share over supper. It also roiled through Washington. Johnson's liberal critics seized on the violence as proof that the war wasn't winnable and therefore had to be ended by negotiations, while the Right hammered away at his refusal to unleash the full force of American power and thus bring the war to a quick conclusion. The liberals had the more powerful voices, the Right the numbers: according to a mid-February Gallup poll 61 percent of Americans wanted the United States to escalate the fighting, almost three times the number who wanted to scale it back. Johnson tried to fend them off with assurances that all was well; the Communists' offensive had been "a complete failure," he told a packed press conference four days after the initial assault.[7] But he didn't believe it. Night after night he sat in the Situation Room poring over battle reports, sometimes to 2:00 or 3:00 a.m., for whatever reassurance he might find there.

Then the crisis intensified. It began on February 27, when the Joint Chiefs of Staff formally requested that the president increase the American military commitment to Vietnam by 40 percent, from the half million men already in-country to 700,000. It was a power play, the Joint Chiefs' attempt to trade on LBJ's fear of failure to dramatically increase the number of troops at their disposal, and it triggered a furious debate that raged for twelve days inside the White House. The military's supporters argued that the war's success hinged on the request, their opponents that the generals couldn't ensure that such a massive call-up would tip the war's balance, while there was no doubt that it would carry enormous costs, both economic and political. Johnson seemed genuinely torn, so unsure what to do that he ordered his speechwriter to prepare two major addresses to the nation, one announcing the escalation the military wanted, the other rejecting it.

On the thirteenth day, Sunday, March 10, the ground abruptly shifted. That morning the *New York Times* ran a front-page story detailing the Joint Chiefs' proposal, apparently leaked by its opponents in hopes of building pressure against it. That it did. "This is the hour to decide whether it is futile to destroy Vietnam in an effort to save it," NBC News's anchorman told his audience on Sunday evening. The next morning the *Times's* editorial board called the possibility of sending so many more men into Vietnam "a suicidal escalation." In Congress the doves spent Monday in open revolt. Giving in to the generals' request would be "nothing short of disastrous," insisted Arkansas' J. William Fulbright, while Oregon's Wayne Morse warned of "an incipient uprising in this country in opposition to this war—and it's going to get worse."[8] But the pivotal response came the following day, Tuesday, March 12, primary day in New Hampshire.

In early February the polls had put LBJ ahead of McCarthy by 53 points. Insiders knew that the race had tightened since then. Still, no one expected McCarthy to take 42 percent of the vote, just seven points behind the president's total. Later studies would show that a substantial portion of McCarthy's supporters didn't know he was an anti-war candidate; they were just lodging protest votes against LBJ. But the next day's papers saw in the returns unmistakable evidence that the doves' critique of the war was surging through the Democratic Party. Robert Kennedy read the vote that way too. The previous Sunday he'd gone back to California's Central Valley to attend Mass alongside Cesar Chavez, who'd be breaking a twenty-five day water-only fast by taking communion. In the subsequent speech he was too weak to deliver, Chavez spoke of courage and sacrifice, attributes that Kennedy in his caution hadn't managed to find. On Tuesday night the primary results came in. On Wednesday morning, March 13, RFK told the reporters trailing him around the Senate Office Building that he was "reassessing" his decision not to seek the nomination, now that New Hampshire had shown that Johnson really could be toppled.[9]

The political turmoil caused a terrifying turn in the global financial markets. Its roots lay in the war's spiraling expense. In 1965 the Defense Department had budgeted $47 billion for military outlays. The 1968 figure was $30 billion higher. Much of that spending went into the American economy, where it triggered the familiar cycle of war-induced inflation: in 1966 and 1967 the rate ticked up by a combined 6.5 percent. The war also sent a good deal of money abroad, to pay for the sprawling infrastructure the fighting required. As the cash flowed out, the nation's deficit in its balance of payments widened, precisely the dynamic that Eisenhower had told Kennedy to avoid in 1960, for fear of the damage it would do to international investors' faith in the dollar. Mid-March's events—the *Times*'s revelation, the possibility that LBJ might markedly escalate the American commitment to Vietnam, the firestorm in the media and on Capitol Hill, the Democrats' splintering—gave those investors every reason to abandon whatever faith they had left. So they mounted a run on gold.

On March 13 they drained $200 million from the United States' gold reserves, more than on any previous day. On March 14 they doubled that amount. On Friday, March 15, the day before RFK made his entry into the race official, the losses threatened to reach a billion dollars. At that rate, experts said, the United States would soon be forced to shut off its gold exchange or drop the dollar's value, in the process setting off shock waves so severe they were likely to topple the foundational economic structures of the Western world. "The world is lost," a British economist told the press as the panic peaked. ". . . We're in the first act of a world depression."[10]

The White House spent the day frantically searching for some way to prevent that from happening. By Friday evening the secretary of the treasury had arranged a weekend summit with his counterparts in

Western Europe, out of which came a set of modifications to the gold exchange that cut off investors' ability to renew their run when the markets opened on Monday morning. But it was clear that more fundamental changes had to follow if the panic wasn't going to flare again. "We are at a most important moment in postwar history," LBJ's national security advisor, himself an acclaimed economist, wrote the president on Tuesday, March 19. "The outcome—whether in Vietnam or the gold crisis—depends on how free men behave in the days and weeks ahead."[11]

Thus began one of the most agonizing weeks of Johnson's presidency. Around him the discussions moved, his political advisers running through the campaign's course now that Kennedy was in the race, his foreign policy advisers trying to unravel the tangle of war and money that had created the crisis, the military still pushing for more. Those closest to him could the see the weight of it bearing down on him—the stoop in his walk, the sag of his face, the red-raw sties around his eyes—but they couldn't be sure of his thinking until March 27, four days before he was scheduled to speak to the nation in a televised address, when he finally accepted one of the two drafts his speechwriter had prepared for him. Even then some of the specifics remained unresolved. For three more days his aides argued over particular passages, while LBJ drafted a closing he wanted almost no one to see. On Sunday evening, March 31, he brought the final version into the Oval Office, set his copy on the desk in front of him, waited for the network cameraman to signal that the feed had gone live, and told his fellow Americans of the decisions he'd made.

His delivery was flat, as it tended to be, much of his text wrapped in language so precisely phrased its significance was hard to see. He was sending 13,500 more troops to Vietnam, he said, without mentioning that the Joint Chiefs had requested fifteen times that number. He talked at length about the South Vietnamese army's growing ability to assume control of the ground war, without making clear that he was doing so because he'd decided that once the latest increase was complete there'd be no more major American deployments. And he gave investors a detailed accounting of how he'd pay for his final increase—by raising taxes and cutting domestic spending—without a single reference to the contagion that had run through the markets two weeks before.

But two pieces of the night's address were too stunning to miss. Since 1965 the entire American strategy had rested on the assumption that the continual bombing of North Vietnam would force the Communists to abandon their subversion of South Vietnam. Now LBJ announced that he'd ordered the bombing stopped over 75 percent of the North, even though the fighting was still raging in the South. All he asked in return was that the North's representatives enter into peace talks wherever and whenever they wanted, "to discuss the means of bringing this ugly war to an end." As for himself, that decision Johnson left for last. "With America's sons in the fields far away," he said, "with America's future under challenge right here at home, with our hopes and the world's hope for peace in the balance every day, I do not believe that I should devote an hour or a day . . . to any duties other than the awesome duties of this office. . . . Accordingly I shall not seek, and I will not accept, the nomination of my party for another term as your president."[12]

When he was done they went up to the White House's private quarters, LBJ and his wife Lady Bird, their two daughters, a son-in-law, and assorted insiders. "Nearly everybody just looked staggered and struck silent," Lady Bird confided in her diary, "and then the phones began to ring."[13] Calls from the secretary of state, old Senate colleagues, Texas oil men, and, oddly enough, Eugene McCarthy's wife, wanting to express her concern. LBJ handled them all with grace, even Abigail McCarthy's. "No one man can stand in the way of history," he told her, though that's exactly what he'd tried to do that evening: to stand up to the twisted history of a war he'd never wanted and the politics that had defined his life, and in a remarkable demonstration of courage, cowardice, and naivete, to reverse their courses.[14]

The Pain Which Cannot Forget

JOHNSON'S DECISIONS THREW the race for the Democratic presidential nomination into utter confusion. After New Hampshire, McCarthy had headed to Wisconsin, where the next primary was to be held on April 2, for another round of cerebral campaigning against the war, while Kennedy—too late into the race to get on Wisconsin's ballot—barnstormed the country, ruthlessly attacking the president. Neither had known that LBJ was going to withdraw, nor did they have any idea of how to react when he did. McCarthy went off to read some poetry, Kennedy to phone leading Democrats to see if he could win them over now that he was the only powerhouse candidate still standing.

He couldn't. By the next day some of the party's most influential figures were urging Johnson's vice president, Hubert Humphrey, to announce his candidacy. Not that Humphrey needed much encouragement. He was a devoted liberal, a champion of civil rights, union rights, and government's responsibility for the nation's well-being. He was also the Democrats' self-proclaimed Happy Warrior, the ebullient son of a small-town pharmacist who couldn't imagine anything better than giving a stem-winding speech followed by an extended stretch of shaking hands along the rope line. Johnson had turned his vice presidency into an ordeal, dominating him, humbling him, and occasionally humiliating him as only LBJ could. Humphrey took it all, burying both his pride and his doubts—about Vietnam most of all—beneath effusive displays of devotion to the president's agenda. So he'd enter the race as the administration's man, a cheerful face for the policies Johnson had put in place.

For a few days that appeared to be a promising position to occupy. McCarthy easily won the Wisconsin primary. But LBJ took 36 percent of the vote, despite having dropped out of the race two days before: a clear indication that the administration still enjoyed solid support inside the party. On April 3 the North Vietnamese accepted Johnson's offer of peace talks. It was a tentative agreement, circumscribed by Hanoi's insistence that there'd be no meaningful discussions until the United States completely stopped its bombing and agreed to include the NLF in the talks, concessions LBJ had no intention of making. Still, McCarthy and Kennedy had to admit that the talks were a significant step toward the policies they'd entered the race to promote, a victory for the pressure they'd created but a blow to the necessity of their nomination. Or so it seemed until the following afternoon, April 4, when Martin Luther King stepped out onto the balcony of Memphis' Lorraine Motel.

A year and a half had passed since he limped out of Chicago. In that time King had engaged in a fierce round of moral witness, speaking out against the destruction the United States had visited on Vietnam, Black Power's provocations, the inequalities that plagued the nation, and the injustices that made its central cities burn. Only in late 1967 did he begin to move from condemnation to mobilization. He'd spend the first part of the new year organizing among the poor, he announced. In the spring of 1968 he'd bring his recruits to Washington, DC, a nonviolent army of the dispossessed camped on the Mall, demanding that the federal government take explicit action to ensure economic justice for all. When Congress refused, as King expected it would, the poor would take to the streets in a massive demonstration of civil disobedience— and shut the city down.

The winter didn't go as King had hoped. Some of his long-standing allies refused to endorse his Poor People's Campaign. Black Power's most prominent spokesmen dismissed it. He had trouble rallying those grassroots organizations that could mobilize substantial numbers of poor people on his behalf. And he was repeatedly pulled away from his own organizing by the multiple demands the civil rights movement made on him. One of these was the call he received in February from the pastor of Memphis' Centenary Methodist Church, the Reverend James Lawson, asking him to support a struggling strike by the city's 1,300 sanitation workers. By all rights he should have declined. But almost all the strikers were African American. Their employer, Memphis' white mayor, was refusing to bargain. And Lawson was one of the movement's towering figures, the radical pacifist who'd taught SNCC's founders to believe in the Beloved Community. King said he'd do what he could.

He came to Memphis three times that spring, on March 18 to preach, on March 28 to lead a demonstration down Beale Street that went disastrously wrong, and on April 3 to make amends. That night he spoke to a packed house at a church on the African American south side, a talk he didn't want to give, building to a haunting evocation of Moses on Mount Nebo, looking longingly into the Promised Land. Much of the next day he spent with his brother A.D. and his closest friend, Rev. Ralph Abernathy, in his motel room, waiting to hear about his lawyers' fight against a court order the mayor had secured to stop him from marching again. Late in the afternoon Andrew Young came back from the courthouse with encouraging news. They talked awhile, clowned a bit as they tended to do when A.D. was around, until their host for the evening, another Memphis minister, arrived to take them to supper. King took a little time to get dressed. When he was ready he came out onto the balcony, in full view of the flophouse across the street.

It took a single shot; one squeeze of the trigger on the high-powered rifle a white supremacist named James Earl Ray had sited through the flophouse's bathroom window; another flash of the violence King had confronted again and again in the dozen years since he'd sat at his kitchen table late on a winter's night and heard God's only begotten Son. He died an hour later, at 7:05 p.m., on an operating table in a local hospital that was still struggling to set aside its segregated wards.

There was no controlling the anger that evening. It raced along with the news reports, flaming into the now-familiar rituals of urban rebellion—crowds on the streets, clashes with the police, shop windows smashed, stores looted, commercial strips torched—this time in more than a hundred cities and towns, most dramatically in Washington, DC, where the rage surged into the downtown shopping district, blocks from the Mall. The next day it flared again, in some cities more intensely than it had the night before. Lyndon Johnson went on national television to plead for calm, backed by a phalanx of civil rights leaders he'd rushed to the White House for moral support. But there were gaps in the line behind him. From Atlanta, King's widow Coretta issued a scalding statement on white America's complicity in her husband's murder. He "knew . . . that this was a sick society," she said, "totally infested with racism and violence, that questioned his integrity, maligned his motives and distorted his views which would ultimately lead to his death. . . ."[15] And from the heart of Washington's African American community Stokely Carmichael tossed aside the possibility of peace. "White America has declared war on black people," he announced. "The only way to survive is to get some guns. Because that's the only way white America keeps us in check, because she's got guns."[16]

The power clearly rested on the other side of the color line. Over the weekend state authorities sent 35,000 National Guardsmen into twenty-two cities. LBJ added almost 24,000 federal troops: 5,000 to Baltimore, another 5,000 to Chicago, and 13,600 to Washington, DC, where combat-ready units took up positions on the White House lawn and the Capitol steps for the first time since the Civil War. Within a few days the riots had been suppressed, though only through a stunning number of arrests—20,000 in all—and the occasional application of fatal force. Of the thirty-nine people who were killed in the week's unrest, thirty-four were African American, among them the Black Panthers' first recruit, seventeen-year-old Bobby Hutton, gunned down in a firefight with the Oakland police on April 6. He was shot twelve times.

King was buried three days later, on Tuesday, April 9; his memory honored in a searing service at his home church, followed by a long procession to Morehouse College, his casket carried by a mule-driven cart in solidarity with the poor he'd planned to organize. George Wallace didn't attend. But the other candidates did, before filtering back onto the campaign trail to address the damage done by the week's carnage. Polls showed a dramatic increase in the number of African Americans who felt alienated from American society, up twenty points—from 32 percent to 52 percent—since the previous sampling, while the violence seemed to play into whites' most deeply rooted racial fears. Shortly after the April upheavals a Gallup poll asked respondents to explain the causes of urban unrest. Forty-one percent of whites said African Americans rioted because they hated white people, and another 25 percent because Blacks were prone to violence. Behind those numbers lay nightmarish visions. In early 1968 Detroit's mayor set up a rumor-control center he hoped might prevent panics from gripping the city's neighborhoods. In the three days following King's murder the center was flooded with calls. The most common asked whether it was true that on Friday, April 12—Good Friday in the Christian calendar—Blacks were going to march into the suburbs to kill all the white children. A modern American Passover timed to coincide with the faithful's commemoration of Christ's crucifixion.

In those fears Wallace saw opportunity. The "shindigs" after King's murder were sure to win him a larger share of the "little people" who "are tired of the pseudo-intellectuals telling them the reasons and causes of riots," he told the *Wall Street Journal.* "There is no reason and cause for riots. . . . The people know that the way to stop a riot is to hit someone on the head."[17] Wallace couldn't fully exploit the moment, since his wife's collapsing health had pulled him off the trail; not until the end of April, a week before she died, did he start campaigning again. But his absence hardly seemed to matter. May's polls put his share of the presidential vote at 14 percent, up five points since King's assassination. He still hadn't reached double digits outside the South. Inside it, though, he was polling at 27 percent.

Those weren't the numbers Richard Nixon wanted to see. The Republicans had won the Upper South in three of the last four presidential elections and had taken the Deep South in 1964, the only bright spot in an otherwise disastrous year. Now Wallace was cutting into those states with a belligerent version of Nixon's law-and-order appeal. If he added in just four or five percent of the vote in a couple of key northern states, like Michigan or Illinois, he could cut off Nixon's path to the presidency. But Nixon couldn't harden his position without soiling his image as the campaign's voice of reason and moderation. So his speechwriters went to work, putting together a new pitch Nixon unveiled in a national radio address on May 16. He was running as the champion of "the silent center," he said, "the millions of people in the middle of the political spectrum who do not demonstrate, do not picket or protest."[18] It was a marvelously conceived appeal, an invitation to Wallace's waitresses and cabbies to join Detroit's terrified suburbanites and reclaim their country through a nationwide coalition that wasn't going to bash anybody over the head. Then the Supreme Court handed down an unexpected ruling, and a clever turn of phrase wasn't enough anymore.

The ruling probably shouldn't have been too surprising. In the spring of 1967 the justices had handed down two major civil rights decisions. First, they'd blocked the Georgia legislature's attempt to prevent a young civil rights activist from taking the seat he'd won in a fair and open election. Then, in the landmark case of *Loving v. Virginia*, they'd struck at one of the defining fears of the nation's racial order— the fusion of race and sex—by declaring unconstitutional a state's right to outlaw interracial marriage. The day after *Loving* came down, LBJ announced that he was planning to fill the Court's latest vacancy with its first African American nominee. To give the moment the weight it deserved, he chose Thurgood Marshall, whose brilliant work for the NAACP had shattered Jim Crow's legal foundations. The Senate confirmed him in the midst of 1967's racial rebellions, so he could be on the bench in time to hear the new term's cases. If ever there was a Court likely to make a major move on racial justice, this was it.

Still, there was something shocking about how major a move it turned out to be. On the day before King's murder the justices had heard oral arguments on another school desegregation case, this one out of New Kent County, Virginia, just east of Richmond. The district had long had two schools, one for Black kids and another for whites. In 1965—eleven years after the *Brown* decision—district officials finally announced a desegregation plan, built on what seemed like a reasonable arrangement: at the start of the year parents could petition to have their children assigned to either school, regardless of race. But everyone knew that no white parent was going to send his or her child to the Black school. And as long as the white kids stayed in place, there wouldn't be room for African American kids to transfer should their parents want them to move. The NAACP filed suit, arguing that the plan was nothing more than a subterfuge, designed to create the illusion of integration.

The justices delivered their decision in *Green v. County School Board*

of New Kent County on May 27. The district's policy was in fact duplici-
tous, William Brennan wrote for a unanimous court, and therefore had
to be set aside. But the ruling didn't stop at New Kent County's schoolhouse doors. "The burden on a school board today is to come forward
with a plan that promises realistically to work," the opinion read, "and
promises realistically to work now."[19] The last word was the crucial one.
No longer could southern officials hide behind *Brown's* ambiguous
order that they desegregate their schools "with all deliberate speed." Six
weeks after April's violence the Court had told the white South that it
had to end school segregation *now.*

African Americans rushed to bring the ruling home. Across the
South families went to court to demand that their children's schools
put in place the required integration plans. The Johnson administration joined them with a vigor only a president not running for reelection would dare. The Department of Justice announced that it was
reopening stalled suits against 193 southern school systems, while the
Department of Health, Education, and Welfare said it would cut off
federal funding to any southern district that hadn't integrated by the
beginning of the 1969–70 school year. If that order held, most districts
couldn't afford to defy it. So in a little more than a year's time Black kids
and white kids would be sitting side by side in the most sweeping act of
integration the nation had ever seen.

This was a possibility George Wallace was happy to exploit. When
he was in the White House, he took to saying in his stump speech,
communities would run their schools as they saw fit, a promise that
immediately became his biggest applause line. Nixon couldn't match
him, not publicly at least. But privacy had its purposes. Five days after
the Court's decision Nixon flew to Atlanta for an off-the-record meeting with the South's most prominent Republicans. The *Brown* decision
was settled law, he told them. With its new ruling, though, the justices
had overstepped their constitutional limits. And the next president
was duty bound to rein them in by filling any vacancies that opened
with justices who believed that the Court shouldn't engage in social
engineering.

Three weeks later Earl Warren announced that after fifteen landmark years as chief justice he was retiring. It was an obviously political move, meant to give the president plenty of time to replace him with the sort of justice who'd maintain the court's progressive bent. LBJ obliged by nominating one of Warren's reliably liberal colleagues, Abe Fortas, to move up to the chief's chair. No one could question Fortas's qualifications: when Johnson had nominated him as associate justice in 1965, the Senate had approved him by a voice vote. But almost immediately some of the most powerful Republicans insisted that it wasn't right for Johnson to nominate anyone in an election year: the seat should stay open, they said, so that whoever won the election could fill it. In the lead stood South Carolina's Strom Thurmond, leaning on a newly invented principle that—if the voting broke the right way—would give Nixon that change to live up to the off-the-record promises he'd made.

For the Democrats, race ran in different ways. Humphrey finally announced his candidacy on April 27. He brought with him deep connections to the older generation of civil rights activists, built over his two decades of commitment to the cause. But he had no intention of using those connections to reach a broad swath of Black voters. In fact he wouldn't try to reach voters at all; rather than running in the seven remaining primaries he'd focus exclusively on caucuses and closed-door meetings, where he could appeal directly to the party insiders who would make up the vast majority of convention delegates. It was a perfectly reasonable strategy, completely within party rules. But it meant that in the course of the nominating process he'd never have to face the passions raging out on the streets.

McCarthy and Kennedy worked the caucuses and back rooms too. But they knew that they wouldn't make much headway with the party's power brokers unless they proved in the final primaries that they could mobilize the Democrats' rank and file more effectively than Humphrey could. Through the rest of the spring they ran head-to-head, from Indiana through the District of Columbia, Nebraska, Oregon, and South Dakota to California on June 5. On the central issues they were barely distinguishable. Both insisted that Johnson ought to order an immediate end to the bombing of North Vietnam, a position made all the more urgent once the peace talks opened—in Paris on May 13—and the North Vietnamese followed through on their promise not to negotiate until the bombs stopped falling. And they both hammered away at the administration's decision to strengthen its bargaining position by intensifying the war in South Vietnam with a massive search-and-destroy operation meant to obliterate the gains the NLF had made during Tet. From the field the bodies came flooding back: more Americans were killed in action in May 1968 than in any other month of the war. "Here while the sun shines, men are dying on the other side of the earth," Kennedy told a crowd at a Sacramento shopping center. ". . . [T]hat is why I run for president of the United States."[20]

They also agreed on the desperate need to confront the nation's racial tensions. Both had built solid records in support of civil rights, Kennedy's more visible and volatile than McCarthy's, given his complex relationship with the movement as attorney general and the transformation he'd undergone in his Senate years. Both put together specific policy proposals meant to address the tangle of race, poverty, segregation, and oppression, McCarthy's slightly to the left of Kennedy's. But in one critical respect they couldn't have been more different. McCarthy spoke of race as he did every other issue, with the studied detachment of the intellectual he knew himself to be, while RFK seemed to feel the injustice of the moment with a fierce immediacy.

The first sign came on the night King was murdered. Kennedy heard the news on his way to a street-corner rally in a Black neighborhood in Indianapolis. He could have canceled it. Instead he stood on the back of a flatbed truck and talked quietly of his brother's assassination, of the rage he'd felt at the cruelty of such a brutal act, of the "pain which cannot forget"—an anguished admission, taken from the ancient Greeks—and of the country he wanted to lead. "What we need in this country is not division," he said, "what we need in the United States is not hatred, what we need in the United States is not violence or lawlessness, but love and wisdom and compassion toward one another, and a feeling of justice towards those who suffer in our country, whether they be white or whether they be black," a vision shaped by the gaping wounds the evening had opened, his and the nation's both.[21]

He didn't always live up to the standard he set that night. During the Indiana primary he made a pitch for the white working class with his own appeal to law and order. And in the spring's only debate, on June 1, he claimed that McCarthy wanted to move African Americans from the cities to the suburbs, a moment of fearmongering that would have fit comfortably within the Wallace campaign. But he also tried again and again to reach across the racial divide: in Washington, DC, three days after King's assassination, where he walked through the still-smoldering center city accompanied only by his wife, the pastor of a local Baptist church, and a gaggle of kids; at a bruising private meeting in Atlanta, where he sat silently while King's grieving aides berated him for the limits of his liberalism; in an auditorium at the Indiana University medical school, where he lectured the almost-exclusively white student body on the obligations their privilege imposed; on the Oglala Lakota's Pine Ridge Reservation in western South Dakota, one of America's most impoverished places, where he ducked into a one-room shanty to talk with the children living there; in California's Central Valley, where he spent an emotional day with the Mexican-American and Filipino farmworkers whose cause he'd embraced; and in the motorcades that served as the high point of each of his primary campaigns, RFK standing in the back of his open-topped limousine as it crawled through the African American sections of Gary, Omaha, Oakland, and LA, throngs of people surging around him, grabbing his hands as he grabbed theirs, his bodyguards gripping him around the waist so he wouldn't be pulled into the crowds, the passions so intense his advisers feared that the images would frighten away the whites who saw them on television. But RFK insisted that the motorcades run.

Maybe his advisers were right. Kennedy carried all but one of April and May's primaries with overwhelming support in minority precincts and whatever share of white working-class wards he could claim. But he couldn't win over the Democrats' share of the middle- and upper-class doves who resented his having entered the race only after McCarthy had cleared the way, the liberal-leaning professionals who liked their politics calmer than Kennedy made them, and the indeterminate number of whites who might have been just a little scared seeing those crowds pressing in around RFK's limo. So they kept slogging through the primary season, McCarthy's chances of taking the nomination shrinking with each loss, Kennedy's margins of victory too narrow to convince the party's insiders that he deserved to be their nominee. Without a viable alternative to block him, Humphrey gradually consolidated his support. By the California primary, on June 5, he had preliminary pledges from over 1,000 of the 1,312 delegates necessary to secure the nomination.

Kennedy won California as he had the previous primaries, the returns from Oakland, Watts, and the Central Valley strong enough to offset his losses in the small towns and suburbs that had become McCarthy's redoubt. Around midnight he came into the ballroom of Los Angeles' Ambassador Hotel, where his campaign workers had gathered for the victory party. He took the stage—his wife standing behind him, aides and supporters circling around him, his sisters somewhere in the crowd—and said a few encouraging words, thanked some people, made fun of himself, and promised to take the fight on to the convention. When he was done the hotel's maître d' led his entourage out through the ballroom pantry.

This time it was four shots fired by a twenty-four-year-old Palestinian American enraged by Kennedy's support for Israel, a troubled young man from Pasadena who'd squeezed himself in by the steam tables an hour before on the chance that his target might pass by. The moment they realized what was happening Kennedy's bodyguards slammed the gunman into the table, but he kept firing wildly, four more shots, four more bodies down. Someone shouted at them to crush his fingers. There was so much screaming, though, it was impossible to sort out the noise, so many reporters and photographers and panicked aides pushing against each other the pantry had become a scrum—except around RFK, who lay splayed on the floor, a Mexican-American busboy kneeling beside him, cradling the senator's head in his hands.

Law and Order

THE NETWORKS CARRIED Kennedy's funeral live as they had King's: another church full of dignitaries, another widow sitting with her children in the front pew, another wrenching eulogy, a second day of national mourning in two months' time. Four days later pollster Louis Harris asked a representative sample of Americans whether they thought "something was deeply wrong" with the country.[22] Two-thirds said they did. But that perception didn't lead them to the politics King and Kennedy had preached. When Harris asked them to define the nation's problems they didn't talk about inequality, injustice, the weight of the war, or the plight of the poor but about violence, lawlessness, and the breakdown of social order, which they attributed by overwhelming margins to radicals, racial agitators, common criminals, and madmen with guns. Within a month George Wallace had moved up another two points in the polls, to 16 percent, the increase driven largely by his support outside the South, which had more than doubled in the weeks since RFK's murder.

Wallace's campaign had its limits, to be sure: 55 percent of Americans considered him an extremist, unfit to be president. But almost a third thought "he would keep law and order the way it ought to be kept." When he swept up north in July—to Maryland, Massachusetts, and Rhode Island—he packed almost every appearance. In Cranston he drew a raucous crowd of three thousand, among them a contingent of protesters, Black and white. At first he let them heckle. But halfway through his speech he'd had enough. "These are the folks that people in our country are getting sick and tired of," he growled. "You'd better have your day now because after November, I tell you, you're through." The rest of the crowd cheered. A few people shouted racial slurs. And somewhere in the hall they started to chant, "We want Wallace! We want Wallace!"[23]

A week later the Republicans met in Miami Beach to make Richard Nixon their nominee. By all accounts it was a dull four days: 1,333 delegates sitting in the air-conditioned comfort of a convention center cut off from the city by the Intracoastal, voting their way to a foregone conclusion. But there were moments when Wallace's spirit haunted the hall: during Nixon's quiet tour of the southern delegations, which he took as an opportunity to repeat his opposition to activist judges and the immediate integration of the region's public schools; in his choice of Maryland governor Spiro Agnew as a running mate purely on the strength of his combative responses to protesters, rioters, civil rights advocates, and just about anyone else he thought disrupted the proper order of things; and in the convention's culminating event, when Nixon finally accepted the nomination he'd spent five years working to secure.

He began with a telling tribute to Ike, who'd recently suffered a major heart attack. "General Eisenhower, as you know, lies critically ill in the Walter Reed Hospital tonight," he said. "I have talked, however, with Mrs. Eisenhower. . . . And she says that there is nothing that he lives more for and there is nothing that would lift him more than for us to win in November and I say let's win this one for Ike." Then he moved to the text of his speech. It was a disciplined piece of work, built around the themes that had defined his campaign from the start, wrapped in a refined version of the pitch his team had developed to counter Wallace's rise. "As we look at America, we see cities enveloped in smoke and flame," he said. "We see Americans dying on distant battlefields abroad. We see Americans hating each other; fighting each other; killing each other at home. And as we hear and see these things millions cry out in anguish. Did we come all the way for this? Did American boys die in Normandy, and Korea, and in Valley Forge for this? Listen to the answer to those questions. It is another voice. It is a quiet voice in the tumult and the shouting. It is the voice of the great majority of Americans, the forgotten Americans—the non-shouters, the non-demonstrators. . . . This I say to you tonight is the real voice of America."[24] The impact wasn't perfectly clear. Post-convention polls showed Nixon's share of the vote up enough to give him a six-point lead. But Wallace ticked up another point too. And the Democrats had yet to hold their convention, with all its attendant publicity.

Lyndon Johnson had selected the timing and the site: late August so that the convention would be in place to celebrate his sixtieth birthday, Chicago to please Dick Daley. Plenty of people were saying that LBJ would pick the nominee too. It wasn't true. Hubert Humphrey had piled up his lead in April and May without Johnson's help. And it was the delegates' calculations in the weeks after Kennedy's murder and not the president's intervention that turned the vice president into the party's presumptive nominee. But Humphrey's devotion to the administration made him look like Johnson's proxy, which was exactly what LBJ wanted him to be.

There was a great deal of power and more than a share of pride at play: the once master politician clinging to his ability to dominate those around him; the president who'd passed the greatest wave of reforms since the New Deal insisting that his successor run on the record he'd built. But mostly there was Vietnam. Johnson wanted nothing more than to see the sacrifices he'd made at the end of March lead to the war's conclusion. His scaling back of the bombing had gotten North Vietnam to the bargaining table but no further; after two months of talks they were still deadlocked. Johnson could break the impasse by giving in to North Vietnam's demands that the United States end its bombing altogether and give the NLF a seat at the table. That's what McCarthy, Kennedy, and the doves had said he should do, though. And the moment he did, they'd get the credit—not LBJ but the very people who'd haunted him, criticized him, defied him, and all but driven him from the Oval Office. That was an outcome Johnson simply couldn't countenance. So the bombs kept falling and the talks stayed stalled, even as the Democrats lurched toward their convention.

Everyone knew a fight was coming. Kennedy's primary victories had denied McCarthy any chance of taking the nomination. Still he insisted on carrying his campaign to the convention. For a while it seemed that the Kennedys might too, through the family's last living son, Ted, the thirty-six-year-old senator from Massachusetts, who was said to be considering a run. Eventually he decided that it wasn't his time. But that didn't mean the delegates his brother had won would let the convention pass without challenging the president. Through July and early August the Democrats' doves made it clear that, at a minimum, they'd press the party to formally endorse an immediate cessation of the bombing and the expansion of the peace talks. For his part, Johnson saw the threat as the affront it was meant to be, an explicit rejection of his leadership, delivered at an event he'd planned as a celebration of his achievements. To make matters worse, his vice president wanted to side with the doves.

Humphrey had started his campaign fully, volubly supportive of LBJ's Vietnam policies. There he remained as the peace talks froze and the body count mounted. More and more, though, the press was hammering away at his obeisance to the president: *Esquire* ran a cover of him as a ventriloquist's dummy, sitting on LBJ's lap. Some of his closest advisers were pleading with him to stake out his own position, and almost everywhere he went he was hounded by the anti-war movement's radical wing. It had been a militant spring, with dozens of protests and confrontations, the most dramatic coming at Columbia University, on Manhattan's Upper West Side, where turmoil over race and war had led to a seven-day occupation of five campus buildings, broken finally through a frontal assault by 1,000 New York City policemen. In the aftermath the movement's most celebrated militant, Tom Hayden, promised "two, three, many Columbias." Humphrey saw his share. In New York 1,000 protesters tried to shut down the streets around his hotel; 300 were arrested. In San Francisco radicals disrupted his photo ops with chants of "Wash the blood off your hands." And in Cleveland a young woman got close enough to call him a murderer to his face. Publicly he refused to be moved. But in private he rattled against the cage he'd locked himself into. "The president didn't run because he knew he couldn't make it, and he clothed me in nothing," he told his aides in mid-June. "To pull ourselves up from these ashes and the humiliation . . . is the most difficult thing in the world."[25]

At the end of July he finally tried. Humphrey's foreign policy team had been working for weeks on a statement that delicately, cautiously, but unmistakably aligned him with the doves. When it was done, on the 25th, he brought it to the White House for the president to see.

Johnson read it over and went for the jugular. The statement was playing politics with the lives of American soldiers, he said—among them
LBJ's two sons-in-law, both recently deployed—and undercutting the
administration's last, best hope for peace. He could do as he pleased,
Johnson told him. But if Humphrey made this statement public, LBJ
would do everything in his power to destroy his candidacy. After the
meeting one of the vice president's aides found him in his office bathroom furiously washing his hands, his breakout statement tossed aside.

The timing of Humphrey's retreat couldn't have been worse. For
half a year the anti-war activists who'd hoped to re-create the Pentagon march at the Democratic convention had been struggling to hold
the project together. First, most of the liberals had been pulled away by
the McCarthy campaign. Then some of the most radical groups had
dropped out too, for fear of being co-opted by mainstream politics.
That left the protest in the hands of the pacifists, some of SDS's most
famous alumni—Hayden among them—and the hippie provocateurs
who'd given the Pentagon protest its surreal edge. By coincidence they
announced their plans just a few days after Humphrey's emasculation.
In keeping with the movement's commitment to radical democracy,
there'd be a swirl of events: for the hippies a "festival of life" in one
of the city parks, with the requisite psychedelic shocks; for the pacifists and the SDSers a series of workshops and rallies leading to a mass
march on the convention the evening Humphrey was nominated; and
for anyone willing, acts of resistance scattered around the city, maybe
peaceful, maybe not. Hayden thought not. "We are coming to Chicago
to vomit on the politics of joy," he declared, "to expose the secret decisions, upset the night club orgies, and face the Democratic Party with
its illegitimacy and criminality."[26]

To face down the Democrats, though, the protesters would have to
get past Dick Daley. For most of the summer his city hall simply didn't
process the organizers' requests for the permits they needed. Finally the
hippies' front men, Jerry Rubin and Abbie Hoffman, announced they'd
hold their festival in Lincoln Park, a mile north of downtown, whether
or not they had the required paperwork. The park was open to visitors,

officials replied, but it closed at 11:00 p.m. each night, so they'd have to be out by then. The pacifists and the SDSers, meanwhile, took the city to court to demand that their right to assemble be honored. But somehow their case ended up before Daley's former law partner, who ruled that while they could have their nomination-day rally in downtown Grant Park there'd be no march on the convention hall, about five miles away. The pacifists immediately announced that they'd march regardless, though it wasn't clear how they'd get around the 11,900 policemen the mayor planned to have on duty during the convention—the entire force split into two twelve-hour shifts—or the 5,600 National Guardsmen he'd had the governor put on call just outside the city, or the 7,500 federal troops held in reserve. Not that he expected trouble, because as Daley explained to reporters, in Chicago people behaved themselves.

Some of them did, anyway. Humphrey bounded into his suite at downtown's elegant Conrad Hilton hotel the day before the convention opened—Sunday, August 25—hoping to squeeze into an opening between Johnson and the doves. While he played the happy host to a stream of politicians, his aides worked both sides, one set huddled with the president's men—Johnson himself having retreated to his ranch for a few days of swimming, eating, and politicking—another with the Kennedys at their compound on Cape Cod; yet another with the McCarthy team, camped in their own suite ten floors down. They were still talking that evening when 120 policemen lined up to clear Lincoln Park for the night. It was the festival of life's opening day, and a couple thousand people turned out. Trouble started with skirmishes around the bathrooms as it was getting dark, kids taunting cops, cops swinging back, rumors flying around that there was going to be bloodshed come closing time. As 11:00 p.m. approached, SDS organizers roamed through the park, trying to get the crowd out before the curfew hit. The police gave them forty minutes' grace. Then the line started moving, across the lawn and into the parking lot where most of those remaining had gathered. There it broke. Into the crowd the cops surged, nightsticks out, nameplates removed, a full-on police assault to get convention week underway.

In the morning the politicians' talks collapsed. Fresh from a dip in the pool, Johnson sent word that he expected the convention to endorse his Vietnam policies fully. In response the doves demanded that the convention vote on their peace proposals, the president's wishes be damned. And suddenly Humphrey the Happy Warrior had no opening to squeeze through. A few hours later the protests started swirling through the city center: an afternoon march toward police headquarters to protest the department's arrest of Tom Hayden on charges no one cared to define; an impromptu rally in Grant Park, across the street from Humphrey's hotel, the NLF flag waving above the crowd until the police ripped it down; a feverish evening in Lincoln Park, as militants and local kids stacked torn-up park benches, trash barrels, and tree branches into a makeshift barrier they thought might stop another assault. But the night brought street fighting, bloodshed on both sides this time, after 300 cops stormed the barricades.

On Tuesday, LBJ's birthday, the bitterness flooded onto the convention floor. Most of the day was consumed by bruising battles over the racial makeup of southern delegations: Mississippi again, as in 1964, and this time Georgia and Texas too. But everyone knew that the fiercest combat was going to come in the evening, when the convention took up the party's platform position on Vietnam. Humphrey couldn't prevent it, but his supporters could push it off prime-time television. So they slowed the evening's proceedings to a crawl, until even the most brain-addled political junkies had gone to bed. Finally, at 12:37 a.m.— 1:37 on the East Coast—the chair put the war before the delegates. Immediately the doves revolted, shouting down the chair's manipulation, calling for an immediate recess so that the issues could be debated in the light of day. For a while the Humphrey forces tried to block them, on the premise that Wednesday was supposed to be devoted to the nominating process, not party policy. But the uproar on the floor was too great. At 2:30 a.m. the chair closed the convention for the evening, with the Vietnam fight still pending.

That night the police choked Lincoln Park with tear gas.

The convention reconvened at 1:00 p.m. on Wednesday, August 28, with two hours set for debate, to be followed by the vote the doves demanded. Already Grant Park was filling with protesters—10,000, the police estimated—come for the nomination-day rally the court had granted the radicals. From 2:00 p.m. to somewhere around half past four they ran together—the doves in the amphitheater pleading with the party to endorse an end to the bombing and a diplomatic drive toward peace; the radicals at the park band shell, calling for moral witness, massive resistance, and revolutionary change, the crowd ringed by a cordon of cops and National Guardsmen sent to ensure that the organizers couldn't turn the rally into the march they'd threatened to mount. Then the voting started, the rally ended, and everything unraveled.

The balloting followed the party's fault lines: the McCarthy and Kennedy delegates on the dove side, Humphrey's delegates under his agonized order to back the president's position, as loyalty required. The moment the result was announced—the doves defeated by 526 votes—the protest started, hundreds of delegates up on their seats, singing chorus after chorus of "We Shall Overcome," others snaking through the convention floor behind a banner reading "Stop the War," some of them weeping, the chair desperately trying to gavel the convention back to order so that it could move on to Humphrey's nomination.[27]

Up on the band-shell stage the pacifists called for volunteers to join them in marching on the convention amphitheater, down on the South Side. Gradually they pieced together a line of six or seven thousand. But the police and the guardsmen had them hemmed in. For almost two hours the organizers tried to negotiate an acceptable path, while their volunteers sat in the grass and waited. The cops had their orders, though, the pacifists their principles, and eventually the discussions stalemated, the march collapsed, and the crowd was on its own.

Some people shoved their way past the guardsmen and out of the park. About fifty managed to get through a minor breach in the line before the troops shut it down. Most streamed through an undefended street on the park's northern edge. From there a solid share of the crowd drifted away. But a portion—maybe three or four thousand—swung a few blocks south, along downtown's Michigan Avenue, toward Humphrey's hotel. It was seven thirty, eight o'clock, darkness descending.

Later Humphrey said that he didn't see it as it happened. Not the wall of policemen across Michigan Avenue directly below his suite or the crowd of protesters facing them, chanting the brutal slogans he'd heard all year: Dump the Hump, Fuck the Pigs, Fuck you LBJ. Not the bottles and stones hurled at the line. Not the cops charging forward, the sudden surge of blue helmets, the nightsticks, the mace, and the tear gas, though a trace of it filtered into his rooms. Not the kids retching on the sidewalk, the kids with their scalps lashed open, the kids being hauled away. But he saw it an hour later, when the networks broke into the middle of the nominating process to show the carnage. And he saw the chaos as the news reached the convention floor: already enraged delegates shouting at each other, pushing each other, occasionally swinging at each other; cops thundering down the aisle to eject three delegates who refused to show their credentials; newsmen knocked to the floor. The dovish senator from Connecticut, Abraham Ribicoff, up on the podium for a nominating speech, denounced "gestapo tactics on the streets of Chicago," prompting the red-faced Richard Daley to growl back on live television, "Fuck you, you Jew son of a bitch, you lousy motherfucker, go home," a string of obscenities to mark the pinnacle of Hubert Humphrey's political career.[28]

A Riven Nation

IT TOOK TWO weeks for Chicago to register in the polls. The results were as devastating to Humphrey as his nominating night had been. He was hemorrhaging support inside the Democratic Party, primarily because of the massive defection of the doves, almost half of whom were refusing to line up behind him. Beyond the party his numbers were even worse. Only 26 percent of those polled thought he was the candidate best equipped to handle the Vietnam War. Only 25 percent thought him the most likely to maintain law and order. Only five percent thought he'd make an excellent president. And 51 percent said he was too close to LBJ to be president at all. Perceptions so debilitating drove his support down to 31 percent, eight points behind Richard Nixon's in one poll, a catastrophic twelve points in another. The gap would have been even greater except for one small point in the polling. Nixon's numbers had fallen too.

He'd come out of his own convention with the autumn perfectly planned. He would stop talking about Vietnam for fear, Nixon said, of undermining the peace process. And he'd say nothing at all about the September filibuster that Strom Thurmond and his fellow southerners mounted to block Abe Fortas's ascension to chief justice, the first time in thirty-eight years that the Senate had rejected a president's nominee. But there'd be plenty of rallies for folks to come out and cheer—one or two a day timed to appear on the nightly news—along with a series of televised town halls, a brand-new format designed by an up-and-coming young operative named Roger Ailes, in which the candidate would field unscripted questions from an audience handpicked by Nixon's advance men. Mostly there'd be a barrage of arresting television commercials designed around a vertiginous rush of still images: shots of combat and weathered GIs for the Vietnam ad, concerned cops and an addict with a needle in his arm for the crime-in-the-streets ad, burning ghettos and raging protesters out on Michigan Avenue for the law-and-order ad, each spot ending with the campaign's new catch phrase, "This time vote like your whole world depended on it."[29] But the plans didn't work quite as his handlers had hoped. Between mid-August and mid-September Nixon lost two points in the polls, while George Wallace surged up four, to 21 percent of the vote.

The experts had been tracing Wallace's ascent all summer. Still, it was a shock to see a leap that large less than two months from Election Day. He had a lock on the Deep South. He was gaining in the border states, his support spiking among small-town voters, independents, and the well-to-do. He was cutting deeper into the rest of the country than ever before, with 10 percent of the Northeast behind him, 11 percent of the West, and 16 percent of the Midwest. And there was every reason to believe he could do better still, given the huge crowds he was drawing, the passions that pulsed through his audiences—the populist pride, the barely disguised bigotry, the threat of retribution, the frisson of violence—and the ever-expanding pool of reporters come to see the spectacle.

Pollster Lou Harris ran the projections. If Wallace's numbers continued to trend through October as they had since August, he was likely to carry about 30 percent of the electorate, enough to deny either Nixon or Humphrey an electoral majority. Were that to happen, the election would be thrown into the House of Representatives, where the South's congressional delegations would hold the balance of power. They wouldn't give Wallace the presidency. But they would give him the leverage he needed to wring from the other candidates fundamental concessions on Supreme Court appointments, civil rights, voting rights, criminal justice, free speech, and foreign aid. The national agenda could be transformed, the white South rising again just three years after the last piece of Jim Crow had come crashing down, thanks to Wallace's primal appeals.

For Humphrey, the break began the day Wallace swept into Cicero. As badly as the vice president had done in the first half of September, the second half was worse. Everywhere he went protesters followed. The pundits panned his speeches. His fundraising collapsed. And the late-September Gallup poll showed him down another three points, to 28 percent, a number so abysmal it set him free. "If the polls are really what they stand to be, I don't stand a chance," Humphrey said to his closest confidant the day the results were released. "I don't give a shit anymore, I'm saying what I want to say."[30] His aides borrowed $100,000 to buy him a half-hour slot on NBC on Monday evening, September 30. He used it to make the commitment he'd wanted to make in July and August, the promise that turned him into a dove. If elected, Humphrey finally said, he'd stop the bombing of North Vietnam.

Three days later the Wallace campaign took up talk of bombing too. For almost a month Wallace had been trying to settle on a vice-presidential pick. It hadn't gone well: his first choice, former Kentucky governor and onetime baseball commissioner A. B. "Happy" Chandler, was forced to withdraw after Wallace's hard-core supporters objected that Chandler was too soft on race, as evidenced by his support back in '47 of a promising second baseman named Jackie Robinson. Soft wasn't an attribute anyone applied to Wallace's next choice. On October 3 he presented to the press his new running mate, Curtis LeMay.

It had been six years almost to the day since LeMay had called John Kennedy a coward for his handling of the missile crisis in Cuba. After finishing out his term on the Joint Chiefs in 1965, LeMay entered a restless retirement. He lacerated LBJ for trying to restrain North Vietnamese aggression with precision bombing when only devastation would do. "There came a time when the Nazis threw the towel into the ring," he wrote in 1965. "Same way with the Japanese. We didn't bring about that day by sparring with sixteen-ounce gloves. My solution to the problem would be to tell them frankly that they've got to draw in their horns . . . or we're going to bomb them back into the Stone Age."[31] So it was only natural for reporters to ask him whether he might consider using nuclear weapons in Vietnam.

LeMay didn't have to give it a second thought. "I think there are many times when it would be most efficient to use nuclear weapons," he replied. "To me, if I had to go to Vietnam and get killed with a rusty knife or get killed with a nuclear weapon I would rather get killed with a nuclear weapon. . . . I don't want to use them unless I have to. I don't want to stick a rusty knife into anyone's belly unless I have to." Wallace cut in to insist that the general wasn't saying that the quickest route out of Vietnam ran under a mushroom cloud. But LeMay wasn't given to retreating. On he went, explaining that Americans had "a phobia" about nuclear weapons, that there was really nothing to fear, that even in nuclear test sites the vegetation eventually grew back, though some of the animal life remained a little hot, until Wallace finally managed to steer him off the stage.[32]

He hadn't moved fast enough. The crowds kept coming after LeMay's debut: 8,000 in downtown Baltimore; 10,000 in Flint, Michigan's quintessential factory town; 20,000 on the Boston Common. But so did the stories about the general's long history of inflammatory comments,

the newspaper columns condemning Wallace's recklessness for thinking that such a man ought to be anywhere near the Oval Office, and
his opponents' declarations of shock and outrage. Humphrey's attacks
were made all the stronger by his pledge to ground the bombers. The
next round of polls showed how sharply sentiment had turned. In the
first two weeks of October, Wallace's share of the vote tumbled from
21 to 15 percent, while Humphrey's shot up to 36 percent, eight points
behind Nixon in one poll, just five points in another: a gap almost small
enough, Lou Harris said, to make the race between them too close
to call.

The race's sudden flux, in turn, wrenched through the delicate politics of peace. On October 9 the White House heard through a back
channel that LeMay's selection had unnerved the North Vietnamese
as much as it had a share of the American electorate. They understood
that Wallace wasn't going to win, the sources said. But they feared that
Nixon might seal his election by striking a deal that would let Wallace
and LeMay influence the next administration's foreign policy in horrific ways. So North Vietnam was willing to make a deal of its own. If
LBJ stopped his bombing, the North Vietnamese would welcome the
South Vietnamese government into the Paris peace talks. There were no
assurances of subsequent steps. Once Saigon was at the table, though,
the negotiations might well move toward a comprehensive settlement.

The North Vietnamese made their offer official on October 11. At
first LBJ hesitated, as he grappled with the thought of doing precisely
what the doves had been demanding of him for three years. But this
was his last chance to end the war that had destroyed his presidency,
and he couldn't let it go. Late on October 14 he told the US representatives in Paris to accept Hanoi's terms. It took two weeks of haggling
to set the schedule. Johnson would announce that he was ending the
bombing of North Vietnam in a speech to the nation on October 31,
with the South Vietnamese joining the talks two days later: the Paris
negotiations finally prized open, a path to peace cleared three days
before Election Day.

LBJ told the candidates of the agreement in a confidential conference call on the 16th, before the details were finalized. Each offered his support, Wallace his prayers. But Nixon had back channels too, his running from his old anti-Communist network to the presidential palace in Saigon. Sometime in the next few days he put them to use. Reject Johnson's invitation to the peace talks, his emissaries quietly said to the South Vietnamese government. Let the negotiations fail. And when he was president Nixon would reach a settlement far more advantageous to South Vietnam than LBJ ever would.

The Gallup organization conducted its last poll as the peace agreement collapsed. It started its surveys on October 29, the day LBJ learned of Nixon's intervention; carried them through the 30th and the 31st, when South Vietnam's president officially informed the White House that his nation wouldn't agree to the terms Johnson had set and then fought off LBJ's ferocious efforts to force him into line; and ended on November 1 and 2, amid the ruins of Johnson's last, best hope of peace. The newspapers released Gallup's results on election eve, November 4. Fifteen percent for Wallace, 42 percent for Humphrey, 43 percent for Nixon: another razor-thin margin for a repackaged politician who'd always thought that nothing mattered more than winning.

LBJ spent election night tracking the vote from his ranch, Humphrey from a Minneapolis hotel room, Nixon from a suite at the Waldorf in New York, Wallace at the house in Montgomery Lurleen had begged him to buy so they'd have somewhere to go when his term was done. The early returns pointed toward an upset: an unexpectedly strong showing for Humphrey in the Northeast, the urban vote solid enough to win him both New York and Pennsylvania; a Wallace sweep in the Deep South, virtually all the states Goldwater had carried in 1964 gone his way, Nixon's electoral path narrowing as they fell. But Wallace took only a third of the vote in the Upper South, not enough to stop Nixon from holding on to what was now clearly Republican territory. The industrial Midwest split: Michigan to Humphrey, Ohio to Nixon, Illinois too close to call. And the Plains went to the Republicans, as they almost always did. There the returns stalled until 8:00 the following morning, when the television networks gave Nixon California's forty electoral votes, enough to bring him within striking distance of the 270 he needed. Immediately Dick Daley called Humphrey to say that he still had ballots to count, in the fine Chicago tradition. But the numbers out of the African American wards weren't strong enough to offset the losses in neighborhoods like the Cahills', where Humphrey's vote tumbled to 37.6 percent, the Democrats' worst showing since Eisenhower's landslide reelection in 1956. At noon the networks gave Nixon Illinois too, and with it the presidency.

Shortly thereafter Humphrey went down to the hotel ballroom to concede. When he was finished LBJ had an aide phone the Waldorf to congratulate the president-elect on his behalf, his mood too dark to do the job himself. The final count put Humphrey within half a million votes of Nixon, a margin even tighter than the polls had predicted. But it wasn't the narrowness of the loss that stung. It was the breadth of it. In four years the Democrats' share of the vote had plunged from 61 to 42.7 percent. It had been pulled down partly by Humphrey's inability to win over independents, partly by a dramatic decline in support from some of the party's core constituencies. Humphrey barely carried the Catholic vote, the union vote, and the working-class vote, all of which LBJ had taken by at least forty points in 1964. And except for Texas, which Johnson refused to surrender, the Democrats lost every southern state, the first time that had happened in the party's history. Beneath those changes lay a tectonic shift in the political order. In 1964 Johnson had won 59 percent of the white vote. Four years later—after the Edmund Pettus Bridge and the Cicero line, after three long hot summers and a single sickening moment at the Lorraine Motel, after the grief and the anger and the rumors of revenge, after all the talk of law and order and local control—Humphrey took 38 percent. That wasn't a frustratingly slim defeat for a candidate making a late rush in the polls. It was a repudiation of the president and his policies.

Half an hour after Humphrey conceded, Nixon entered the Waldorf's ballroom to make his victory speech. He followed the rules of the form, praising the opposing party for fighting the good fight, thanking his campaign workers for their tireless efforts, humbly acknowledging his family's devotion. Toward the end he told a mawkish story of seeing a teenager at a rally in a small Ohio town, holding up a sign that said, "Bring Us Together."[33] That was the message he took from the campaign trail, he said, that Americans wanted their new president to bring them together again. It was the sort of thing he was supposed to say. But it wasn't true. In the end Wallace carried 13.5 percent of the vote—almost 9 percent around Eddy Street—well below his peak but still the strongest showing by a third-party candidate in almost half a century, a testament to the appeal of division and the enduring power of deeply rooted injustice. As for Nixon, he'd come into the campaign committed to reclaiming Eisenhower's middle ground and the electoral majorities it had produced. In pursuit of that goal he'd played on the country's divisions too, albeit in softer, more sophisticated, and, in the race's final days, unconscionably manipulative ways. With that cynical politics, he'd held off Humphrey's October charge, pieced together the thinnest of pluralities, and won the right to govern a fiercely riven nation.

CHAPTER 10

NOBODIES

The first time she became pregnant Norma McCorvey was living in Los Angeles with her husband, a drifter with a vicious streak who'd won her over by saying he wanted to be a rock star. On the night she told him she was expecting, he beat her unconscious. The next morning a friend drove her to the airport, put a roll of cash in her hand, and sent her up to the counter to buy a ticket on the first flight to Dallas, so she could get back to her mother's house, though that had never been a safe place either. Seven months later, in May 1965, she gave birth to a girl she named Missy. McCorvey was seventeen.

She and her mother tried to make a go of it. But there was too much history between them, too much anger, too much alcohol, and far too many complications. In McCorvey's telling the fissures began to crack open at a gay bar called Sue's, where she finally admitted to herself that she was more attracted to women than to men. When she brought the truth home, she says, her mother claimed custody of Missy and threw McCorvey out of the house. Her mother told the story a different way. She never could stand Norma's defiance. "I beat the fuck out of her," she said much later. "You can only take so much of nerviness. She was wild. Wild."[1] But it wasn't her daughter's lesbianism that made her take Missy from her, she insisted. It was the drinking, the dope, and the sleeping around. She told her she had to straighten out. But McCorvey didn't listen.

She got pregnant again in 1967. She was living with a woman she'd met in a bar, working a job her partner had gotten her on the night shift at the Baylor University hospital, when one of the orderlies started hitting on her. She told him she was gay. He said it didn't matter. They spent a week together while her girlfriend was out of town, long enough for the sex to lose whatever allure it had. McCorvey thought he'd taken up with her for the thrill of being with a bad girl. What she was looking for she couldn't say. But it wasn't a baby. That much she knew.

She delivered her second child alone, her partner having broken off their relationship and tossed her out of the apartment as soon as she'd heard what had happened, the hospital having fired her once her supervisor discovered that she was expecting out of wedlock, her mother having decided that there wasn't any point in trying to salvage her. By arrangement the medical staff whisked away the baby before McCorvey came out of the anesthetic, so that the adopting family wouldn't have any contact with the young woman who'd given them their newborn. Afterward the doctor said she'd had a son, though one of the nurses was sure it was a girl.

As soon as she could she went back to the bars, working days at a gay place, evenings at a straight one, still drinking, still smoking weed, and now dropping and occasionally dealing acid too. From there she took to hustling pool alongside yet another drifter, this one a middle-aged good old boy who drove a two-year-old Olds, drank as hard as she did, and made a living reeling in the marks. Eventually she "shacked up with him and his liquor and his music," she said. "And a few pills of course."[2] It lasted just a week; in her version of events relationships with men always seemed to last a week. Then he left for Vegas.

Somehow she hooked on to a roadside carnival, the sort of operation that set up for a couple of days in a parking lot, selling rides on the whirligig, thrills at the motor dome, and a look at the five-legged cow, before moving on to the next town. The last stop was Fort Lauderdale, where the carnival shut down for the season. The owners told the hands who had nowhere else to go that they could stay with the flatbeds as long as they wanted, though they wouldn't be paid for their time. That's where she was in September 1969, a twenty-one-year-old nobody, as she put it, living in a truck on a Florida blacktop, sharing joints with her fellow carnies, drinking what little savings she had, too scared to admit that she was pregnant again.

Nixon Now

RICHARD NIXON KNEW that Dwight Eisenhower was dying. The old man had been admitted to Washington's Walter Reed Hospital in May 1968 with congestive heart failure. There he'd stayed through the election, the December marriage of his grandson David to Nixon's younger daughter Julie, and the January inauguration of the man he'd set on the path to the presidency back in 1952. Nixon had gone to see him twice, the first time just hours after Hubert Humphrey's concession— it was his first official visit as president-elect—and again on Thanksgiving Day, when the Nixon and Eisenhower families had gathered together in the hospital cafeteria for the turkey dinner the army made for them. After that there'd been any number of phone calls and messages, interspersed with an expanding set of reports on the general's gradual decline.

Still, his passing, in the early afternoon of March 28, 1969, came as a shock. The president was in the Oval Office with the secretary of defense when Bob Haldeman came in to give him the news. Nixon started to talk about funeral arrangements. But partway through he got up from his desk, turned his back to the room, and started to cry.

After a couple of minutes he slipped into an anteroom off the Oval Office for some time alone. When he returned, still half-crying, a handful of aides were waiting for him. They stood around awkwardly, Haldeman wrote in his diary that evening, until one of them thought of the perfect thing to say. Eisenhower had seen "all his checkpoints, the nomination, the wedding, the inaugural, the P[resident]'s success," he told Nixon. "So he could go freely now," as dying fathers do when they know that their sons have secured their legacy.[3]

Nixon wove that legacy through his new administration as thoroughly as he'd drawn it through the campaign. Some of his most important appointments came straight from the Eisenhower years—

his secretary of state had been Ike's last attorney general, his secretary of commerce Eisenhower's budget director—and he filled almost every other cabinet post with the moderate Republicans Ike had always favored. Inside the White House he re-created the organizational structure Eisenhower had imported from the military, with strict lines of authority leading up to a chief of staff who controlled access to the president. JFK and LBJ had reverted to the somewhat looser structure previous presidents had used. But Nixon liked the precision—and isolation—that Ike's system offered.

Its operation turned out to be a grim business. According to the White House's PR machinery, the New Nixon was running his administration with the same quiet reason he'd brought to his campaign. His staffers knew better. Most days he bunkered himself into the Oval Office or the hideaway he claimed in the Old Executive Office Building next to the West Wing, alone with the stack of memos funneled through the only three aides whose company he cared to keep: Haldeman, the campaign's leading ad man, as chief of staff; domestic affairs adviser John Ehrlichman; and Henry Kissinger, the ruthlessly ambitious and relentlessly manipulative Harvard professor he'd made his national security advisor. Out of his seclusion flowed a stream of "action items," some scrawled in the memos' margins, others embedded in the rambling, brooding, often angry soliloquies he delivered, mostly to Haldeman and Ehrlichman, who'd been protecting him for years—though Kissinger also heard his share. He'd settle into his favorite chair and talk, sometimes late into the night, obsessing over appearances, raging against slights, slashing away at the enemies he saw all around him, the Old Nixon through and through.

He took a few months to settle on a domestic agenda, but its guiding principles were set from the start. He'd tinker around the edges of the Great Society, moving a handful of programs from one spot in the bureaucracy to another and changing up their funding streams. But the key programs would stay in place, as he'd said they would during the campaign. And from the pile of proposals LBJ had left behind he'd pick out a few to extend, just as Ike had expanded the New Deal's public works programs to build the nation's freeway system. Nixon found two he liked. One of them would remake the New Deal's piecemeal welfare state by replacing the mix of monthly support poor families received with a guaranteed annual income. The other resurrected a mandatory hiring program Lyndon Johnson had put in place to combat racial discrimination in Philadelphia's congenitally discriminatory construction work. There'd been so much pushback from the building trades that Johnson had abandoned it. In June 1969 Nixon revived it, under the legalistic name of "affirmative action."

When it came to his broader racial policies, though, Eisenhower's moderation wouldn't do. Postelection studies showed that two-thirds of Wallace's voters would have supported Nixon in 1968 had the governor not been in the race. With those returns Nixon would have won 52.3 percent of the popular vote, less than three points shy of Ike's percentage in 1952. And he probably would have carried every southern state he failed to carry, from Georgia all the way through Texas. Losses that serious couldn't be allowed to stand. So Nixon spent the winter and spring piecing together a robust racial agenda, the process shaped by his furious marginalia, occasional racist rants—"Went through his whole thesis re: blacks and their genetic inferiority and the hopelessness of any early change in the situation," Haldeman wrote after one session with the president, "have to wait for in-breeding"[4]—and an abiding fear of being outflanked by George Wallace again.

The civil rights movement's most dynamic centers were already struggling. Its southern wing was still reeling from the loss of Martin Luther King, while Black Power had suffered a serious blow from Stokely Carmichael's December decision to abandon the United States for a new life in Guinea. A sudden surge in membership had turned the Black Panther Party into the new face of African American radicalism. But it also strained the leadership's ability to control the party they'd created; in January its Central Committee launched what would turn into a series of purges, a sign of fierce conflicts to come. Nixon wanted to speed the spiral. King's successors should be discreetly marginalized, he said, and Black Power broken by a dramatic intensification of the clandestine operation the FBI had launched against it in 1967. Those quiet moves would then be coupled with two very public ones, the first aimed at the inner cities, the second at the Supreme Court's assault on segregated schools.

The 1968 Safe Streets Act had given Nixon a hundred million dollars to distribute to states and cities to intensify policing. But it hadn't given him the ability to tell state and local authorities what form the intensification should take. At the end of January 1969 the White House offered them a model to follow by submitting to Congress a bill to combat crime in the District of Columbia, where the federal government set the rules. The details were draconian. The district police would be given the right to enter suspects' homes without announcing themselves. Judges would be allowed to detain arrestees for up to sixty days without bail whenever they thought the suspects posed "a danger to the community." Anyone convicted of an armed crime of violence was to receive a mandatory minimum sentence of three years; a second conviction carried a mandatory minimum of twenty years; and a third, life imprisonment. The counting could begin as early as age fifteen, since prosecutors would be given the discretion to have kids that young tried as adults. This wasn't an anti-crime bill, said a Senate critic. It was "a blueprint for a police state," to be imposed on the only major American city with an overwhelmingly African American population: a terrifying escalation of the racalized law and order that had already done so much damage to the nation.[5]

In the summer Nixon turned to the Supreme Court. A scattering of rural southern school systems had already integrated in accordance with the previous year's *New Kent County* decision. But most had preferred to plod through the cases Black parents had brought to force their compliance. Not that the districts had decent defenses to mount, since the vast majority of them had been sustaining their color lines through the same disingenuous transfer plans the justices had declared unconstitutional in *New Kent*. All through the year the rulings came down as the law required, so that by the time classes let out in June 1969 a substantial portion of the southern countryside was facing the imminent integration of its schools.

In the cities the legal question grew more muddied. Many of the South's urban school systems also had deceptive transfer programs. For the most part, though, they just assigned students to their neighborhood schools. That policy produced segregated systems, their lawyers argued, but not because of any discriminatory intent. It was simply a matter of geography: neighborhoods were segregated, so their schools were too. That put southern cities on what had long been thought of as the northern side of the de facto/de jure divide. On that side, the southern lawyers said, the courts had no right to require schools to integrate.

The NAACP's attorneys knew the argument far too well: by 1969 the association's legal files were full of failed attempts to bring court-ordered desegregation to schools outside the South. In the summer of 1968 they'd tried again, with a filing against Los Angeles' sprawling system. This time they handed the court a new argument. LA's segregated neighborhoods had indeed produced segregated schools, they said. But that connection wasn't simply a matter of geography. Government officials had actively divided neighborhoods through a host of programs, from redlining to highway construction. The LA school board then reinforced the division by manipulating ostensibly neutral processes like the drawing of attendance zones. Los Angeles' schools therefore weren't segregated by de facto discrimination, the argument ran. They were segregated by law. And the courts had every right to demand their immediate integration.

The LA case was still underway in the winter of 1969, when the NAACP brought the argument south on behalf of a long-standing suit against the Charlotte, North Carolina, schools. At first the presiding judge, James McMillan, a farmer's son trained at Harvard Law, wasn't convinced that the definition of de jure discrimination could be stretched so far. But the more he heard the more sense it made. The courtroom phase ended in March. The next month he dismissed Charlotte's de facto defense—"the neighborhood school theory has no standing to override the Constitution," he said—and ordered integration so thorough that every school in the district was to have a balance of Black and white students equal to the racial makeup of the city as a whole.[6]

It was only a district court decision, sure to be appealed. But its implications were enormous. New Kent County had about 1,300 students in its schools, a reasonable number for a rural system. Charlotte had 85,000. To meet McMillan's order, the school board would have to move a substantial portion of them across the color line, busing white children into Black neighborhoods and Black children into white ones. Some of those moves would run between abutting communities. Others would stretch across Charlotte, from its northwest corner where 90 percent of African Americans lived to the leafy subdivisions of the southeast, where there were no Blacks at all. When the buses rolled into that section of the city—as the court expected them to do in September 1969—the NAACP's lawyers would have finally breached the barriers that had protected middle-class whites from any personal experience of the civil rights revolution. They'd have done it, moreover, by flipping the formula SCLC had used to shatter Jim Crow in the spring of 1963. Then the movement had put African American children into the streets. This time the movement would bring white kids into the center of the struggle.

The protests started as soon as the ruling came down. Some of them embraced the explicit racism that had infused the massive resistance campaigns of the 1950s. But the largest rallies ran in a different direction. We have nothing against integration, the parent organizers told the families who filled the church halls and high school gyms of Charlotte's suddenly imperiled subdivisions. But they'd worked hard to get their kids into decent schools close to home. And it wasn't right for the courts to wrench them away solely because of the color of their skin. So the organizers flipped the movement's formula too, appropriating its promise of a color-blind America to defend those long-standing barriers the neighbors who were packed onto the bleachers had never even noticed.

The school board filed its appeal in June, late enough that the superior court couldn't possibly rule in time for integration to begin by the deadline Judge McMillan had set. A few weeks later the Fifth Circuit Court ordered thirty-three Mississippi districts to integrate when their schools reopened in September, as Charlotte was supposed to do. Thirty of them asked that they be given until December 1 to comply, a request the Department of Justice quickly and very publicly endorsed. On its face a three-month delay seemed a minor concession. But the NAACP feared that the administration was actually signaling to every school system under court order—from New Kent to Charlotte—that it should stall integration with whatever legal means it could find. When the Fifth Circuit gave the schools the extension they wanted, the association's lawyers appealed its decision to the Supreme Court. And the White House announced that at oral arguments the Justice Department's lawyers would stand with Mississippi.

Nixon combined that subtle move with a far blunter one. He'd come into office knowing that he'd have one Supreme Court seat to fill, thanks to the Senate's conservatives blocking Abe Fortas's ascension to chief justice the previous September. In May 1969 the conservatives drove Fortas from the Court altogether, forcing him to resign over financial improprieties, with the threat of a homosexual scandal tossed in. For the new chief justice, Nixon nominated longtime circuit court judge Warren Burger, who'd come to his attention by publicly embracing the administration's defense of law and order. For Fortas's seat he went with Clement Haynsworth of the Fourth Circuit, a fifth-generation South Carolinian with an imposing pedigree, impeccable manners, and a judicial record unequivocally in support of segregated schools. Haynsworth had already ruled in the mid-1960s to protect Charlotte's segregated school system, which was clearly part of his appeal. Two appointments weren't enough to break the bench's liberal bloc, but once they were confirmed, Nixon would have begun to build a counterweight.

Vietnam required a long game too. He was facing short-term pressures, to be sure. LBJ's dramatic moves in March 1968 had calmed the international markets. But in the course of the year the inflationary spiral had hit 4.7 percent, its highest level since 1950. In response the

Federal Reserve was starting to raise interest rates, which would likely push the economy into a recession, all because of the economic tangle the war had created. Then there was the inescapable fact that Nixon had spent the campaign promising that he would bring the war to an honorable end. When reporters pushed for details at his first press conference as president, he stumbled a bit. But the fundamental point came through clearly enough. He wanted to reach a settlement with North Vietnam that preserved South Vietnam's independence, the same goal LBJ had pursued for five blood-soaked years.

The difference lay in the details. Like Johnson before him, Nixon assumed that the North Vietnamese wouldn't begin serious negotiations until they were convinced that a brokered peace was in their best interest. He saw two ways to push them to that conclusion, one strikingly strategic in its conception, the other brutal. For years the North Vietnamese had exploited the tension between the Soviet Union and China, playing the two nations off each other to maximize the support they drew from both. Nixon wanted to turn that dynamic around with a stunning bit of *realpolitik*. He'd quietly offer the Soviets improved relations on a number of fronts, while simultaneously probing the possibility of opening relations with China for the first time since the 1949 revolution had brought Mao Zedong to power. Each side would be anxious to cut off his overture to the other, for fear that if it didn't it would be isolated in a superpower realignment. From that fear Nixon could wrench concessions on various issues, from nuclear weapons to trade. But most of all he could insist that both Moscow and Beijing push Hanoi toward a settlement.

Such a grand strategy would take time to develop. Within a month of his inauguration Nixon had established a secret channel to the Russian ambassador, to be run through Kissinger, who shared the president's love of the clandestine. China was harder to reach. Not until midsummer did Nixon manage to even hint at the possibility of an opening, and then only through an intermediary. In the meantime he put the more brutal piece of his Vietnam policy into place. He came into office with the military still fully engaged in South Vietnam, its troops still slogging through the countryside in search of Viet Cong to destroy, its bombers still pounding the nation it had pledged to protect. That clearly wasn't enough. So he ran through other options. For a while he considered launching a Curtis LeMay–style air assault on North Vietnam, far more vicious than anything LBJ had tried. But having promised Americans peace he was hesitant to give them an intensified war. Or at least one they could see.

Since 1965 the military had been running a covert bombing campaign against the supply lines the North Vietnamese snaked through Laos, the tiny country on North Vietnam's western border. On March 17 Nixon extended that campaign to Cambodia, immediately west of South Vietnam, ordering the first of what would be almost 4,000 American bombing runs against the supply lines' southern stretch. It was a fourteen-month assault on a neutral nation meant solely to intimidate Hanoi, just as LBJ had believed Rolling Thunder would do back in 1965, the entire operation wrapped in a secrecy so complete Nixon didn't even tell his secretary of state what he'd done until the bombers were airborne.

There the war remained for the next three months, to all appearances the fighting precisely where Johnson had left it—1,316 Americans were killed in combat in March 1969, 847 in April, 1,209 in May—the peace talks as deadlocked as they'd ever been. Then, on June 8, Nixon announced that he was going to start bringing the boys back home. He couched his decision in long-standing policy. The United States had always intended the South Vietnamese to assume responsibility for their own defense, he said. Now they were ready, and the Pentagon could begin to draw down its troops. The reductions would be handled with the utmost caution, he insisted: the first round would shrink the American force in South Vietnam by 25,000, less than five percent of the number in-country, with more to follow as circumstances allowed. Even his closest advisers were surprised by the decision, which seemed to run counter to his intention of battering the North Vietnamese into a settlement. But really it was all of a piece. Nixon was slowly pulling the troops out of combat so as to drive down the casualties Americans couldn't stand to see, while hiding the violence he'd unleashed by turning it into covert action. He was still going to fight LBJ's bitch of a war, in other words, but he was going to do it the way Dwight Eisenhower had taught him.

Nixon mixed in a bit of McCarthyism. Under the president's prodding, the FBI's covert campaign against the Panthers reached a feverish level, fueled by the informants and provocateurs the bureau flooded into the Panthers' chapters across the country. Official repression quickly followed, nowhere more brutally than in Chicago, where the police used the FBI's subversions to justify their murder of the city's most prominent Panther, twenty-one-year-old Fred Hampton, in an early morning raid on his apartment three blocks west of Vacuum Can. The cops shot him two times in the head before he could even get out of bed.

To the bureau's secret crusade against the Panthers, Nixon added a public show of force aimed at the anti-war movement's militant wing. A week after the inauguration the White House had a letter out to college presidents, reminding them that Washington had the right to withdraw federal funding from any student who committed a crime during a campus protest. That small slap was followed by a tougher blow: in March the Justice Department indicted the seven radicals who'd organized the Chicago convention actions, with an eighth— Black Panther Bobby Seale—added in for symmetry's sake. They were charged with conspiracy to incite a riot, a tough case to make, since the week's worst violence had come not from the protesters but from Chicago's rampaging police. But the point wasn't to secure a conviction, or even to make prospective radicals think twice before taking to the streets. In fact Nixon hoped for a spike in campus unrest come spring. Or so he said in another of his marginal notes, this one written the week the indictments were handed down, presumably on the assumption that any disruption would play in his favor now that he'd proved to those Americans who couldn't stand anti-war protesters that he was on their side.

He got what he was looking for. Through April and May, confrontations swept across the country's colleges and universities, some fed by the war, others by race, still others by administrators' determination to assert their authority. There were hundreds of small-scale protests, larger ones at some of the nation's best-known schools. Down went Harvard, shut by a three-day student strike that started as a campaign against the campus military training program the university had long run. Down went Stanford, crippled by student protests over military-funded research. Down went Cornell, paralyzed by an armed occupation of the student union by Black students demanding that the university create an African American Studies Department. And down went two of the campuses that had given student activism its shape—North Carolina A&T and the University of California, Berkeley, both hit with massive state repression after student-led marches went horribly wrong. Hundreds of students were injured in the fighting that followed, two of them killed: a twenty-one-year-old farmer's son gunned down at A&T in a drive-by that may or may not have involved the police, and a twenty-five-year-old in Berkeley hit in the back by a load of buckshot the Alameda County sheriff's department was using in lieu of bullets. This wasn't dissent, Nixon told the 10,000 people who came to his only campus appearance, at South Dakota's placid little General Beadle State College. This was insurrection.

SDS promised worse to come. At the end of June its most devoted members swept into Chicago, of all places, for their annual convention. Their aim was to set the nation's surging students on the road to revolution. But they couldn't agree on which road to follow. For four fevered days they argued over principles, tactics, comportment, and the finer points of revolutionary thought. On the fifth day they split, one faction claiming the hall for the student-worker alliance that would topple the capitalist order, the other stalking out to build the vanguard that would lead the masses of radicalized youth into the anti-imperialist war raging among the world's oppressed.

Theorizing a revolution wasn't the same as delivering it. For the first time since 1964 the summer passed without any major urban unrest, except for a few tense nights in the streets around a Greenwich Village gay bar called the Stonewall Inn. Talk of building a "gay power" move-

ment had been circulating around the edges of gay and lesbian communities for a couple of years. On the West Coast there'd been a scattering
of actions too, mostly protests against police harassment of homosexual social spaces and public demonstrations of gay pride. But it wasn't
until eight New York cops raided the Stonewall early in the morning
of June 28 that the movement started to surge. It was the force of the
response that did it—crowds of young gay and trans people filling the
streets for three nights of clashes with the cops—and the media attention that dramatic events in the heart of Manhattan inevitably drew.
Within a few weeks activists had formed the Gay Liberation Front, the
first decisive step in a national mobilization that didn't fit neatly into
any of SDS's radical categories.

As for the surging students, their greatest show of force came on a
dairy farm a hundred miles north of New York City, a world away from
the anti-imperialist struggle. Since 1967 the hippie ethos had seeped
into popular culture as a pastiche of rebellion for sale in the record
stores and on the edgy end of Broadway—its allure heightened by the
drug panic that refused to give way, though the most careful studies
showed that while marijuana use was rapidly rising, only about six percent of Americans younger than twenty-five had ever tried a harder
drug. That was the combination that the summer's most successful
promoters put together. They called it the Woodstock Music & Art
Fair, though it wasn't in Woodstock and there was no fair: just three
days of rock and roll, much of it transplanted from the 1967 Monterey
Pop Festival, the best of it mesmerizing, even without the pot and the
pills passing through the crowd. It was a late-summer revival of the
Haight's hippie glory for 400,000 kids to share, an appeal SDS's splintered vanguards couldn't come close to matching.

They tried, most provocatively with a call on young militants to join
them for three "Days of Rage" to mark the October opening of the Chicago conspiracy trial. The organizing cadre, rebranded as the Weath-
ermen, imagined "a huge action," as one of its leading figures put it.
"Thousands upon thousands will be on hand, and the whole wide world
will see what a radical fighting force in the mother country can look

like."[7] They got 300 militants smashing windows on Chicago's upscale North Side and a bit of the Loop until the cops beat them into submission. The news gave it heavy play. But the White House paid almost no attention, preoccupied as it was by another demonstration scheduled for the following week, to be led not by Maoists-in-the-making but by the Democrats' growing number of doves.

Nixon had always assumed that the most prominent liberals would take him on. And they had, in bits and pieces. Some of them had objected to his crime bill's most aggressive provisions, more to his nomination of Judge Haynsworth, who it turned out had some financial indiscretions of his own to go with his troubling racial record. Vietnam built more slowly. At first almost everyone was willing to give the president time to put his policy into place. But the spring was so violent—and the administration's initial troop reduction so small—that the doves decided they couldn't wait any longer. Since 1965 they'd centered their dissent on the extent of American bombing and the desperate need for negotiations. In the summer of 1969 they coalesced around a far more fundamental demand, built on Nixon's June drawdown. It was time, they said, for the United States to bring its entire force home in a single sustained withdrawal, to be completed within a year or two, and by so doing to shut down the American share of the war altogether.

But beyond the occasional op-ed, some sharply argued speeches, and hollow threats of congressional action, they had no way to pressure the president—until they joined the Moratorium to End the War in Vietnam. The idea had come from a progressive businessman in suburban Boston, who imagined a national day of peaceful protest to demand that the war be brought to an end, centered on the sort of moral witness that had seemed to slip away since the mid-1960s. He passed it on to two protégés of Allard Lowenstein, the liberal provocateur who'd brought Eugene McCarthy into the previous year's presidential race. Together they gave the protest a sophisticated-sounding title, picked a date for it to run—October 15—used the businessman's cash to open an office in Washington, DC, and set to organizing along the networks Lowenstein provided. First they brought in liberal student groups, then those segments of the radical anti-war movement that had no interest in SDS's rush to the barricades, and finally, at summer's end, the liberal portions of the middle and professional classes that had sustained the McCarthy campaign.

The leading liberals started signing on when it became clear that the moratorium's organizers were taking anti-war protest into the mainstream. In poured offers of support from New York's celebrity mayor, the NAACP's executive director, the leaders of the nation's two largest unions, the president of Yale, Harvard's entire faculty, Congress's most outspoken doves—McCarthy, Ted Kennedy, William Fulbright, Albert Gore, Frank Church, George McGovern—and a coterie of notables from the Johnson administration who wouldn't have dared to be seen in such company the year before. Together they'd give the day a great deal of respectability, wrote an administration analyst as the momentum mounted, and maybe even a claim to patriotism.

That was exactly what Nixon feared they'd do. For weeks beforehand he scrambled for ways to undermine the moratorium's reach. He tried dismissing it, deflecting it, preempting it, and in the final rush dispatching handpicked proxies to say that it was aiding and abetting the enemy. Nothing worked. Somewhere around a million people turned out for one or another of the day's events, ten times the number who'd marched on the Pentagon in 1967, a hundred times the number who'd gone to Chicago to confront the Democrats in 1968, and five hundred times the number who'd joined SDS's Days of Rage. Most of their gatherings were small and somber—a nationwide sprawl of prayer vigils and anti-war lectures, well-mannered marches and memorials to the dead—though there were massive rallies as well: 10,000 at Rutgers, 15,000 at the University of Wisconsin, 20,000 at the University of Michigan, 25,000 on Wall Street, 30,000 on the New Haven green, 35,000 at midtown Manhattan's Bryant Park, 50,000 for a candlelit procession around the White House, 100,000 overflowing the Boston Common. And everywhere the crowds came out there were liberals up on the stage, demanding that the president bring the war to an end.

Nixon spent the day running through an unusually intense round of meetings meant to show that he was far too busy with matters of state to notice the 50,000 Americans marching around his home. In private the White House staff was badly shaken by the staggering number of people the moratorium had mobilized. But no one was sure how to react. "Great debates rage on the tactics for the future," Haldeman wrote in his diary, with one faction urging the president to mount a vigorous defense of his policies, another pressing for a conciliatory gesture, maybe even a concession or two. At first Nixon seemed torn too. The moment didn't last. A couple of days after the marchers went home he sat down with a yellow legal pad to start sketching out his response, already scheduled as a major address to the nation on Monday, November 3. "Don't get rattled," he wrote on the top of the page. "Don't waver. Don't react."[8]

From there the drafts developed. Nixon wrote at least a dozen over the next two weeks, mostly in the long blocks of private time he insisted Haldeman carve into his schedule. The final version he finished over a secluded Halloween weekend at Camp David, alone in his cabin in the Maryland woods, writing late into the night. He waited until Monday afternoon to return to the White House, then immediately went off to his Executive Office hideaway, his only contact until the evening a series of phone calls to Haldeman obsessing over the networks' plans for makeup and lighting. When he went live at half past nine Eastern time, seventy million Americans were watching.

He spoke for thirty-two minutes, almost perfect timing for the television age. The first two-thirds of his address he used to construct the contrast he wanted Americans to see. The fundamental question facing the nation wasn't whether the United States ought to continue the war or seek peace, he insisted, but rather what sort of peace it ought to pursue. On one side of the divide lay those who wanted the United States out of Vietnam immediately, on the other his administration, working methodically to extract the nation from the slog of a war he'd inherited from his predecessors. He walked through the steps he'd taken, though there were a few details—his disruption of LBJ's October agreement and his secret bombing of Cambodia—he failed to mention. When he reached the end of that recitation he acknowledged that some "honest and patriotic Americans" disagreed with what he'd done. Then the speech abruptly shifted. Not the tone, which remained as calm and reasonable as it had been from the start, but the message.

He made the pivot with a variation of the story he'd told on election night, another sign in another rally, this one a world away from the Ohio teenager pleading with Nixon to bring the nation together. "In San Francisco a few weeks ago," he said, "I saw demonstrators carrying signs reading 'Lose in Vietnam, bring the boys home.' Well, one of the strengths of our free society is that any American has a right to reach that conclusion. . . . But as President of the United States, I would be untrue to my oath of office if I allowed the policy of this nation to be dictated by the minority who hold that point of view and who try to impose it on the nation by mounting demonstrations in the street." All of a sudden his opponents weren't patriotic Americans anymore. They were subversives undermining the Constitution he'd pledged to defend, radicals and liberals together, rooting for the nation's defeat. To complete the turn he reached back to the campaign again, to the pitch his handlers had given him to undercut George Wallace's appeal. "And so tonight," he said as his half hour closed in, "to you—the great silent majority of my fellow Americans—I ask for your support. . . . Let us be united for peace. Let us be united against defeat. Because let us understand: North Vietnam cannot defeat or humiliate the United States. Only Americans can do that."[9]

It worked even better than he'd hoped it would. Fifty thousand telegrams poured into the White House the following day, almost all of them supportive, the largest number of wired messages any presidential address had ever drawn, followed by 30,000 letters. Shortly thereafter CBS asked a representative sample of Americans what they thought of the war now that the president had spoken. Sixty-two percent of them said public protest harmed the administration's search for a settlement. Sixty-seven percent said that they opposed the immediate withdrawal of American troops. And 74 percent said that they considered themselves to be in the silent majority.

Norma

WHEN MCCORVEY FINALLY told the other carnies she was pregnant, they said she needed a plan. She spent a little time making the rounds of the nearby restaurants in hopes of finding some waitressing work. But no one was willing to hire a vaguely strung-out twenty-one-year-old whose only address was a parking lot. That left her no choice, really, but to fall back on the one set of connections she had left. So she put together a pile of dimes, planted herself at a pay phone, and called every gay bar she knew in Dallas until she reached someone willing to wire her the money to buy a bus ticket home.

She got back to Dallas, she said later, with three dollars in savings, two packs of cigarettes, and a sense of failure so severe she spent the next five days in the bus station, because walking out the door seemed way too hard. On the sixth day she called the bar that had paid her way home. The manager sent a friend round to pick her up, get her a decent meal, a shower, and a clean set of clothes. Once they had her looking better, the manager offered her a couple of shifts a week and a lead on a room to rent. A lifeline, McCorvey called it, which seemed about right.

A few weeks later she grabbed hold of what she thought might be another. It was an ordinary evening, in her telling, a handful of regulars sitting in the bar drinking Lone Star, McCorvey sharing her troubles with one of her customers, telling her how unhappy she was to be expecting again. If you don't want another baby, the woman said, why don't you get rid of it? McCorvey was stunned. "Get rid of it?" she remembered thinking. "Get rid of it? How?"[10] For most of her shift she left the question hanging for fear of sounding stupid. Come closing time she took aside another regular, a nurse's aide, who she knew wouldn't laugh at her when she asked whether it was true that she didn't have to see her pregnancy through. The next day she asked the doctor who'd delivered her first two children to abort the fetus she was carrying.

He turned her down, as Texas law required him to do. So she found another doctor, a younger one who handled unwanted pregnancies as something of a specialty. It turned out he didn't perform abortions either; he simply referred his patients to one of several adoption lawyers with whom he'd made arrangements. But the attorney he suggested refused to take her case, on the assumption, she said later, that she might be carrying a biracial baby no white family would want to adopt. From there she went searching for back channels. Somebody told her about an illegal clinic on Dallas' ragged West Side, someone else that she could self-induce with a mix of castor oil and peanuts. But the clinic had been shuttered—the cops had raided it, she was told when she showed up at its door—and the castor oil just made her sick. That's when she circled back to the second doctor to see if he knew another lawyer she could talk to. He sent her to Henry McCluskey.

McCorvey went over to McCluskey's office sometime in January 1970, early in her second trimester. From the start she liked him. He was younger than the other lawyer had been—barely older than her, in fact— less buttoned-down, and much more willing to listen. But when she asked him to help her get an abortion, he turned her down too. For a while he talked to her about adoption, gently enough she thought, until she said that if he wasn't going to help her she was going to find another back-alley place. He stopped for a second, as she remembered it. Then he told her about a lawyer he knew who was looking for a woman like her for a court case she was hoping to file. The rest McCorvey didn't really understand, except for a couple of things. McCluskey wanted her to talk to his lawyer friend. And more than likely she was going to have this baby.

Linda Coffee told her that too, when they met a few days later. She and another young attorney, a woman named Sarah Weddington, were indeed preparing a lawsuit, just as McCluskey had said: a case designed to challenge the constitutionality of Texas' abortion law. They wanted to argue that women had a right to end their pregnancies for whatever reason they chose—or no reason at all. But to get a hearing they had to have a client who'd been denied that right. There'd be no cost, Coffee said, no demands on McCorvey's time, and no trouble: they could even keep her name out of the official documents they'd be filing. But they needed her to be pregnant.

What Coffee didn't say was how preposterous it was that she and Weddington were doing such a thing. They'd known each other since the summer of 1965, when they'd both started at the University of Texas Law School, two of five women in an incoming class of 120. It was one of the first cohorts admitted after the 1964 Civil Rights Act had prohibited job discrimination on the basis of gender. But most Texas law firms still wouldn't consider hiring a woman, no matter what the law said. So when Coffee and Weddington finished they didn't receive any offers. Coffee took a state job instead and then, with a bit of luck, landed a clerkship with one of the few female judges in the federal judiciary, Sarah Hughes, who happened to be based in Dallas. Weddington never made it out of the law school: two years after getting her JD she was still working as a research assistant to one of her professors, the only position she could get. That's where she was on a November afternoon in 1969, tucked away in her little office on UT's campus, when a law student she vaguely knew stopped by with a proposition. A tiny group of radical grad students was interested in trying to overturn Texas' abortion law in federal court. They were hoping that Weddington would be their lawyer.

She heard him out—a preacher's kid from small-town Texas wasn't raised to turn people away—though a proposal so naive didn't really deserve the time she gave him. It had been five years since the measles scare had intensified talk of reforming the nation's abortion laws. In the measles' aftermath the groups willing to back change had expanded dramatically. The American Medical Association had endorsed the idea, on the principle that doctors ought to decide what was best for their patients. The ACLU signed on too, timidly at first and then with growing conviction. Planned Parenthood offered its support after a long struggle to decide whether abortion was, in fact, a form of birth control. The fledgling National Organization for Women did the same after a divisive debate over whether abortion was a women's issue. And a number of mainline Protestant denominations declared reform a moral imperative, as did some of the nation's most influential news sources, from CBS's Walter Cronkite to the *New York Times*. "Obviously there is latitude for expert medical judgement," the *Times*'s editorial board wrote in 1965. "The present barbarous law ought to be revised to permit that judgement to be exercised."[11] The reformers couldn't have agreed more. The next year they used their momentum to launch a series of campaigns meant to soften state laws by giving doctors permission to abort pregnancies that had been caused by rape or incest or were going to result in disabled babies.

Mobilization bred resistance. A few prominent pastors broke with their brethren as the campaigns got underway, a scattering of doctors with the AMA, a handful of feminists with NOW. But the most powerful opposition came from the Catholic Church, which mobilized its thick network of parishes, hospitals, and schools, confraternities, sodalities, guilds, and social clubs in defense of what Los Angeles cardinal James McIntyre called "the right to life," the fundamental conviction that from the moment of conception a fetus was a human being, which made abortion nothing less than infanticide, even in those devastating circumstances the reformers had targeted.[12] In state after state the battle ran, two intensely powerful blocs clashing over a tangle of law, morality, philosophy, and mercy. The results were mixed. Between 1967 and 1969 ten legislatures added the exemptions the reformers wanted. But when they pushed into states with a strong Catholic presence—among them some of the nation's largest—they were beaten back. Three times the reformers tried to amend New York's abortion laws. Each time the Church stopped them.

Then the battle lines shifted. There was no defining moment. But in 1969 reformers began to set aside modification of abortion law and put in its place outright repeal. The change came partly from some of the campaign's established supporters, who'd long felt that governments had no right to regulate abortion; partly from a couple of high-profile court cases working their way through the legal system; and partly from a new wave of feminists, inspired by the revolutionary fervor and deepseated misogyny of the student Left, who injected into the campaign an often searing analysis of oppression and liberation centered on a woman's right to control her own body. As the stakes rose, so did emotions.

"We are tired of paying for the sins of men," declared one of the new wave's leading figures, Shulamith Firestone. "So we must say to those bishops and pompous lawmakers and self-righteous men, we will no longer be shoved around. We will no longer submit to your definitions of what we should not be or do. . . ." The bishops replied with their own broadsides. To claim that a woman had a right to choose, said Washington's formidable cardinal, was to endorse "murder on demand."[13]

Behind their fierce rhetoric lay complicated alignments. By 1969 most Americans—whatever their religion—had come to approve of a woman's right to abort her pregnancy when it threatened her health or when she was carrying a malformed fetus. But only 19 percent of Americans, and 15 percent of Catholics, supported abortion as a matter of choice. The strongest backing for that position came not from young women, 82 percent of whom opposed the idea, but from non-Catholic, college-educated white men: a solidly Republican demographic that would have been appalled to think of itself standing alongside feminists like Firestone. Into that convoluted politics stepped UT's little radical group, somehow imagining that a twenty-four-year-old attorney with no money, no staff, no standing, and no commitment to the cause could topple Texas' abortion laws.

Weddington tried to tell them that they needed someone better positioned. But the truth is she wanted the case, out of ambition to be sure, maybe even hubris, but also because of the abortion she'd hidden away, a half-day trip to a clinic just across the Mexican border sometime in 1967, her last year in law school. So she agreed to think through how a legal challenge could be shaped. There were the obvious questions of precedent and standing. And there was the practical problem of navigating the federal court system, which Weddington had never done. She had a classmate who'd clerked in the United States District Court in Dallas, though, and would know its procedures inside and out. A couple of days into December 1969 she gave Linda Coffee a call.

As soon as Weddington explained the idea Coffee started making connections. She'd recently read an important September decision from the California Supreme Court concerning a doctor's right to refer a patient to an abortion provider. The ruling had centered on the imprecision of the state law's language. But in its opinion the court had suggested that abortion fell under the right to privacy the *Griswold* decision had created in 1965. Coffee also knew of a case before the court for which she had clerked, this one filed by her friend Henry McCluskey. It had been five years since Bruce Scott had challenged the federal government's ban on hiring gay employees. Washington's Mattachine Society had followed his small victory with a set of cases that in 1969 toppled the government's ability to fire gay employees too. The judges had based their decision on the equal protection arguments embedded in *Brown*, a striking extension of gay rights. In his case, McCluskey was pushing for an even more fundamental turn. He was using *Griswold* to challenge the constitutionality of the state sodomy law Dallas' authorities had used to convict his client, a gay man who'd been caught having sex in a public bathroom. The court had yet to rule. But if it sided with McCluskey there'd be every reason to believe that it would be open to a matching challenge to Texas' abortion law. Weddington was so impressed she asked Coffee to consider taking over the case. Coffee suggested that they work on it together.

That still left a couple of potentially crippling complications. There was a very good chance that the court would deny Weddington's clients—those radical grad students—the standing to bring suit, since Texas' abortion law hadn't affected them directly. What's more, a case coming out of UT wouldn't go before Coffee's court, whose jurisdiction didn't reach down to Austin. What they needed was a pregnant woman in Dallas who'd been prevented from getting the abortion she wanted by the state's restrictive rules, a profile so precise they had no idea how to find her, until McCluskey called Coffee with word of Norma McCorvey.

Later McCorvey said that she didn't follow Coffee's talk about plaintiffs and constitutional tests any more than she had McCluskey's. But she agreed to be their client on the off chance that when the case was over she could have her abortion. Then nothing happened, as far as she could tell. She had no idea that in mid-January Henry McCluskey won his sodomy case in Dallas' federal court; that in late February the Hawaii legislature became the first in the nation to repeal its state's abortion laws and by so doing made the procedure freely accessible to its residents; that in the same month a Republican state representative introduced a repeal bill in New York's legislature; and that on March 3, 1970, Linda Coffee filed a three-page complaint on McCorvey's behalf with the clerk of the federal court in downtown Dallas, alleging that by enforcing state law the county's district attorney, Henry Wade, had infringed upon her client's "fundamental right . . . to choose whether to bear children."[14] But McCorvey did know that when the case went to court she'd still be a nobody, her identity hidden behind Coffee's decision to call her Jane Roe.

Nixon Redux

THE NIGHT OF his "silent majority" speech the president was too excited to sleep. The next day he spent reading through the stack of congratulatory telegrams Bob Haldeman piled on his desk, the day after that laying plans for a PR blitz on behalf of national unity and an assault on the liberal press for not giving him the credit he deserved. Then the siege began again. On November 13, 1969, the anti-war forces returned for two days of demonstrations in DC. Up went the defenses: troops stationed in federal buildings around the capital, plans in place to circle the White House with a fleet of buses parked bumper-to-bumper so that the culminating march couldn't get too close, Haldeman directing operations from the White House's bomb shelter, Nixon marking the opening event—a candlelight procession from Arlington Cemetery to honor the 40,000 Americans killed in the war—with two hours in the basement rec center, bowling alone.

That same day the My Lai massacre broke in the press. The secretary of defense had told the White House in September that a court martial was coming. But the news had arrived just as Nixon was trying to suppress an army investigation that had already made the front page of the *Times*, a potentially explosive story of a Special Forces unit having assassinated a South Vietnamese official. In the middle of that tangle—the president pressing the Pentagon to back off, the generals pushing back, the CIA caught in between—no one in Nixon's little circle had the time or inclination to deal with a case that wasn't drawing any attention. Now here was this thoroughly sourced piece from a young freelancer, Seymour Hersh, reporting that the army had recently charged twenty-six-year-old Lieutenant William Calley of Waynesville, North Carolina, with murdering 109 civilians in a South Vietnamese village, a total so shocking that thirty-five newspapers had picked up the story, though it had come to them through an obscure wire service.

Over the next six days the story inched forward. On the seventh it exploded. After his first report appeared Hersh tracked down three men who'd served under Calley. In his second installment he used their accounts to piece together exactly what had happened in My Lai. On the morning of March 16, 1968, while the Tet Offensive was raging, their company had been helicoptered into what they'd been told was a Viet Cong hot zone in Quang Ngai Province, on South Vietnam's northeast coast. They'd trooped into a cluster of hamlets, rounded up as many villagers as they could find, and slaughtered them. "They just started pulling people out and shooting them," said Michael Terry. "They had them in a group standing over a ditch—just like a Nazi-type thing. . . . One officer ordered a kid to machine-gun everybody down, but the kid just couldn't do it. He threw the machine gun down and the officer picked it up. . . . I don't remember seeing any men in the ditch. Mostly women and kids." There were "piles of people all through the village, all over," Michael Bernhardt told Hersh. "The whole thing was so deliberate. It was point-blank murder and I was standing there watching it."[15]

From there the revelations mounted. There hadn't been 109 casualties in My Lai, said the *Times*; there'd been 576. The killing hadn't been restricted to Calley and a few of his men. Much of the company had joined in, Private Paul Meadlo told CBS's Mike Wallace in an interview made all the more disturbing by the young man's utter lack of affect. On the day of the massacre a helicopter pilot had reported the savagery to his commanding officers, but instead of punishing the perpetrators or passing the information up the line, they sat on it. Had it not been for a recently discharged GI sending his congressman the details months later, the slaughter never would have been exposed.

The pictures made it even worse. Alongside Hersh's second story the *Cleveland Plain Dealer* ran eight photos of the massacre taken by one of the company's men. But the paper didn't have the right to distribute them to other publications. So almost no one beyond Cleveland saw them until November 30, when they were published in *Life*, the nation's fabled news magazine. A couple of the images were standard shots from the war: troops scurrying out of a helicopter, a GI burning a villager's thatch-roofed house. The rest were absolutely appalling. One showed a mother frantically trying to block a group of soldiers from assaulting her teenage daughter, the first time an American news outlet had suggested that a share of the men had raped some of their victims before gunning them down. Another showed a father and his four- or five-year-old son lying side by side, the little boy's blood pooled beneath him; yet another a jumble of bodies on a road leading out of My Lai, the corpses of a toddler and two infants among the dead.

The shock of it reverberated through the country as none of the war's previous reporting had done. Most public analyses stressed that something systemic had led to the slaughter, though they struggled to say what it was. "My Lai—those women and children are in our consciousness now," ABC's highly respected anchor Frank Reynolds told his audience, "and they are also on our conscience. The national soul is wounded and because those men came *from* us and acted *for* us, the wound is self-inflicted."[16] Public opinion seemed more pointed. By mid-December 94 percent of Americans had heard of the massacre. Twenty percent thought that Calley and his men bore primary responsibility for what they'd done, while 55 percent thought that the government was turning them into scapegoats for its policies.

The president's public response was as muted as the New Nixon was supposed to be. He made his first public comment—an anodyne statement about American virtue and justice—on December 8, almost a month after Hersh's initial report came out. A week later he announced he'd be bringing home another 50,000 soldiers, enough to reduce troop levels to where they'd been in the summer of 1967, and hopefully to contain the damage the slaughter had caused to his handling of the war.

His larger move he wrapped in absolute secrecy. The Paris peace talks had been meandering along since the middle of 1968 without any meaningful progress. On January 1, 1970 Kissinger sent word to the North Vietnamese that he'd be willing to open a parallel set of negotiations, hidden from public view, so that their governments could speak to each with a frankness that the formal talks didn't provide. Not quite two months later they held their first session in the sitting room of a little house the North Vietnamese quietly maintained at 11 rue Darthé, in a working-class neighborhood on the outskirts of Paris: Kissinger on one side, the high-ranking diplomat Le Duc Tho on the other, a chasm of mistrust between them.

In the meantime a new round of revelations hit. The trouble started at home. The Senate had confirmed Warren Burger as chief justice in June. At the end of October he joined with his seven new colleagues in rejecting the Justice Department's argument that Mississippi's segregated school systems be given more time to erase their color lines. The districts could still appeal specific portions of the lower courts' orders, the justice said. But they had to integrate while those appeals were pending, a move that obliterated the administration's strategy of stalling integration through endless legal maneuvers. The following month the Senate voted against the confirmation of Clement Haynsworth, whose nomination had been crippled by his less-than-ethical finances. Nixon responded by doubling down. His administration had to make it perfectly clear that it didn't support forced integration, the president told his closest aides shortly after the Mississippi decision. "We do what the law requires, nothing more," he said. "This is politics, and I'm the judge of the politics of schools."[17] As for the Court seat, he wanted his staff to find him a new nominee even more southern and more conservative than Haynsworth had been.

They came back with G. Harrold Carswell, a forty-nine-year-old Georgian who'd spent the previous decade on the U.S. District Court in northern Florida. The White House scoured through his finances to make sure there weren't any improprieties. They were clean. So, on January 19, 1970, Nixon announced him as his nominee. Two days later CBS News uncovered a speech young Mr. Carswell had given in 1948. "Segregation of the races is proper and the only practical and correct way of life," he'd said. "I have always so believed and will always so act."[18]

All the major civil rights organizations immediately denounced him as unacceptable, the NAACP furiously so. Nixon waved them off. "I'm not concerned about what Judge Carswell said twenty-four years ago," he told the press as the confirmation hearings got underway. "I'm very much concerned about his record [since then] . . . a record that is impeccable and without a taint of any racism."[19] That wasn't quite the case. Carswell had created an all-white booster club at Florida State in 1953, his former law partner told the confirmation committee. In 1956 he'd helped a Tallahassee golf club beat back demands that it desegregate, said another witness. He'd maneuvered to get voter registration workers arrested in 1963 and berated the lawyers who tried to defend them, said a third. Still he managed to get through the committee, which sent him on to the full Senate by a surprisingly strong margin on February 16. But no one was thinking of him as impeccable anymore.

That same week the Laotian revelations started to appear. The story had almost cracked open the previous October, when the *Times* had published a short series describing the United States' covert support for Laos' decade-long war against its Communist insurgency. But the White House had managed to seal it up with a vigorous application of obfuscation and denial. There it remained, hidden away in the Eisenhower style, until Nixon decided to extend the bombing campaign from the Laotian border to the country's central plateau. The first assault was launched in secret—Cambodia again—on the Monday that Judge Carswell slipped through committee. By Thursday all the major papers had news of the Laotian bombing on their front pages. With that wedge reporters pried open the rest of the story: the fifty-odd military bases the CIA operated deep in the Laotian countryside; the private air force the agency ran, its pilots so engaged in the fighting they

received combat pay; the five years of continual bombing along the border, more extensive than the bombing of North Vietnam had been; and
the 200 American airmen who'd been lost in the process, their place of
death never acknowledged. A secret war, the reporters called it, passed
from president to president, newly intensified by the sorties Nixon had
ordered without a word to the American people.

He knew they'd be coming for him. He'd known it since the My Lai
firestorm, when he'd sat in the serenity of the Oval Office, his inner circle ringed around him, and ranted against the massive conspiracy that
was driving the coverage, its tentacles stretching from those suspicious
vets who'd exposed the massacre to the Jewish media moguls who
wanted nothing more than to undermine his presidency. He scrawled
it in the margins of an article John Ehrlichman had put in his briefing
book shortly after CBS had dug up Carswell's speech, an angry little
note about the pressure "the professional civil-righters" were going to
bring to bear. And he'd said it to Haldeman two weeks before the Laotian secrets came crashing in. The "establishment" was getting ready
to reopen the autumn's anti-war offensive, he told Haldeman, and they
had to be prepared to hit back.[20]

But the White House wasn't prepared. Otherwise Nixon's congressional liaisons would have pushed the full Senate to approve Carswell's
nomination immediately after he'd gotten through committee, instead
of letting the liberals delay the vote for more than a month, long enough
for more revelations to surface and the opposition to expand—from
the NAACP to the AFL-CIO, the American Bar Association, dozens
of law school deans, and 200 former Supreme Court clerks. In the first
week of March the liberals thought they had about twenty colleagues
opposed to Carswell's confirmation. By the middle of the month their
count was up to thirty-one, a bloc of them moderate Republicans, with
the final vote still weeks away.

Laos caught the White House off guard as well. As soon as the
bombing made the news the doves started slashing away. There was
Mike Mansfield, the Senate majority leader, telling reporters that
Americans were "up to our necks" in the fighting; and George McGov-

ern claiming that the road Nixon was following into Laos looked an awful lot like the road that had led the United States into Vietnam; and William Fulbright, the powerful chair of the Foreign Relations Committee, raising the possibility of a resolution requiring congressional approval for any additional moves into Laotian territory, a direct attempt to reclaim the war-making powers LBJ had usurped with the Gulf of Tonkin Resolution.[21]

For almost two weeks the White House didn't respond, a delay almost as long as the one following the news of My Lai. Finally, on March 6 the president issued a 3,000-word statement acknowledging much of what had been reported, a show of candor to quiet his critics. But the details he revealed didn't mean that the United States was fighting a secret war in Laos, he said. How could it be, when not a single American had ever been killed in combat there? Two days later the *Los Angeles Times* published a detailed account of what turned out to be one of twenty-seven American deaths on Laotian soil since 1965, seven of them in the previous year alone: another revelation to add to the pile, another sign that the president couldn't be trusted to tell the truth. Three days after the story appeared, Fulbright put his resolution before the Senate.

Over the next few weeks the pressures escalated. The administration had already angered some of the Senate's most powerful southerners by pushing past them a dramatic extension of its singular civil rights initiative—affirmative action—from its narrow base in Philadelphia's construction trades to almost every company that held a government contract, a move that put about a third of the nation's workforce under its provisions. The growing federal threat to segregated schools heightened the tensions. Since the Supreme Court's Mississippi ruling the previous October, the White House's attempt to contain integration had crumbled. The thirty districts that had triggered the case had fallen first, on the December deadline the justices had imposed. The circuit courts ordered another forty to follow on February 1. After that there was supposed to be a lull until the start of the next school year—August 31 in most of the South—when 600 districts were to integrate, among them a number of major urban systems.

But the February integration didn't go to plan. Some of the affected districts shut down rather than break their color lines. Others were crippled by white boycotts. Several simply refused to comply with their court orders. And in rural Darlington County, South Carolina, a white mob attacked two buses filled with African American children on the way to their new school. In the midst of the resistance the two most consequential integration cases flared again. On February 5 Judge McMillan used the Supreme Court's Mississippi ruling to reinstate his comprehensive busing plan for Charlotte's schools, though the circuit court had yet to say whether it should stand. Six days later the Los Angeles Superior Court finally ended its two-year-long litigation by ordering LA to integrate the 674,000 students in its system, a decision that—if it withstood the inevitable appeal—would obliterate the distinction between southern schools and the rest of the nation.

Suddenly the old Dixiecrats were down in the well of the Senate, thundering against the "educational butchery" of forced integration, as if it were 1954 all over again. And the letters were pouring into the White House, 5,000 from Charlotte alone, pleading for the president to block the buses from running come September, because "the white majority has civil rights too," as one parent put it, "and we can't be expected to keep turning the other cheek forever." And LA's school superintendent was telling the press that the court's new ruling would require him to bus a quarter million kids every day, at a cost that would bankrupt his district within a year. Nixon's aides battled over how he ought to reply. The most conservative thought he should condemn the courts outright. "The second era of Reconstruction is over," his young speechwriter Pat Buchanan told him. "The ship of integration is going down . . . and we ought not to be aboard." The moderates pushed back, arguing that the president couldn't align himself against the courts any more than Eisenhower had after *Brown*. Nixon was too torn to choose between the sides, so the fight dragged on. "School statement still in great agony," Haldeman wrote in mid-March, both the president and his staff split between enforcing the law and defying it.[22]

Then Vietnam twisted again. On March 17 the army shattered the administration's efforts to keep the My Lai story under control by indicting fourteen officers for covering up the massacre, the highest ranking a major general then serving as commandant of West Point. The next day Cambodia's long-serving monarch, Prince Norodom Sihanouk, was toppled in a coup virtually no one saw coming, not even the CIA, though the coup's central figure, Prime Minister Lon Nol, had been working with the agency since the 1950s. From the capital the new government pushed its precarious power into the countryside, looking to root out the North Vietnamese bases Sihanouk had tolerated. The North Vietnamese struck back with a wave of counterattacks. As the fighting accelerated, talk of a widening war intensified in the press—the *Washington Post* came dangerously close to exposing Nixon's still-secret bombing of the Cambodian countryside—and up on the Hill, where Fulbright ordered closed-door hearings on the administration's intentions toward the new regime. It reached into Kissinger's clandestine Parisian talks too, which the North Vietnamese cut off after an angry exchange over the new fronts that seemed to be opening.

Nixon released his school statement on March 24. In the end he settled on a lawyerly warning to the Supreme Court not to blur the de jure/de facto divide, coupled with an emotional defense of the neighborhood school as "the focal point of community life . . . a place not only of learning but of living" that shouldn't be sacrificed "in a tragically futile effort to achieve in the schools the kind of multi-racial society which the adult society has failed to achieve for itself."[23] The NAACP replied with a scalding statement of its own, promising more suits to come. Through it all Carswell kept bleeding out. The Senate finally scheduled his confirmation vote for April 8. In the run-up, the *New York Times* put the number of senators opposing him at forty-nine, two shy of the total needed to reject the president's second straight nominee, a humiliation that had last been inflicted on Grover Cleveland almost a century before.

Nixon's inner circle could see the tension mounting. At times the president seemed cool and collected, even happy to have crises to confront. But he was also hiding away more than he ought to, Haldeman thought, brooding over his shrinking support—at the end of March his approval rating fell to 53 percent, the lowest of his presidency—and seething over his staff's shortcomings. "No one takes the offensive, all just lie down," he told Haldeman in a long harangue the day before Carswell's nomination went before the Senate. "[N]o fire except after [the silent majority speech] and then didn't follow up."[24]

Still they were surprised by how furiously he responded to a vote everyone knew could go against him. The news came on the afternoon of April 8: forty-five senators in favor of Carswell's confirmation, fifty-one opposed, the last two votes lost on the final day. The president spent the rest of the afternoon raging in the Oval Office. An evening cruise down the Potomac with the attorney general only seemed to make him angrier. The next morning he stormed into the West Wing, canceled the day's cabinet meeting, and put in its place an off-the-record session with the handful of staffers who knew how to get things done. He wanted Buchanan to get him a scalding statement denouncing the Senate for its malicious assault on his nominees' character when their only real fault was to be southern-born. He wanted a strong statement on crime too, something he could give on television, to start squeezing the Senate on his next nominee. But speeches weren't enough. He wanted his political operatives brought in for a private meeting so he could fire them up. He wanted investigators out in the field digging for dirt on the liberals and the groups that backed them. He wanted to hit his contributors for the cash he'd need for a full-out assault. He wanted, he said, to go to war.

The Incursion

FOR TWO WEEKS after his day of rage Nixon acted with the calm assurance he was supposed to exude. On April 14 he conceded the court fight by naming as his new nominee Harry Blackmun, a sixty-one-year-old U.S. Court of Appeals judge from Minnesota whose opinions were so circumspect the Senate couldn't conceivably object to him. Six days later he announced yet another Vietnam drawdown, this time of 150,000 men, to be completed by the end of the year. Then he reached the third week.

The Joint Chiefs had already urged him to couple his withdrawal announcement with a ground assault across the Cambodian border to destroy the North Vietnamese sanctuaries Lon Nol's teetering regime had failed to clear. It remained nothing more than a provocative proposal, though, until Nixon went to Hawaii for a weekend photo op with the recently rescued astronauts of Apollo 13. He was scheduled to leave Sunday afternoon, April 19, which left just enough time for a breakfast briefing from the commander of the U.S. Pacific Fleet. Nixon had met John McCain once or twice. But he hadn't experienced the passion McCain brought to his briefings, a style rooted in a devotion to the military's mission that stretched across three generations, from his admiral father to his pilot son, then in his third year as a prisoner of war in Hanoi. Here was the commander's plan laid out in detailed maps of the Cambodian borderland dripping in Communist red, the specifics of the American thrust draped in duty, sacrifice, and the defense of the West. It was a patriot's mission to be fought by hard-driving men like McCain and the president he'd enthralled. On the flight home Nixon announced to the staffers traveling with him that he was putting Cambodia at the top of his agenda.

Nixon spent the rest of the week relentlessly reviewing his options, his focus so intense even his most devoted aides found it unnerving. "P roars on . . . with little sleep," Haldeman wrote in his diary on Wednesday, April 22. "He was up at 5:00 this morning dictating. Really in high gear when got to the office, wanted everything possible cancelled so he could concentrate on Cambodia decisions." But Nixon cut out of the process anyone likely to oppose a strike—from the State Department, through the civilian leadership of the Defense Department, to Congress—while making it obvious to those on the inside the conclusion he wanted to reach. They read the early morning memos he filled with talk of "bold strokes" and "lily-livered diplomats" too scared to fight. They took his angry late-night phone calls demanding action. And they sat through the week's soliloquies. "Everyone comes into my office with suggestions on how to lose," he said to Kissinger on Wednesday. "No one ever comes in here with a suggestion on how to win."[25] Kissinger came away convinced that Nixon wasn't thinking through the consequences of a strike across the border. But he didn't dare say that to the president.

Nixon told his closest aides of his decision on Friday morning, April 24. Later that day, he made a single surreptitious contact on Capitol Hill, with Mississippi's John Stennis, the reliably hawkish chair of the Senate Armed Services Committee. On Sunday evening he brought in the secretaries of state and defense for what turned out to be the first in a series of angry meetings that ended only when Nixon said that they had no choice but to fall in line. Early in the week he put the White House staff to work on the details, Buchanan to draft his speech announcing the move, his press secretary to get him network airtime and to plant fake stories in the media so as to throw reporters off track. At 8:15 Thursday evening, April 30, 1970, he finally informed the congressional leadership. Forty-five minutes later he told the American people.

He started by trying to channel McCain, pivoting between his text and an oversized map of Cambodia, Laos, and South Vietnam propped next to his desk, the sanctuaries set off in the admiral's red. But he struggled to explain how sending 35,000 US soldiers into yet another southeast Asian country fit into his pledge to bring the war to an honorable end. He tried an Orwellian turn. This wasn't an invasion of a neutral country, he insisted. It was an incursion into enemy territory, a constricted unleashing of American power to secure the peace he'd promised.

Then he lurched in a different direction entirely. "We live in an age of anarchy," he said, marked by "mindless attacks on all the great institutions which had been created by free civilizations in the last five hundred years." In the United States those attacks targeted the great universities, in other countries a nation's very right to exist. In the face of those threats some of America's most influential figures call for caution and retreat. Standing against them might make him a one-term president, he said. But he had no choice, because "it is not our power but our will and character that is being tested tonight."[26] His own will and character pitted against enemies that stretched far beyond those vivid red sanctuaries.

Delivery

AT SOME POINT or another Norma McCorvey lost track of her pregnancy. Maybe it was in the spring of 1970, after she'd gotten into a fight with the manager at the bar, walked out on the only job she was likely to find, gave up the apartment that went with it because she couldn't pay the rent without some work coming in, and shuttled between her father's place and wherever she could crash after a night of smoking dope and drinking cheap wine. It might have been years later, when she tried to bring some order to her memories and got the facts all jumbled up. She was in her sixth month when Linda Coffee and Sarah Weddington first argued her case in court, she said then, and was still clinging to the hope that once the judges ruled in her favor she'd finally get her abortion. In fact she was halfway through her eighth month when the district court held its hearing in May 1970. And she'd already agreed that as soon as her baby was born the hospital would hand it over for adoption to the couple Henry McCluskey had found, exactly as she'd handed over her second baby back in '67.

But she also got some details right. She was right when she said that between the time she became Jane Roe and the initial hearing she saw Weddington and Coffee only once, when they needed her to sign an affidavit they'd written on her behalf. She was right when she said that they didn't want her in the courtroom on the day they argued her case because she was so visibly pregnant. And she was right when she said that after the hearing no one called to tell her how it had gone, as if she didn't matter. It's possible that she got the more intimate details right as well, the ones only she could know, though with Norma McCorvey it was always hard to tell where the truth ended and the stories began.

Her water broke in the middle of the night as she remembered it, amniotic fluid and blood together on the bed her father let her use whenever she slept over. She stumbled into the bathroom to clean herself, terrified that the blood was a sign of serious trouble. Then she woke her father, who gathered her up, led her out to his truck, and drove her to the emergency room. By the time they got there she was having intense contractions, "by far the worst I'd ever felt," she said. "The pain was horrible, and my clothes were soaking wet. . . . I could feel the baby coming out of my body. The baby was being born. And I was bleeding to death."[27]

The rest she remembered in snatches. The nurse taking down her vital information—her name, her address, her arrangement with Henry McCluskey—the orderlies prepping her, the rush into the delivery room, the final contractions, the last moment of the baby inside her, more pain, more blood, the exhaustion sweeping over her as they moved her out of delivery and into recovery, the baby gone to wherever it was supposed to go. When she woke up she was in an ordinary room in the maternity ward, the daylight streaming through the window.

How long she lay in bed before the nurse came in she couldn't recall, though she thought it was a couple of hours. "Feeding time," the woman said in the insistently encouraging way of maternity wards, and handed McCorvey an expertly swaddled newborn.[28] She might have objected, might have raised her hands or crossed her arms or told the nurse not to get within a foot of her. But she didn't. For a moment she just sat there, cradling the baby, feeling it breathe, forcing herself to stare straight ahead because she knew that the worst thing she could do was look down and see its face. Then she started to cry—to keen—and the nurse realized what she had done. Within a minute or so the baby was gone, hustled out of the room by one of the orderlies who'd rushed in at the sound of her wailing. Gone forever, McCorvey wrote a quarter century later, when the memory of her third child nestled in her arms had yet to ease.

CHAPTER 11

COMING HOME

It was less than a year since Allison Krause had graduated from John F. Kennedy High. But when the *Washington Post*'s reporter came round to ask about her, the staff had to pull out her file to have anything to say. They listed the courses she'd taken, the grades she'd received, and her score on the SAT. And they showed him the recommendation letter the counselor had written when she was applying to college. "Allison is a very stable and mature young woman," it read. "She possesses a very positive approach to life. . . ."[1] Beyond that the only thing anyone seemed to recall was how pretty she'd been, though they might have just been thinking of her yearbook photo, which had already made it into the papers by the time the reporter arrived.

Not that they should have remembered her. The Krauses had come to the area the way families sometimes did, trailing behind a father's corporate career. Her dad had started with Westinghouse in Cleveland in 1949, a couple of years before Allison was born. In 1963 the company brought him to Pittsburgh, where Westinghouse had its headquarters. Three years later he was transferred again, this time to the Baltimore plant. Her parents did what they could to make the latest move work, settling into a nice split level on a curving street in Wheaton, Maryland, barely beyond the Capital Beltway. Her dad got the daily drive up to Baltimore, while Allison and her little sister Laurie got glistening new suburban schools; Kennedy High had been open all of two years when Allison enrolled. For whatever reason, though—maybe because she was already a sophomore, maybe because she was fifteen—she didn't join any of the activities that made a kid stand out. Nor did she get the sort of grades that drew a teacher's attention. And when it came time to think about colleges, her only application went to an obscure state university in Ohio, a place she'd seen on Sunday drives in the countryside with her family when she was small. A place closer to home.

Her family left Wheaton shortly after her graduation in June 1969, when Westinghouse decided it wanted her dad back in Pittsburgh. Since then the staff had heard from her just once, in April 1970. She'd written to ask that her transcript be sent to the University of Buffalo, where she was hoping to transfer come summer. It wasn't an obvious move to make, but she didn't explain it and they didn't ask. So they had no idea that she was planning to go with her new boyfriend, a quiet young man from Long Island whose roommates called him "a fag" because he wore his hair too long and cared about politics more than football.[2] He had a few friends on the Buffalo campus and wanted to join them there. She was going to follow him, like her mom had followed her dad over the years. They were together when she was shot, crouching side by side in the parking lot below the National Guardsmen, the bullet tearing through the Kennedy High T-shirt she wore that day.

The next morning some of the kids gathered in front of the high school to lower the flag to half-staff in her honor, others to stop them. Already there'd been clashes on college campuses across the country. Emotions surged out on the Kennedy High lawn too, the kids screaming and shoving each other, until the principal stepped in to impose a compromise. The flag on the main pole would be lowered, he said, but they'd raise another flag outside the building to its full height. That got everyone back to class. But a little while later someone went out to the pole again, pulled the first flag down, and burned it in a trash can.

The *Post* reporter showed up that afternoon. After he talked to the staff he wandered the halls to ask the kids what had happened. They talked about the school and the war and whether it was right to honor a dead protester when no one honored the GIs who were killed in combat. "Why wasn't the flag lowered then?" one of them said. "They're in there fighting to keep the flag up."[3] As for that pretty girl whose picture had run in the morning's paper, a few kids thought they'd seen her once or twice. But the truth of it was nobody really knew her at all.

Anarchy

RICHARD NIXON WAS up early on the first full day of the Cambodian incursion, almost giddy with the thought of pressing the fight. He started by telling Bob Haldeman and Henry Kissinger how he wanted the day's news spun. "Cold steel, no give, nothing about negotiations," he said. "Stay strong, whole emphasis on 'back the boys,' sell courage of [the] president." Then he went off to the Pentagon to deliver the message himself. Officially he was there for another briefing. But the critical moment came in the hallway, when a secretary whose husband was in Vietnam stopped him to say how much she'd loved his speech. "Oh, how nice of you," he replied. "You finally think of all those kids out there. I say kids. I've seen them. They're the greatest. You see these bums, you know, blowing up their campuses. Listen, the boys that are on the college campuses today are the luckiest people in the world, going to the greatest universities, and here they are, burning up the books, storming around about this issue," loosing anarchy upon the world.[4]

Already there'd been a few demonstrations, the worst at Stanford in the hours after his speech. On Friday and Saturday, May 1 and 2, the resistance swelled. Some of it came from the congressional doves outraged by the president's blatant abuse of his power as commander in chief. The deeper fury roiled the nation's colleges and universities, from the Ivies through the big state schools to places that hadn't seen much activism before. Most of it was peaceful. But there was violence too, at Rutgers, Maryland, UC Berkeley, Wisconsin, and Kent State in northeast Ohio, where two nights of clashes between protesters and the police—and a fire at the ROTC building—led the governor to send in the National Guard.

All weekend there was talk of the opposition solidifying, maybe through a nationwide student strike or another march on Washington or a renewed push by the doves to defund the war. It didn't matter,

Nixon told Haldeman on Sunday afternoon, because this time there'd be no backing down. "Don't play a soft line—no aid and comfort here," he said. "Congressmen, really put it to them, sticking the knife in the back of US troops, not supporting the president. . . . Giving aid and comfort to the enemy—use that phrase. Don't worry about divisiveness. Having drawn the sword, don't take it out. Stick it in hard. . . . Hit 'em in the gut."[5]

On the fourth day, Monday, May 4, he spent the morning in the Oval Office before heading off to his hideaway for the afternoon. He was still there three hours later, coming out of a nap, when Haldeman brought over the news. The National Guard had been moving away from an angry midday rally on the Kent State campus, tramping up a little hill overlooking the college green. Then, for reasons Haldeman couldn't explain, some of the troopers had pivoted around and fired down into the crowd. Thirteen students had been hit. Four of them—two young men and two young women—had been killed.

Bob Haldeman saw it right away. Not the full depth of it, but enough to note it during that long afternoon in the hideaway, while he listened to the president talk through how the killings might be handled, how the story might be spun, and what his condolence letter ought to say. That evening Haldeman turned his notes into his diary entry, as he did almost every night. Maybe it wasn't the most generous way to describe what he'd seen. But it wasn't a generous day. "P is troubled by all this," he wrote, "although it was predicted as a result of the Cambodian move."[6]

On Tuesday the spiral set in. They'd known since the previous evening that a student strike was coming. Still it was a shock to see it surging across the country: fifty, a hundred, a hundred and fifty schools shut in a rush of walkouts and boycotts and barely planned protests, most of them swirling around their campuses, some of the largest spilling into the streets, the most volatile edged with the anarchic violence of the mob—windows smashed, cars overturned, a handful of ROTC buildings burned—and the repressive power of the policemen and guardsmen sent out to stop them.

But it wasn't the strike alone that made the day so dangerous. It was also the organizers of the previous November's march on Washington promising to bring 30,000 protesters to a Saturday rally at the White House gates. It was the congressional doves saying again and again that the president's war-making power had to be constrained. It was the stock market plunging to its lowest point since the summer of 1963 in a panic that looked an awful lot like the one that brought down LBJ. And it was those devastating few minutes on the nightly news, when David Brinkley showed millions of Americans the faces of the dead—four clean-cut kids smiling for their yearbook photos—followed by footage of the youngest victim's hollowed-out father in his suit and tie, struggling through the statement he'd written for the president to hear. "She resented being called a bum because she disagreed with someone else's opinion," Arthur Krause said. "She felt war in Cambodia was wrong. Is this dissent a crime? Is this a reason for killing her?"[7]

On Wednesday the strike shut another 150 schools. More walkouts meant more confrontations, more clashes, more injuries, and another death, this one at tiny Wabash College in Crawfordsville, Indiana, where twenty-seven-year-old Rex Vice drenched himself in gasoline and, like Norman Morrison five years before, set himself aflame. "As the day went on, concern from outside about the campus crisis built rapidly," Haldeman wrote that night. "Very aware . . . that goal of the Left is to panic us, so we must not fall into their trap."[8] By then the secretaries of state and defense had already leaked to the press details of Nixon's rush into Cambodia so as to make it clear that they weren't to blame, and the secretary of the interior had quietly passed to reporters a supposedly private letter he'd sent Nixon, pleading with him to reach out to the kids in the streets, whose rebellion he compared to the founding fathers'. As for the president, he spent the evening with his wife and daughters—his Julie having been brought home from shuttered Smith College—watching *Sunrise at Campobello*, a ten-year-old movie about vibrant young Franklin Roosevelt waking one morning to find himself paralyzed.

He'd finally gone to bed around half past four. Three hours later he was up again, pushing through a schedule so packed it dragged on to

10:45 that night. Thursday was harder still. In the morning he had a tense meeting with a select group of university presidents, the first in a series of events his aides had organized to show that he had the crisis under control. Afterward Haldeman had him whisked off to Camp David so that he could get some rest before the next event, a Friday night news conference the television networks had agreed to carry live. But Nixon wouldn't let himself relax. Between 5:00 and 8:00 p.m. Thursday he phoned the White House eight times, with calls to Ronald Reagan and Nelson Rockefeller pressed in between. Most of Friday he spent with his briefing books, though he kept the calls coming too: Haldeman at 9:49 a.m., Kissinger at 10:06, Haldeman again at 10:38, Kissinger again at 11:36, back to Haldeman at 11:48 and 1:01 p.m., as reports of the day's violence started filtering in and the evening's stakes began to rise.

There'd been signs of a mounting backlash throughout the week. On Wednesday somebody had fired buckshot into a crowd of protesters at the University of Buffalo. On Thursday a gang of club-wielding men had stormed across the University of Washington campus. On Friday the violence reached Manhattan. Right around noon, 200 construction workers from the new World Trade Center site descended on an antiwar rally on Wall Street, chanting, "All the way, USA!"[9] As they closed in, the protesters tried to scatter. But the workers chased them down, pummeling anyone too slow to get out of the way. When they were finished they marched on city hall, where they forced the deputy mayor to raise to full height the rooftop flags his boss, a liberal Republican, had lowered in mourning. Then they turned on nearby Pace University to find more college kids to kick around before heading back to work, public order having been righted by a rampage fascism's bully boys would have been proud to call their own.

Nixon helicoptered to the White House at half past six on the evening of May 8. The first lady and their daughters had followed him to Camp David that afternoon, presumably to protect themselves from whatever Saturday's protest might bring. So he ate dinner alone, then hid away in the empty family quarters until 10:00 p.m., when he walked into the East Room to face the nation.

He stood stiffly in front of a single microphone, his hands clasped behind his back, the beads of sweat on his forehead glistening under the television lights, his voice carefully modulated to project a calm he clearly didn't feel. The first round of questions focused on his reaction to the week's turmoil. No, he wasn't surprised by the protests' intensity, he said. Yes, he welcomed the weekend rally, in fact was pleased that it'd be so close to the White House. No, he didn't think the United States was lurching toward revolution. Finally someone asked about the invasion. Everything was going so well, he said, the first American units would be pulled out of Cambodia within a few days, the vast majority within a month, the remainder—every last American—by June 30.

A reporter asked the obvious follow-up. Now that he'd set a hard date for a complete withdrawal, wouldn't the North Vietnamese simply wait for the troops to be gone and then rebuild their sanctuaries? If that was the case, had the invasion been worth the cost? Nixon replied with a measured statement about the attack having bought the South Vietnamese army six more months of the intense training it needed to assume full responsibility for the war: the incursion suddenly turned into another way of bringing the boys home, the previous week's test of will abandoned for a barely disguised retreat.

He'd told Haldeman that after the press conference he'd be going straight back to the family quarters, where he wanted to be left alone. But as soon as he was upstairs he started making phone calls. The first went to Haldeman at 10:37 p.m. By midnight he'd made sixteen more, all but one back-to-back. In the next two hours he made another twenty-three, his only break the eleven minutes he spent trying to reach people who didn't answer. The frenzy ended at 2:00 a.m., only to start again an hour and a half later. He spent six minutes talking to a California television producer, one minute with his press secretary, three minutes with Kissinger, and a rambling four minutes with UPI's longtime White House correspondent. Then he took a half-hour break to listen to Sergei Rachmaninoff's relentlessly romantic Piano Concerto No. 2 before calling his valet, Manolo Sanchez, to ask if he'd ever seen the Lincoln Memorial at night.

It was still dark when the limousine left—Nixon, Sanchez, and three panicked Secret Service agents slipping past the barricade of buses that had been placed around the White House overnight for the quick drive to the Memorial. When they arrived a few minutes before 5:00 a.m., Nixon took Sanchez up the steps to read the inscriptions on either side of the statue, both of them meditations on a time of civil war. As they turned back a small group of students in Washington for the day's protests came up to shake hands. Nixon responded with the sort of casual conversation starters he'd never mastered. But they seemed a bit nervous, so he just started to talk.

Once he got going he couldn't stop. For almost an hour he roamed from topic to topic—from Vietnam to the nation's racial divisions to his own troubled childhood to the importance of travel—while the gradually growing cluster of students tried to make sense of what he was saying. "He wouldn't look anyone in the eyes," one of them said afterward. "He was mumbling. When someone asked him to speak up he would boom one word and no more." Eventually someone cut in. "I hope you realize that we're willing to die for what we believe in," he said.

"I certainly realize that," Nixon replied. "Many of us when we were your age were also willing to die for what we believe in and are willing to do so today. The point is, we are trying to build a world in which you will not have to die for what you believe in,"[10] as if that's what he'd been trying to do when he extended the war he'd promised to end. As if he hadn't told his aides that he wanted the nation divided. As if he didn't know what he had done.

Secrets

HALDEMAN LEARNED THAT the president was at the Lincoln Memorial in a 5:00 a.m. phone call. By the time he got into the White House at 6:15, Nixon had moved on to the Capitol for a meandering tour that culminated in the House's empty chamber, where he sent Sanchez up to the Speaker's podium to give an impromptu speech while he sat in his old seat and applauded. They came out to find Haldeman waiting for them, desperate to get him back to the White House. But Nixon insisted that they get breakfast first. Off they went to the dining room of Washington's most exclusive hotel for another hour of the president's ramblings, until Haldeman finally convinced him that it was time to go home. "The weirdest day so far," he told himself that night, a phrasing that left open the possibility of worse to come as Nixon buckled under the crisis he'd created.[11]

In fact the crisis had peaked. Saturday's rally passed with a shapelessness to be expected of an event that had been organized so quickly. Over the next few days the student strike faded too, its reach undermined by the inevitable problem of sustaining passions that had reached such an intense pitch. There were still protests and counterprotests, some of them fiercely confrontational. But by the end of the week only a dozen campuses were shut and the nation's streets were largely clear—except in New York, where the city's suddenly militant hard hats were drawing thousands of supporters to their now daily marches through Wall Street.

Only then did Nixon start to recover. A long weekend in Florida helped. The polls helped more. Though Americans hadn't rallied behind him as they usually did when a president sent troops into combat—a striking 43 percent thought he'd been wrong to push into Cambodia—the invasion hadn't damaged his approval rating. And despite all the agonies that had followed the Kent State killings, public support for the anti-war movement had clawed up only a few points, to 27 percent of Americans, ten points below the share who thought anti-war activism ought to be made illegal. Haldeman saw the effect on the flight back from his weekend away. "P had me up alone for the first hour," he wrote once they were in Washington. "He was in a good mood, relaxed, confident, optimistic, not driving hard," a month of frenzy finally behind him.[12]

He spent the next few weeks worrying his wounds with more early-morning action items, brooding sessions in his hideaway, and occasional backsliding into the Old Nixon. The most public came in late May, when he had the hard hats' leaders in for a photo op; they handed him a yellow helmet with "commander in chief" stenciled across the front, in case he wanted to join them the next time they stomped some doves. The more dangerous turn came in early June, when he authorized a deeply conservative young staffer he liked, twenty-nine-year-old Tom Huston, to prepare a highly classified plan for undermining the anti-war movement. Huston returned with a proposal packed with illegalities, among them a suggestion that the government break into activists' offices to rifle their files and tap their phones. Nixon loved it. But he wasn't willing to meet FBI director J. Edgar Hoover's insistence that he sign off on every illegal activity he wanted the bureau to undertake, a classic bit of bureaucratic self-preservation that put the Huston Plan on the shelf, waiting for someone to revive it.

The remaining American soldiers were withdrawn from Cambodia at the end of June, just as Nixon had said they would be. He marked the moment by announcing a new peace initiative, though the real negotiations remained hidden in the apartment on Paris' rue Darthé, where Kissinger and the North Vietnamese resumed their secret meetings on September 7. A month later the Pentagon reduced the number of troops in South Vietnam by 50,000, the first step toward meeting the 150,000-man withdrawal Nixon had set as a goal in April, while it intensified the air war against Cambodia under the president's direct order. So the administration slipped back into the strategy the incursion had broken, May's horrific miscalculation having been wiped away by the declining casualties the drawdown produced and the brutal bombing Americans didn't see.

It wasn't as if the counterpressures dissipated. Congress's leading doves kept hammering away at Nixon's inability to end the war, while the protesters kept coming into the streets. In their most powerful moments the two intertwined. A generous count gave Vietnam Veterans Against the War about 12,000 members, a minute fraction of the millions of soldiers who'd cycled through Vietnam since 1965. Of that number, only a few thousand made it to Washington in April 1971. But for the better part of a week they dominated the news with scalding demonstrations, capped by two dramatic events on Capitol

Hill. First, a line of 800 vets marched, one by one, to a fence that had been put around the Capitol to keep them out, and tossed over it the medals they'd been awarded for their service. Then their spokesman went inside to talk to the Senate Foreign Relations Committee. John Kerry was that rare young man who'd set aside the protections of privilege to go to Vietnam, in his case straight from Yale. He'd come back with two Purple Hearts and a deep conviction that the war had been a terrible mistake, as he told the committee's doves in the relentlessly articulate, profoundly moving televised testimony they'd arranged because they knew he'd say exactly what they wanted the nation to hear.

The further Nixon got from Cambodia, though, the more confidence he had in his ability to hold the center. He'd decided on another major drawdown in early 1971, this one to bring the total number of troops in Vietnam below 200,000 by the end of the year. But he waited until early April to announce it, so as to undercut the spring protest season. When the federal courts ordered the veterans to be removed from their encampment on the Mall, he refused to enforce the ruling. But when radical activists tried to shut down the city a few weeks later, he had 12,000 of them arrested. And he made his own appeal to vets in the final act of the My Lai massacre. A year of legal procedures had dwindled the army's fourteen indictments down to a single court-martial, of Lieutenant William Calley, the lowest-ranking soldier it had charged. On March 30 he was convicted of murdering twenty-two civilians—a fraction of those he'd actually killed—and sentenced to life imprisonment. Nixon let him serve three days. Then he publicly ordered the army to move him from his cell to his apartment at Fort Benning, pending a presidential review of his conviction.

Together those moves set a floor beneath the public's support for his handling of the war; only once in the first half of 1971 did it drop below 40 percent, and by spring it was closer to 50. On particular policies his support spiked. Seventy percent of Americans approved of his latest troop withdrawal. Seventy-six percent approved of May's mass arrests. And 80 percent approved of his putting a convicted war criminal into a comfortable house arrest, two and a half times the number who approved of the Vietnam Veterans Against the War.

There were also promising signs in the peace process. From his secret Parisian meetings Kissinger brought back hints of progress, some of them substantive, others purely symbolic: he returned from one session thrilled to report that the North Vietnamese had set the apartment's chairs around a table they'd covered with a green tablecloth, an arrangement diplomats traditionally considered the mark of formal negotiations. The more significant possibilities came from another direction. For two years Kissinger had been quietly working his back channels to Moscow and Beijing, in pursuit of Nixon's grand strategy for pressuring the North Vietnamese into a settlement. In January 1971 the Soviets finally sent word that they were willing to discuss the details of a presidential visit. On April 27 the Chinese did the same with a personal note passed through the Pakistani ambassador. Kissinger read it to the president with a coda to match the moment's significance. "We have done it now," he said over the brandy Nixon had brought out to toast their triumph. "We have got it all hooked together."[13]

Nixon insisted that the opening be wrapped in absolute secrecy until the arrangements were complete; not even the secretary of state was to be informed. There it stood two months later—Kissinger still feeling his way through the opaque diplomacy the Chinese had placed around the process, Nixon still waiting for confirmation—when the first of the summer's crises hit. Timing was everything. In his last year as secretary of defense, Bob McNamara had commissioned a tiny group of high-level staffers to conduct a study of the United States' disastrous path into Vietnam. They produced a forty-three volume, two-and-a-half-million-word history of the presidential decisions and deceptions that had shaped America's Vietnam policy from 1945 to mid-1968. When they finished they made fifteen strictly classified copies. On Sunday morning, June 13, 1971, the *New York Times* announced that it had a copy too, and would be publishing detailed analyses and key excerpts day by day on the paper's front pages.

The White House knew that the stories would reveal a great deal, from Jack Kennedy's complicity in Ngo Dinh Diem's death through the manipulations LBJ used to draw the United States into a war he knew to be unwinnable. But the study stopped half a year before Nixon took office, so at first no one seemed particularly concerned about its release. Then Kissinger called from his weekend away in Los Angeles. It wasn't the study's details that mattered, he insisted. It was the fact that someone had leaked to the press forty-three volumes of classified material just as Nixon was in the most delicate negotiations of his presidency. How were the Chinese supposed to trust him now that his government had shown that it couldn't keep its secrets? How was his foreign policy supposed to survive now that he looked so weak?

If Kissinger was baiting Nixon, as Haldeman later claimed, it worked. Within a day and a half the administration was in federal court, seeking to stop the *Times* from running the rest of its series. From that first motion the case spun into an epic two-week battle over the press's right to publish free of government constraint, the fight spreading from the *Times* to the *Washington Post*, which started to run its own series based on the copy it had obtained, and then to almost a dozen papers as the original leak turned into a flood. The Supreme Court agreed to hear the case on June 25, held oral arguments on the 26th—for a while Nixon thought of presenting the government's side himself—and handed down its ruling four days later: a six-to-three decision clearing the *Times* to resume its publication of the Pentagon Papers under the First Amendment's protection.

That was only half the fight, though. It took Kissinger about a day to decide who'd leaked the study to the *Times*. Daniel Ellsberg was an ex-marine with a Harvard PhD, a specialist in game theory who'd spent most of the Johnson years in the Pentagon's proudly analytical inner rings, first as an aide to McNamara and then—after a stint as an expert adviser in Vietnam—as a researcher on the Pentagon Papers. Along the way he'd turned against the war, as Kissinger knew from the couple of months in 1969 that Ellsberg had spent on his staff before he moved to the RAND Corporation, the Defense Department's favorite think tank. According to the government's records RAND had two of the study's fifteen copies, which gave Ellsberg the perfect combination of motive and opportunity. The FBI put him under investigation three days after the *Times*'s first story appeared. The following week he was charged with theft of government property and possession of documents relating to national defense, crimes that carried a ten-year prison term.

Nixon wanted more. From the start he was convinced that the leak had come through some sort of conspiracy, likely leading up from Ellsberg to the study's director, Leslie Gelb, another Harvard PhD who was now working at Washington's Brookings Institution, an even more prestigious think tank than Ellsberg had managed to find. Nixon's first thought was to expose him to the press as a threat to the nation, just as he had Alger Hiss all those years before. But on June 17, halfway through the first week of the leak, Haldeman happened to mention a rumor that Gelb was holding another file, this one detailing the peace deal LBJ had almost put in place in October 1968. And Nixon's thinking lurched back to the spate of illegal actions he'd wanted to pursue after the Cambodian demonstrations. "Bob, now you remember Huston's Plan," he snapped. "Implement it. . . . I mean, I want it implemented on a thievery basis. Goddamn it, go in there and get those files. Blow the safe and get it."[14]

Haldeman let it go, as he often did with presidential orders he considered too preposterous to pursue. When the Supreme Court ruled against the government a week later, Nixon brought it roaring back. At 9:00 the next morning he gave Haldeman three hours to find someone to head the new unit he wanted to run the Huston Plan's covert operations. Not just anyone would do. "I want a son of a bitch," he said. "I want someone just as tough as I am for a change. . . . These goddamn lawyers, all whining around about, you know. . . . Do you think, for Christ's sake, the *New York Times* is worried about all these legal niceties? . . . We're up against an enemy, a conspiracy. They're using any means. We are going to use any means. Is that clear?" Then he swung back to Gelb's supposed files. "Did they get the Brookings Institute raided?" he asked, though he knew they hadn't. "No? Get it done! I want it done! I want the Brookings Institute safe cleaned out," a crime to cover up his role in extending the war that had already come close to breaking him; secrets in defense of secrets; the beginning of the end.[15]

De Jure

VIRDA BRADLEY'S SUIT started with her frustration that things weren't the way they ought to be. When she'd moved into her house in the mid-1960s there'd still been plenty of whites in the neighborhood: factory workers and their families mostly, living in the solid little homes their union wages bought them; people no different from Bradley really, except for the color of their skin. Most mornings from the day after Labor Day to early June their younger kids would troop into the grade school across the street from Bradley's house, a brown-brick pile of a place opened in the 1920s, during Detroit's great building boom. Her youngest two would troop in too—Richard right away; Ronnie, her baby, in September 1969. That was one of the reasons she'd settled on her house, so her boys could go straight out the front door into school.

By the time Ronnie started kindergarten most of Bradley's white neighbors were gone. They'd cleared out the way they always did, selling their houses as quickly as they could once the color line was broken—always to Black buyers of course—tripping over each other on their way to the city's fringes or out to the suburbs. The pace had picked up after the rebellion of 1967, the flight turning into a flood, not because the looting and burning had reached into their area but because the fear and anger had. It was startling how quickly things changed, even by Detroit's fevered standards. The year Bradley arrived in the neighborhood about half the people living there were white. In the autumn of 1969 more than 80 percent of them were Black, as were 97 percent of the kids in the school across the street.

It didn't bother Bradley that the whites had left. What rankled was the way the money followed them. She could see the cost of it in the books that didn't get replaced; the supply shelves that were never restocked; the bathrooms that ran out of toilet paper; the dingy portable classrooms the district slapped up behind the school when the influx of Black kids made it too crowded inside the building; the snow that nobody shoveled off the playground anymore, and the mud pits they'd stopping filling now that the color line had been redrawn. There was no denying that the situation was complicated, as tangled as it was in falling property values and failed millage votes, indecipherable funding formulas and convoluted politics. But for Bradley the bottom line was simple enough. When she was a girl back in Jim Crow Tennessee she'd gone to schools whites had stripped bare, and it wasn't right that her little boys were going to do the same. That's what drew her to the integration suit the NAACP's lawyers were putting together in the spring of 1970: the injustice across the street and the intimate history behind it.

As for the attorneys, they saw the case as an obvious addition to the association's surging school campaign. They already had a number of test cases underway to extend integration to cities in the north and west, led by the sprawling Los Angeles litigation. The really dramatic movement, though, was coming in the South. Despite the resistance that the latest round of court orders had faced, the 1969–70 academic year ended with almost 75 percent of southern districts having integrated at least some of their schools. Six hundred more districts would be added to the list when the new year began in September, among them Strom Thurmond's hometown of Aiken, South Carolina, and bloody Birmingham. And there was good reason to believe that the Charlotte case was about to break in just the right way. In late May the circuit court upheld Judge McMillan's integration order, albeit with a few alterations. Both the school board and the NAACP immediately appealed to the Supreme Court, which set oral arguments for October 12, 1970. But the justices refused to delay the order's September implementation date. So Charlotte would get its chance to stop the racial transformation of its schools—five weeks after the court-ordered buses started running.

The promise of progress met a fierce reaction. When George Wallace lost Lurleen to cancer in May 1968 he also lost Alabama's governorship to her successor, Albert Brewer. Wallace wasn't particularly interested in governing the state again, but he needed the base the office provided to make another run for the presidency. So as soon as Brewer announced that he'd be seeking the Democratic nomination in the June 1970 primary, Wallace launched a challenge drenched in the most savage race-baiting of his career. Out came the television ads warning of Black domination, the radio spot hinting at Black rapists about to stalk the state, and the campaign flyer—spread from Selma—featuring a white girl of four or five surrounded by seven Black boys of roughly the same age. "This could be Alabama four years from now," read the accompanying text, the racists' nightmare of radical rule revived with a photo of eight little kids sitting side by side.[16] Brewer still managed to win half a million votes. Wallace won 30,000 more.

To Alabama's east and west the politics of rage gave way to repression. On the May 1970 weekend that the Cambodian protests peaked, African Americans in tiny Perry, Georgia, mounted a series of marches against the county's tepid desegregation plan. State troopers arrested 430 of them, crammed them onto buses, and shipped them to a prison farm the state had closed because it wasn't fit for human habitation, where some of them were brutalized in the course of their processing. Two days later the Savannah police killed six African Americans after a demonstration against police brutality turned into a night of looting. Three days after that the Mississippi highway patrol met a student protest at Jackson State College with a fusillade of buckshot that killed two more young men. "This is war," Georgia's rabidly segregationist governor Lester Maddox told 800 cheering members of the Georgia Peace Officers Association shortly thereafter, though he forgot to mention that the war ran only one way. None of the week's eight victims had been armed. Six had been shot in the back, five of them multiple times.[17]

After a summer of such brutality, there was no telling what might happen when the new school year began. Through much of August districts were swept by talk of crippling boycotts and pledges of defiance in defense of the parental rights the courts were trying to rip away, threats Washington took so seriously that the Justice Department sent a hundred lawyers down South to deal with the confrontations to come. But beyond a few ugly incidents—a predawn bombing of an African American grade school in North Carolina, a brawl in a Mobile high school, race-laced protests in a number of towns and cities—nothing much happened. Even the boycotts faded within a couple of weeks: a sign, said the *Times*, of white southerners' weariness with a struggle that many of them secretly wanted to put behind them, though it was just as reasonable to see in September's success whites' grudging capitulation to orders the courts wouldn't let them circumvent any longer.[18] And white schools could be very grudging places, shot through with assertions of white superiority and Confederate pride. Still, the change was striking. In 1968 68 percent of southern African American children attended all-Black schools. By December 1970 18.4 percent did, a rate the rest of the country couldn't come close to matching.

Not yet, anyway. Charlotte's lawyers went into their October appearance before the Supreme Court arguing that their city's schools had been segregated exactly as Chicago's or Detroit's had. The courts hadn't ordered those systems to integrate, they said, because the de facto discrimination that had segregated them was beyond the court's reach. So they had no right to integrate Charlotte's schools either. The NAACP attorneys turned that argument in the other direction. The courts had every right to integrate Charlotte's schools, they insisted, as Judge McMillan had realized once he'd accepted the association's broadened definition of de jure discrimination. By that standard they'd have every right to integrate Chicago's and Detroit's schools too.

The justices handed down their decision in *Swann v. Charlotte-Mecklenburg Board of Education* on April 20, 1971. It was a carefully hedged, often convoluted opinion, written by the chief justice to wring a unanimous vote out of colleagues who couldn't agree on how far the definition of de jure ought to be extended. But on the particulars it was decisive. McMillan had acted within the law when he'd ordered Charlotte's schools to integrate, the ruling read, and when he'd required kids to be bused as the best way to achieve that end. The next morning's papers laid out the obvious implication: if Charlotte's school system had to bus its kids to achieve integration, then other southern cities had to do the same. The director of the NAACP's legal team pushed the logic further. The federal court in northern California had just ruled in an association suit against the segregation of San Francisco's public schools. The Tenth Circuit's Court of Appeals was about to rule on an NAACP challenge to Denver's schools. Behind them loomed the Los Angeles case, with its enormous reach. Once the Supreme Court affirmed one of those decisions, he told the *Times*, the rest of the nation's cities would have to start busing too.

The thought of it appalled a huge swath of the population. According to the polling that followed the Charlotte ruling, 85 percent of whites and 65 percent of African Americans opposed busing kids to integrate their schools. By the summer that opposition was feeding another wave of protests, more intense than the previous year's, the South's swirling around the busing that would begin in September, the North's and the West's around the possibility that the buses would soon start rolling in their cities too. Much of it was driven by whites' enduring opposition to integration. But the thought of moving huge numbers of kids around their cities raised all sorts of fears. In Florida's Broward County Black parents objected to the danger of sending their children into hostile white communities. In San Francisco Chinese-American parents vehemently objected to their kids losing the Chinese culture classes that their neighborhood schools provided. Denver's Latino parents raised a similar warning about the fate of the bilingual education they'd fought to secure in their neighborhood schools. And at a mass rally in Nashville a white mother raged against racial mixing while another told a reporter that what really scared her was the thought of her nine-year-old getting sick at a school fifty minutes from home.

Then there was Virda Bradley's suit, which in the spring of 1971 went to trial in the federal courthouse in Detroit, the Honorable Stephen J. Roth presiding. It seemed like a far from perfect fit. Born in Hungary and raised in blue-collar Flint, sixty miles north of Detroit, Roth had reached the federal bench through the political pathways the New Deal had created for sons of the immigrant working class. He'd never given much thought, he said later, to how government power had served a very different purpose on the other side of the racial divide. Over the next three months the NAACP's lawyers led him through a painstaking reconstruction of Detroit's systemic segregation. Roth took another two months to process what he'd heard. When he finally issued his decision in September, he swept past the Supreme Court's caution with the assurance of someone who'd seen the truth revealed.

From the stack of evidence the NAACP had presented it was clear that the school board had manipulated some of its rules to maintain the system's color line. But the problem stretched far beyond those specific offenses, Roth said. In Detroit, school segregation was inextricably linked to neighborhood segregation, which had been driven by a fusion of public policies and private actions so complete it turned the entire process into an overpowering case of de jure discrimination. Whatever segregation government entities had imposed the courts were obliged to undo. Detroit's schools therefore had to be integrated just as southern schools had been.

How that was to be done Roth would determine through another set of hearings. But he'd be working under one obvious constraint. Detroit's schools were already losing about 40,000 white kids a year. If his implementation order stopped at the city limits those losses would reach such an intensity the entire system would soon be segregated as the Bradleys' school had been, by the overwhelming force of white flight. So, Roth told the press, any integration plan was likely going to require the busing of Black students out to the all-white suburban schools that ringed Detroit and the busing of suburban kids into the city schools, as a matter of practicality, law, and justice. Within a week almost 20,000 families in suburban Warren had joined a boycott of their schools, triggered by a rumor that Judge Roth was about to send buses full of kids like Mrs. Bradley's little boys across the suburban color line.

Appeals

ON JUNE 17, 1970, a week or so after Norma McCorvey gave birth to her baby, the circuit court's three-judge panel issued its ruling on *Roe v. Wade*. In nine precise pages it aligned with Sarah Weddington and Linda Coffee on almost every point, including the decisive one that a woman's decision to have an abortion was protected by the right of privacy *Griswold* had created. Even its one major reservation broke their way. For reasons that weren't completely clear, the judges declined to stop Dallas County from prosecuting abortion providers, a decision that—through the technicalities of federal law—gave Weddington and Coffee the ability to appeal their entire case directly to the Supreme Court. They submitted the required paperwork on October 6, as the politics of abortion was spiraling through its most ferocious phase yet.

The turmoil was sparked by a turn no one saw coming. Reformers had been trying to liberalize New York's restrictive abortion law since 1966. Every year they brought a bill to Albany. Every year the legislature rejected it on the order, people said, of the state's enormously influential Catholic bloc. That's what everyone was expecting to happen in 1970 too, until the Senate majority leader put before his colleagues a proposal not to soften the state law but to repeal it altogether, without the residency requirements or strict time limits that Hawaii, the only other state to repeal its abortion law, had put in place. Pro-choice supporters saw it as a cynical maneuver, meant to kill reform by replacing it with a bill so extreme it couldn't possibly pass. But it did pass, after three brutal weeks of debate, the decisive vote coming from a conservative Democrat—and former marine—so agonized by what he'd just done he slumped at his desk on the House floor and buried his head in his hands.

He had good reason. Half a decade of reform had broadened the circumstances under which women could have abortions in a dozen states. The procedure was still wrapped up in layers of regulations, though, mostly controlled by medical professionals. Now New York was going to allow any woman who wanted an abortion in the first twenty-four weeks of her pregnancy to have one, no questions asked or reasons demanded. Because it hadn't adopted any residency rules, it was also extending that possibility to the millions of women who lived within a bus-ride's reach of the state. Only the courts could establish a woman's right to an abortion. But on the day the repeal took effect, July 1, 1970, New York's legislature had moved the United States as close to that standard as it had ever been.

"The new law should offend the conscience of no man," said the *Times*'s editorial board on the day the bill was passed. But it did, profoundly. From their chanceries New York's Catholic bishops condemned it as a desecration of the founding fathers' principle that life was an inalienable right. Billy Graham's influential monthly magazine *Christianity Today* followed with a methodically searing piece denouncing the state's "war on the womb," a first step toward evangelicals' embrace of what they had considered a Catholic cause. At the grass roots, passions moved in even more visceral ways. "It is difficult to describe one's feelings as a resident of New York City during those days before July 1," a woman involved in Catholic action wrote late in the year; ". . . the passage of each twenty-four hours was bringing closer the killing of the children, atrocities in which one could not avoid being implicated oneself," as the faithful were when they failed to stand against society's sins.[19]

Atrocity and complicity. That was the connection Martin Luther King Jr. had made from his Birmingham jail cell in 1963, that Norman Morrison had made in his last letter to his wife in 1965, and that Bobby Kennedy had made in his anti-war speech from the Senate floor in 1967. Pro-choice activists had made it too in the run-up to the repeal vote, when they'd rallied in front of midtown Manhattan's St. Patrick's Cathedral with blood-red coat hangers in their hands, to lay the brutality of back-alley abortions at the steps of the Church. In the months after the New York breakthrough anti-abortion activists embraced the politics of moral confrontation with a fury.

The idea of publicizing the disturbing details of abortion procedures had started to gain traction in more militant anti-abortion circles in early 1970. That spring a scattering of Catholic newspapers published vivid descriptions, most of them wrapped in the most lurid language the authors dared to use. Then the photos of aborted fetuses began to appear on the anti-abortion lecture circuit, images so wrenching that the first speakers to employ them reported audience members fainting at the sight of them. From there they passed to right-to-life flyers and fundraising appeals. And in 1971 two of the leading lecturers—a gynecologist and his wife, a former nurse, both long involved in Catholic sex education—reprinted a set of photos in a 141-page handbook meant to confront its readers with the only choice they faced. "Is this unborn being, growing within the mother, a human person?" it read. "Judge it to be a mass of cells . . . ? Then vote for abortion-on-demand. Judge it to be a human person? Then join us in fighting for his right to live, with all the energy and resources at your command."[20] Within a year they'd sold about a million copies.

The movement had its quieter strains, to be sure, shaped by a range of ideas on the complex obligations that a right to life imposed. But it was the furious version that raged through the legislative fights that followed New York's repeal. Twenty-five states took up bills to change their abortion laws in 1971. Out came the photos, for the rallies the pro-life forces mounted, the expert testimony they put before the considering committees—more anti-abortion doctors with shocking slides to show—and the postcards that flooded into legislators' offices, a graphic image on one side, a personal demand for a vote on the other. Down went the bills, every single one.

Weddington and Coffee spent much of that spring lobbying for Texas' version, a repeal bill that was sliding toward defeat when the Supreme Court ruled on jurisdictional grounds that the Dallas court had been wrong to overturn Texas' sodomy law. For a while they feared that the justices would do the same with their case. But on May 3 the Court announced that it would indeed hear *Roe*, with oral arguments to be held sometime in the Court's fall term. And suddenly there was a chance that abortion's place in American life could be settled not by a brutal slog through the states but by nine aging men sitting in judgment of a case created by two young women barely out of law school.

The movement's legal experts had already started to press them on preparations, in anticipation of the Court taking their appeal. Coffee didn't have time to spare from her firm's work. So it was Weddington who gave up the job she'd finally secured for a minuscule stipend from a New York legal institute that promised her the help she needed; Weddington who holed up in the broken-down Manhattan office the institute provided for the summer, writing the case's brief with the makeshift staff its director assembled; and Weddington who made the rounds of the movement's leading figures—Planned Parenthood's powerhouse doctors and lawyers, the woman with ties to the Rockefeller fortune, the prickly law professor from NYU—to lock down the supporting briefs she had to have and cover the costs the institute couldn't manage. On August 17 she submitted every document the Court required, a foot-high stack of paper, and headed home to wait for *Roe* to be assigned an argument date.

She was still waiting a month later, when two of the justices announced that their collapsing health made it impossible for them to continue on the Court. Insiders told her that their resignations would probably put arguments off for a year, since an issue of such importance shouldn't be settled by a shrunken bench, much less by one tangled up in another round of political warfare over the president's search for just the right replacements. So it was something of a surprise when the clerk of the Court finally sent word in mid-November that the justices would be hearing the case on December 13, and even more of a surprise when the director of the New York institute promptly informed the Court that he'd be making the argument on *Roe*'s behalf. The justices would expect their side's most skilled attorney to appear, he told Weddington, though she ought to be "relatively well-prepared on all the issues" in case some terrible accident prevented him from taking the place he clearly deserved.[21] She didn't reply. But Linda Coffee did, with a sharp-edged letter to the clerk reminding him that her client had the right to be represented by a lawyer of her choosing. And Jane Roe wanted Weddington.

The chief justice opened the session at 10:07 a.m. on the 13th, with

Weddington standing at the podium, the youngest woman ever to appear before the Court. In the half hour she'd been given she made a quietly impassioned plea for a woman's right to an abortion as "fundamental," the word she and Coffee had used in their original filing. She walked the justices through the constitutional bases of that claim, which she rooted in individuals' right "to determine the course of their own lives." And she tried to sidestep their questions about whether the state had a compelling interest in protecting the fetus at any point in a pregnancy.[22] It was a solid, at times eloquent presentation, an impressive achievement by any measure. And when her thirty minutes expired she had no idea how she'd done with those seven aging men sitting in front of her.

Calculations

NIXON DIDN'T GET anyone to burglarize Brookings in the summer of 1971. But he did get the covert team he wanted to implement the most far-reaching parts of the Huston Plan. On the White House organizational chart it was listed as the Special Investigations Unit, though its small collection of political operatives and former federal agents preferred to call themselves the Plumbers, since it was their job to plug the administration's leaks. Once they were up and running they gave the president a different break-in—at the office of Daniel Ellsberg's psychiatrist, where they spent the better part of a night rifling through the filing cabinets in search of something damning to bring back to their boss. Later Nixon said that he didn't remember hearing anything about it. More than likely no one told him, on the principle that the president shouldn't know about the felonies his staff committed on his behalf, though it's possible that the memory of it just got lost in the sweep of events that were moving in Nixon's direction.

Kissinger put the final pieces of the China opening into place during a secret three-day visit to Beijing in early July, a suitably clandestine way to seal the deal. He left with a two-paragraph communiqué simply stating that Nixon would visit China at some point before May 1972 as a step toward reopening the diplomatic relations the United States had severed in 1949. It took two days of circuitous travel for him to bring it back to Nixon, and another two days to reach the agreed-upon release date of July 15. The president used just seven minutes of the networks' time to read it to the nation and offer a couple of comments about his commitment to securing world peace for generations to come. Then he took Kissinger, Haldeman, and a couple others off to one of his favorite restaurants to celebrate with dinner and a very expensive magnum of wine in anticipation of the reviews coming in.

The announcement brought the inevitable attacks from the far Right, including a grandstanding condemnation from Nixon's Orange County congressman, a devout member of the John Birch Society, who said that by going to China the president was "surrendering to international communism."[23] Almost everyone else lined up behind it: the Senate's leading hawks and doves, the television anchors, the most prominent newspaper columnists, and the major editorial boards, among them the *Post*'s and the *Times*'s, which set aside the bitterness of the previous month's battles for glowing pieces in praise of the president's breakthrough. But the most important response arrived almost a month later. On August 10 the Soviets privately invited the president to follow his China trip with a Moscow summit in May or June 1972. It had taken almost three years of painstaking diplomacy. But now he really did have the pieces of his grand global strategy hooked together.

The next day the international financial system pitched into its third crisis in a dozen years. The problem had started in the winter of 1971, when the economy began to improve after two sluggish years. The numbers weren't exactly spectacular: between January and April the unemployment rate fell by 0.2 percent, the inflation rate by 1.0 percent. But that was enough to intensify the flow of dollars out of the country. And that was enough to make the international money markets nervous. By May Western Europe's central bankers had traded in so many dollars that the American gold supply had reached its lowest point since 1936.

Over the next few months the trades slowed down, in the mystifying ways of high finance. Then a congressional report supporting the devaluation of the dollar turned the spring's unease into a run. Between August 9 and August 12 the gold supply fell by at least $200 million, with the British government hinting that it might draw down $750 million more. Suddenly Nixon was facing the same choice Eisenhower had faced in 1960 and Johnson in 1968: salve the investors' fears by pushing the American economy into recession a year before the next election, or let the nation's gold reserves drain away—which was to say that he had no choice at all.

Except the one his predecessors would have thought anathema. The secretary of the treasury, a hard-headed pol from Texas, had raised the possibility after the spring gold drain. As Friday's rush mounted he raised it again. Avoid the political devastation of another recession, he said, by abandoning the gold exchange and letting the dollar's value float to whatever level the global markets thought it might be worth. The chairman of the Federal Reserve—an old Eisenhower hand— countered with a reminder that the exchange anchored an international order that the wartime generation had built to prevent the world from tumbling into the catastrophic economic conflicts of the 1930s. Currency wars, trade wars, political friction: we risk them all, the Fed chair told the president, by allowing the order to fall. It was a powerful presentation, shaped by the most fearsome specter he could raise, and it never stood a chance.

At 3:00 a.m. Saturday Nixon was up sketching out the speech he'd have to give before the markets' Monday opening: something "concise, strong, confident," he thought, without any "gobbly-gook about [a] crisis in international monetary affairs." He finally decided to say that he was ending the gold exchange to create "a new era of prosperity" to accompany the "generation of peace" he was building abroad—to suggest that he was working from a master plan rather than political calculation—and then hope that the markets would absorb the shock.[24] They did, in the United States at least, though European and Japanese currencies took a terrible hit, the first hint of the volatile new order that would replace the old. But most Americans weren't worried about the value of the franc and the yen. In the late August polls Nixon's approval rating hit 56 percent, his best showing in almost a year, while 70 percent thought he'd done the right thing by freeing the dollar from gold.

In September Nixon heard that he'd have two more Supreme Court seats to fill. It was an opening created by the accidental timing of age and illness: eighty-five-year-old Hugo Black was dying when he stepped down on September 17, and seventy-one-year-old John Marshall Harlan was wracked with cancer when he resigned on the 23rd. Harlan had been willing to delay his departure as long as he could, to keep the bench from narrowing to seven justices. But Nixon sent word that he'd prefer he resign immediately. That way, Haldeman wrote on the day Harlan made his offer, "the P [would be in] the unique position of appointing two justices at once, which will give him his four on the Court and darn near control of it" just as busing was bearing down on him.[25]

In his first statement on the Charlotte decision Nixon had said that as president he was obligated to enforce the Court's order no matter what he thought of it. But he hadn't anticipated how severe the backlash would be. By midsummer Republicans across the South were telling him that any administration support for busing was going to be politically devastating. Worse, George Wallace was telling Alabama's urban districts to defy the Court and daring Nixon to stop him in what everyone could plainly see was the first flamboyant act of his next presidential campaign. Nixon tried to counter by threatening to pull federal funding from busing plans that his own administration was backing, a move so contradictory even Haldeman couldn't defend it. Then Black and Harlan tendered their resignations.

He devoted about a month to floating the names of potential nominees. Almost all of them were southerners, mostly respectable segregationists like the ones he'd tried to put on the Court in 1969 and 1970. He also threw in a few inflammatory possibilities, among them the lawyer who'd represented Little Rock's schools in 1957 and Democrat Harry Byrd, the senator from West Virginia who'd started out his public life as a recruiter for the Klan. Some of them Nixon actually wanted to appoint. Others were just for show, a way to enrage the civil rights forces while playing to all those folks who wanted the Court reined in.

In mid-October he finally made his nominations. One seat he offered to yet another courtly southerner, a sixty-four-year-old corporate lawyer from Richmond named Lewis Powell; the other to William Rehnquist, a forty-seven-year-old assistant attorney general who'd come into the Justice Department through the intercession of his old friend Barry Goldwater. Compared to some of the other possibilities they were impeccable choices, with perfect legal pedigrees, sterling connections, and almost no records on civil rights. Neither in fact had much of a public record at all, which made it highly unlikely that anyone could uncover the sort of damning material that had toppled Nixon's previous nominees. What made them most attractive, though, was the depth of their conservatism: Lewis's in his view of the law as a bulwark of proper order, Rehnquist's deeper still. "Bill Rehnquist makes Barry Goldwater look like a liberal," said one of his White House supporters in a private aside, the ideal endorsement for a president who saw in his two new nominees his chance to change the Court's sense of racial justice rather than flail against it.[26] In December 1971 the Senate confirmed them both by comfortable margins.

Shortly thereafter Nixon approved a major round of bombing in North Vietnam, to coincide with the Christmas holidays. The hopes that Kissinger had carried out of his clandestine meetings with the North Vietnamese had faded over the summer. There were occasional sessions through September, but the negotiations deadlocked over the administration's support for the current government in Saigon, which was in the midst of reelecting its president in a blatantly fraudulent fashion. Once the October results were in—the president having squeaked by with 94 percent of the vote—the talks shut down. Shortly thereafter military intelligence picked up signs that the North Vietnamese were preparing for a major assault on the South sometime in early 1972, in hopes of winning on the ground what they couldn't get in negotiations.

The possibility of attack didn't slow Nixon's drawdown. On November 12 he stopped by the White House press room to say that he'd be withdrawing another 45,000 soldiers by February 1, 1972, which would bring the total number of Americans in Vietnam down to 140,000, its lowest level since 1965. A few days later a Pentagon source told the *Times* that the president planned to pull out another 100,000 by the end of June, leaving behind a force so small it couldn't really fight at all. Even as the news went out, Nixon was quietly adding to the United States' already enormous air forces in Thailand, Guam, and South Vietnam. On December 26, 1971, he unleashed them for five days of sorties deep in the North, a brutal reminder of the power he wielded and a vicious conclusion to what had turned out to be a very good year for the president.

The Campaign Season

THE CAMPAIGN APPARATUS was set well before the new year began. The unfortunately named Committee to Re-elect the President (CREEP) had opened its offices across the street from the White House gates. The cabinet was being reshuffled to give the committee the senior leadership Nixon wanted it to have. Corporate donations were pouring in. And the West Wing was freeing up whatever additional resources CREEP would need. Even the Plumbers unit would have its place, working on the dark side of a campaign whose candidate planned to present himself as the statesman he'd become, floating above the slightly unseemly world of politics much as Eisenhower had always managed to do.

Two steps got the campaign underway. On January 25, 1972, Nixon went on national television to reveal Kissinger's two years of secret talks with the North Vietnamese, the latest installment of the dramatic announcements he'd come to love, this one meant to eviscerate the doves' claims that he wasn't committed to pursuing peace. Three weeks later he went to China, trailing a planeload of reporters, anchormen, and cameramen behind him. Back flowed seven days of brilliant images: Nixon at the Great Wall; Nixon at the Ming tombs; Nixon at the opera; Nixon trading banquet toasts with Premier Zhou

Enlai in the Great Hall of the People; Nixon sitting alongside an aging Mao Zedong in his book-lined study next to the Forbidden City, quietly talking politics. What the world was seeing, *Time* said in its breathless report from Beijing, was Nixon freeing the nation's foreign policy of the anti-Communist obsession that he'd once helped to start, a perfectly crafted story of transformation to begin the campaign season.

The Democrats were changing too, though without a sense of where they wanted to go. After 1968 the party had reformed its rules to open up its nominating process. No longer could a candidate take the nomination as Hubert Humphrey had, by lining up the party's leaders. Now he or she would have to run through a series of primaries that would select well over half of the convention's delegates, a far more democratic system that gave the party plenty of opportunity to splinter, which was precisely what it did.

Two of the first five primaries, in New Hampshire and Illinois, went to Humphrey's running mate in 1968, Senator Ed Muskie. The son of a Polish-born tailor who'd settled in a Maine mill town, Muskie had risen through the political world the New Deal created. There he stayed, a pro-life Catholic with an abiding faith in the virtue of government action whose greatest appeal was to the working-class ethnics who saw him as one of their own. Muskie followed his wins with two losses, in Massachusetts and Wisconsin, to the race's most prominent anti-war candidate. South Dakota's George McGovern had been one of the first senators to turn against LBJ's escalation in Vietnam, a position he'd built from the deep faith he'd inherited from his father, a Methodist minister; his nightmarish experience of flying almost two years of bombing runs over German-occupied territory in World War II; and the nuances of global politics he'd learned while earning his PhD in American history in the late 1940s. He brought to the race an earnest, cerebral style that allowed him to re-create the coalition Eugene McCarthy had put together for his anti-war campaign in 1968—young liberals providing its energy, progressive suburbanites providing its votes. Down in Florida the last of the first five primaries went to George Wallace, back in the Democratic fold after his 1968 run and furiously trading on the anti-busing fervor that had exploded the year before.

Muskie was the first to fall, brought down by the fractured field and the vicious acts of sabotage CREEP's operatives secretly launched to smear his record, his character, and his family. For a short stretch of the spring it seemed that Humphrey might step into his place. But the polarization was too strong to counter. By early May the party was split down the middle, with McGovern solidifying his hold on its left wing, Wallace gripping its right, and Nixon perfectly positioned to claim its crumbling center.

Nixon staked his claim in a swirl of presidential actions. There was the bill he sent to Capitol Hill, linking a proposed yearlong moratorium on court-ordered busing that Congress had no right to impose with a $2.5 billion increase in federal funding for public schools in poor neighborhoods. The bill would allow those Democrats who couldn't stomach Wallace's white supremacy to wrap their opposition to busing in something suitably progressive. There was the supposedly private letter he sent to New York City's cardinal praising the Church's defense of the unborn—a position that as a mildly pro-choice Republican he didn't share—duly leaked as a direct appeal to the working-class Catholics Muskie's defeat had set adrift. And there were the two new justices he'd put on the Court, making their presence felt.

Toward the close of its term the Court announced that instead of handing down its ruling in *Roe* it would rehear the case now that the bench was back to full strength. No one knew precisely what the delay meant, not even the justices who, a couple of days after the December oral arguments, had voted, five to two, in Sarah Weddington's favor. But the papers were filled with speculation that Nixon's appointees were tipping the balance against abortion rights. Around the same time the Court issued its first integration decision with the new justices in place. It wasn't a major case except for the signal it sent. Since *Brown* the justices had unanimously supported every integration ruling. This time they split five to four, with Nixon's appointees all in dissent, an unmistakable sign that his remade Court was close to bringing the age of integration to an end.

Of all the actions Nixon took that spring, though, none mattered more than the violence he unleashed in Vietnam. The warning he'd tried to send with his Christmas bombing hadn't worked; by early January the evidence of a North Vietnamese buildup was so strong that the Pentagon warned the offensive could come within a month. But the North Vietnamese couldn't afford to embarrass the Chinese with an attack while Nixon was in Beijing, nor the Soviets during his Moscow summit, set for late May. So they squeezed it in between, starting with a massive artillery barrage in the closing days of March—the heaviest since the Tet offensive four years before—followed by 150,000 troops in motorized units pouring into South Vietnam from the North, with supporting divisions striking from Cambodian and Laotian bases to the west.

Kissinger delivered the news to Nixon in the middle of a morning meeting in the Oval Office on March 30. Almost immediately he ordered the bombing strikes he'd built up the air forces to deliver. Most of them served as support for the South Vietnamese troops who were doing the frontline fighting in place of the American boys he'd brought home. But he also insisted on hitting North Vietnam harder than he had before: for the first time in his presidency he turned loose the military's biggest bombers, the devastating B-52s, for a mid-April assault on Haiphong, the North's major port, while fighter jets struck military sites around Hanoi in yet another warning of the damage US forces could inflict.

It wasn't enough. Quang Tri City, on South Vietnam's northern coast, fell to the Communists on the first of May. Hue could go next, the American commander told the White House that afternoon; already refugees were streaming out of the city amid credible reports that the South Vietnamese army was losing its will to fight, a danger so great Nixon decided he had to escalate. Over the next few days he settled on his strategy. Hue he'd defend with waves of B-52s. And the North he would break by severing its access to the military materiel Hanoi had to have to wage its war. The sea routes he'd shut by seeding North Vietnam's harbors with mines, the land routes by blanket bombing of its roads and rail lines, switching yards and fueling stations. He expected precision, he told the Joint Chiefs. But if the bombing "slops over" to civilian targets, "that's the way it's going to be, because we—I've made the decision and we now have no choice . . . but to avoid the defeat of the South" whatever the costs might be.[27]

He told the nation of the escalation on the evening of May 8. It was a careful speech, the specifics of the assault surrounded by another explication of failed negotiations and repeated declarations of his desire to end the war. As soon as he went off the air the leading doves fired off their condemnations—from the campaign trail McGovern called it "a reckless . . . flirtation with World War III"—while the universities braced for a repetition of those terrible May days two years before.[28] There were certainly protests through the balance of the week. But the numbers weren't big enough for anyone to imagine turning them into a student strike, much less a revolution. Only one governor bothered to call up his National Guard. And the requisite Saturday march on Washington drew just 2,000 people.

The escalation drew far more public support. On the night of Nixon's speech the White House switchboard was overwhelmed by the congratulatory calls pouring in. Western Union delivered some 40,000 telegrams, the vast majority of them supportive. And the first poll to reach the president's desk put public support for the attack at 72 percent, almost exactly the share of Americans who'd said they were in the silent majority during those tense days of protest in November 1969. Almost none of them thought that the assaults would end the fighting. But that wasn't the point. With his latest turn Nixon had given much of the nation the Vietnam War they'd always wanted: a sharp, decisive, devastating strike at the enemy that didn't require them to sacrifice their sons—four weeks into the North's offensive only thirty-five Americans had been killed in action—and didn't put the consequences of the military's ferocious power on the nightly news for everyone to see. By the end of May, Nixon's approval rating had reached 62 percent, ten points above where it had been before he'd ordered in the bombers.

In the intervening weeks the violence had lurched in another direction. Wallace swept the last two southern primaries in early May. After a quick swing out to the Plains he moved on to the May 16 contests in Maryland and Michigan, the testing grounds for the northern stage of his campaign. Wallace already had a base in Maryland, where he'd run up the vote in his 1964 primary drive to embarrass LBJ. This time he had an opening in the suburbs too, roiling as they were with talk of busing. The possibilities in Michigan were stronger still. In late March Judge Roth handed down his long-awaited ruling on the integration of Detroit's schools. It read exactly as Wallace thought it would. The city's system couldn't be integrated, Roth said, without integrating the suburban systems too. The details weren't yet settled. But whatever emerged was going to encompass Detroit's entire suburban ring: fifty-three districts linked to the center city in a comprehensive plan that on any given day would be busing more than 300,000 children. Into the ensuing panic strode Wallace, his anti-busing pitch polished to a hard-edged sheen. For a while it was like the glory days of 1968, the governor on the stage slashing away at the judges, the liberals, and the bureaucrats who didn't give a damn for the rights of the working man while his overflow crowds stomped and cheered.

He was back in Maryland on the day before the primaries, shaking hands along a rope line in a suburban shopping center, when a young man with a handgun and a deep psychosis pushed to within a couple feet of him and opened fire. Wallace couldn't tell how many times he was shot. But even in the first horrifying moments—before the race to the hospital, the hours of emergency surgery, the months of rehabilitation, and the years of withering pain—he knew that one of the bullets had hit his spine. Otherwise he'd have been able to feel his legs.

Wallace won both of the next day's primaries, Maryland with a solid plurality, Michigan with a clear majority. Afterward the experts said that he would have done about the same had he not been shot, because it wasn't sympathy that had driven the vote but the strength of his appeal. Where his campaign might have gone next wasn't clear: maybe to another win or two, and from there to a convention fight split along the divides he'd been exploiting since the Wisconsin night eight years before when the Herbstreiths phoned to offer him a national career shaped by hate and fear. Without him the race was essentially done. McGovern took six of the seven remaining primaries, capped by a victory in California that all but made the Democrats' leading dove the party's nominee.

The results were everything Nixon wanted them to be. The last week of May he spent in the Soviet Union, piling up more fabulous images of his statesmanship to go with the nuclear arms agreement he signed as the summit's culminating achievement. He came home to a 15-point lead over McGovern in the polls. Behind that gap lay even more promising numbers. Americans favored his position on abortion over McGovern's by 11 points; his position on the economy by 23 points; his position on busing by 26 points as Wallace's voters swung his way. Best of all, he had a 19-point advantage on his Vietnam policies, a devastating deficit for McGovern to overcome with a campaign rooted in an anti-war movement that most Americans had never trusted. In that opening Nixon saw the rest of the election unfolding. "Get McGovern tied as an extremist," he told Haldeman on June 9, "while we go for the all-out-square America."[29]

The balance of the summer went almost perfectly to plan. It was true that in the middle of June they had a serious scare from those sons of bitches Nixon had wanted hired in the Plumbers unit. On the night of May 28 five of its operatives had broken into the Democratic National Committee's headquarters in Washington's Watergate complex to plant bugs on the office's phones. They'd planned it as another search for dirt on the president's enemies, a high-tech version of the Ellsberg break-in crosscut with the sabotage they'd been committing throughout the campaign. But one of the bugs didn't work. Early on the morning of Saturday, June 17, they'd gone back to replace it. In the middle of the operation they managed to get themselves arrested.

Nixon hadn't known about the burglary beforehand. But he knew that the Plumbers' reporting lines ran up to the Oval Office. So he plunged into his inner circle's attempts to contain the damage. They unfolded as Nixon's crises always did, in obsessive Oval Office conversations and long rambles in his Executive Office Building hideaway. Out of them flowed a series of orders to impede the FBI's investigation and get the story out of the papers. By the end of June he was confident enough in what they'd done to call a prime-time press conference. He used it to announce that the North Vietnamese offensive had stuttered to an end and that the peace talks would be resuming, though the bombing would continue for as long as he thought necessary. From there the session spun through twenty-one questions, not one of them on Watergate.

Two weeks later McGovern formally received the Democratic nomination in a high-minded, occasionally chaotic convention broadened by the party's reforms. Gone were many of the old pols who'd dominated in 1968—Dick Daley didn't even get a seat—replaced by more women and people of color than ever before, many of them embedded inside the anti-war bloc McGovern had assembled. The principle that had put them there was the right one for a party that called itself democratic. But the television coverage of a convention floor filled with unexpected faces reinforced the message Nixon wanted to send, as did the platform they produced, with its promise to end the bombing of North Vietnam immediately and the war within ninety days, its explicit embrace of busing, and its subtle nod to the abortion rights and gay rights that a share of the Democratic base couldn't abide. Shortly after the convention closed Lou Harris put out a poll asking whether McGovern had too many ties to radicals and protest groups. Fifty percent of his respondents said he did.

August was even better for the president. Watergate bubbled up a few times, mostly through revealing reporting from the *Washington Post* and the *New York Times*. But it didn't seem to have much of a hold; according to the White House's polling, 40 percent of Americans hadn't even heard of the break-in, and only one percent of those who had thought the president had anything to do with it. McGovern ate up a huge portion of the media's attention by stumbling through a series of missteps—the worst choosing a running mate he then had to remove from the ticket eighteen days later—while Nixon quietly worked to seal him off from much of his own party; for weeks he courted LBJ, just to convince him not to give McGovern his endorsement. At the end of the month the Republicans swung into their perfectly stage-managed convention: an opening-night tribute to Ike that ended with his widow praising the president from her Gettysburg farm; a second-night tribute to the first lady, narrated by Jimmy Stewart; and on the final night Nixon's triumphant acceptance speech, built around his invitation to both Republicans and Democrats to "come home to the great principles we Americans believe in together."[30] By the time he was done his lead had swollen to 34 points.

He barely campaigned in the fall, having decided that he was better off staying in the White House: an "Eisenhower father figure," as Billy Graham called him in September, too busy caring for the nation to devote any time to his reelection.[31] But he made a few carefully controlled appearances, at the Statue of Liberty on September 26 for a celebration of immigration with a multiethnic contingent of school kids, in Chicago to lead the Columbus Day parade, at Philadelphia's Independence Hall on October 19 to sign a revenue bill. On October 23 he spent an afternoon barnstorming through the upscale suburbs of New York's Westchester County. On the 28th he went to Ohio for one of the last campaign swings of his career.

Two days before, the press had reported that Kissinger and the North Vietnamese had reached a settlement that would finally bring the Vietnam War to an end. Hanoi said they had. Kissinger said they were working on it, though in fact he had a deal in hand. And Nixon said nothing at all, for fear that an agreement announced before the election would leave him open to attacks from the Right that he'd appeased the Left by selling out the South—the same fear that had coursed through America's Vietnam policy for more than twenty years. Still, there wasn't much harm in having the news packed with talk of impending peace.

From Cleveland his motorcade headed southeast into the rolling countryside. He stood in the back of the limousine for the entire afternoon, the first lady at his side, the two of them waving to the small-town folks who'd come out to greet them. At tiny Mantua Corners he saw a couple holding a sign saying that they'd lost their son in Vietnam. It was a hook he often took from the campaign trail, spotting a homemade sign that moved him; he had put the story of one, also from Ohio, into his victory speech back in 1968. This time he had the limo pull over so he could offer his condolences. What he noticed was the mother's rough hands, he told his cabinet the next day. A workingwoman's hands that reminded him of his mother's, which he always thought were beautiful. There was another detail of that moment that he didn't mention. Maybe he didn't even know it. As he was standing on the roadside talking to those grieving parents, he was just fourteen miles from the Kent State campus, where the war had claimed another mother's child two years before in what he'd come to consider the darkest day of his presidency. He remembered writing her family a condolence letter and seeing her father on the nightly news, struggling to read the statement he'd written on his daughter's death. He even seemed to remember how pretty she'd been. But he couldn't remember her name.

EPILOGUE

The Cahills voted for George McGovern in 1972.

They were fifty-five now, Stella closing in on fifty-six. Twenty-four of those years they'd spent together on Eddy Street, long enough to have buried Ed's dad, raised their three kids, and sent them out to lives of their own. After eight years in New Jersey, Judy had recently moved to one of the western suburbs so that she could bring up her kids closer to home. Terry had taken his electrical engineering degree from Notre Dame—maxima cum laude, class of '69—straight into a promising job with a major firm north of Chicago. And Kathy was at the start of her junior year in South Bend, a place she never would have gone had her mother and brother not cleared the way back in 1965. That had been their route into the solid center of the middle class: a step up from their parents' world, though on the salary Ed brought home he and Stella could have moved up as well, into something bigger and better than an aging bungalow with boxes full of flags in the basement. But they couldn't imagine why they'd want to.

That's how they felt about politics too. They'd started voting Democratic when they were young, as almost everyone like them did. There they'd remained, supporting candidates they loved—like Dick Daley, who understood them better than any other politician was ever going to do—and candidates who didn't get them at all, like George McGovern, because in the end voting for a party wasn't a deal to be made every time an election rolled around. It was a commitment to be maintained, just like all the others that the Cahills had made.

Their neighbors didn't agree. In 1968, 62 percent of whites nation-wide had voted for either Nixon or Wallace. In 1972, Nixon alone took 70 percent. He reached that figure by cutting deeply into some of the Democrats' core constituencies. Sixty-one percent of blue-collar voters went his way, 57 percent of union households, and 57 percent of Catholics, a transformation driven by widespread defection among a number of the Democrats' old ethnic blocs. In the Cahills' ward, those realignments combined to give Nixon 66 percent of the vote, six points above a national total so lopsided it won him forty-nine states: a stunning sweep for the emerging Republican majority Eisenhower had envisioned in 1952, sealed by Nixon's four years of appeals to the nation's silent center.

Five weeks later Nixon sent the bombers back over North Vietnam, though much of their impact was aimed at Saigon. Kissinger and the North Vietnamese had in fact reached a comprehensive settlement in mid-October. With its signing would come an immediate cease-fire to finally bring the fighting to an end. Beyond that, the entire agreement pivoted on South Vietnam. Officially the United States recognized the possibility of a unified Vietnam. In reality the South Vietnamese government would remain in place—the Americans wouldn't agree to anything else—though its dynamics would change in fundamental ways. Within six months the United States would withdraw all of its troops from the South and dismantle its sprawl of bases; the North Vietnamese would keep its forces in the South; and the NLF would be given a formal role in shaping South Vietnam's direction—in recognition, Kissinger insisted, of the realities on the ground.

But when he brought the agreement down to Saigon for approval in late October, South Vietnam's president Nguyen Van Thieu rejected it as far too weak to protect his interests. He had a point. Once the settlement was signed and its provisions put in place, Thieu would be heading a country that looked a lot like the one Ngo Dinh Diem had led in the darkest days of his regime—holding power in Saigon while the Communists controlled the countryside, slicing into his authority bit by bit. And this time the Americans would not be willing to intervene.

Kissinger tried to salvage the deal by proposing changes to the North Vietnamese that he hoped would calm Thieu's fears. For weeks the two sides probed around the agreement's edges, searching for subtle shifts that might satisfy Saigon, but nothing worked. On December 13, Kissinger told the White House that the negotiations had deadlocked. The next day Nixon decided to bomb again, both to bludgeon Hanoi back to bargaining—just as Eisenhower had bludgeoned North Korea into a settlement in 1953—and to remind Thieu of the enormous damage the United States could inflict on the North should conditions require it.

The assault began on December 18, paused for Christmas Day, and then resumed until December 29, when the North Vietnamese agreed to go back into negotiations. In between, the military unleashed an orgy of violence. Every night the bombs came raining down—20,000 tons of them in all, mostly from B-52s—lacerating targets around Hanoi, the sites chosen so that the city's civilian population would feel the explosions rattling through their homes, the timing set so that no one would be able to sleep, the collateral damage to Hanoi's neighborhoods the cost of securing peace with a final blast of brutality.

The talks reopened in Paris on January 2, 1973. Seven days later— Nixon's sixtieth birthday—Kissinger and the North Vietnamese reached a settlement that in its essentials matched the one they'd had in October. Over the next two weeks their staffs perfected its language, while the White House strong-armed Thieu into abandoning his objections. He capitulated on January 21, two days before a signing ceremony that Nixon had authorized Kissinger to hold whether or not Saigon approved.

On January 22 the Supreme Court handed down its ruling in *Roe v. Wade*. The justices had reheard oral arguments on October 11, 1972. In their subsequent conference they voted seven to two in support of *Roe*, up from the five-to-two-margin of the previous year. The chief justice assigned the opinion to Nixon's second appointee, Harry Blackmun, precisely the sort of mainstream Republican who, according to the polls, was most likely to support abortion rights. He took about a month to finish a detailed draft based on the extensive reading he'd completed over the summer in anticipation of the case coming his way, though its general outline was never in doubt. His colleagues offered their critiques, in the Court's tradition, which he incorporated into a revised opinion in time for Christmas. It took a couple more weeks for the two opposing justices to write their dissents and for the chief justice to settle on a concurrence. Only then was the Court ready to release its ruling.

Blackmun announced it from the bench with his colleagues arrayed alongside him, a practice the justices reserved for their most important decisions. His opinion opened by acknowledging "the deep and seemingly absolute convictions" that abortion inspired. But the Court was required, he said, to "resolve the issue by constitutional measurement free of emotion and predilection." That's what he tried to do in the fifty-one pages that followed. Its opening sections dealt with jurisdictional questions, its long middle piece with a detailed history of abortion law. On page thirty-six Blackmun finally reached the central issue. "The Constitution does not explicitly mention any right of privacy," he said, but in its 1965 *Griswold* ruling the Court had recognized that such a right existed. With *Roe*, the justice had decided that it was "broad enough to encompass a woman's decision whether or not to terminate her pregnancy."[1]

Blackmun immediately narrowed that right to the first trimester of a woman's pregnancy. After that date, he said, a state could regulate abortion to protect her health. And once the fetus reached viability, it could limit or even outlaw abortion to protect "the potentiality of human life," a carefully constructed way of saying that the fetus had no rights of its own.[2] The decision's significance didn't lie in its limits, though, but in its breadth. When Estelle Griswold set up her Connecticut clinic in 1961, a state still had the power to prohibit a couple from using any form of birth control. Twelve years later the United States Supreme Court was guaranteeing women access to the most controversial of procedures as a matter of right—and by so doing truncating the government's ability to control its citizens' sexuality to a degree that would have been unimaginable at the start of the 1960s. The revolution was far from complete—it would take the Court another thirty years and another Texas sodomy case to extend *Griswold* to gay and lesbian Americans—but with Harry Blackmun's painstaking opinion it had moved dramatically forward.

All the major morning papers put the decision on their front pages, but it wasn't the lead story. That belonged to Lyndon Johnson, who late on the afternoon of January 22 had suffered a massive heart attack. His Secret Service detail found him collapsed on his bedroom floor and tried to revive him with heart massage and mouth-to-mouth resuscitation. It didn't work. The doctors pronounced him dead at 4:33 p.m. Texas time, at the age of sixty-four. Twelve hours later Henry Kissinger and his North Vietnamese counterpart met in Paris' once elegant Hotel Majestic to initial the agreement that ended his bitch of a war.

Nixon formally announced the settlement that evening with the latest in his long line of television addresses. In a tight ten minutes on the air he offered North Vietnam "a peace of reconciliation" to follow the devastation the United States had inflicted, congratulated South Vietnam on securing the "precious right" of self-determination the agreement didn't ensure, and thanked the American people for the sacrifices that they hadn't wanted to make.[3]

The accounting would follow. The Defense Department set the cost of the war at $140 billion. That was purely a measure of military expenses, divorced from the war-induced inflation that would take another decade to break and the international financial transformations that would play a central part in the reconfiguration of the American economy. The Pentagon also counted the precise force its strategy had required: the seven million tons of bombs it dropped on Vietnam, Cambodia, and Laos; the eleven million gallons of Agent Orange it spread across the Southeast Asian countryside; and the two million soldiers it passed through its grinding ground war. But there was no way to measure with any precision the damage that terrifying force had produced, just as there had been no way for Americans to measure the fighting's progress, except through the body count. From the United States' tentative steps toward escalation in the early 1960s to the imposition of its cease-fire shortly after Nixon's nighttime address, the war had killed 2 million Vietnamese civilians, almost 1.5 million North and South Vietnamese troops, and 58,000 Americans, among them Lyndon Johnson.

Over the next few months the Watergate story broke open in a burst of revelations. Up the line they raced as Nixon had feared they could, from a first confession by one of the burglars to the White House lawyer he implicated, who knew exactly how the cover-up had been shaped inside the Oval Office. By mid-April 1973, the Democratically controlled Senate was preparing to open investigative hearings. The U.S. Attorney's Office was moving toward new indictments, with the head of CREEP—Nixon's former attorney general—at the top of its list. The *Washington Post* was regularly running damning stories sourced from somewhere inside the government. And Nixon was scrambling to build a firewall around himself by forcing his inner circle to accept sole responsibility for the crimes he'd pressed them to commit. On April 29 he brought Haldeman into his office one last time to tell him he had to resign, as a final act of loyalty to the president who was about to betray him. As they finished Nixon shook his hand, the first time he'd ever done such a thing.

Even as his administration was crumbling, one crucial piece of Nixon's legacy was taking shape. In October 1972 the Supreme Court had heard oral arguments in *Keyes v. School District No. 1, Denver, Colo.*, the NAACP's long-sought test of whether the Charlotte decision applied to school districts outside the South. On June 21, 1973, the justices ruled by a vote of seven to one that Denver's school board had, in fact, segregated its schools through many of the same manipulations Charlotte's board had used. Denver therefore had to implement a court-directed process of integration as Charlotte had, with busing at its center. The ruling was tempered by technicalities, as the Court's recent decisions almost always were. But the implications were enormous. If Denver's schools met the Court's standard for de jure discrimination, then almost every other urban system in the nation did as well. Already many of them were in litigation in the lower courts. So it wouldn't be long before the buses started rolling in cities that *Brown* had never touched, from Boston to Los Angeles.

But what about Detroit? In June 1972, two months after George Wallace's imposing victory in Michigan's presidential primary, Judge Roth had finalized the comprehensive busing plan that would connect the city's schools to the fifty-three surrounding suburban districts. It was the largest integration order ever issued, encompassing 780,000 children, 40 percent of whom were to be bused to new schools, the most distant 45 minutes away. Most of the affected districts and the State of Michigan immediately appealed to the Sixth Circuit Court, which upheld Roth's ruling in June 1973. So the districts appealed again.

The Supreme Court heard oral arguments in the case, now formally titled *Milliken v. Bradley*, on February 28, 1974. The justices waited six months, until July 25, to issue their decision, which the chief justice read from the bench as Blackmun had read *Roe* the year before. Since its *New Kent* decision in 1968, the Court had moved relentlessly against segregated schools, first in the rural South, then in southern cities, and finally in cities across the nation. Now, in a five-to-four ruling anchored by Nixon's four appointees, the justices announced that they had gone far enough. Detroit's suburban schools had been segregated as a matter of course, the ruling read, and not by state action. So Judge Roth had no right to order their integration, much less to tie them to the racial transformation of the center city's schools.

To so conclude, wrote Thurgood Marshall in a blistering dissent, was to ignore the tangle of state actions that had divided increasingly Black cities for the all-white suburbs that encircled them. Worse, by exempting those suburbs from the necessity of integration, the Court's majority was giving white families the ability to flee the integration of city schools simply by moving across the suburban color line, as Judge Roth had warned they would in his initial ruling three years before. In the process, Marshall said, the Court would reverse the progress the nation had finally made in dismantling its ignoble tradition of separate and unequal schools, deny Black children the rights that were their due, and bring to an end the era that he himself had opened with his brilliant victory before the Court twenty years before.

Marshall had it exactly right. Nixon hadn't appointed his four justices to roll back the legislative triumphs African Americans had won in the course of the 1960s, as Goldwater or Wallace would have done. The Court he shaped would never undermine the fundamentals of the Civil Rights Act, and it would be forty years before another set of justices eviscerated the Voting Rights Act. What Nixon wanted was a Court that would stop the civil rights movement's drive to break through the racial barriers that surrounded his majority's middling classes, where segregation wasn't defined by a "Coloreds Only" sign hanging over a waiting-room door, or a mob out on the street, but by structures so deeply embedded even his justices could insist that they didn't exist.

That's what his appointees did. After their ruling in *Milliken*, school integration slowed, stalled, and then gave way to a gradual resegregation inside an enduring system of neighborhood segregation. Four decades on, the percentage of Black children in hyper-segregated schools was eight points above where it had been at the peak of integration, and the color line remained almost as starkly drawn across the nation's major metropolitan areas as it had been when the NAACP's lawyers put Virda Bradley's case before the Court—or even as it had been when Martin Luther King Jr. dared to march into Marquette Park in the summer of 1966, hoping that by re-creating the moral witness that had brought down Jim Crow's segregation of social space he could destroy Chicago's as well.

Nixon was in California when the *Milliken* ruling came down, stumbling toward his final days in office. For over a year he'd been trying to hold off investigators' demands that he turn over evidence he knew would implicate him in the Watergate cover-up. The harder he resisted the more they seemed to close in: by the start of 1974 he was under investigation by a special prosecutor appointed by the attorney general; the Senate's select committee, which had staged a spectacular series of hearings over the summer of 1973; and the House Judiciary Committee, which had its staff working on the possibility of impeachment. The conflict reached a dangerous level in April 1974, when the special prosecutor subpoenaed the material. Nixon countered with claims of executive privilege, which the prosecutor then asked the Supreme Court to review. The justices unanimously rejected the president's position on July 24, 1974, the day before their *Milliken* decision, on the grounds that the privileges of his office didn't grant him the right to impede the pursuit of justice. Nixon resigned two weeks later.

Ed Cahill put up the flags again that year, though he'd started to think that the celebrations weren't what they used to be. There wasn't any reason for him to feel that way, beyond the ordinary changes that made the day seem different: kids growing up, neighbors moving away, the excitement fading with routine. But that was enough, even for Ed. So he'd run it for a few more Fourths, for his grandkids more than anyone else. Then he'd let it go as the creaking tradition it had become, the vestige of another age, when draping Eddy Street in the Stars and Stripes seemed just the right thing to do.

ACKNOWLEDGMENTS

ACADEMIC HISTORIANS OFTEN talk about how they might bring their scholarship into the undergraduate classes they teach. For me it's been much more valuable to think about how to bring my teaching into my scholarship. This time the connection is straightforward. *The Shattering* has its roots in a course on the 1960s I first offered at Ohio State University in 2006 and a course on the civil rights movement that I created at Northwestern University in 2014. I owe an enormous debt to the hundreds of undergrads who took one or the other of those classes—among them many of the finest students I've taught in the course of my career—as well as to the superb graduate students who served as their teaching assistants. Together they made those classes come alive.

The debts began to accumulate when I decided to move from teaching the courses to writing a book. I contacted Judy Kagan out of the blue to ask if she might be willing to tell me the story behind Eddy Street's Fourth of July celebration. She responded with extraordinary generosity, even as our conversations ranged well beyond her dad draping their block in flags. It's impossible to say just how grateful I am for her willingness to open her family's history to me. I filled in the Cahills' story with the invaluable assistance of Meg Hall, the director of the Archives and Records Center at Chicago's Catholic Archdiocese; Patty Chavez of DePaul University's Special Collections and Archives; Rachele Esola, the library media specialist at St. Patrick's High; Mech Frazier, Anne Zald, and the incomparable Harriet Lightman of Northwestern's library; the reading room staff of Chicago's marvelous Newberry Library; the staff of the Harold Washington Library Center's Municipal Reference Collection; and the extremely helpful staff of the Cook County Recorder of Deeds Office.

My thanks as well to Fr. Kevin Feeney of Northwestern's Sheil Center, who made some valuable introductions; to Don Brown, who in the course of a fascinating conversation helped me understand the power of the networks that ran through Catholic Chicago; to Peter Hallam, who took the time to explain to me the intricacies of Chicago real estate; and to the audiences at the Chicago Humanities Festival, the Bay View Association's American Experience Week, the National Humanities Center, the Alumnae of Northwestern University's Continuing Education Program, and the Newberry Library Teachers' Consortium, all of whom asked such searching questions when I finally stopped talking. I owe Jon Elfner a special thanks for his interest, his perspective, and his help. Someday I'll manage to get down to Jon's class, if he'll have me.

The Shattering bears the mark of the wonderfully stimulating and encouraging world of Northwestern's History Department. It's an enormous privilege—and still a bit of a surprise—to have a place among my fellow Americanists Henry Binford, Martha Biondi, Caitlin Fitz, Leslie Harris, Daniel Immerwahr, Doug Kiel, Michaela Kleber, Kate Masur, Bob Orsi, Mike Sherry, Keith Woodhouse, and Ji-Yeon Yuh. Ken Alder, Brett Gadsden, and Danny Greene talked through portions of the book during some luxurious conversations in those halcyon days when it was possible to go out for a beer. Laura Hein offered her always original insights during discussions on our respective decks and then went above and beyond by reading and commenting on chapter seven. Deborah Cohen gave me a gentle push at a difficult moment. Gerry Cadava, Susan Pearson, Amy Stanley, and Helen Tilley extended valuable advice during our fellowship year writing group get-togethers. I'm particularly indebted to Michael Allen, who challenged me to think much harder than I had about the arguments I was making. I'm not sure he'd agree with where I ended up. But I wouldn't have gotten there without him.

Sidney Fine passed away before I began *The Shattering*, George Hodgman while I was deep in its writing. But I like to think that they knew how much they shaped me. So have the grad students I've had the great luck to work with, some as TAs, some as advisees, many as both. Alvita Akiboh, Joe Arena, Ashley Johnson Bavery, Michelle Bezark, Chris Elias, Erica Gilbert-Levin, Andy Holter, Katie Harvey, Jenny Hasselbring, Ryan Irwin, Brian Kennedy, Greg Kupsky, Danielle Olden, Sian Olson Dowis, Lucy Reeder, Ana Rosado, Charlotte Rosen, William Sturkey, and Tyran Steward have taught me much more than I ever taught them, as brilliant young scholars and teachers will do. Since coming to Chicago I've reveled in the chance to talk about writing—and other things—with Elliot Gorn, Alex Kotlowitz, and Peter Slevin, whose remarkable talents I admire so much. Kathy Peiss gave me just the right encouragement over a New York City lunch a year and a half ago. I have only a casual acquaintance with Matt Lassiter and Jacquelyn Dowd Hall and haven't even met Fredrik Logevall, David Garrow, or George Chauncey. But they have my deepest thanks for the inspiration I've taken from their dazzling scholarship. And I'll always dream of writing with the power and grace of Taylor Branch, David Levering Lewis, and Isabel Wilkerson, since there isn't any harm in dreaming.

Christy Fletcher has been incredibly supportive, even when I didn't deserve her backing. And Steve Forman has been the finest editor I could have hoped to have. Steve signed *The Shattering* when it was nothing more a vague idea. Over the years he must have wondered whether it was ever going to be anything more than that. Instead of giving up on it—as I would have had I been in his place—he gently moved it forward with perfectly timed phone calls, comfortable conference lunches, and encouraging readings of developing chapters. When I stumbled he understood. When I felt overwhelmed he calmed me down. And when I got close to finishing he pushed with the ideal combination of pressure and empathy. It's tempting to say that the book wouldn't be the same without him. The truth is it wouldn't exist at all. Thank you for everything, Steve, though thanks alone hardly seem sufficient. I'm also grateful to Nancy Palmquist for her exemplary copyediting and to W. W. Norton's outstanding production team for its great work.

Then there's my enduring debt to friends and family. I'm not sure I could explain how much I owe Jon Crosthwaite, Brad Cwycyshyn, Dave Giovannucci, Terry and Cindy Hopman, Kevin Hurst, Rudy Mui, John Reswow, Joe and Nancy Tolkacz, and Joe and Paula Zehetmair, who have been a part of my life for almost half a century. I don't see Rich Bodek, Steve Conn, Marty Hershock, Janet and Jed Kuhn, Mike Smith, Suzy Smith, and Chuck Trierweiler as much as I'd like. But when we do get together it's such a joy to be in their company again. The same is true of our extended Columbus family: Bill and Sandy Cohn, Alice Conklin, Susan Hartmann, Terry and Denece Kemp, Mark and Pam Lytle, Angie Mally, Geoffrey Parker, and Birgitte Soland. And it's been far too long since we've been back to see the Harkins, the Kenneys, the Parsonages, the O'Heas, and the Walshes, who together make up my Irish family. I miss you all.

I also look forward to the day when I can finally sit down with Art Getis again to talk about history, geography, politics, academics, and a fair share of baseball. What I really want, though, is just to spend some time with a man I've long admired. To the rest of the clan—Hilary, Jamal, and Christina Tarazi, Sophie Tarazi and Anuj Patel, and Annie, Tony, Darby, Trevor, and Matthew Tibbetts—everyone should be lucky enough to be in a family like yours.

My parents are gone now, my dad nine years, my mom not quite two. The end was hard. Maybe that's why I can't yet see their lives with the clarity I hope to have one day. But I'm absolutely sure of the fundamentals. Kevin and Anne Boyle were good and decent people who gave their sons security, stability, opportunity, and unconditional love. Gifts that great can't be repaid. They can be honored, though, which is why *The Shattering* is dedicated to my parents' memory.

There's another dedication alongside theirs, as there should be. Late last year Abby and Nan came home for a month of decompression and relaxation. They certainly deserved the down time: Abby had just finished working as the digital media director on a tough senatorial campaign, and Nan was nearing the end of the first semester in her masters of education program, barely half a year past her return from her tour with the Peace Corps in Malawi. So naturally I asked them to spend their break tracking down the photos that would appear in the book. They could have begged off. Instead they took on the job—slogging through the manuscript, digging through websites, piling up potential images—with the graciousness, generosity, sensitivity, and great humor that have made them the spectacular young women they are. I'm thankful for their help. And I am so very proud to be their father.

As for Vicky—there words start to fail me. I can talk about all that she's done on behalf of the book: the many drafts she read, the insightful revisions she suggested, the countless problems she talked me through, the repeated doubts she assuaged, the gorgeous photo section she organized, and the endless Eddy Street monologues she endured. I can talk about her taking on those burdens while managing her own massive workload as director of Northwestern IT's Office of Teaching and Learning Technologies. I can talk about the remarkable job she and her staff did in moving our faculty online in the first frenzied days of pandemic; without their brilliant performance the university would have tumbled into crisis. I can talk about her commitment to our daughters, her dad, her sisters and brothers-in-law, our nieces and nephews. No matter what I say, though, I'm not going to capture the depth of her devotion, the breadth of her love, or everything she means to me. The best I can do is offer *The Shattering*'s dedication. For Vicky, Abby, and Nan with all my love and admiration.

NOTE ON SOURCES

THE SHATTERING HAS its distant origins in Eddy Street's Fourth of July photo, which I first saw many years ago in *The American Image: Photographs from the National Archives, 1860–1960* (New York: Pantheon Books, 1979). For reasons I can't explain, the image fascinated me, so much so that when I started teaching an undergraduate course on the 1960s sixteen years ago, I used it to open the first lecture. At the time I knew that it had been taken somewhere in Chicago in 1961. There its story stopped as far as I was concerned, until I set out to write *The Shattering.*

The most important sources for my re-creation of the Cahills' story are the long conversations and subsequent email exchanges I had with Judy Kagan, Ed and Stella's first child, whose generosity opened up her family's history as nothing else could. My notes of those conversations and the emails themselves are in my possession. Around Judy's memories I arrayed a wide range of primary sources. Ship manifests marked the immigration of Stella's parents, Adam Rompala and Stefania Gorska. The United States manuscript census lays out the Cahill family's path in the United States from 1860 onward, and the Rompala family's path from 1910. The 1930 and 1940 manuscript censuses also allowed me to re-create the Eddy Street neighborhood. The Catholic Archdiocese of Chicago holds the records of Stella's parents' marriage and her father's burial. Her mother's remarriage, along with the marriage of Ed's parents, his father's remarriage, and Ed and Stella's marriage, are recorded in the Cook

County, Illinois, marriage index. The timing of Ed's military service is noted in the United States Department of Veterans Affairs BIRLS Death File, 1850–2010. All of those sources are available through the invaluable website ancestry.com.

Stella's peripatetic childhood can be traced through Chicago's city directories, published annually in the 1920s and available at Chicago's fabulous Newberry Library. Details on Stella's schooling come from *The Harrisonian: A Chronicle of Harrison Technical High School and Harrison Activities* (Chicago: Senior Class Publisher, 1932), which is in the possession of the Chicago History Museum. Ed's education I followed through his high school record at the Chicago Archdiocese Archives. The home ownership records for the house Stella's mother bought, and the Cahills' bungalow, can be found at the Cook County, Illinois, Recorder of Deeds, and the election results for the Cahills' ward in the records of the Chicago Board of Election Commissioners at the Municipal Reference Collection of the Chicago Public Library's Harold Washington Library. For Judy Cahill's college career I drew on *The DePaulian* (Chicago: DePaul University, 1962). Terry Cahill's high school experience comes from the 1961 to 1965 editions of the St. Patrick High School yearbook and a selection of unprocessed papers about the school, which were made available to me by St. Patrick's librarian. Terry's college career and that of his younger sister Kathy are detailed in the digitized material on the Notre Dame University Archives website, http://archives.nd.edu/digital/.

As I moved beyond the Cahills' story, I turned to other primary sources. Digitization has given historians immediate access to the newspapers and magazines that were central to the media markets of the 1960s. I made particularly heavy use of the *New York Times* and the *Washington Post*, though I also read my share of stories in the *Chicago Tribune*, the *Los Angeles Times*, the *Detroit Free Press*, the *Boston Globe*, the *Atlanta Constitution*, *Time*, *Life*, *Look*, *Newsweek*, and—for Joan Didion's early work—the *Saturday Evening Post*. The poll results that appear throughout *The Shattering* come primarily from the extraordinary collections of Cornell University's Roper Center for Public Opinion Research, available through the center's iPoll database. I supplemented those figures with Gallup Poll data published in the period's newspapers. The demographics of postwar presidential elections I drew from Warren E. Miller and Santa Traugott, *American National Election Studies Data Sourcebook, 1952–1986* (Cambridge, MA: Harvard University Press, 1989), and from Gallup postelection surveys, some published in the newspapers and others available at gallup.com.

I followed the hesitant and uneven development of postwar prosperity through a series of revealing government reports: U.S. House of Representatives, Subcommittee on Study of Monopoly Power of the Committee on the Judiciary, *Hearings*, May 21–July 26, 1951 (Washington, DC: Government Printing Office, 1951); U.S. Department of Commerce, "Current Population Reports: Consumer Income," April 27, 1954, December 1955, and April 1958; United States Department of Labor, *Nonfarm Housing Starts, 1889–1958* (Washington, DC: Government Printing Office, 1959); U.S. Bureau of the Census, *Construction Reports: Value of New Construction Put in Place, 1946–1963* (Washington, DC: Government Printing Office, 1964); and the comprehensive data sets put together by the Federal Reserve Bank of St. Louis, available at https://fred.stlouisfed.org/categories/. For illuminating material on white flight in Chicago, I turned to the United States Commission on Civil Rights, *Hearings*, May 5–6, 1959 (Washington, DC: Government Printing Office, 1959). And I traced the cost of the Vietnam War partly through William W. Kaufman, "Choices and Trends in the Defense Budget," February 16, 1970, William Kaufman Papers, John F. Kennedy Presidential Library, available at https://www.jfklibrary.org/asset-viewer/archives/WWKPP/001/WWKPP-001-003.

I also relied on a number of collections of presidential documents: Robert Ferrell, ed., *The Eisenhower Diaries* (New York: W. W. Norton, 1981); Ernest May and Philip Zelikow, eds., *The Kennedy Tapes: Inside the White House During the Cuban Missile Crisis* (Cambridge, MA: Belknap, 1997); Michael Bechloss, ed., *Taking Charge: The Johnson White House Tapes, 1963–1964* (New York: Simon & Schuster, 1997); Michael Bechloss, ed., *Reaching for Glory: Lyndon Johnson's Secret*

White House Tapes, 1964–1965 (New York: Simon & Schuster, 2001), and H. R. Haldeman, *The Haldeman Diaries: Inside the Nixon White House* (New York: G. P. Putnam's Sons, 1994). I read the diary—which in its published version is far from complete—alongside Douglas Brinkley and Luke Nichter, eds., *The Nixon Tapes, 1971–1972* (Boston: Houghton Mifflin, 2014). I made frequent use of the spectacular collection of presidential speeches and taped conversations at the University of Virginia's Miller Center. Visit https://millercenter.org/the-presidency to see the center's holdings. Richard Nixon's daily diary provided compelling detail at several key points in the narrative. A digitized version is available through the Richard M. Nixon Presidential Library, at https://www.nixonlibrary.gov/president/presidential-daily-diary.

Although primary sources were fundamental to shaping the story I tell, *The Shattering* is a synthesis, built on and profoundly indebted to the many scholars and journalists who have defined the history of the postwar era. I had superb examples of syntheses to follow, foremost among them David Farber, *Age of Great Dreams: America in the 1960s* (New York: Hill and Wang, 1995); and Maurice Isserman and Michael Kazin, *America Divided: The Civil War of the 1960s* (New York: Oxford University Press, 2000). As I explain in the prologue, *The Shattering* also reframes the 1960s in ways inspired by important recent developments in the historical literature. That's not to suggest that I'm leaving older histories behind; some of the finest historical writing on the 1960s stretches back decades. My goal is to fuse those histories with the best of the newer scholarship. What follows is a record of my largest debts. Anyone interested in a comprehensive bibliography can follow the links at https://history.northwestern.edu/people/faculty/core-faculty/kevin-boyle.html.

My sense of the postwar political order starts with two indispensable histories of the New Deal and World War II: David Kennedy, *Freedom from Fear: The American People in Depression and War, 1929–1945* (New York: Oxford University Press, 1999); and Ira Katznelson, *Fear Itself: The New Deal and the Origins of Our Time* (New York: Liveright, 2013). For the intricacies of the wartime and immediate postwar domestic front, I am particularly indebted to James Sparrow, *Warfare State: World War II Americans and the Age of Big Government* (New York: Oxford University Press, 2011); Alonzo Hamby, *Man of the People: A Life of Harry S. Truman* (New York: Oxford University Press, 1995); and Ellen Schrecker, *Many Are the Crimes: McCarthyism in America* (Boston: Little, Brown, 1998). The most insightful analyses of Dwight Eisenhower are Robert Griffith, "Dwight D. Eisenhower and the Corporate Commonwealth," *American Historical Review* 87 (February 1982); Fred Greenstein, *The Hidden-Hand Presidency: Eisenhower as Leader* (New York: Basic Books, 1982); and William Hitchcock, *The Age of Eisenhower: America and the World in the 1950s* (New York: Simon & Schuster, 2019). Tracing the complexities of the defense budget was challenging. I relied on three outstanding Defense Department studies: Doris M. Condit, *The Test of War, 1950–1953* (Washington, DC: Historical Office, Office of the Secretary of Defense, 1988); Richard Leighton, *Strategy, Money and the New Look, 1953–1956* (Washington, DC: Historical Office, Office of the Secretary of Defense, 2001); and Robert Watson, *Into the Missile Age, 1956–1960* (Washington, DC: Historical Office, Office of the Secretary of Defense, 1997).

There is now a profoundly important literature on the repression and restrictions of the mid-twentieth century. On the constriction of gay life, see George Chauncey, *Gay New York: Gender, Urban Culture, and the Making of the Gay Male World, 1890–1940* (New York: Basic Books, 1994); Margot Canaday, *The Straight State: Sexuality and Citizenship in Twentieth-Century America* (Princeton: Princeton University Press, 2009); and David Johnson, *The Lavender Scare: The Cold War Persecution of Gays and Lesbians in the Federal Government* (Chicago: University of Chicago Press, 2004). Also see Christopher Elias's outstanding *Gossip Men: J. Edgar Hoover, Joe McCarthy, Roy Cohn, and the Politics of Insinuation* (Chicago: University of Chicago Press, 2021). The key studies of race and housing policy are Richard Rothstein, *The Color of Law: A Forgotten History of How Our Government Segregated America* (New York: Liveright, 2017); and Mehrsa Baradaran, *The Color of Money: Black Banks and the Racial Wealth Gap* (Cambridge,

MA: Belknap, 2018). My understanding of Chicago's postwar segregation comes from Laura McEnaney's splendid *Postwar: Waging Peace in Chicago* (Philadelphia: University of Pennsylvania Press, 2018); Arnold Hirsh, *Making the Second Ghetto: Race and Housing in Chicago, 1940–1960* (New York: Cambridge University Press, 1983); Adam Cohen and Elizabeth Taylor, *American Pharaoh: Richard J. Daley: His Battle for Chicago and the Nation* (Boston: Little, Brown, 2000); and Amanda Seligman, *Block by Block: Neighborhoods and Public Policy on Chicago's West Side* (Chicago: University of Chicago Press, 2005).

The following were particularly useful in shaping my reading of the early Cold War, the other critical component of the postwar political order: Melvyn Leffler, *A Preponderance of Power: National Security, the Truman Administration, and the Cold War* (Stanford, CA: Stanford University Press, 1992); Michael Hogan, *A Cross of Iron: Harry S. Truman and the Origins of the National Security State, 1945–1954* (Cambridge: Cambridge University Press, 1998); John Lewis Gaddis, *George Kennan: An American Life* (New York: Penguin, 2011); and Bruce Cumings, *The Korean War: A History* (New York: Modern Library, 2010). Odd Arne Westad, *The Global Cold War: Third World Interventions and the Making of Our Time* (Cambridge: Cambridge University Press, 2005) expanded my perspective. My account of the United States' deepening involvement in Vietnam in the 1950s relies to a considerable extent on Fredrik Logevall's magnificent *Embers of War: The Fall of an Empire and the Making of America's Vietnam* (New York: Random House, 2012). On the Eisenhower-era gold tangle, see Francis Gavin, *Gold, Dollars and Power: The Politics of International Monetary Relations, 1958–1971* (Chapel Hill: University of North Carolina Press, 2004).

There is a vast and uneven literature on John Kennedy. Among the best studies is Robert Dallek, *An Unfinished Life: John F. Kennedy, 1917–1963* (Boston: Little, Brown, 2003), a balanced biography deepened by unprecedented access to primary sources. The best sources on JFK's family history, which I see as pivotal, are David Nasaw, *The Patriarch: The Remarkable Life and Turbulent Times of Joseph P. Kennedy* (New

York: Penguin, 2012); and Fredrik Logevall, *JFK: Coming of Age in the American Century, 1917–1965* (New York: Random House, 2020). Of the many books on the Cuban Missile Crisis, Aleksandr Fursenko and Timothy Naftali, *"One Hell of a Gamble": Khrushchev, Castro, and Kennedy, 1958–1964* (New York: W. W. Norton, 1997) remains unmatched. On Kennedy's Vietnam policy and the toppling of Diem, see David Kaiser, *American Tragedy: Kennedy, Johnson, and the Origins of the Vietnam War* (Cambridge, MA: Belknap, 2000).

In recent decades historians have dramatically expanded the length and breadth of the civil rights movement. Among the many exemplary studies of the nation's racial regime and the movement's long campaign to break it, I am most indebted to Ibram Kedzi, *Stamped from the Beginning: The Definitive History of Racist Ideas in America* (New York: Nation Books, 2016); Grace Hale, *Making Whiteness: The Culture of Segregation in the South* (New York: Pantheon Books, 1998); Steven Hahn, *A Nation Under Our Feet: Black Political Struggles in the Rural South, from Slavery to the Great Migration* (Cambridge, MA: Belknap, 2003); Patricia Sullivan, *Lift Every Voice: The NAACP and the Making of the Civil Rights Movement* (New York: New Press, 2009); Colin Grant, *Negro With a Hat: The Rise and Fall of Marcus Garvey* (New York: Oxford University Press, 2008); Robin D. G. Kelley's brilliant *Hammer and Hoe: Alabama Communists during the Great Depression* (Chapel Hill: University of North Carolina Press, 1990); John D'Emilio, *Lost Prophet: The Life and Times of Bayard Rustin* (New York: Free Press, 2003); Barbara Ransby, *Ella Baker and the Black Freedom Movement: A Radical Democratic Vision* (Chapel Hill: University of North Carolina Press, 2003); Thomas Sugrue, *Sweet Land of Liberty: The Forgotten Struggle for Civil Rights in the North* (New York: Random House, 2008); Richard Kluger, *Simple Justice: The History of Brown v. Board of Education and Black America's Struggle for Equality* (New York: Knopf, 1976); Danielle McGuire, *At the Dark End of the Street: Black Women, Rape and Resistance—A New History of the Civil Rights Movement from Rosa Parks to Black Power* (New York: Knopf, 2010); Jeanne Theoharis, *The Rebellious Life of Mrs. Rosa Parks* (Boston: Beacon Press, 2013); and

David Margolick, "Through a Lens, Darkly," *Vanity Fair*, September 24, 2007, for his evocative retelling of Elizabeth Eckford's experience in front of Little Rock High School.

My account of the civil rights movement in the 1960s draws a good deal of information and inspiration from Taylor Branch's magisterial three-volume narrative, *America in the King Years* (New York: Simon & Schuster, 1989–2006); David Garrow, *Bearing the Cross: Martin Luther King, Jr. and the Southern Christian Leadership Conference* (New York: William Morrow, 1986); Clayborne Carson's classic *In Struggle: SNCC and the Black Awakening of the 1960s* (Cambridge, MA: Harvard University Press, 1981); John Lewis, *Walking with the Wind: A Memoir of the Movement* (New York: Simon & Schuster, 1998); Raymond Arsenault, *Freedom Riders: 1961 and the Struggle for Racial Justice* (New York: Oxford University Press, 2006); Charles Payne, *I've Got the Light of Freedom: The Organizing Tradition and the Mississippi Freedom Struggle* (Berkeley: University of California Press, 1995); Diane McWhorter, *Carry Me Home: Birmingham, Alabama: The Climactic Battle of the Civil Rights Revolution* (New York: Simon & Schuster, 2001); William Jones, *The March on Washington: Jobs, Freedom and the Forgotten History of Civil Rights* (New York: W. W. Norton, 2014); and James Ralph Jr., *Northern Protest: Martin Luther King, Jr., Chicago and the Civil Rights Movement* (Cambridge, MA: Harvard University Press, 1993).

For the Nationalist side of the movement I relied particularly on Malcolm X with the assistance of Alex Haley, *The Autobiography of Malcolm X* (New York: Grove Press, 1965); Manning Marable, *Malcolm X: A Life* (New York: Viking, 2011); Les Payne and Tamara Payne, *The Dead Are Arising: The Life of Malcolm X* (New York: Liveright, 2020); Peniel Joseph, *Waiting 'Til the Midnight Hour: A Narrative History of Black Power in America* (New York: Henry Holt, 2006); Peniel Joseph, *Stokely: A Life* (New York: Basic Civitas, 2014); Hasan Kwame Jeffries, *Bloody Lowndes: Civil Rights and Black Power in Alabama's Black Belt* (New York: New York University Press, 2009); and Joshua Bloom and Waldo Martin Jr., *Black Against Empire: The History and Politics of the Black Panther Party* (Berkeley: University of California Press, 2013).

As civil rights history has expanded, so has the history of modern American conservatism. For its suburban and corporate strands, I turned to Lisa McGirr's pathbreaking *Suburban Warriors: The Origins of the New American Right* (Princeton: Princeton University Press, 2001); Rick Perlstein, *Before the Storm: Barry Goldwater and the Unmaking of the American Consensus* (New York: Hill and Wang, 2001); Darren Dochuk, *From Bible Belt to Sun Belt: Plain Folk Religion, Grassroots Politics, and the Rise of Evangelical Conservatism* (New York: W. W. Norton, 2011); and Kim Phillips-Fein's invaluable *Invisible Hands: The Businessmen's Crusade Against the New Deal* (New York: W. W. Norton, 2010). Conservatism's southern strand is powerfully explicated in Dan T. Carter, *The Politics of Rage: George Wallace, the Origins of the New Conservativism, and the Transformation of American Politics* (New York: Simon & Schuster, 1995), a book whose influence runs through *The Shattering*; and Joseph Crespino, *Strom Thurmond's America* (New York: Hill and Wang, 2012).

The long histories of civil rights and conservatism intersect with the mid-1960s burst of reform in complex ways. On Lyndon Johnson, civil rights, and social policy, see Doris Kearns Goodwin's still-revealing *Lyndon Johnson and the American Dream* (New York: Harper & Row, 1976); Robert Caro, *The Passage of Power: The Years of Lyndon Johnson, Volume Four* (New York: Vintage, 2013); Clay Risen, *The Bill of the Century: The Epic Battle for the Civil Rights Act* (New York: Bloomsbury, 2014); Gary May, *Bending Toward Justice: The Voting Rights Act and the Transformation of American Democracy* (New York: Basic Books, 2013); and Julian Zelizer, *The Fierce Urgency of Now: Lyndon Johnson, Congress, and the Battle for the Great Society* (New York: Penguin Press, 2015). On the contested relationship between the Great Society and racialized policing, see Michael Flamm, *Law and Order: Street Crime, Civil Unrest, and the Crisis of Liberalism in the 1960s* (New York: Columbia University Press, 2005); and Elizabeth Hinton, *From the War on Poverty to the War on Crime: The Making of Mass Incarceration in America* (Cambridge, MA: Harvard University Press, 2017). Michael Flamm, *In the Heat of the Summer: The New York Riots of 1964 and the War on Crime* (Philadelphia: University of Pennsylvania Press, 2017) is an excellent study of the first urban rebellion of the mid-1960s. The other rebellions await comparable treatment.

The mid-1960s reformation of the state's relationship to sexuality also intersects with a long history of activism. I began with updated versions of two brilliant foundational books: John D'Emilio and Estelle Freedman, *Intimate Matters: A History of Sexuality in America,* 3rd ed. (Chicago: University of Chicago Press, 2012); and Linda Gordon, *The Moral Property of Women: A History of Birth Control Politics in America* (Urbana: University of Illinois Press, 2002). Valuable entry points into midcentury gender politics include Stephanie Coontz, *A Strange Stirring: The Feminine Mystique and American Women at the Dawn of the 1960s* (New York: Basic Books, 2011); Dorothy Sue Cobble, *The Other Women's Movement: Workplace Justice and Social Rights in Modern America* (Princeton: Princeton University Press, 2004); Johnson, *The Lavender Scare,* cited above; and Eric Cervini, *The Deviant's War: The Homosexual vs. the United States of America* (New York: Farrar, Straus and Giroux, 2020). My tracing of the long road to *Griswold* draws particularly on David Garrow, *Liberty and Sexuality: The Right to Privacy and the Making of Roe v. Wade* (New York: Macmillan, 1994); Rickie Solinger, *Pregnancy and Power: A Short History of Reproductive Politics in America* (New York: New York University Press, 2005); Jonathan Eig, *The Birth of the Pill: How Four Crusaders Reinvented Sex and Launched a Revolution* (New York: W. W. Norton, 2014); and Sarah Igo's imposing *The Known Citizen: A History of Privacy in Modern America* (Cambridge, MA: Harvard University Press, 2018). Also see Leslie Reagan's essential *When Abortion Was a Crime: Women, Medicine and Law in the United States, 1867–1973* (Berkeley: University of California Press, 1997).

I give the counterculture far less attention than do other historians of the 1960s. For a sweeping analysis see Arthur Marwick, *The Sixties: Cultural Transformation in Britain, France, Italy, and the United States, c. 1858–c. 1974* (New York: Oxford University Press, 1998). Also see Bill Morgan, *The Typewriter Is Holy: The Complete, Uncen-*

sored History of the Beat Generation (New York: Free Press, 2010); and Michael Kramer, *The Republic of Rock: Music and Citizenship in the Sixties Counterculture* (New York: Oxford University Press, 2013). The details of Ken Kesey's story and Joan Didion's reporting from the Haight come from two classic pieces of 1960s journalism: Tom Wolfe, *The Electric Kool-Aid Acid Test* (New York: Farrar Straus and Giroux, 1968); and Joan Didion, "Slouching Toward Bethlehem," *Saturday Evening Post*, September 23, 1967. Didion describes her history in portions of *The White Album* and *Where I Was From*, reprinted in Joan Didion, *We Tell Ourselves Stories in Order to Live: Collected Nonfiction* (New York: Knopf, 2006).

The literature on the Vietnam War is enormous. The best introduction remains George Herring, *America's Longest War: The United States and Vietnam, 1950–1975*, 6th ed. (New York: McGraw-Hill, 2019). Of the many books on LBJ's escalation, I found most valuable Lloyd Gardner, *Pay Any Price: Lyndon Johnson and the Wars for Vietnam* (Chicago: I. R. Dee, 1995); Fredrik Logevall, *Choosing War: The Lost Chance for Peace and the Escalation of War in Vietnam* (Berkeley: University of California Press, 1999); Kaiser, *An American Tragedy*, cited above; and Brian VanDeMark, *Road to Disaster: A New History of America's Descent into Vietnam* (New York: William Morrow, 2018). Christian Appy, *Working-Class War: American Combat Soldiers in Vietnam* (Chapel Hill: University of North Carolina Press, 1993), is indispensable, as is Christian G. Appy, *Patriots: The Vietnam War Remembered from All Sides* (New York: Viking, 2003). For the financial cost of the war I used Edward Drea, *McNamara, Clifford, and the Burdens of Vietnam, 1965–1969* (Washington, DC: Historical Office, Office of the Secretary of Defense, 2011). My descriptions of James Farley's combat trauma and Norman Morrison's self-immolation come from Paul Hendrickson's extraordinary *The Living and the Dead: Robert McNamara and Five Lives of a Lost War* (New York: Knopf, 1996). The story of Ben Suc's destruction is from Jonathan Schell, "A Reporter at Large: The Village of Ben Suc," *The New Yorker*, July 15, 1967, 28–93.

On the origins and complications of the New Left, see Jim Miller,

Democracy Is in the Streets: From Port Huron to the Siege of Chicago (New York: Simon & Schuster, 1987); Maurice Isserman, *If I Had a Hammer: The Death of the Old Left and the Birth of the New Left* (New York: Basic Books, 1987); Sara Evans's important *Personal Politics: The Roots of Women's Liberation in the Civil Rights Movement and the New Left* (New York: Knopf, 1979); and Robert Cohen, *Freedom's Orator: Mario Savio and the Radical Legacy of the 1960s* (New York: Oxford University Press, 2009). On the breadth of the movement, see Charles DeBenedetti and Charles Chatfield's encyclopedic *An American Ordeal: The Antiwar Movement of the Vietnam Era* (Syracuse, NY: Syracuse University Press, 1990). Kenneth Heineman, *Campus Wars: The Peace Movement at American State Universities in the Vietnam Era* (New York: New York University Press, 1993) is crucial for contextualizing Kent State. The scholarship has almost completely overlooked the conservative side of the movement. An exception is Sandra Scanlon, *The Pro-War Movement: Domestic Support for the Vietnam War and the Making of Modern American Conservatism* (Amherst: University of Massachusetts Press, 2013).

My retelling of 1968 is indebted to Rick Perlstein, *Nixonland: The Rise of a President and the Fracturing of America* (New York: Scribner, 2008); John Farrell, *Richard Nixon: The Life* (New York: Doubleday, 2017); Robert Collins, "The Economic Crisis of 1968 and the Waning of the 'American Century,'" *American Historical Review* 101 (April 1996): 396–422; Michael Honey's beautiful *Going Down Jericho Road: The Memphis Strike, Martin Luther King's Last Campaign* (New York: W. W. Norton, 2007); Jason Sokol, *The Heavens Might Crack: The Death and Legacy of Martin Luther King, Jr.* (New York: Basic Books, 2018); Evan Thomas, *Robert Kennedy: His Life* (New York: Simon & Schuster, 2000); Arnold Offner, *Hubert Humphrey: The Conscience of the Country* (New Haven: Yale University Press, 2018); David Farber, *Chicago '68* (Chicago: University of Chicago Press, 1988); Carter, *Politics of Rage*, and Cohen and Taylor, *American Pharaoh*, both cited above. Also see the best of that year's election chronicles, Lewis Chester, Godfrey Hodgson, and Bruce Page, *An American Melodrama: The Presidential Campaign of 1968* (New York: Viking, 1969).

My interpretation of the Nixon presidency is derived from the brilliant reconceptualization of late twentieth-century politics that Matthew Lassiter offers in *The Silent Majority: Suburban Politics in the Sunbelt South* (Princeton: Princeton University Press, 2006), and "Political History beyond the Blue-Red Divide," *Journal of American History* 98 (December 2011): 760–64. My descriptions of the politics and policies of the Nixon White House benefited enormously from Richard Reeves, *President Nixon: Alone in the White House* (New York: Simon & Schuster, 2001); Farrell, *Richard Nixon*; Perlstein, *Nixonland*; Hinton, *From the War on Poverty to the War on Crime*, cited above; Jeffrey Kimball, *Nixon's Vietnam War* (Lawrence: University Press of Kansas, 1998); Henry Kissinger, *White House Years* (Boston: Little, Brown, 1979), which should be read alongside Larry Berman, *No Peace, No Honor: Nixon, Kissinger and Betrayal in Vietnam* (New York: Free Press, 2001); and Barry Gewen, *The Inevitability of Tragedy: Henry Kissinger and His World* (New York: W. W. Norton, 2020); and Joanne Gowa, *Closing the Gold Window: Domestic Politics and the End of Bretton Woods* (Ithaca: Cornell University Press, 1983). Stanley Kutler, *The Wars of Watergate: The Last Crisis of Richard Nixon* (New York: W. W. Norton, 1990) is still the best narrative of the Watergate affair.

I built Norma McCorvey's story from her first memoir (with Andy Meisler), *I Am Roe: My Life, Roe v. Wade, and Freedom of Choice* (New York: HarperCollins, 1994); and Joshua Prager's powerful article, "The Accidental Activist," *Vanity Fair*, January 18, 2013. For the politics of abortion in the late 1960s and early 1970s and the route to *Roe*, I relied on Alice Echols, *Daring to Be Bad: Radical Feminism in America, 1967–1975* (Minneapolis: University of Minnesota Press, 1989); Reagan, *When Abortion Was a Crime*, cited above; Garrow, *Liberty and Sexuality*, cited above; Sarah Weddington, *A Question of Choice* (New York: G. P. Putnam's Sons, 1992); Robert Self, *All in the Family: The Realignment of American Democracy since the 1960s* (New York:

Hill and Wang, 2012); and Daniel Williams's valuable *Defenders of the Unborn: The Pro-Life Movement before Roe v. Wade* (New York: Oxford University Press, 2016). There are excellent studies of school integration and busing in particular locations, among them Brett Gadsden's *Between North and South: Delaware, Desegregation, and the Myth of Southern Exceptionalism* (Philadelphia: University of Pennsylvania Press, 2012). But there isn't a broad history of busing. Lassiter, *Silent Majority*, cited above, is essential on Charlotte's school integration. Sugrue, *Sweet Land of Liberty*, cited above, contextualizes *Milliken v. Bradley*. On George McGovern's base, see Lily Geismer's valuable *Don't Blame Us: Suburban Liberals and the Transformation of the Democratic Party* (Princeton: Princeton University Press, 2014).

NOTES

PREFACE

1. The term originates with Arthur Marwick, *The Sixties: Cultural Revolution in Britain, France, Italy and the United States, c. 1958–1974* (Oxford: Oxford University Press, 1998). It has since passed into wide usage. Historians disagree about the precise boundaries of the "long sixties." I think of it as a slightly shorter period than Marwick does.
2. Daniel Bell, *The End of Ideology: On the Exhaustion of Political Ideas in the Fifties* (New York: Free Press, 1960), 373, 375.
3. Rick Perlstein, *Nixonland: The Rise of a President and the Fracturing of America* (New York: Scribner, 2008), 747.
4. Fred Greenstein, *The Hidden-Hand Presidency: Eisenhower as Leader* (New York: Basic Books, 1982), 52.

CHAPTER 1: EDDY STREET

1. J. E. Cahill, "Flags for July 4," *Chicago Tribune*, June 21, 1961, 10.
2. Franklin Roosevelt, "Acceptance Speech at the Democratic National Convention," July 27, 1936, available at https://teachingamericanhistory.org/library/document/acceptance-speech-at-the-democratic-national-convention-1936/ [last accessed January 22, 2020].
3. David Kennedy, *Freedom from Fear: The American People in Depression and War, 1929–1945* (New York: Oxford University Press, 1999), 618.
4. "Truman: We're Not at War," *Chicago Tribune*, June 30, 1950, 1.
5. "New War Aide Served with MacArthur," *Washington Post*, February 23, 1942, 18.
6. Dwight Eisenhower diary entry, January 14, 1949, reprinted in Robert H. Ferrell, ed., *The Eisenhower Diaries* (New York: W. W. Norton, 1981), 153.
7. Robert Taft to Prescott Bush, August 4, 1952, reprinted in Clarence E. Wunder-

lin Jr., ed., *The Papers of Robert A. Taft*, vol. 4 (Kent, OH: Kent State University Press, 2006), 406.

8. Quoted in Peter Guralnick, *Last Train to Memphis: The Rise of Elvis Presley* (New York: Back Bay, 1994), 284.

CHAPTER 2: TWILIGHT WARS

1. Richard Rhodes, *Dark Sun: The Making of the Hydrogen Bomb* (New York: Simon & Schuster, 1995), 21–22.

2. Rhodes, *Dark Sun*, 566.

3. The exchange is reprinted in Ernest May and Philip Zelikow, eds., *The Kennedy Tapes: Inside the White House During the Cuban Missile Crisis* (Cambridge, MA: Belknap, 1997), 178.

4. Robert Dallek, *Franklin D. Roosevelt and American Foreign Policy, 1932–1945* (New York: Oxford University Press, 1979), 166.

5. Harry Truman Address before a Joint Session of Congress, March 12, 1947, available at https://avalon.law.yale.edu/20th_century/trudoc.asp [last accessed March 1, 2021].

6. Joseph McCarthy, "Enemies from Within," February 9, 1950, available at http://historymatters.gmu.edu/d/6456/ [last accessed February 23, 2021]; George Sokolsky quoted in David K. Johnson, *The Lavender Scare: The Cold War Persecution of Gays and Lesbians in the Federal Government* (Chicago: University of Chicago Press, 2004), 30.

7. "President Bitter," *New York Times*, March 31, 1950, 1; "Text of President's Broadcast on the Korean Crisis," *New York Times*, July 20, 1950, 15.

8. Eisenhower diary entry, November 6, 1950, reprinted in Robert H. Ferrell, ed., *The Eisenhower Diaries* (New York: W. W. Norton, 1981), 181.

9. Eisenhower quoted in Robert Griffith, "Dwight D. Eisenhower and the Corporate Commonwealth," *American Historical Review* 87 (February 1982): 95. Almost thirty years after its publication Griffith's article remains the best analysis of Eisenhower available.

10. Joseph McCarthy speech before the U.S. Senate, June 14, 1951, available at https://sourcebooks.fordham.edu/mod/1951mccarthy-marshall.asp [last accessed March 1, 2021]; Eisenhower diary entry, June 14, 1951, in Ferrell, ed., *Eisenhower Diaries*, 195.

11. John Lewis Gaddis, *Strategies of Containment: Critical Appraisal of American National Security Policy During the Cold War* (New York: Oxford University Press, 2005), 131; Dwight Eisenhower hand-edited draft of public statement on Korean armistice, July 26, 1953, available at https://www.eisenhowerlibrary.gov/sites/default/files/research/online-documents/korean-war/armistice-draft-1953-07-26.pdf [last accessed March 1, 2021].

12. Eisenhower diary entry, March 17, 1951, in Ferrell, ed., *Eisenhower Diaries*, 181.

13. Robert McClintock quoted in Fredrik Logevall's brilliant study, *Embers of War: The Fall of an Empire and the Making of America's Vietnam* (New York: Random House, 2012), 591.

14. Logevall, *Embers of War*, 679.

15. Rick Perlstein, *Before the Storm: Barry Goldwater and the Unmaking of the American Consensus* (New York: Hill and Wang, 2001), 66, 76.

16. David Nasaw, *The Patriarch: The Remarkable Life and Turbulent Times of Joseph P. Kennedy* (New York: Penguin, 2012), 498.

17. Robert Dallek, *An Unfinished Life: John F. Kennedy, 1917–1963* (Boston: Little, Brown, 2003), 118.

18. Dallek, *Unfinished Life*, 225.

19. David Pietrusza, *1960: LBJ vs. JFK vs. Nixon: The Epic Campaign That Forged Three Presidents* (New York: Union Square Press, 2008), 344.

20. Nasaw, *Patriarch*, 751.

21. Dwight Eisenhower Farewell Address, January 17, 1961, available at https://avalon.law.yale.edu/20th_century/eisenhower001.asp [last accessed March 1, 2021].

22. Edward Lansdale memorandum, January 17, 1961, Pentagon Papers, Part IV-A-5, available at https://nara-media-001.s3.amazonaws.com/arcmedia/research/pentagon-papers/Pentagon-Papers-Part-IV-A-5.pdf [last accessed March 1, 2021].

23. Louis J. Smith, ed., *Foreign Relations of the United States, 1961–1963*, Volume X (Washington, DC: Government Printing Office, 1997), p. 666.

24. Aleksandr Fursenko and Timothy Naftali, *"One Hell of a Gamble": Khrushchev, Castro, Kennedy, and the Cuban Missile Crisis, 1958–1964* (London: John Murray, 1997), 182.

25. Rusk quoted in May and Zelikow, eds., *Kennedy Tapes*, 60.

26. John Kennedy address to the nation, October 22, 1962, available at https://www.mtholyoke.edu/acad/intrel/kencuba.htm [last accessed October 30, 2020].

27. Robert Kennedy memorandum to Dean Rusk, October 30, 1962, reprinted in May and Zelikow, eds., *Kennedy Tapes*, 607.

CHAPTER 3: THE BELOVED COMMUNITY

1. The mob is quoted in David Margolick's powerful article "Through a Lens, Darkly," *Vanity Fair*, September 2007, available at https://www.vanityfair.com/news/2007/09/littlerock200709 [last accessed December 5, 2020]. I supplemented his account with details from *Life*'s photos of her arrival, available at https://www.life.com/history/little-rock-nine-1957-photos/ [last accessed December 5, 2020].

2. Tillman quoted in Joel Williamson, *The Crucible of Race: Black-White Relations in the American South Since Emancipation* (New York: Oxford University Press, 1984), 135.

3. W. E. B. Du Bois, "The Talented Tenth," 1903, available at https://glc.yale.edu/talented-tenth-excerpts [last accessed March 1, 2021]; "Platform Adopted by the National Negro Committee," 1909, available at https://www.loc.gov/exhibits/naacp/founding-and-early-years.html [last accessed November 9, 2020].

4. Gandhi thought of *satyagraha* as "perhaps the mightiest instrument on earth." See Rmachandra Guha, *Gandhi Before India* (New York: Knopf, 2014), 550.

5. Barbara Ransby, *Ella Baker and the Black Freedom Movement: A Radical Democratic Vision* (Chapel Hill: University of North Carolina Press, 2003), 112.

6. Richard Kluger, *Simple Justice: The History of Brown v. Board of Education and Black America's Struggle for Equality* (New York: Vintage Books, 2004), 681–82.

7. Patricia Sullivan, *Lift Every Voice: The NAACP and the Making of the Civil Rights Movement* (New York: New Press, 2009), 420; John Egerton, *Speak Now Against the Day: The Generation Before the Civil Rights Movement in the South* (New York: Knopf, 1994), 609; Gene Roberts and Hank Klibanoff, *The Race Beat: The Press, the Civil Rights Struggle, and the Awakening of a Nation* (New York: Random House, 2006), 62.

8. Kluger, *Simple Justice*, 745–49.

9. For Parks's thinking, see Jeanne Theoharis, *The Rebellious Life of Mrs. Rosa Parks* (Boston: Beacon Press, 2013), 62.

10. David Garrow, *Bearing the Cross: Martin Luther King, Jr. and the Southern Christian Leadership Conference* (New York: William Morrow, 1986), 58.

11. John D'Emilio, *Lost Prophet: The Life and Times of Bayard Rustin* (Chicago: University of Chicago Press, 2003), 239.

12. Margolick, "Through a Lens Darkly."

13. Faubus quoted in National Park Service, "Crisis Timeline," *Little Rock Central High School National Historic Site*, available at https://www.nps.gov/chsc/learn/historyculture/timeline.htm [last accessed November 14, 2020].

14. John Lewis (with Michael D'Orso), *Walking with the Wind: A Memoir of the Movement* (New York: Simon & Schuster, 1998), 66.

15. Lawson quoted in Taylor Branch, *Parting the Waters: America in the King Years, 1954–63* (New York: Simon & Schuster, 1988), 291.

16. Lewis, *Walking with the Wind*, 78.

17. Malcolm X (with the assistance of Alex Haley), *The Autobiography of Malcolm X* (New York: Random House, 1965), 193.

18. Manning Marable and Garrett Felber, eds., *The Portable Malcolm X Reader* (New York: Penguin Books, 2013), 154–55.

19. Marable and Felber, eds., *The Portable Malcolm X Reader*, 150.

20. The passage appears in James Baldwin's 1972 essay collection, *No Name in the*

Street, reprinted in Toni Morrison, ed., *James Baldwin: Collected Essays* (New York: Library of America, 1998), 410.

21. Lewis, *Walking with the Wind*, 142.

22. Raymond Arsenault, *Freedom Riders: 1961 and the Struggle for Racial Justice* (New York: Oxford University Press, 2006), 181.

23. Garrow, *Bearing the Cross*, 159–60.

24. Arthur Schlesinger Jr. *Robert Kennedy and His Times* (New York: Ballantine Books, 1978), 342.

25. Kevin Boyle, *The UAW and the Heyday of American Liberalism, 1945-1968* (Ithaca: Cornell University Press, 1995), 153; Branch, *Parting the Waters*, 695.

CHAPTER 4: THE DEAD

1. Taylor Branch, *Parting the Waters: America in the King Years, 1954–63* (New York: Simon & Schuster, 1988), 759.

2. Diane McWhorter, *Carry Me Home: Birmingham, Alabama: The Climactic Battle of the Civil Rights Revolution* (New York: Simon & Schuster, 2001), 48.

3. McWhorter, *Carry Me Home*, p. 311; Dan T. Carter, *The Politics of Rage: George Wallace, the Origins of the New Conservatism, and the Transformation of American Politics* (New York: Simon & Schuster, 1995), 109.

4. Martin Luther King Jr., Draft of Chapter XV, "The Answer to a Perplexing Question," July 1962–March 1963, available at http://okra.stanford.edu/transcription/document_images/Vol06Scans/July1962-March1963DraftofChapterXV,TheAnswerstoaPerplexingQuestion.pdf [last accessed February 8, 2021].

5. Martin Luther King Jr., "Letter from a Birmingham Jail," April 16, 1963, available at https://www.africa.upenn.edu/Articles_Gen/Letter_Birmingham.html [last accessed March 2, 2021].

6. Gene Roberts and Hank Klibanoff, *The Race Beat: The Press, the Civil Rights Struggle, and the Awakening of a Nation* (New York: Random House, 2006), 323.

7. Manning Marable, *Malcolm X: A Life of Reinvention* (New York: Viking, 2011), 238.

8. John Kennedy, Address on Civil Rights, June 11, 1963, available at https://millercenter.org/the-presidency/presidential-speeches/june-11-1963-address-civil-rights [last accessed December 5, 2020].

9. Kevin Boyle, *The UAW and the Heyday of American Liberalism, 1945–1968* (Ithaca: Cornell University Press, 1995), 176.

10. Todd Purdum, *An Idea Whose Time Has Come: Two Presidents, Two Parties, and the Battle for the Civil Rights Act of 1964* (New York: Henry Holt, 2014), 87–88.

11. William P. Jones, *The March on Washington: Jobs, Freedom, and the Forgotten History of Civil Rights* (New York: W. W. Norton, 2013), 193.

12. Boyle, *UAW and the Heyday of American Liberalism*, 180.

13. Martin Luther King, Address Delivered at the March on Washington for Jobs and Freedom, August 28, 1963, available at https://kinginstitute.stanford.edu/king-papers/documents/i-have-dream-address-delivered-march-washington-jobs-and-freedom [last accessed February 6, 2021].

14. Carter, *Politics of Rage*, 157; Rick Perlstein, *Before the Storm: Barry Goldwater and the Unmaking of the American Consensus* (New York: Hill and Wang, 2001), 115.

15. Lloyd Gardner, *Pay Any Price: Lyndon Johnson and the Wars for Vietnam* (Chicago: Ivan Dee, 1995), 77; George Herring, *America's Longest War: The United States and Vietnam, 1950–1975*, 3rd ed. (New York: McGraw Hill, 1996), 109.

16. "Vatican Deplores Bombings," *New York Amsterdam News*, September 28, 1963.

17. Herring, *America's Longest War*, 118.

18. Robert Dallek, *An Unfinished Life: John F. Kennedy, 1917–1963* (Boston: Little, Brown, 2003), 693.

CHAPTER 5: BENDING

1. Quotes in this and the previous paragraph are from Robert Caro, *The Passage of Power: The Years of Lyndon Johnson, Volume Four* (New York: Knopf, 2012), 313–14, 319.

2. Lyndon Johnson, *The Vantage Point: Perspectives of the Presidency, 1963–1969* (New York: Holt, Rinehart and Winston, 1971), 10.

3. Caro, *Passage to Power*, 198.

4. Robert Caro, *Means of Ascent: The Years of Lyndon Johnson, Volume Two* (New York: Knopf, 1990), 387.

5. Joseph Rauh quoted in Kevin Boyle, *The UAW and the Heyday of American Liberalism* (Ithaca: Cornell University Press, 1995), 182.

6. Ward S. Just, "What Ever Happened to Lyndon Johnson?" *Reporter*, January 17, 1963, 27.

7. Doris Kearns Goodwin, *Lyndon Johnson and the American Dream* (New York: Harper & Row 1977), 191.

8. Lyndon Johnson, Address to Joint Session of Congress, November 27, 1963, available at https://millercenter.org/the-presidency/presidential-speeches/november-27-1963-address-joint-session-congress [last accessed February 7, 2021].

9. Lyndon Johnson State of the Union Address, January 8, 1964, available at https://millercenter.org/the-presidency/presidential-speeches/january-8-1964-state-union [last accessed March 2, 2021].

10. Kim Phillips-Fein, *Invisible Hands: The Businessmen's Crusade Against the New Deal* (New York: W. W. Norton, 2009), 132.

11. Rick Perlstein, *Before the Storm: Barry Goldwater and the Unmaking of the American Consensus* (New York: Hill and Wang, 2001), 214.

12. Dan T. Carter, *The Politics of Rage: George Wallace, the Origins of the New Conservatism, and the Transformation of American Politics* (New York: Simon & Schuster, 1995), 203.

13. Carter, *Politics of Rage*, 207.

14. Carter, *Politics of Rage*, 205.

15. Carter, *Politics of Rage*, 215.

16. Perlstein, *Before the Storm*, 215, 374.

17. Students for a Democratic Society, "Port Huron Statement," June 15, 1962, available at https://history.hanover.edu/courses/excerpts/111huron.html [last accessed March 2, 2021].

18. Faith Holsaert et al., eds., *Hands on the Freedom Plow: Personal Accounts by Women in SNCC* (Urbana: University of Illinois Press, 2010), 51.

19. Clayborne Carson, *In Struggle: SNCC and the Black Awakening of the 1960s* (Cambridge, MA: Harvard University Press, 1984), 98.

20. Carson, *In Struggle*, 115.

21. Malcolm X, "Message to the Grass Roots," November 10, 1963, available at https://www.csun.edu/~hcpas003/grassroots.html [last accessed March 2, 2021]; Manning Marable, *Malcolm X: A Life of Reinvention* (New York: Viking, 2011).

22. "Eruption," *Washington Post*, July 21, 1964, A14.

23. "Families of Rights Workers Voice Grief and Hope," *New York Times*, August 6, 1964, 16; Taylor Branch, *Pillar of Fire: America in the King Years, 1963–1965* (New York: Simon & Schuster, 1998), 438; Seth Cagin and Philip Dray, *We Are Not Afraid: The Story of Goodman, Schwener, and Cheney and the Civil Rights Campaign for Mississippi* (New York: Macmillan, 1988), 410.

24. Fannie Lou Hamer, Testimony before the Democratic National Committee Credentials Committee, August 22, 1964, available at https://www.americanrhetoric.com/speeches/fannielouhamercredentialscommittee.htm [last accessed March 2, 2021].

25. Harvard Sitkoff, *King: Pilgrimage to the Mountaintop* (New York; Hill and Wang, 2008), 140; Carson, *In Struggle*, 126.

26. "Texas-Sized Boardwalk Fete Honors Johnson on 56th Birthday," *New York Times*, August 28, 1964, 12.

27. Betty Freidan, *The Feminine Mystique* (New York: W. W. Norton, 1963), 15, 282.

28. Hugh Davis Graham, *The Civil Rights Era: Origins and Development of National Policy, 1960–1972* (New York: Oxford University Press, 1990), 133.

29. Mary King, *Freedom Song; A Personal Story of the 1960s Civil Rights Movement* (New York: William Morrow, 1987), 569.

30. Robert Cohen, ed., *The Essential Mario Savio: Speeches and Writings That Changed America* (Berkeley: University of California Press, 2014), 87.

31. Robert Cohen, *Freedom's Orator: Mario Savio and the Radical Legacy of the 1960s* (New York: Oxford University Press, 2009), 99.

32. Mario Savio Sit-In Address, December 2, 1964, available at https://www

.americanrhetoric.com/speeches/mariosaviosproulhallsitin.htm [last accessed March 2, 2021].

33. David Burner, *Making Peace with the '60s* (Princeton: Princeton University Press, 1996), 142.

34. Both Kerr quotes from Cohen, *Freedom's Orator*, 211, 214.

35. Cohen, *Freedom's Orator*, 218–19.

36. "Barry Denounces Unfair Rights Act," *Atlanta Journal and Constitution*, November 1, 1964, 2; "Goldwater Sees Rights Act Flaw," *New York Times*, October 28, 1964, 1; "Goldwater Links the Welfare State to a Rise in Crime," *New York Times*, September 11, 1964, 1.

37. "Transcript of Goldwater Speech Accepting Republican Presidential Nomination," *New York Times*, July 17, 1964, 10.

38. Branch, *Pillar of Fire*, 491.

39. "President Urges Big Vote Turnout," *New York Times*, October 29, 1964, 1.

40. Perlstein, *Before the Storm*, 426; "It's All Over with Goldwater," *Guardian*, October 28, 1964, 1.

41. "Johnson Victory Speech," *New York Times*, November 4, 1964, 22.

CHAPTER 6: THE REVOLUTIONS OF 1965

1. Justice Felix Frankfurter majority opinion in *Poe et al. v. Ullman, State's Attorney*, June 19, 1961 available at http://law2.umkc.edu/faculty/projects/ftrials/conlaw/poe.html [last accessed March 3, 2021].

2. David Garrow, *Liberty and Sexuality: The Right to Privacy and the Making of Roe v. Wade* (New York: Macmillan, 1994), 203, 207.

3. Lyndon Johnson Inaugural Address, January 20, 1965, available at https://avalon.law.yale.edu/20th_century/johnson.asp [last accessed March 3, 2021].

4. George Herring, *America's Longest War: The United States and Vietnam, 1950–1975*, 3rd ed. (New York: McGraw Hill, 1996), 122; Michael Bechloss, ed., *Taking Charge: The Johnson White House Tapes, 1963–1964* (New York: Simon & Schuster, 1997), 200.

5. Lloyd Gardner, *Pay Any Price: Lyndon Johnson and the Wars of Vietnam* (Chicago: Ivan Dee, 1995), 98.

6. Doris Kearns Goodwin, *Lyndon Johnson and the American Dream* (New York: Harper & Row, 1976), 196.

7. "The President's Address," *New York Times*, August 5, 1964, 1.

8. "Message and Draft Text in Congress," *New York Times*, August 6, 1964, 8; "Resolution Wins," *New York Times*, August 8, 1964, 1.

9. Lyndon Johnson Remarks at the Dedication of the Eufaula Dam, September 25, 1964, available at https://www.presidency.ucsb.edu/documents/remarks-oklahoma-the-dedication-the-eufaula-dam [last accessed March 3, 2021].

10. Fredrik Logevall, *Choosing War: The Lost Chance for Peace and the Escalation of War in Vietnam* (Berkeley: University of California Press, 1999), 346.

11. Maxwell Taylor to the State Department, February 22, 1965, available at https://www.mtholyoke.edu/acad/intrel/pentagon3/pent8.htm [last accessed March 3, 2021].

12. Clayborne Carson, *In Struggle: SNCC and the Black Awakening of the 1960s* (Cambridge, MA: Harvard University Press, 1984), 128, 151.

13. Carson, *In Struggle*, 127.

14. Bayard Rustin, "From Protest to Politics: The Future of the Civil Rights Movement," *Commentary*, February 1965, 28, 31.

15. Gary May, *Bending Toward Justice: The Voting Rights Act and the Transformation of American Democracy* (New York: Basic Books, 2014), 48.

16. Harvard Sitkoff, *King: Pilgrimage to the Mountaintop* (New York; Hill and Wang, 2008), 150.

17. Taylor Branch, *Pillar of Fire: America in the King Years, 1963–1965* (New York: Simon & Schuster, 1998), 599.

18. John Lewis, *Walking with the Wind: A Memoir of the Movement* (New York: Simon & Schuster, 1998), 338.

19. Transcript of "Bridge to Freedom," *Eyes on the Prize: America's Civil Rights Movement, 1954–1985* (Blackside Productions, 1987), available at http://www.shoppbs.pbs.org/wgbh/amex/eyesontheprize/about/pt_106.html [last accessed March 6, 2021].

20. "Congressmen Assail Alabama Beatings," *Atlanta Constitution*, March 9, 1965, 15; Taylor Branch, *At Canaan's Edge: America in the King Years* (New York: Simon & Schuster, 2006), 60.

21. "Civil Rights: The Central Point," *Time*, March 19, 1965, 25.

22. May, *Bending Toward Justice*, 114.

23. Lyndon Johnson Speech before Congress, March 15, 1965, available at https://millercenter.org/the-presidency/presidential-speeches/march-15-1965-speech-congress-voting-rights [last accessed March 3, 2021].

24. Oral argument in *Griswold v. Connecticut*, March 29, 1965, available at http://academic.brooklyn.cuny.edu/history/johnson/griswoldoral.htm [last accessed March 6, 2021].

25. Garrow, *Liberty and Sexuality*, 244.

26. Garrow, *Liberty and Sexuality*, 255.

27. Garrow, *Liberty and Sexuality*, 245–46.

28. Justice William O. Douglas majority opinion, quoted in "Excerpts from Opinions of Supreme Court in Barring Curbs on Birth Control," *New York Times*, July 8, 1965, 34.

29. "Birth Curb in Wedlock Held Legal," *Washington Post*, June 8, 1965, A1; "Ct. Birth Control Ban Is Ruled Unconstitutional," *Boston Globe*, June 8, 1965, 1.

30. James Patterson, *The Eve of Destruction: How 1965 Transformed America* (New York: Basic Books, 2012), 160.

31. Michael Beschloss, *Reaching for Glory: Lyndon Johnson's Secret White House Tapes, 1964–1965* (New York: Simon & Schuster, 2001), 388.

32. Lyndon Johnson, Remarks in the Capitol Rotunda on the Signing of the Voting Rights Act, August 6, 1965, available at https://www.presidency.ucsb.edu/documents/remarks-the-capitol-rotunda-the-signing-the-voting-rights-act [last accessed February 7, 2021].

CHAPTER 7: TURNING AND TURNING

1. Joan Didion, "On Morality," reprinted in Didion, *We Tell Ourselves Stories in Order to Live: Collected Nonfiction* (New York: Everyman's Library, 2006), 120.

2. Joan Didion, "Slouching Towards Bethlehem," *Saturday Evening Post*, September 23, 1967, 26.

3. Martin Lee and Bruce Shlain, *Acid Dreams: The Complete Social History of LSD: The CIA, the Sixties, and Beyond* (New York: Grove Press, 1985), xviii, 47.

4. Lee and Shlain, *Acid Dreams*, 120.

5. Rick Dodgson, *It's All a Kind of Magic: The Young Ken Kesey* (Madison: University of Wisconsin Press, 2013), 157.

6. David Courtwright, *Forces of Habit: Drugs and the Making of the Modern World* (Cambridge, MA: Harvard University Press, 2001), 89.

7. Taylor Branch, *At Canaan's Edge: America in the King Years* (New York: Simon & Schuster, 2006), 200.

8. Branch, *At Canaan's Edge*, 296, 319.

9. David Garrow, *Bearing the Cross: Martin Luther King, Jr., and the Southern Christian Leadership Conference* (New York: William Morrow, 1986), 444.

10. Garrow, *Bearing the Cross*, 448.

11. "Dr. King's Campaign Welcomed by Daley," *New York Times*, February 1, 1966, 24.

12. Garrow, *Bearing the Cross*, 468.

13. "Interview with New SNCC Chairman," *Militant*, May 23, 1966, 8.

14. Rick Perlstein, *Nixonland: The Rise of a President and the Fracturing of America* (New York: Scribner, 2008), 98–99.

15. "Civil Rights: The New Racism," *Time*, July 1, 1966, 11.

16. "Director of CORE Criticizes Non-Violence as a Dying Principle," *Los Angeles Times*, July 3, 1966, 1; "Excepts from the Speech by Wilkins," *New York Times*, July 6, 1966, 14.

17. "'Black Power,'" *New York Times*, July 10, 1966, 143.

18. "White power" and "burn them" quotes both from Branch, *At Canaan's Edge*, 508.

19. Perlstein, *Nixonland*, 119; Branch, *At Canaan's Edge*, 511.

20. Branch, *At Canaan's Edge*, 515.

21. Garrow, *Bearing the Cross*, 508.

22. Harvard Sitkoff, *King: Pilgrimage to the Mountaintop* (New York; Hill and Wang, 2008), 204

23. Paul Friedlander (with Peter Miller), *Rock and Roll: A Social History*, 2nd ed. (New York: Routledge, 2018), 192.

24. Lee and Schlain, *Acid Dreams*, 160.

25. "San Francisco: Love on Haight," *Time*, March 17, 1967, 27.

26. Stokely Carmichael, Speech at the University of California–Berkeley, October 29, 1966, available at http://americanradioworks.publicradio.org/features/blackspeech/scarmichael.html [last accessed March 3, 2021].

27. "Guards at Capitol Called 'Helpless,'" *Los Angeles Times*, May 5, 1967, 3.

28. "Curfew Imposed on City," *New York Times*, July 15, 1967, 1; "Strategy of Riot Control," *New York Times*, July 20, 1967, 1.

29. "Johnson TV Talk on Troop Order," *New York Times*, July 25, 1967, 20.

30. "Carmichael, at Havana Parlay, Urges Negro 'Revolution' in U.S.," *New York Times*, August 2, 1967, 12.

31. Ray Girardin, "After the Riots: Force Won't Settle Anything," *Saturday Evening Post*, September 23, 1967, 10.

32. Stewart Alsop, "Why Juanita Enjoyed the Riot," *Saturday Evening Post*, September 23, 1967, 16.

33. Didion, "Slouching Towards Bethlehem," 26.

CHAPTER 8: WAIST DEEP IN THE BIG MUDDY

1. Paul Hendrickson, *The Living and the Dead: Robert McNamara and Five Lives of a Lost War* (New York: Knopf, 1996), 137.

2. Hendrickson, *Living and the Dead*, 136.

3. Robert Pearce, ed., *Patrick Gordon Walker: Political Diaries, 1932–1971* (London: Historians' Press, 1991), 305.

4. Doris Kearns Goodwin, *Lyndon Johnson and the American Dream* (New York: Harper & Row, 1976), 251.

5. Lloyd Gardner, *Pay Any Price: Lyndon Johnson and the Wars for Vietnam* (Chicago: Ivan Dee, 1995), 238.

6. Larry Berman, *Planning a Tragedy: The Americanization of the War in Vietnam* (New York: W. W. Norton, 1982), 179, 184.

7. George Herring, *America's Longest War: The United States and Vietnam, 1950–1975*, 3rd ed. (New York: McGraw Hill, 1996), 168.

8. J. E. Cahill, "Voice of the People: Flags on Eddy Street," *Chicago Tribune*, July 2, 1966, 12.

9. Christian Appy, *Patriots: The Vietnam War Remembered from All Sides* (New York: Viking, 2003), 326.

10. Quoted in Christian Appy's superb book, *Working-Class War: American Combat Soldiers and Vietnam* (Chapel Hill: University of North Carolina Press, 1993), 130.

11. Jonathan Schell, "A Reporter at Large: The Village of Ben Suc," *The New Yorker*, July 15, 1967, 38.

12. Tim O'Brien, *If I Die in a Combat Zone Box Me Up and Ship Me Home* (New York: Delacorte, 1975), 124; Appy, *Patriots*, xx.

13. Appy, *Working Class War*, 163.

14. Appy, *Working-Class War*, 184.

15. James Miller, *Democracy Is in the Streets: From Port Huron to the Siege of Chicago* (New York: Simon & Schuster, 1987), 199.

16. Tom Wells, *The War Within: America's Battle Over Vietnam* (Berkeley: University of California Press, 1994), 14.

17. Miller, *Democracy Is in the Streets*, 233–34.

18. Hendrickson, *Living and the Dead*, 214–15.

19. Hendrickson, *Living and the Dead*, 223; Miller, *Democracy Is in the Streets*, 232, 236.

20. Fredrik Logevall, *Choosing War: The Lost Chance for Peace and the Escalation of War in Vietnam* (Berkeley: University of California Press, 1999), 250.

21. Ronald Steel, *Walter Lippmann and the American Century* (Boston: Little, Brown, 1980), 565.

22. Charles DeBenedetti and Charles Chatfield, *An American Ordeal: The Antiwar Movement of the Vietnam Era* (Syracuse, NY: Syracuse University Press, 1990), 197.

23. Arthur Schlesinger Jr., *Robert Kennedy and His Times* (New York: Ballantine Books, 1978), 832.

24. Martin Luther King Jr., "Letter from a Birmingham Jail," April 16, 1963, available at https://www.africa.upenn.edu/Articles_Gen/Letter_Birmingham.html [last accessed February 7, 2021].

25. Martin Luther King, Jr., "Beyond Vietnam," April 4, 1967, available at https://kinginstitute.stanford.edu/king-papers/documents/beyond-vietnam [last accessed February 7, 2021].

26. Miller, *Democracy Is in the Streets*, 238.

27. Miller, *Democracy Is in the Streets*, 267–68.

28. Robert C. Cottrell, *All-American Rebels: The American Left from the Wobblies to Today* (Lanham, MD: Rowman and Littlefield, 2020), 114.

29. Norman Mailer, *The Armies of the Night: History as a Novel, the Novel as History* (New York: New American Library, 1968), 246.

30. "Observer: Dove Antics," *New York Times*, October 24 1967, 45.

31. "Vietnam 'Teach-ins' Bring Out Contrasts," *Los Angeles Times*, June 21, 1965, 8.

32. "70,000 Turn Out to Back U.S. Men in Vietnam War," *New York Times*, May 14, 1967, 1; "Vigil at the Battery: Backing Up the Troops," *Village Voice*, October 26, 1967, 11.

33. "70,000 Turn Out to Back U.S. Men in Vietnam War"; "Vigil at the Battery"; "100,000 in New York Area Show Support of War," *Los Angeles Times*, October 23, 1967, 18.

CHAPTER 9: THE CRUELEST MONTHS

1. Dan T. Carter, *The Politics of Rage: George Wallace, the Origins of the New Conservatism, and the Transformation of American Politics* (New York: Simon & Schuster, 1995), 293.

2. For Wallace's speech and the crowd's reaction, see Theodore White, *The Making of the President 1968* (New York: Atheneum, 1969), 349.

3. "Four View Nixon in TV 'Obituary,'" *Baltimore Sun*, November 12, 1962, 1.

4. White, *Making of the President 1968*, 129.

5. "The Wallace Phenomenon," *Boston Globe*, March 10, 1968, F6.

6. William Chafe, *Never Stop Running: Allard Lowenstein and the Struggle to Save American Liberalism* (New York: Basic Books, 1993), 264.

7. "Johnson Says Foes' Raids Are a Failure Militarily," *New York Times*, February 3, 1968, 1.

8. "NBC Hardens Line on Vietnam Policy," *Atlanta Constitution*, March 11, 1968, 19; "Suicidal Escalation," *New York Times*, March 11, 1968, 40; Rusk Tells Panel of 'A to Z' Review of Vietnam War," *New York Times*, March 12, 1968, 1; "Excerpts from Rusk Testimony on Vietnam and Exchanges with Senate Panel," *New York Times*, March 12, 1968, 16.

9. "Kennedy Is Ready to Run; Says Vote for M'Carthy Discloses Split in Party," *New York Times*, March 14, 1968, 1.

10. Robert Collins, *More: The Politics of Economic Growth in Postwar America* (New York: Oxford University Press, 2000), 69.

11. Walt Rostow quoted in Robert Gavin, *Gold, Dollars and Power: The Politics of International Monetary Relations, 1958–1971* (Chapel Hill: University of North Carolina Press, 2004), 1. Also see Robert Collins's enlightening article, "The Economic Crisis of 1968 and the Waning of the 'American Century,'" *American Historical Review* 101 (April 1996): 396–422.

12. Lyndon Johnson, Remarks on Decision Not to Seek Re-Election, March 31, 1968, available at https://millercenter.org/the-presidency/presidential-speeches/march -31-1968-remarks-decision-not-to-seek-re-election [last accessed February 7, 2021].

13. Lady Bird Johnson, *A White House Diary* (Austin: University of Texas Press, 2007), 646.

14. White, *Making of the President 1968*, 124.

15. Jason Sokol, *The Heavens Might Crack: The Death and Legacy of Martin Luther King, Jr.* (New York: Basic Books, 2018).

16. Peniel E. Joseph, *Stokely: A Life* (New York: Basic Civitas, 2014), 258.

17. "Wallace Plugs Away," *Wall Street Journal*, April 25, 1968, 1.

18. William Safire, *Before the Fall: An Inside View of the Pre-Watergate White House* (Garden City, NY: Doubleday Publishing, 1975), 50. Safire, Nixon's speechwriter, says he took the "silent center" phrase from a speech by Illinois' reliably liberal senator Paul Douglas.

19. *Charles C. Green et al. v. County School Board of New Kent County, Virginia et al.*, May 27, 1968, available at https://www.law.cornell.edu/supremecourt/text/391/430 [last accessed February 6, 2021].

20. Jack Newfield, *Robert Kennedy: A Memoir* (New York: Dutton, 1969), 238.

21. Robert Kennedy, "Statement on the Assassination of Martin Luther King, Jr.," Indianapolis, Indiana, April 4, 1968, available at https://www.jfklibrary.org/learn/about-jfk/the-kennedy-family/robert-f-kennedy/robert-f-kennedy-speeches/statement-on-assassination-of-martin-luther-king-jr-indianapolis-indiana-april-4-1968 [last accessed February 6, 2021].

22. Louis Harris, "In-Depth Poll Shows Public Reaction to Kennedy's Death," *Los Angeles Times*, June 16, 1968, 17.

23. "Wallace in the North: Friends and 'Anarchist' Critics Cheer and Scream," *New York Times*, July 27, 1968, 1.

24. Richard Nixon, Address to the Republican National Convention, August 8, 1968, available at https://www.presidency.ucsb.edu/documents/address-accepting-the-presidential-nomination-the-republican-national-convention-miami [last accessed November 24, 2020].

25. "University Must Accept Students' Challenge," *Boston Globe*, June 21, 1968, 14; Carl Solberg, *Hubert Humphrey: A Biography* (New York: W. W. Norton, 1980), 342–43.

26. Quoted in David Farber's wonderful *Chicago '68* (Chicago: University of Chicago Press, 1988), 114.

27. "Defeat for Doves Reflects Deep Divisions in the Party," *New York Times*, August 29, 1968, 1.

28. Ribicoff and Daley both quoted in David Paul Kuhn, *The Hard Hat Riot: Nixon, New York, and the Dawn of the White Working-Class Revolution* (New York: Oxford University Press, 2020), 25–26. Whether Daley said precisely those words remains a point of debate.

29. "TV Viewers Target for Saturation Sell on Nixon," *Boston Globe*, September 23, 1968, 10.

30. Solberg, *Hubert Humphrey*, 380.

31. Kenneth Williams, ed., *LeMay on Vietnam* (Washington, DC: Air Force History and Museums Program, 2017), 23.

32. "LeMay, Named Wallace's VP, Might A-Bomb Vietnam, But . . . ," *Boston Globe*, October 4, 1968, 1.

33. "Nixon's 'Great' Goal: 'Bring Us Together,'" *Washington Post*, November 7, 1968, 1.

CHAPTER 10: NOBODIES

1. Joshua Prager, "The Accidental Activist," *Vanity Fair*, February 2013, available at https://www.vanityfair.com/news/politics/2013/02/norma-mccorvey-roe-v-wade -abortion [last accessed December 5, 2020].

2. Norma McCorvey (with Andy Meisler), *I Am Roe: My Life, Roe v. Wade, and Freedom of Choice* (New York: HarperCollins, 1994), 95.

3. H. R. Haldeman diary entry, March 28, 1969, reprinted in H. R. Haldeman, *The Haldeman Diaries: Inside the Nixon White House* (New York: Putnam, 1994), 44.

4. Haldeman quoted in Richard Reeves, *President Nixon: Alone in the White House* (New York: Simon & Schuster, 2001), 110.

5. Senator Sam Ervin quoted in "Four Major Crime Bills Cleared 91st Congress," *Congressional Quarterly*, 1970, available at https://library.cqpress.com/ cqalmanac/document.php?id=cqal70-1292693 [last accessed March 4, 2021].

6. Matthew Lassiter, *The Silent Majority: Suburban Politics in the Sunbelt South* (Princeton: Princeton University Press, 2006), 136.

7. Bill Ayers, *Fugitive Days: Memoir of an Anti-war Activist* (Boston: Beacon Press, 2001), 173.

8. Haldeman diary entry, October 16, 1969, in Haldeman, *Haldeman Diaries*, 100; Reeves, *President Nixon*, 139.

9. "Text of President Nixon's Speech to the Nation on U.S. Policy in the War in Vietnam," *New York Times*, November 4, 1969, 16.

10. McCorvey, *I Am Roe*, 104.

11. "A New Abortion Law," *New York Times*, February 13, 1965, 20.

12. Daniel Williams, *Defenders of the Unborn: The Pro-Life Movement before Roe v. Wade* (New York: Oxford University Press, 2016), 76.

13. Shulamith Firestone, "On Abortion," 1968, available at https://www.marxists.org/ subject/women/authors/firestone-shulamith/on-abortion.htm [last accessed February 23, 2021]; Cardinal Patrick O'Boyle in Daniel Williams, *Defenders of the Unborn: The Pro-Life Movement before Roe v. Wade* (New York: Oxford University Press, 2016), 102.

14. David Garrow, *Liberty and Sexuality: The Right to Privacy and the Making of Roe v. Wade* (New York: Macmillan, 1994), 406.

15. "GIs Call Viet Killings 'Point-Blank Murder,'" *Cleveland Plain Dealer*, November 20, 1969.

16. Kendrick Oliver, *The My Lai Massacre in American History and Memory* (Manchester: Manchester University Press, 2006), 137.

17. Reeves, *President Nixon*, 158.

18. "Excerpts from Carswell Talk," *New York Times*, January 22, 1970, 22.

19. "Transcript of the President's News Conference on Foreign and Domestic Matters," *New York Times*, January 31, 1970, 14.

20. Haldeman diary entries, February 4 and 7, 1970, in Haldeman, *Haldeman Diaries*, 125, 126.

21. "Mansfield on Laos: 'Up to Our Necks,'" *Washington Post*, March 3, 1970, A1.

22. Mississippi senator John Stennis quoted in "South Opens Fight to Save School Choice: Senators Attack Edicts," *Atlanta Constitution*, February 6, 1970, 1A; Lassiter, *Silent Majority*, 142; Haldeman, *Haldeman Diaries*, p. 139.

23. "Nixon on School Desegregation, 'Not Backing Away,'" *Washington Post*, March 25, 1970, A12.

24. Haldeman diary entry, April 7, 1970, in Haldeman, *Haldeman Diaries*, 147.

25. Haldeman diary entry, April 22, 1970, in Haldeman, *Haldeman Diaries*, 153; Jeffrey Kimball, *Nixon's Vietnam War* (Lawrence: University Press of Kansas, 1998), 203; Henry Kissinger, *White House Years* (Boston: Little, Brown, 1979), 490.

26. Richard Nixon, "Address to the Nation on the Situation in Southeast Asia," April 30, 1970, available at http://www.presidency.ucsb.edu/ws/?pid=2490 [last accessed October 13, 2017].

27. McCorvey, *I Am Roe*, 130.

28. McCorvey, *I Am Roe*, 131.

CHAPTER 11: COMING HOME

1. "Kent Death Splits Victim's Old School," *Washington Post*, May 6, 1970, A1.

2. Allison Krause's boyfriend, Barry Levine, recounts the "fag" comment in Jeff Kisseloff, *Generation on Fire: Voices of Protest from the 1960s, an Oral History* (Lexington: University of Kentucky Press, 2006).

3. "Kent Death Splits Victim's Old School," A1.

4. Rick Perlstein, *Nixonland: The Rise of a President and the Fracturing of America* (New York: Scribner, 2008), 482; Richard Reeves, *President Nixon: Alone in the White House* (New York: Simon & Schuster, 2001).

5. Reeves, *President Nixon*, 211.

6. Haldeman diary entry, May 4, 1970, in H. R. Haldeman, *The Haldeman Diaries: Inside the Nixon White House* (New York: Putnam, 1994), 160.

7. Haldeman, *Haldeman Diaries*; "4 Kent State Victims Were Not Known as Campus Activists," *Boston Globe*, May 6, 1970, 10.

8. Haldeman diary entry, May 6, 1970, in Haldeman, *Haldeman Diaries*, 161.

9. "War Foes Here Attacked by Construction Workers," *New York Times*, May 9, 1970, 1.

10. Quote in this paragraph and the previous from Tom McNichol, "I Am Not a Kook: Richard Nixon's Bizarre Visit to the Lincoln Memorial," *Atlantic*, November 11, 2014, available at https://www.theatlantic.com/politics/archive/2011/11/i-am-not-a-kook-richard-nixons-bizarre-visit-to-the-lincoln-memorial/248443/ [last accessed September 28, 2018].

11. Haldeman diary entry, May 9, 1970, in Haldeman, *Haldeman Diaries*, 163.

12. Haldeman diary entry, May 18, 1970, in Haldeman, *Haldeman Diaries*, 167.

13. Henry Kissinger, *White House Years* (Boston: Little, Brown, 1979), 716.

14. Oval Office recording, June 17, 1971, available at the Miller Center Presidency Project, University of Virginia, https://millercenter.org/the-presidency/educational-resources/breaking-brookings [last accessed December 15, 2020].

15. Oval Office recording, July 1, 1971, available at the Miller Center Presidency Project, https://millercenter.org/the-presidency/secret-white-house-tapes/i-want-brookings-institute-safe-cleaned-out [last accessed December 15, 2020].

16. Dan T. Carter, *The Politics of Rage: George Wallace, the Origins of the New Conservatism, and the Transformation of American Politics* (New York: Simon & Schuster, 1995), 393.

17. "'Floor' Any Attacker, Maddox Urges Patrol," *Atlanta Constitution*, May 14, 1970, 1A.

18. "South on Verge of Carrying Out '54 School Ruling," *New York Times*, August 30, 1970.

19. "Abortion Reform at Last," *New York Times*, April 11, 1970; "The War on the Womb," *Christianity Today*, June 3, 1970, 24–25; Williams, *Defenders of the Unborn*, 128.

20. Dr. and Mrs. J. C. Wilke, *Handbook on Abortion*, reprinted in Linda Greenhouse and Reva B. Siegel, eds., *Before Roe v. Wade: Voices that Shaped the Abortion Debate before the Supreme Court's Ruling* (2012), 102–3, available at http://documents.law.yale.edu/sites/default/files/BeforeRoe2ndEd_1.pdf [last accessed February 23, 2021].

21. David J. Garrow, *Liberty and Sexuality: The Right to Privacy and the Making of Roe v. Wade* (New York: Macmillan, 1994), 514.

22. Sarah Weddington, *A Question of Choice* (New York: G. P. Putnam's Sons, 1992), 116; Garrow, *Liberty and Sexuality*, 525.

23. "Nixon's China Travel Plans Stir Some Discordant Notes," *Baltimore Sun*, June 17, 1971, A4.

24. Reeves, *President Nixon*, 358–59, 362.

25. Haldeman diary entry, September 20, 1971, in Haldeman, *Haldeman Diaries*, 357. While appointing two justices simultaneously was unusual, it wasn't unique. Franklin Roosevelt had done the same in 1941.

26. John Dean quoted in Elizabeth Tandy Shermer, "Phoenix's Cowboy Conservatives in Washington," in Shermer, ed., *Barry Goldwater and the Remaking of the American Political Landscape* (Tuscon: University of Arizona Press, 2013), 204. Rehnquist's record wasn't as clean as Nixon had hoped it would be. Shortly before his confirmation vote, *Newsweek* revealed that as a Supreme Court clerk in 1952 he'd written a memo urging the justice he served to affirm *Plessy v. Ferguson* rather than vote in support of *Brown*. He contained the damage by saying

that he was stating the justice's view and not his own, a claim that remains controversial.

27. Transcript of recorded conversation, May 4, 1972, reprinted in Douglas Brinkley and Luke Nichter, eds., *The Nixon Tapes, 1971–1972* (Boston: Houghton Mifflin, 2014), 541.

28. "U.S. Political Leaders Split Over Wisdom of Nixon's New Move," *Los Angeles Times*, May 9, 1972, A1.

29. Haldeman diary entry, June 9, 1972, in Haldeman, *Haldeman Diaries*, 470.

30. "Transcript of Nixon's Acceptance Address and Excerpts from Agnew's Speech," *New York Times*, August 24, 1972, 47.

31. Haldeman diary entry, September 16, 1972, in Haldeman, *Haldeman Diaries*, 505.

EPILOGUE

1. Opinion of the Court, *Roe et al. v. Wade, District Attorney of Dallas County*, January 22, 1973, U.S. Reports: Roe v. Wade, 410 U.S. 113, 116, 152, 153, available at https://tile.loc.gov/storage-services/service/ll/usrep/usrep410/usrep410113/usrep410113.pdf [last accessed February 14, 2021].

2. Opinion of the Court, *Roe v. Wade*, 162.

3. "Text of Nixon's Talk on Vietnam," *Los Angeles Times*, January 24, 1973, 11.

INDEX